Programming
Visual Basic 2005

Other Microsoft .NET resources from O'Reilly

Related titles   Visual Basic 2005: A   Programming ASP.NET
                      Developer's Notebook   Visual Basic 2005 Jumpstart
                      ASP.NET 2.0: A Developer's
                      Notebook

.NET Books   *dotnet.oreilly.com* is a complete catalog of O'Reilly's books on
Resource Center   .NET and related technologies, including sample chapters and
                      code examples.

ONDotnet.com provides independent coverage of fundamental, interoperable, and emerging Microsoft .NET programming and web services technologies.

Conferences   O'Reilly brings diverse innovators together to nurture the ideas that spark revolutionary industries. We specialize in documenting the latest tools and systems, translating the innovator's knowledge into useful skills for those in the trenches. Visit *conferences.oreilly.com* for our upcoming events.

Safari Bookshelf (*safari.oreilly.com*) is the premier online reference library for programmers and IT professionals. Conduct searches across more than 1,000 books. Subscribers can zero in on answers to time-critical questions in a matter of seconds. Read the books on your Bookshelf from cover to cover or simply flip to the page you need. Try it today for free.

Programming
Visual Basic 2005

Jesse Liberty

Beijing · Cambridge · Farnham · Köln · Paris · Sebastopol · Taipei · Tokyo

Programming Visual Basic 2005
by Jesse Liberty

Copyright © 2005 O'Reilly Media, Inc. All rights reserved.
Printed in the United States of America.

Published by O'Reilly Media, Inc., 1005 Gravenstein Highway North, Sebastopol, CA 95472.

O'Reilly books may be purchased for educational, business, or sales promotional use. Online editions are also available for most titles (*safari.oreilly.com*). For more information, contact our corporate/institutional sales department: (800) 998-9938 or *corporate@oreilly.com*.

Editor:	John Osborn
Developmental Editor:	Ralph Davis
Production Editor:	Matt Hutchinson
Production Services:	Octal Publishing, Inc.
Cover Designer:	Karen Montgomery
Interior Designer:	David Futato

Printing History:

September 2005:	First Edition.

 This book uses RepKover™, a durable and flexible lay-flat binding.

ISBN: 0-596-00949-6
[M]

This book is dedicated to two young women: one who is braver and stronger than anyone I know, and the other who is the definition of love and compassion. And this book is dedicated to their mother, who provides us all a zone of safety.

Table of Contents

Part II.   Building Web Applications

Preface

This is not your typical Visual Basic book.

This is not a reference book. This is not a primer on the language. This is not a book of white papers hyping .NET.

The goal of this book is to make you immediately productive, creating Windows and Web applications using Visual Basic and its associated tools.

By creating applications, you will learn Visual Basic as it has evolved for .NET. You'll see how to use the tools effectively, and you'll learn the details of building robust object-oriented applications.

The focus of this book is on building Windows applications and building Web applications (including Web Services). In a sense, this is really two books in one. The first book could have been called *Building Windows Applications with Visual Basic and Visual Studio 2005*, and the second *Building Web Applications And Web Services with Visual Basic and Visual Studio 2005*. By putting them in a single volume, we can combine all the supplemental and background material, and give you more bang for your buck.

 If you only want to build web applications, skip right to Part II. Don't worry, you'll be fine, and you can always come back to Part I when you need to build a Windows application.

What You Need to Know About This Book

This book assumes you are already a Visual Basic programmer (probably VB6, but possibly VB.NET Version 1.x). Thus, I'm not going to explain what an if statement is. (If you don't *know* what an if statement is, or if you just want a thorough review, please read Chapters 16 to 18, which provide a primer on the Visual Basic 2005 language and object-oriented programming. We stuck them in the back so that you can ignore them if you'd like.)

If this is your first programming language, don't panic, you will learn everything you need to know as we go. You might want to take a quick peek at Chapter 16 now and again if you're feeling lost.

This book includes notes along the way pointing out especially dangerous pitfalls for VB6 and VB.NET 1.x programmers.

While Visual Basic is now a fully object-oriented language, we're not going to start with an introduction to the theory of object-oriented programming. It will be much more satisfying, and much more effective, just to start programming with objects, and I'll include sidebars that explain the theory in context.

 If you really want a primer on object-oriented programming, be sure to read Chapter 18, which I wrote at the insistence of my editor. It is boring, but at least it is short.

Most important, I'm *not going to waste your time*. You won't find a long treatise on why .NET is great. (It *is* great, but you are here already, and what is the point of selling you on a technology you've already bought?) You also won't find a theoretical exposition on the role of .NET framework or on all the associated tools; instead you'll use the tools and the framework, and I'll put it all in context as we go about our business of building applications.

Finally, I'm not going to waste your time by filling pages with material that is otherwise freely available. I'll show you *how* to get the information you need, but I won't waste page after page with tables listing all the properties and methods of each class; that information is already available to you in the built-in help files.

What You Need to Use This Book

To get the most out of this book, you'll need either Visual Studio (with Visual Basic) *or* Visual Basic Express.

You'll also need some sort of database software. Best bet is either SQL Server or SQL Server Express. You can get away with using Microsoft Access in a pinch. Anything else and you're on your own.

That's all you need.

I suggest typing in the code, but you are free to download all of the examples from my web site, *http://www.LibertyAssociates.com* (click on Books), where you'll also find an errata (with, I hope, very few entries), a FAQ, and a link to my private support discussion group.

If you find an error that isn't already listed in the errata, please send it to me at *jliberty@LibertyAssociates.com*. If you have a question about a topic in this book, please post it in the discussion group, under this book's folder, and make sure you tell me which edition you were reading, what page or example you were looking at, what you did, what you expected, and what you got.

What I Threw Away

Chapter 1 was going to be an introduction to Visual Basic and an explanation of how it fits into the .NET world. But that would be a waste of time. You'll see how things fit together when you start creating applications. I threw it away.

Chapter 2 was going to be devoted to writing your first "Hello World" program. Another waste of time. I threw that away too.*

Let's get started building something useful.

How This Book Is Organized

Part I: Building Windows Applications

Chapter 1, *Design and First Forms*
> Get right to work creating Windows Applications using drag and drop in Visual Studio 2005. Understand how to respond to events to build interactive applications.

Chapter 2, *Data Access*
> Most meaningful applications interact with a database. This chapter shows you how to use drag-and-drop controls to create that connectivity, how to query with parameters, and how to build master/detail pages

Chapter 3, *Cool Controls*
> Go beyond the standard form controls to enhance your Windows application with built-in browser controls, masked text boxes, and sophisticated tree controls.

---

* There, isn't that better? We haven't even begun, and I've already saved 100 pages. At this rate, you'll finish reading this book before you pay for it. Oops. Go pay for it. I'll wait.... Got your receipt? Good. Then we're ready.

Chapter 4, *Custom Controls*
When the controls that Microsoft provides are not quite enough, you are free to create your own by modifying an existing control, combining two or more existing controls, or creating an entirely new control from scratch

Chapter 5, *GDI+ and Drawing*
When you need to take absolute control of what is drawn on your form, turn to GDI+ and the techniques shown here to draw dynamic applications.

Chapter 6, *Mice and Fonts*
Learn how to detect mouse events and respond to them. While you're at it, explore the use of fonts to enhance the presentation of your application.

Chapter 7, *Integrating Legacy COM Controls*
Many Windows Forms applications will interact with legacy COM controls. This chapter shows you how to do so in a managed environment.

Part II: Building Web Applications

Chapter 8, *Web Application, Design, and First Forms*
Visual Basic 2005 and Visual Studio make a powerful combination for creating sophisticated web applications. The same drag-and-drop technology you used to create Windows applications can be used to create complex and sophisticated Windows applications.

Chapter 9, *Validation Controls*
Validating the user's input to ensure that fields are filled, that values are appropriate, that passwords match, and so forth was tedious job for many web programmers. This chapter shows you the library of controls created for you to greatly simplify these tasks.

Chapter 10, *Master Pages and Navigation*
Providing a unified look and feel for your site is made much easier though the innovation of Master Pages. A second requirement for modern web applications is to provide "bread crumbs" to show the user how she arrived at the current page and to provide a site map to show the user how to get to the page he wants. This chapter walks you through the controls that make this a very easy task.

Chapter 11, *Web Data Access*
As with Windows applications, most meaningful web applications need to interact with data. We'll show you how to do so with a single control, and how to update the database and manage multiuser applications.

Chapter 12, *Personalization*
Creating forms-based security is now a matter of dragging and dropping controls onto the form and hooking them into a database provided for you by .NET. Once your user is validated and assigned a role, it is easy to remember your user's preferences. With just a few controls, you can allow your user to customize not only

the look and feel of your pages, but also which data is presented and at what part of the page.

Chapter 13, *Custom Controls*
When the web controls provided by Microsoft are not quite enough to accomplish your task, you are free to create your own by modifying an existing control, combining two or more existing controls, or creating an entirely new control from scratch. You can also extract part of an existing web page and use it repeatedly throughout your application by creating a user control.

Chapter 14, *Web Services*
Web services allow applications to interact with one another using the standard protocols of the Web. This chapter will show you how to create web services and also how to create applications that use web services.

Part III: Working with Visual Basic 2005

Chapter 15, *Visual Studio 2005*
Visual Studio 2005 is a highly sophisticated tool that will greatly enhance your productivity. This chapter will take you into some of the nooks and crannies of this tool.

Chapter 16, *Visual Basic 2005 Fundamentals*
The premise of this book is that you know most of the language from working with previous versions of VB6. If you are new to the language, however, or if you run into syntax that you find confusing, this chapter will provide a review of the language in detail.

Chapter 17, *Using Collections and Generics*
Collection classes are now type safe in Visual Basic 2005, and this chapter will show you how to use the new "Generic" collections to create type-safe stacks, queues, and dictionaries.

Chapter 18, *Object-Oriented Visual Basic 2005*
If you work your way through the exercises in this book, you'll be living and breathing object-oriented programming. This chapter provides a slightly more formal overview.

Conventions Used in This Book

The following typographical conventions are used in this book:

Plain text
Indicates menu titles, menu options, menu buttons, and keyboard accelerators (such as Alt and Ctrl)

Italic
Indicates new terms, URLs, email addresses, filenames, file extensions, pathnames, directories, and Unix utilities

Constant width

Indicates commands, options, switches, variables, attributes, keys, functions, types, classes, namespaces, methods, modules, properties, parameters, values, objects, events, event handlers, XML tags, HTML tags, macros, the contents of files, or the output from commands

Constant width bold

Shows commands or other text that should be typed literally by the user

Constant width italic

Shows text that should be replaced with user-supplied values

 This icon signifies a tip, suggestion, or general note.

 This icon indicates a warning or caution.

Using Code Examples

This book is here to help you get your job done. In general, you may use the code in this book in your programs and documentation. You do not need to contact O'Reilly for permission unless you're reproducing a significant portion of the code. For example, writing a program that uses several chunks of code from this book does not require permission. Selling or distributing a CD-ROM of examples from O'Reilly books *does* require permission. Answering a question by citing this book and quoting example code does not require permission. Incorporating a significant amount of example code from this book into your product's documentation *does* require permission.

The publisher appreciates, but does not require, attribution. An attribution usually includes the title, author, publisher, and ISBN. For example: *Programming with Visual Basic 2005* by Jesse Liberty. Copyright 2005 O'Reilly Media, Inc., 0-596-00949-6.

If you feel your use of code examples falls outside fair use or the permission given above, feel free to contact us at *permissions@oreilly.com*.

I'd Like to Hear from You

Please send comments, suggestions, and (horrors!) errata to *jliberty@libertyassociates. com*. Please check the FAQ and errata on the web site (*http://www.LibertyAssociates.com*;

---

click on Books) first, though, as someone may have already reported your error or asked your question.

You can get extensive help through the private discussion group provided for this book. Sign up through my web site and then follow the link to the discussion forum provided at the top of the Books page.

Comments and Questions

Please address comments and questions concerning this book to the publisher:

O'Reilly Media, Inc.
1005 Gravenstein Highway North
Sebastopol, CA 95472
(800) 998-9938 (in the United States or Canada)
(707) 829-0515 (international or local)
(707) 829-0104 (fax)

O'Reilly maintains a web page for this book, which lists errata, examples, and any additional information. You can access this page at:

http://www.oreilly.com/catalog/progvb2005

To comment or ask technical questions about this book, send email to:

bookquestions@oreilly.com

For more information about O'Reilly books, conferences, Resource Centers, and the O'Reilly Network, see O'Reilly's web site at:

http://www.oreilly.com

Safari Enabled

 When you see a Safari® Enabled icon on the cover of your favorite technology book, that means the book is available online through the O'Reilly Network Safari Bookshelf.

Safari offers a solution that's better than e-books. It's a virtual library that lets you easily search thousands of top tech books, cut and paste code samples, download chapters, and find quick answers when you need the most accurate, current information. Try it for free at *http://safari.oreilly.com*.

Acknowledgments

The book you have in your hands is far better than the book I wrote, and for this I must thank an extraordinary pair of editors, Ralph Davis and John Osborn. If this book feels comfortable to VB6 programmers, as I sincerely hope it will, it is due in large measure to the work of Ron Petrusha and Robert Green. In addition, the folks behind the scenes at O'Reilly Media can never be thanked sufficiently: Caitrin McCullough, Linley Dolby, Matt Hutchinson, and Rob Romano.

This book is a departure from previous programming books; it is targeted at making you instantly productive, teaching the language and the concepts as we go. Approving such a book required a great leap of faith and courage, and I'm deeply grateful to John Osborn and Tim O'Reilly.

PART I

Building Windows
Applications

CHAPTER 1

Design and First Forms

In this chapter you will begin to create a Windows application. You will find that we get down to business *immediately* with as little fuss as possible. The introductory comments are intended to set the stage for everything else we're doing. I'll keep them short.

The requirements for a meaningful Windows application will be spelled out in this chapter, and the rest of the book will focus on implementing that application. We will finesse the design, exploring design decisions as we go, and our general approach will be that of *successive approximation*; that is: get it working and keep it working, as you add new functionality.

At times, this approach will cause us to write and rewrite the same section. One could argue that had we designed in advance we would avoid those cul-de-sacs, but it is exploring these dead ends, and the improvements we can make as we progressively improve our product, that will bring out essential aspects of Visual Basic 2005 programming.

The Requirements

Over the course of part one of this book, we will create an application based on a real-world application I recently built for one of my clients. We will use the application to explore retrieving and updating data from the Northwind Database that comes with SqlServer and SqlExpress.

 At the time of this writing, Microsoft is urging that .NET applications use SqlExpress in preference to Access, and so we shall in this book, though converting the code to support an Access database should not be difficult.

The opening form for the application allows you to search for or display all the Customers, Orders, Suppliers, and Employees listed in the Northwind tables, as shown in Figure 1-1.

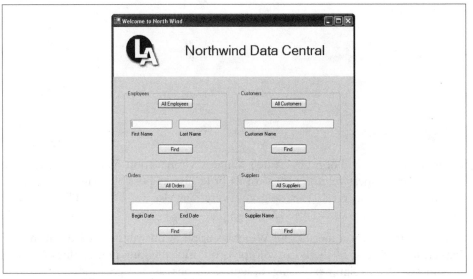

Figure 1-1. Initial form

The details page provides details on one company. It is tabbed and has a menu item, as shown in Figure 1-2. (Actual fields to be displayed will correspond to what is in the database.)

Figure 1-2. Customer detail

This form will be used to demonstrate menus, events, data display, data binding, data updating, and so on.

If you click All Customers from the main menu, you will be brought to a custom Rolodex®, as shown in Figure 1-3.

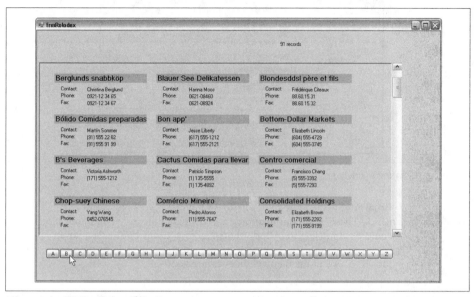

Figure 1-3. All Customers Rolodex

The user can scroll through all the customers or click on a letter to advance immediately to customers whose name begins with that letter. This will show a fairly sophisticated custom control, as well as advanced use of inheritance and polymorphism, as we reuse the basic structure of the Rolodex to be able to scroll through both customers and suppliers.

Double-clicking the customer entry in the Rolodex will bring you to the details page (as shown earlier).

You'll create the Rolodex in Chapter 4.

Getting Started

The hardest part of any project, for me, is getting started. There is a simple problem of mental inertia that is overcome only by firing up Visual Studio 2005 and dragging some controls onto a form.

To begin, start Visual Studio 2005 and create a Visual Basic 2005 Windows application, as shown in Figure 1-4. (If you are already in Visual Studio 2005, choose File → New project.)

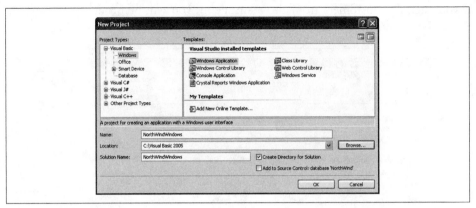

Figure 1-4. Creating the new project

Visual Studio 2005 has short-cut keys for almost every important command. These key combinations are configurable, however, and it would be confusing to include short-cut keys in this book when yours may be different. The best way to learn the short-cut key combinations is to look at the menu choices as you go.

Once the project is created, you are put into the Designer, with a blank form (titled Form1). The Toolbox is typically on the left, the Solution explorer and Properties windows are usually on the right, and a number of other useful windows may be minimized on the bottom, as shown in Figure 1-5.

Rearranging Windows

You can rearrange all of these Visual Studio elements by dragging and dropping the various windows. While you are in the editor, drag one of the windows from its docked position. As soon as you begin to move the window around, the docking diamond appears, as seen in Figure 1-6.

As you move the window, the four arrows of the diamond point to where you may dock. If you place the cursor over one of the arrows, it darkens and the placement for the window is previewed. If the window can join a tabbed group, the center of the diamond darkens as you pass the cursor over it. Hover over the darkened center and release the mouse and your window is automatically added to the tabbed group.

Renaming and Sizing the Form

The very first step will be to rename the *Form1.vb* file to *Welcome.vb*. Visual Studio 2005 will do the necessary work to make the changes throughout the solution. To rename the file click on Form1.vb within the Solution explorer and either right-click and choose Rename or change the File Name property in the Properties window.

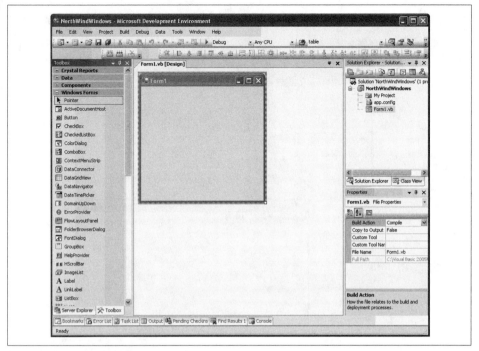

Figure 1-5. Designer window

We'll also change the window caption on the form to say "Welcome to Northwind." Changes to the form are accomplished by clicking on the form and then editing the properties in the Properties window. In VB.NET, the Text property controls the window caption.

VB6 NOTE: If you're familiar with Visual Basic 6 or earlier, you may recall that a form's caption was defined by its Caption property, not its Text property. In addition to the Visual Basic Form object, controls such as Checkbox, CommandButton, Frame, Label, and Option had a Caption property for static, display-only text. In contrast, the Text property was used for text that could usually be modified by the user. In .NET controls, these have been replaced by a single Text property.

The next step is to resize the form, which you can do by grabbing and dragging one of the sizing handles on the form itself, or by setting its Size property (click on the form, then click on the Size property in the Properties window). Notice that Size is expandable, and under Size you can set Width and Height separately. Set the Width to 582 and the Height to 582.

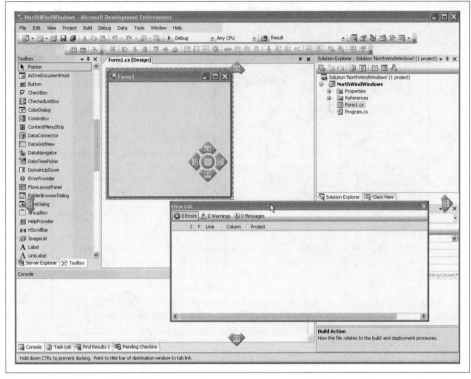

Figure 1-6. Docking windows

The size that looks best for you may depend on your target screen resolution. The projects done in this book were created on monitors set to 1280 × 1024.

MinimumSize and MaximumSize

The form may be resized by your user. You can control how much your form may be made smaller or larger using the MinimumSize and MaximumSize properties. These default to 0,0, which effectively disables these properties.

For this form, you may well want to create a MinimumSize that prevents the user from hiding one or more of the group boxes, or you may choose to leave the properties at their default values, which allows the user to set the form to any convenient size.

Using Picture Boxes, Panels, and Labels

To place the logo in the upper lefthand corner, follow these steps:

1. Right-click on the project in the Solution explorer and add a folder. Name it Images.

2. Copy the *LAlogo.gif* file (downloaded with the source code for this book) into the Images directory.

3. Add a PictureBox control to your form with Location 0, 0.

4. Click on the Ellipsis button within the Image property of the Picture box. Import the GIF file. Size the picture box to fit (133,129).

To create the banner "Northwind Data Central" you'll use two more controls. First, drag a panel into position by just touching the logo. (Its Location property should be 133,0.) Drag the panel's sizing handles to make the panel as tall as the logo, and wide enough to fill the form. (Its Size should be 445,128.) Set its name to pnlBanner. Set its BackColor to White (click on BackColor, drop down the color picker, and pick either a standard or a custom color).

 All links mentioned in this book are available as hyperlinks in the file *ProgrammingVisualBasic2005links.html* included with the downloadable source code.

Next, drag a label onto the Panel. Set its name to lblBanner and its BackColor to White. Set its ForeColor to Blue (type in the name **Blue**, or pick it from Custom colors). Open the Font property and set the font size to 24. In the Text property, type in the text you want, **Northwind Data Central**. The label will expand to fit the text. You may want to click on it and choose Format → CenterInForm → Horizontally—it will center itself in the panel.

Press F5 to run the application. You should see a logo across the top of your form.

Adding Group Boxes, Buttons, and Text Boxes

You are now ready to create your four groups (Employees, Customers, Orders, and Suppliers), as shown in the specification.

Begin by dragging a group box onto the form. Name it grpEmployees and set its Text property to Employees (which sets the text in the border of the group box). Drag a button into the group box and name it btnAllEmployees. Set its Text property to All Employees. Grab the side of the button and stretch it so that the words fit. A reasonable location for the group lbox is 29,162, and a reasonable size is 247,166.

Naming Conventions

The name of the control: *pnlBanner* is an example of "Hungarian Notation," named after Dr. Charles Simonyi, Chief Architect at Microsoft (born in Hungary), who is credited with inventing the idea of prefixing variable names with a letter (or series of letters) that indicates the variable type.

Hungarian notation makes much more sense in a programming language like C with a limited number of types, than it does in an object-oriented language like Visual Basic 2005 that has an unlimited number of types.

Microsoft discourages the use of Hungarian Notation in public variables and properties for .NET. The convention that many Visual Basic 2005 programmers have adopted, and which I will use in this book, is to use Hungarian notation only for controls. For example, text boxes will be named txt??? (e.g., txtName) and group boxes will be grp??? (e.g., grpEmployees), while labels will be named lbl??? (e.g., lblFirstName). And so forth.

For more on Hungarian Notation, see:

> *http://msdn.microsoft.com/library/default.asp?url=/library/en-us/dnvsgen/html/hunganotat.asp*

For more on Microsoft naming conventions, see:

> *http://msdn.microsoft.com/library/default.asp?url=/library/en-us/cpguide/html/cpconimplementingnetdataprovidercodeconventions.asp*

and:

> *http://msdn.microsoft.com/library/default.asp?url=/library/en-us/cpgenref/html/cpconnamingguidelines.asp*

Aligning controls

Visual Studio 2005 provides extensive help for aligning the controls in your form. As you add controls, blue alignment lines appear to show you how to align various controls. Alternately, you are free to select (Shift-click) two or more controls and then use the alignment menu choices under Format.

For example, if you'd like your button centered within the group box, select the button and choose Format → Center In Form → Horizontally.

Drag two text boxes onto the group box, right below the All Employees button, and name them txtEmployeeFirst and txtEmployeeLast. To center the two text boxes, you'll need to select them both (click on the first text box, and Shift-click to highlight the second). This group of two text boxes can now be centered by choosing Format → Center In Form → Horizontally.

Drag two labels onto the group box and use the blue alignment lines to place them below the text boxes. Name them lblEmployeeFirst and lblEmployeeLast and set their text to First Name and Last Name, respectively.

Finally, click on the All Employees button and copy and paste it in place. Drag the new button below the text boxes and labels. Name it btnEmployeesFind and set its Text property to Find.

All of the elements in the group box should now be centered horizontally; let's center them vertically as well. To do so, put the cursor in the upper lefthand corner and drag to the lower righthand corner, marking all the controls. Next, use the menu item Format → Center In Form → Vertically.

You will want to explore the impact of using the various Format options, including aligning objects, equalizing the spacing, and centering objects within the group box. You can also use the blue alignment lines to help you quickly realign the various controls.

Copying and moving controls

Once the group box looks the way you want, use the mouse to select the group box and copy and paste so that you have a duplicate (which is pasted on top of the original, offset slightly). You can now drag the new group box below the first group box. (When you click on the group box, a move handle will appear, as shown in Figure 1-7, which allows you to drag the group box where you desire.)

Figure 1-7. Move handles

Rename the new group box grpOrders and set its text to Orders. Fix the text on the buttons and labels, and rename all the controls (e.g., btnAllOrders, etc.), as shown in Table 1-1.

Table 1-1. Controls for Orders

Control	ControlID	Notes
Button	btnOrders	Centered (like All Employees)
Textbox	txtOrdersBeginDate	Good size is 100,20
Textbox	txtOrdersEndDate	Align with first text box
Label	lblBeginDate	Text: Begin Date
Label	lblEndDate	Text: EdDate
Button	btnFind	Centered as before

Copy and paste a third group box and name it grpCustomers. Delete the text box and label on the left. Move the right text box and label, stretching out the text box for

Customer Name. Change the Text property of the Label to Customer Name. Rename the control and change the Text property of btnAllCustomers to All Customers. The new group box should look like Figure 1-8.

Figure 1-8. Customer group box

Finally, copy this third group box and create a fourth group box for Suppliers, as shown in Table 1-2.

Table 1-2. Controls for Suppliers

Control	ControlID	Notes
Button	btnAllSuppliers	Centered
Textbox	txtSupplierName	Same size as for customers
Label	lblSupplierName	Test: Supplier Name
Button	btnFind	Centered as before

When you are done, you should have a form that looks more or less like Figure 1-9.

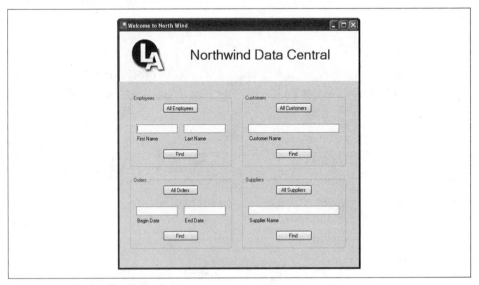

Figure 1-9. Completed welcome form

Once you get comfortable with the tools, this form should take about 10 minutes to create! The good news is you now have a working form; unfortunately, the buttons don't actually do anything yet!

Events

The logic you will eventually implement is this: if the user clicks (for example) All Employees, you will open a form with a Rolodex that will allow the user to scroll through all the Employees. That form will also allow the user to filter which Employees are shown and to jump to those Employees whose name begins with a specific letter. All of that will be implemented with fairly advanced features such as custom controls in Chapter 4, so for now we'll stub out these buttons.

You can, of course, have the buttons do nothing, but it would be nice to have them pop up a message box saying, "Not yet implemented."

To make that work, you'll need to respond to the button click event, and you'll need to put up a message box.

Every control "publishes" a number of *events* that other parts of your program can respond to or *handle*. Buttons, of course, publish a *click* event. The click event "fires" every time the button is clicked.

Buttons also publish events that fire when the button's size is changed, when its background color changes, when its image changes, when its cursor changes, for drag over or drag/drop and so forth. You can find the events for buttons by either checking the documentation, or by selecting a button in the designer and then, in the Properties window, clicking the lightning bolt. This lightning bolt button switches the property window to show the control's events, as shown in Figure 1-10.

Creating Event Handlers

You now have three ways to create the Click event handler:

1. You can type a method name in the property box next to Click, to create a method handler with that name, and press Enter.

2. You can click in that box and drop down the list of already existing event handlers. (In this case, there won't be any yet, but later in the program you can use this approach to share event-handler methods among more than one control. More on that idea shortly.)

3. You can double-click in the property box. Visual Studio 2005 will name the method for you.

Whichever of these you decide on, Visual Studio 2005 will bring you to the code editor for the event handler. If you let Visual Studio 2005 name the method, you will find yourself inside a Sub named btnAllEmployees_Click.

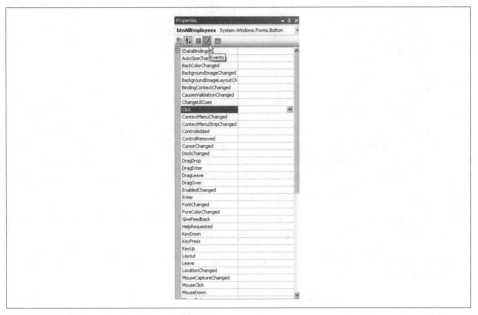

Figure 1-10. Button events

Default Event Handler

Every control has a default event. In the case of the button, it is (no surprise) "Click." That is the event most often handled, and so the Button designer set it to be the default event. You can double-click on the button and Visual Studio 2005 will act as if you had single-clicked on the button and then double-clicked on the Click event—that is, it will create the btnAllEmployees_Click event handler and put the editor into that subroutine.

Event-Handler Parameters

The convention is for .NET Event handlers to take two parameters. The first is of type Object (see sidebar "Classes, Objects, and Derivation") and is filled at runtime with a reference to the object that triggered the event (in this case, the button).

The second is an object of type EventArgs or a type *derived* from EventArgs. EventArgs itself is not useful, but the types derived from EventArgs contain very pertinent information. (See the sidebar "Classes, Objects, and Derivation.")

In this case, we want to put up a message box saying that the handler has not yet been implemented. The Framework Class Library (FCL) that comes with .NET provides you with a number of useful classes, one of which is the MessageBox class. The MessageBox class has a shared method (see sidebar "Shared Methods and Properties") Show that is *overloaded* (see the sidebar "Overloading Methods").

Classes, Objects, and Derivation

A class defines a new type, extending the language beyond the built-in types, such as integer and string.

A type is a general category like car. You drive a particular car, but your car and my car both belong to the class cars; they are of type car.

An object is an individual *instance* of a type. Each individual car (your particular car, my particular car) is an object.

A class has *methods* (that tell you what the class can do) and *properties* (that hold values for instances of the class). For example, the class MessageBox has a Show method that does the work of drawing the MessageBox. It also has a number of properties, such as size. Each *instance* of the MessageBox will have a specific size; one MessageBox may be 100×150, another may be larger or smaller.

It is possible for one class to *inherit* from (or *derive* from) another class. Saying that ListBox inherits from Window indicates that it *specializes* Window (that is, a ListBox is a special type of Window). Inheritance creates the *is-a* relationship: a ListBox *is-a* (specialized form of) Window that includes all the methods and properties of Window but adds additional methods and properties of its own. It is also possible for ListBox to change the way it implements methods inherited from Window. Thus, a ListBox might Draw itself differently than another Window does.

Window is referred to as the *base* class, and ListBox is called the *derived* class. That is, ListBox derives its fundamental characteristics and behaviors from Window, and then specializes to its own particular needs.

When you define a method, you define its parameters. It is permissible to pass a derived type as a parameter in place of a base type. That is, if a Window is expected, it is permissible to pass a ListBox (which derives from Window) because a ListBox *is-a* Window.

Similarly, all event handlers take an instance of type EventArgs, so it is permissible to pass an instance of a class that derives from EventArgs. For example, when you write an event handler for the selection change event in a ListBox, you will be passed an instance of type ListViewItemSelectionChangedEventArgs that is derived from EventArgs. This specialized type of EventArgs class contains additional information that is only relevant to the selection change event, such as the property IsSelected.

.NET has a *rooted* inheritance hierarchy. Every type in .NET is considered to derive from the base class Object. Even built-in types (e.g., integer, Double, etc.) derive from Object. Thus, by declaring a method to take an object of type Object, you can accept any type whatsoever.

For further discussion, see Chapter 18.

Shared Methods and Properties

The methods and properties of a class can be either *instance members* or *shared members*. *Instance* members are associated with an instance of the class (e.g., a particular MessageBox's location), while shared members are associated with the class itself. The advantage of shared methods and properties is that you may access them without first creating an instance of the class.

Thus, in the code for the All Employees button-click event handler, you want to call the Show method on a message box. Rather than having to write:

```
Dim mbox as new MessageBox(…)
mBox.Show( )
```

you can just write:

```
MessageBox.Show(…)
```

The shared Show( ) method is not specific to an instance, but rather is associated with the entire class.

For further discussion, see Chapter 1.

When you type the word MessageBox and then type a period, Visual Studio 2005's IntelliSense will display all the shared members of the MessageBox class. (The shared members are displayed because you placed the dot after a type name; had you typed the dot after an instance variable, the nonshared members would be displayed.

Click on Show and type an open parenthesis, and you'll see a tool tip indicating that there are 21 overloaded versions of this method. You want the one that lets you put in text, a title, and which buttons and icon you want to appear, as shown in Figure 1-11.

As you are about to enter each parameter, the tool tip will describe what it is looking for. When you get to the choice for the MessageBoxButtons, the tool tip will offer you one of the allowed values. These values are enumerated constants (see sidebar "Enumerated Constants") and thus IntelliSense can help you make a valid choice, as shown in Figure 1-12.

Similarly, IntelliSense will help you choose one of the valid options for the icon. When you are done, your event handler will look like Example 1-1.

Overloading Methods

There are many parameters you might want to provide to the MessageBox's Show method depending on the circumstances. In some cases, you'd like to provide just a single string and let the message box worry about its title, buttons, and so forth. In other cases, you'd like to dictate the title, buttons, and icons to use, but you don't care about setting a default button. Rather than creating 24 different methods (e.g., ShowString, ShowStringAndChooseButtons, ShowStringAndChooseButtonsAndSetDefaultButton) the author of the MessageBox class created 21 variations of the Show method. This process of creating more than one method with the same name is called *method overloading*.

Each method must have a unique *signature*. The signature is the name and the parameters. You typically overload a method by varying either the number of parameters or the types of parameters or both (note that changing the *name of a parameter* does *not* vary the signature).

If you look at the help entry for the MessageBox Show method, you'll find 24 overloaded versions of this one method. Each has a unique signature; meaning that no two have the same number and type of parameters, and that is how the compiler knows which version you want.

For further discussion, see Chapter 18.

Figure 1-11. Choosing the overloaded Show method

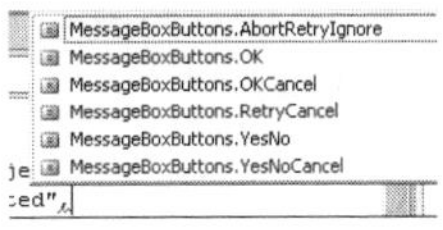

Figure 1-12. Message box button choices

Example 1-1. btnAllEmployees Click event handler

```
Private Sub btnAllEmployees_Click(ByVal sender As System.Object, _
    ByVal e As System.EventArgs) Handles btnAllEmployees.Click
  MessageBox.Show("Not yet implemented", "Not Yet Implemented", _
    MessageBoxButtons.OK, MessageBoxIcon.Exclamation)
End Sub
```

The code in this and all examples has been broken into shorter lines to fit within the book; in Visual Studio 2005 you will find the entire signature (name and parameters) for the method on a single line. If you break a line in Visual Basic 2005 you must use the line continuation character—an underscore (_)—preceded by a space.

Run the application and click on All Employees. A message box will pop up with the message, title, icon, and button you designated, as shown in Figure 1-13. Congratulations! You just wrote your first event handler.

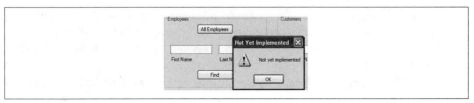

Figure 1-13. Testing the event handler

Enumerated Constants

It is helpful to group related constants into an enumeration. For example, you might declare an enumeration of Fahrenheit temperature constants using the following code:

```
Enum Temperatures
    CelsiusMeetsFahrenheit = -40
    WickedCold = 0
    FreezingPoint = 32
    LightJacketWeather = 60
    SwimmingWeather = 72
    BoilingPoint = 212
End Enum
```

You would refer to one of these enumerated constants through the name of the enumeration. For example, the freezing point of water would be referred to as:

```
Temperatures.FreezingPoint
```

Similarly, the buttons valid for a `MessageBox` are referred to through their enumeration, `MessageBoxButtons`, and this allows IntelliSense to present you with all the valid values.

For more, see Chapter 16.

VB6 NOTE: You may be wondering what happened to the `MsgBox` function, the standard Visual Basic language function for displaying a message box. The answer is that it still exists in Visual Basic (it's a part of the Interaction class of the `Microsoft.VisualBasic` namespace) and can still be called from your Visual Basic code just as you always did. (Interestingly, it can also be called from any other .NET-compliant language, like C#, although it needs to be called as a shared method of the Interaction class.) Moreover, the syntax of `MsgBox` is largely identical to its VB6 counterpart, except that the final two optional parameters (which specify the location of a help file and the help context ID in the help file that contains information about the `MsgBox` display) have been eliminated.

.NET uses the more versatile `MessageBox.Show` method rather than the VB6 `MsgBox`, and we will use `MessageBox` throughout this book.

Sharing Event Handlers

It is possible, and often much cleaner, for more than one event to share a single event handler. Since the functionality of All Employees, All Customers, All Orders, and All Suppliers is very similar, it might make sense to give all four of these a common event handler.

 VB6 NOTE: In VB6 and earlier versions, you could share event handlers by creating a control array. When the control array's event handler was invoked, Visual Basic passed it a single parameter, the index of the control that had fired the event. The VB6 control array, however, is not supported by Visual Basic .NET, which offers a much more flexible method of sharing event handlers.

To do so, open the code editor and change the name of `btnAllEmployees_Click` to `btnAll_Click`. When you do, an underline will appear near the new method name. Clicking on the underline will open a smart tag, and dropping the smart tag will open a command offering to rename the function for you, as shown in Figure 1-14. Clicking this will not only rename the function in place, but will "fix up" all references to this function (including in the designer-generated code).

```
Private Sub btnAll_Click(ByVal sender As System.Object, ByVal
    System.Windows.For       essageBox.Show("Not yet implemented",
        MessageBoxButto
                              Rename 'btnCustomersFind_Click' to 'btnAll_Click'
    End Sub
```

Figure 1-14. Change function name

Return to the design mode, click on the All Employees button, and then click on the lightning bolt in the properties to see the Events. Notice that the handler associated with the click event is now `btnAllClick`. Copy and paste that event handler name to the Click event handler for the other three related buttons, or click on the button and then in the properties/events window click on the "click" event and use the drop-down menu of event handlers to pick the one you want to use. Run the application and you'll see that all four buttons now bring up the same message box.

Differentiating Which Button Was Pressed

While having shared event handlers is fine, you may need to know which button was actually pressed. In our simple case, it would be nice to have the error message reflect the button (e.g., "All Employees not yet implemented.").

You can do this by casting the object passed into the event handler to type `Button` (using the `CType` conversion function):

```
CType(sender, Button)
```

Casting

When you *cast* an object, you tell the compiler "trust me, I know what this is." In the example shown:

```
CType(sender, Button)
```

you are saying to the compiler, "trust me, I happen to know that sender is really of type `Button`." This is perfectly fine, but if you get it wrong, this code will throw an exception.

As an alternative to `CType` you may use the `DirectCast` keyword, providing an expression as the first argument and the type to convert it to as the second argument. You can only do this if the two arguments have an inheritance relationship. Since `Button` does inherit from `Object`, you could have written:

```
DirectCast(sender, Button)
```

Because `DirectCast` can be somewhat more efficient, it is preferred where there is an inheritance relationship.

For still further discussion, see Chapter 16.

This call to `CType` returns an object of type `Button`, representing the button that caused the event to fire. You can ask that button for its `Text` property, and assign the string returned to a variable:

```
Dim buttonName As String = CType(sender, Button).Text
```

You can then add that variable into the message box's message:

```
MessageBox.Show(buttonName + " not yet implemented", "Not Yet Implemented", _
        MessageBoxButtons.OK, MessageBoxIcon.Exclamation)
```

Each button's message is specialized, as shown in Figure 1-15.

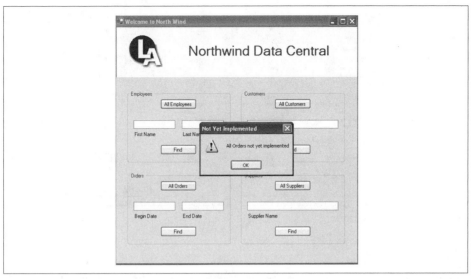

Figure 1-15. Sharing event handlers

Creating the Customer Detail Page

Once the program is fully functional, the Find button will examine the contents of the text boxes and seek to find all the customers that match the text provided. If a single match is found, a form will open with details about that customer.

For now, we'll bypass the issue of what happens when multiple matches are found, and we'll even bypass the database search, and just build the form that will be filled in with the customer's details.

To get started, you need to create a second form, frmCustomerDetails. Right-click on the solution and choose Add Class. From within the dialog, choose Windows Form as the type of item you wish to add, and name the form *frmCustomerDetails.vb*, as shown in Figure 1-16. Click Add to add the new form.

Resize your form to 600,300. Click on your form and change the caption (using the Text property) to Customer Details.

Our task for this form is to add a menu, tab controls, and the controls necessary to display and edit the Customer information. The specifications call for this form to open in Read Only mode; the user must explicitly choose the menu item Edit to make the fields editable, and then Save to save the changes made in Edit mode (which returns the user to Read Mode).

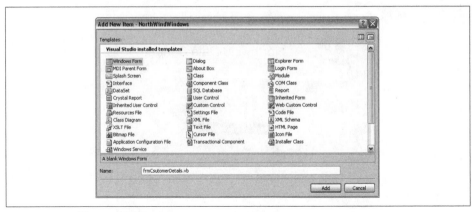

Figure 1-16. Add second form

Adding a Menu

You'll begin by adding a menu to the form. To do so, first drag a menu strip onto the form. Two things will happen: your menu will be represented by a `MenuStrip` instance in the "tray" at the bottom of the form, and the menu itself will be docked to the top of the form. Notice that the menu has an area that says Type Here. Enter the text for the top-level menu, **Customer**, and notice that when you hit enter, two more Type Here boxes appear, one for a second top-level menu item (we won't need this for now) and one for a sub-menu. In that sub-menu enter the word Edit. As you do, another box will open below it. Enter the three remaining choices (Save, Cancel, Close) one by one.

Right-click on a menu item to see some of the common actions you might want to take. This allows you to edit the text or change the behavior of the menu items. For now, you won't need any of these options.

Hooking Up the Second Form to the First

We're going to hardwire this form (for now) to the Find Customer button in the Welcome page. Return to the Welcome page and double-click on the All Customers button in the Customer group box. In the Event handler, enter this one line of code:

```
frmCustomerDetails.Show( )
```

This opens the new dialog, but passes in no information about the customer's name. We'll fix that later when we are ready to search for a customer in the database.

Adding Tab Controls

The Customer Details page has four tabs. Drag a TabControl onto the form, and size it to fill most of the form, as shown in Figure 1-17.

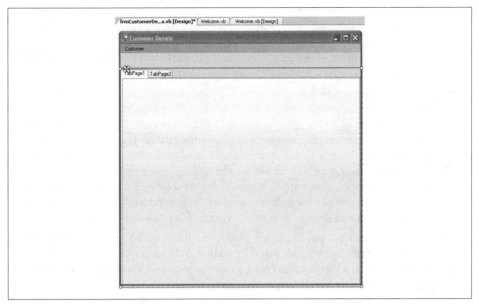

Figure 1-17. New tab control on form

Notice that the TabControl starts with two tabs, labeled `TabPage1` and `TabPage2`. Click on the TabControl itself, then click on the first tab (TabPage1). Look in the Properties window. It should say:

    TabControl1 System.Windows.Forms.TabControl.

Change its `Name` property to `tclCustomerDetails`. The Properties window should now say:

    tclCustomerDetails System.Windows.Forms.TabControl.

Adding Tabs to the TabControl

Click within the first tab and the Properties window should show you that you are in TabPage1. Use the name property to change the name of the tab to `tabCustomerInfo` and the Text field to change the text that appears on the tab to `Customer.Info`.

To get to the second tab, you'll need to click on TabPage2 twice. The first click will choose the TabControl, and the second click will bring TabPage2 forward. You'll then need to click in the page itself to get to TabPage2. Rename it `tabCustomerDemographics` and change its `Text` to `Demographics`.

You are now ready to add a third tab. Click on the TabControl itself, and in the Properties window scroll down to TabPages. Click the Ellipsis button to open the TabPage Collection Editor. Click Add to add a new page, and use the properties to set both the name and the text, as shown in Figure 1-18.

Namespaces, Classes, and Instances

The Properties window is reflecting that tclCustomerDetails is the name for an instance of an object of type System.Windows.Forms.TabControl.

You read this name back to front. TabControl is the class type. System.Windows.Forms is the *namespace* within which TabControl is defined. Namespaces are used to avoid name collisions, and to divide up class libraries to make it easier to find the classes you need. The namespaces can be thought of as concentric circles. The outermost circle is System, which contains nearly all the namespaces used in the framework class library. The Windows namespace (which is within the System namespace) contains all the namespaces used by Windows applications (as opposed to Web applications) and the Forms namespace contains all the classes used by Forms (and itself is contained in the Windows namespace, and thus by extension, within the System namespace).

When referring to a class you must *fully qualify* the name (provide its full namespace identification), or you can use shorthand by adding an Imports statement at the top of your code file. Thus, if you want to create a form in your code, you can either write:

```
Dim myForm As New System.Windows.Forms.Form( )
```

or you can add an Imports statement to the top of your code file:

```
Imports System.Windows.Forms
```

in which case, you can write:

```
Dim myForm As New Form( )
```

In either case, myForm will be considered to be an instance of the class System.Windows.Forms.Form and thus will have all the methods, properties, and events of that class.

Visual Studio automatically adds Import statements when you create a project, appropriate to the kind of project you are creating. For example, Windows Forms project automatically Imports System.Windows.Forms.

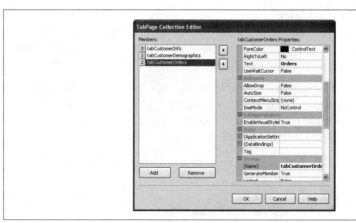

Figure 1-18. TabPage Collection Editor

You now have a details page with three tabs. You are ready to populate these tabs with controls that will reflect the data held in the Customer Database (and that will build on the structure provided by Microsoft).

You can also add and remove tabs using the TabControl's smart tag, as shown in Figure 1-19.

Figure 1-19. The TabControl smart tag

The first tab will be used to display (and update) the information contained in the Customers Table, whose design is shown in Figure 1-20.

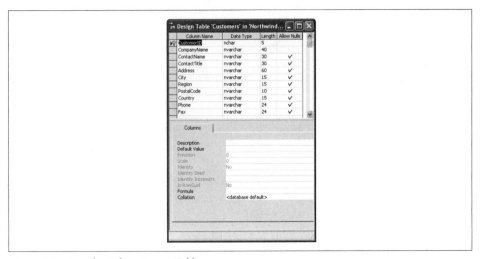

Figure 1-20. Northwind Customer Table

Each of these items can be displayed with a simple combination of labels and text boxes, as shown in Figure 1-21. The label that reads "Company Name Here" should have a font size of 20, with the font's Bold attribute set to True. Also, the field's ForeColor should be Blue. Accept the default field names that Visual Basic assigns. You'll give them more precise names in Chapter 2.

Summary

In this chapter you've seen how to create a form, how to connect that form to other forms, and how to handle events by posting message boxes. In the next chapter, you will see how to connect data stored in a database to the fields in your form, and how to edit, update, and delete that data.

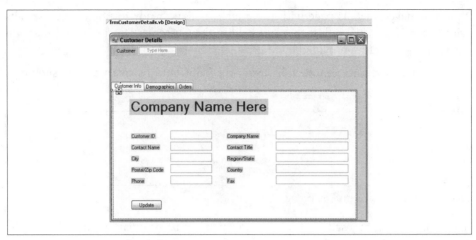

Figure 1-21. Customer info tab design

CHAPTER 2

Data Access

In Chapter 1, you created a couple of forms and some Find buttons, but your forms were left more or less inert; they do not interact with real data.

In this chapter you'll begin to extract data from the Northwind database that comes both with SQL Server and SQL Server Express. You'll use that data to fill in your forms. You'll do this incrementally, adding complexity as you go. You'll put a premium on using data controls provided with Visual Basic 2005 and letting the controls manage the "plumbing" of database interaction for you.

> If you do not have either SQL Server or SQLServer Express you will need to download a copy from Microsoft. There is usually some form of demonstration version available, though the names and conditions change from time to time. As of this writing, SQL Server Express is bundled with all versions of Visual Studio 2005 or is available as a free download on the Microsoft site (*http://www.Microsoft.com*).

Adding Data to the Customer Page

Return to the first tab of `frmCustomerDetails` and give each text box a reasonable name (e.g. `txtCustomerID`, `txtCity`, and so on).

> This chapter picks up on the code from the previous chapter. If you download the source, however, you'll find that we've created folders with snapshots that represent the state of the code at the end of each chapter.

Create a Data Connection

You need a connection to the database. Before you begin, open the Data Sources Window (Data → Show Data Sources). From this floating, dockable window there are a number of ways to create a new data source. The two simplest are either to click the hyperlink Add New Data Source… or to click the Add New Data Source button, as shown in Figure 2-1.

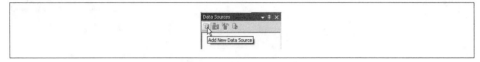

Figure 2-1. Add New Data Source button

Clicking this button opens the Data Source Configuration wizard. On the first tab, you can indicate the type of DataSource you wish to use; in this case, you'll pick Database. The next step is to create a Connection to do that data source.

You can use an existing connection (if you have one) or click New Connection… to create a new connection object. This opens the connection Properties modal dialog box. The first step is to select the server, the second step is to choose between Windows Integrated Security (trusted connection) or a specific database user ID. The third and final step is to choose the database. Be sure to click the Test Connection button to ensure that the connection is working, as shown in Figure 2-2.

Figure 2-2. Configure and test the connection

After you click OK and click the Next button, you will have the option to save the connection information to the application configuration file. Click the check box and name the connection NorthwindConnection, as shown in Figure 2-3.

Figure 2-3. Save NorthwindConnection

Create a Data Set Declaratively

The next step in the wizard asks you to choose the database objects you'll connect to through this Database connection object. You can connect to any number of tables, stored procedures, views, and functions of the Northwind dataset. For this project, expand the tables category and select the Customers table, as shown in Figure 2-4 (you can expand the table to select just certain fields, but in this case you want them all).

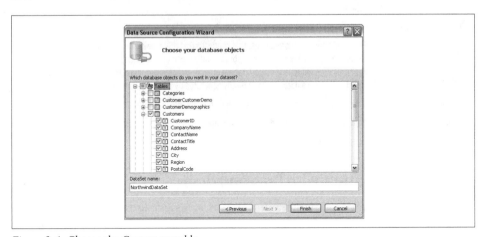

Figure 2-4. Choose the Customers table

Click Finish and the Wizard will create a selection statement for selecting all the fields from the Customers table within the Northwind database. Notice that the Data Sources window now reflects your NorthwindDataSet, with the Customers table beneath the ADO.NET Object Model.

The NorthwindDataSet is an instance of a DataSet object, the heart of the ADO.NET object model. While you don't need to understand the ADO.NET object model in detail to work with data (the controls will hide a lot of the internal plumbing from you), it can be useful to have an idea of what these different objects are and what they are for. This is shown in Table 2-1.

Table 2-1. Principal ADO.NET objects

ADO.NET object	Description
DataSet	A *disconnected* subset of the entire database. In most environments, there are a limited number of connections to the database, such connections are said to be "expensive" and there is strong incentive to use connections to the database as briefly as possible. By making the dataset "disconnected" you are able to work on it at length without tying up a connection to the database. (Periodically, you'll reconnect the DataSet to its parent database, update the database with changes you've made to the DataSet, and update the DataSet with changes in the database made by other processes.)
	A DataSet is composed of DataTable objects as well as DataRelation objects.
DataTable	The DataTable, which represents a database table, can be created programmatically or as a result of a query against the database. The DataTable has a number of public properties, including the Columns collection, which returns the ColumnsCollection object, which in turn consists of DataColumn objects. Each DataColumn object represents a column in a table.
DataRelation	Represents the relation between two columns (typically of different tables).
DataView	Enables you to create different views of the data in a table, allowing for sorting and filtering.
DataConnector	Acts as a data source for controls and mediates between the control and its own data source (typically a dataset). Simplifies binding to a single table within a dataset that may have many tables.
DataNavigator	Provides services for navigating through data bound to a control.
TableAdapter	Designer-generated components that connect a DataSet object to the underlying data source. Similar to DataAdapters (below) but strongly typed (a unique class defined to work only with the fields selected for a specific database object), and can contain multiple queries to support multiple tables from a data source. Typically generated by the Data Source Configuration Wizard.
DataAdapter	Decouples the DataSet from the underlying structure of the physical database.
Command	Command objects are used for Selection, Update, Deletion, and Insertion.
Connection	Connection objects represent a connection from your application to the database.

Binding Data Controls with Drag and Drop

Return to frmCustomerDetails. The first step is to associate the text boxes on the form with the data in the database. You can do this with the DataBindings property, but it is much easier to drag columns from the Customers table onto the appropriate text box. To do so, expand the Customers table in the NorthWindDataSet (within the Data Sources window) and drag the CustomerID column onto the CustomerID text box. Then do the same with the remaining text boxes.

Let's also add text boxes for the Phone and Fax. Click on Phone in the Data Sources window. Notice that there is a drop-down menu available. Click on the drop-down menu and notice that you may choose a TextBox, ComboBox, Label, and so on, to display this data. Set it to TextBox and drag it into place.

Two controls are placed onto your form: a label and a text box. Reposition the label (to align it) and rename the text box to txtPhone. Do the same with the Fax.

 Three controls are added to your tray: a NorthWindDataSet control, a CustomersBindingSource, and a CustomersTableAdapter. These are used to facilitate binding the data from the data source to the actual controls on your form.

You do not want the users setting the Customer ID. You can disable the text box by setting the Enabled property to False.

Querying with Parameters

Now return to the Welcome page (see Figure 1-1). The Find button works great if you want to find the first customer. However, you want slightly more complex behavior. When the user clicks on the Find button, the value in the Company Name field will be examined and used as a search criterion against all the Company Names in the database. Here is the behavior we want to achieve with our code:

- If there is exactly one match, the customer data is displayed.
- If there is more than one match, however, you want to display a list of all the matching customer names, so the user can pick the desired company.
- If no names match, you want to inform the user that no matches were found.

To begin your implementation make the Customers table available to the Welcome page. Drag the Customers table onto the form. Five controls are created:

- NorthWindDataSet
- CustomersBindingSource
- CustomersTableAdapter
- CustomersBindingNavigator
- CustomersDataGridView (visible on form)

Delete the CustomersDataGridView from the form; we won't be using it.

The next task is to write a complete handler for the Customers Find button. The code we'll use is shown in Example 2-1.

Example 2-1. Customers Group Find button

```
Private Sub btnCustomersFind_Click( _
    ByVal sender As System.Object, _
    ByVal e As System.EventArgs) _
    Handles btnCustomersFind.Click

    Dim filteredView As Data.DataView = _
        New Data.DataView(NorthwindDataSet.Customers)
```

Example 2-1. Customers Group Find button (continued)

```
    filteredView.RowFilter = "CompanyName Like '%" + txtCustomerName.Text + "%'"

    Dim rowsFound As Int32 = filteredView.Count
    Select Case rowsFound
        Case 0  ' no records found
            MessageBox.Show( _
            "No matching records found", _
            "No records found", _
            MessageBoxButtons.OK, _
            MessageBoxIcon.Exclamation)
        Case 1
            frmCustomerDetails.CompanyNameParameter = _
                filteredView.Item(0)("CompanyName")
            frmCustomerDetails.Show()
        Case Else
            dlgPickMatchingCompany.FilteredView = filteredView
            Dim result As DialogResult
            result = dlgPickMatchingCompany.ShowDialog()
            If result = DialogResult.OK Then
                Dim rowView As Data.DataRowView
                rowView = dlgPickMatchingCompany.lbMatching.SelectedItem
                Dim companyName As String = rowView.Row.Item("CompanyName")
                frmCustomerDetails.CompanyNameParameter = companyName
                frmCustomerDetails.Show()
            End If
    End Select
End Sub
```

Let's take this step by step.

Open the handler for the customers Find button in the Customers group box and replace it with the following code (you'll need to add the statement Imports System.Data to the top of the code file):

```
    Private Sub btnCustomersFind_Click( _
        ByVal sender As System.Object, _
        ByVal e As System.EventArgs) _
        Handles btnCustomersFind.Click

        Dim filteredView as DataView = new DataView(NorthwindDataSet.Customers)
        filteredView.RowFilter = "CompanyName Like '%" + txtCustomerName.Text + "%'"
```

The first line creates a DataView object based on the Customers table within your data set. As noted in Table 2-1, this view can be used to filter which data is presented.

The second line sets the filter on the DataView to match the partial customer name entered by the user (surrounded by wildcard characters [%]).

This search will find any `CustomerName` that *contains* the text the user enters. If you want to match any name that *starts with* the text the user enters, remove the first wildcard (%).

Thus, if the user enters "BO" and clicks find, four companies will be found: *Bo*n app', *Bo*ttom-Dollar Markets, Lacorne d'a*bo*ndance, and The Cracker *Bo*x. If you change the query to *starts with* (by removing the first wildcard), you will match only the first two of these.

One row found in search

Once you have a filtered view, you can find out how many matches have been returned:

```
Dim rowsFound As Int32 = filteredView.Count
```

If `rowsFound` has a value of exactly one, only one company matches your search criterion, so you want to open the `frmCustomerDetails` page and display the information for that one company.

By inspecting the database you will find that if you query for the name Around, only one company matches (Around the Horn). That makes a good test case.

To implement the case of finding a single company, the first step is to return to the code page of the *frmCustomerDetails.vb* page and notice that the `frmCustomerDetails_Load` method fills the `CustomersTableAdapter` with the entire Customers table within the `NorthwindDataSet`:

```
Private Sub frmCustomerDetails_Load(ByVal sender As System.Object, ByVal e As System.
EventArgs) Handles MyBase.Load
    Me.CustomersTableAdapter.Fill(Me.NorthwindDataSet.Customers)
End Sub
```

You want to fill only the subset of that table that matches the criterion (Company name). So you'll create a parameterized query, which you'll use to pass in the name of the company.

To do so, return to the Designer view of `frmCustomerDetails`. Click on the smart tab for `CustomersTableAdapter` and click Add Query, as shown in Figure 2-5.

Figure 2-5. Add Query to CustomersTableAdapter

This will open the Search Criteria Builder. Select the data source, and create a new query named FillByCompanyName. Modify the query to add a where clause, as shown in the sample on the dialog, and as illustrated in Figure 2-6.

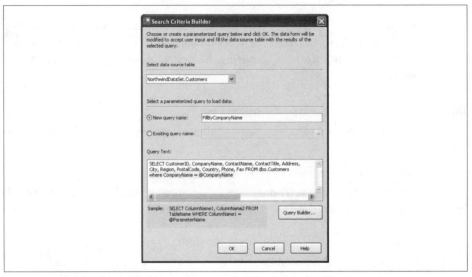

Figure 2-6. Search Criteria Builder dialog

Click OK. A FillByCompanyNameToolStrip is created for you. Delete it; you will not be filling in the company name interactively on this form.

Double-click on *NorthWindDataSet.xsd* in the Solution explorer. This will open the *NorthWindDataSet.xsd* designer and reveal that you now have two methods to fill the CustomersTableAdapter, as shown in Figure 2-7.

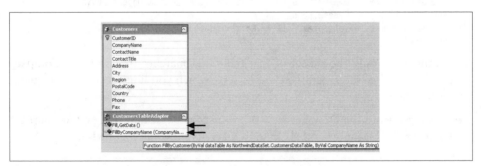

Figure 2-7. NorthWindDataSet.xsd

It is this new method (FillByCompanyName) that you'll want to call, with the name of the company as the second parameter (the first parameter is the table).

To do so, you need a way for the Welcome page to pass the name of the Company to the Customer Details page. The easiest way is to create a public property in the Customer Details form:

```
Private m_CompanyNameParameter As String
Public WriteOnly Property CompanyNameParameter( ) As String
    Set(ByVal value As String)
        m_CompanyNameParameter = value
    End Set
End Property
```

 Properties typically have a *get* and a *set* accessor. Since there is never a reason to get the m_CompanyNameParameter value from outside this class, this property has been marked WriteOnly and provides only a Set accessor.

You can now modify the frmCustomersDetails_Load event to call the new parameterized query, which has four overloads. The one you want takes a DataTable (Customers) and the string representation of the parameter (the company name), as shown in Figure 2-8.

Figure 2-8. Fill by company name

Fill this in with the name of the table and with the name of the company (set by the Welcome form).

```
Me.CustomersTableAdapter.FillByCompanyName( _
    Me.NorthwindDataSet.Customers, _
    Me.m_CompanyNameParameter)
```

 Don't forget to comment out or delete the original call to the unparameterized fill method.
```
'Me.CustomersTableAdapter.Fill( _
    'Me.NorthwindDataSet.Customers)
```

Return to *Welcome.vb*. Still working on the assumption that you found exactly one matching record, you can now set the CompanyNameParameter in the frmCustomerDetails page, and call Show on frmCustomerDetails, which will fire the Load event. This will in turn load the parameterized query and display your company.

```
frmCustomerDetails.CompanyNameParameter = filteredView.Item(0)("CompanyName")
frmCustomerDetails.Show( )
```

Let's unpack the line. The database returned, you'll remember, a filteredView with just one row. That row is stored in the Item property, which is a collection. You want the first (and only) entry, which is at offset 0. That returns a Table row. Within that table row you want the column whose name is CompanyName. It is that value that you are setting to the CompanyNameParameter property of the frmCustomerDetails page.

Finding More Than One Match

If the find returns zero records, you'll post a MessageBox and return the user to the Welcome form. If you match one record, you'll invoke frmCustomerDetails, as shown earlier. If you find more than one record, you'll need to open a modal dialog box that will display all the matching records and let the user pick, as shown in Example 2-2.

Example 2-2. Matching records

```
Select Case rowsFound
    Case 0  ' no records found
        MessageBox.Show( _
        "No matching records found", _
        "No records found", _
        MessageBoxButtons.OK, _
        MessageBoxIcon.Exclamation)
    Case 1
        frmCustomerDetails.CompanyNameParameter = _
            filteredView.Item(0)("CompanyName")
        frmCustomerDetails.Show( )
    Case Else
        dlgPickMatchingCompany.FilteredView = filteredView
        Dim result As DialogResult
        result = dlgPickMatchingCompany.ShowDialog( )
        If result = DialogResult.OK Then
            Dim rowView As Data.DataRowView
            rowView = dlgPickMatchingCompany.lbMatching.SelectedItem
            Dim companyName As String = rowView.Row.Item("CompanyName")

            frmCustomerDetails.CompanyNameParameter = _
                filteredView.Item(0)("CompanyName")
            frmCustomerDetails.Show( )
```

To do this, create a form, *dlgPickMatchingCompany.vb,* with a list box and two buttons: OK and Cancel, as shown in Figure 2-9.

Change the name of the first button to btnOK and the second to btnCancel. Set the DialogResult property for the first to OK and for the second to Cancel. The form itself has a DialogResult property that can be queried after the dialog is closed. By setting the button's DialogResult property, you instruct that button to set the form's DialogResult property when the button is clicked. The net effect is that when the dialog is closed you can test the DialogResult to see if the OK button was clicked.

Figure 2-9. dlgPickMatchingCompany dialog

VB6 NOTE: In Visual Basic 6.0 and earlier versions, it was often difficult to determine whether the Cancel button was pressed to close a
window or terminate a dialog. In Visual Basic 2005, however, the
DialogResult property makes this easy, since, if the DialogResult property of buttons contained on the form is properly set, it reflects the
button used to cancel the dialog.

You'll want to pass the value of the DataView to this dialog box so that you can bind
the list box to the filtered view, and thus display all the companies that match the
user's input. To do so, create a property in the dlgPickMatchingCompany class:

```
Private my_filteredView As Data.DataView
Public WriteOnly Property FilteredView() As Data.DataView
    Set(ByVal value As Data.DataView)
        my_filteredView = value
    End Set
End Property
```

When you load the form, you'll bind the list box to this view by setting its
DataSource property. You'll also set the DisplayMember of the list box to the column
you want to display.

```
Private Sub dlgPickMatchingCompany_Load(ByVal sender As System.Object, _
    ByVal e As System.EventArgs) Handles MyBase.Load
    Me.lbMatching.DataSource = Me.my_filteredView
    Me.lbMatching.DisplayMember = "CompanyName"

End Sub
```

If you match two or more companies (e.g., you enter **bo** into the find control), the
Case Else (shown soon) is triggered and the dlgPickMatchingCompany dialog is displayed, as shown in Figure 2-10.

If the user picks a company (e.g., The Cracker Box) and then presses the OK button,
the dialog is closed (the OK button does this automatically). The result returned to
the calling code (Welcome.btnCustomersFind_Click) is DialogResult.OK

At that point, you can ask the list box for the selected item (which will be of type
DataRowView). You may then ask the DataRowView for its Row property, and within the

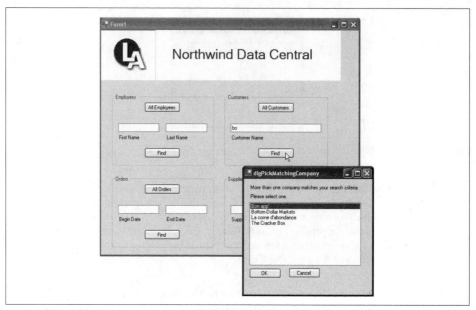

Figure 2-10. dlgPickMatchingCompany dialog displayed

Row, you may ask for the Item property, indexing it by column name. What you get back is a string that you can use to set the CompanyNameParameter property of the frmCustomerDetails form, which you then display. The complete code for the Welcome Page's Customer Find button (in the customer's group) is shown once again in Example 2-3.

Example 2-3. CustomersFind button Click event handler

```
Private Sub btnCustomersFind_Click( _
    ByVal sender As System.Object, _
    ByVal e As System.EventArgs) _
    Handles btnCustomersFind.Click

    Dim filteredView As Data.DataView = _
        New Data.DataView(NorthwindDataSet.Customers)

    filteredView.RowFilter = "CompanyName Like '%" + txtCustomerName.Text + "%'"

    Dim rowsFound As Int32 = filteredView.Count
    Select Case rowsFound
        Case 0  ' no records found
            MessageBox.Show( _
            "No matching records found", _
            "No records found", _
            MessageBoxButtons.OK, _
            MessageBoxIcon.Exclamation)
        Case 1
            frmCustomerDetails.CompanyNameParameter = _
```

Example 2-3. CustomersFind button Click event handler (continued)

```
                filteredView.Item(0)("CompanyName")
            frmCustomerDetails.Show( )
        Case Else
            dlgPickMatchingCompany.FilteredView = filteredView
            Dim result As DialogResult
            result = dlgPickMatchingCompany.ShowDialog( )
            If result = DialogResult.OK Then
                Dim rowView As Data.DataRowView
                rowView = dlgPickMatchingCompany.lbMatching.SelectedItem
                Dim companyName As String = rowView.Row.Item("CompanyName")
                frmCustomerDetails.CompanyNameParameter = companyName
                frmCustomerDetails.Show( )
            End If
    End Select
End Sub
```

Using the Details View to Create the Detail Form

In the same way that you want to allow the user to search for a customer, you'd like to be able to search for a supplier. In addition, when looking at the supplier, you'd like to see which products that supplier offers.

Adding New Tables

The first step is to add new tables to the `NorthWindDataSet`. To do so, choose the menu selections Data → ShowDataSources. Right-click on the `NorthWindDataSet` and choose Edit Data Source With Designer.

This opens the *NorthwindDataSet.xsd* designer. Right-click anywhere in the designer (except on the Customers table) and choose Add → DataTable, as shown in Figure 2-11.

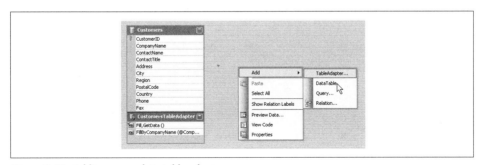

Figure 2-11. Adding a new data table adapter

This opens the DataComponents Configuration Wizard. The first step is to choose the connection you want to use (in this case, you can continue to use the North-Wind Connection).

The next step is to choose whether you are using SQL Statements, new stored procedures, or existing stored procedures. In this case, you'll use SQL Statements.

In the next step, click on the Query Builder window. The Add Table dialog will open, as shown in Figure 2-12.

Figure 2-12. Adding a table

Select the Suppliers table. Click Add and then click Close. When you return to the Query Builder window, select the checkbox beside All Columns, to select all the columns in the Suppliers table, as shown in Figure 2-13.

Figure 2-13. Query Builder window

Click OK and then Next, to open the Choose Methods to Generate dialog box, as shown in Figure 2-14.

The Fill method will fill the `DataTable`, as you saw previously. The `GetData` method will return the `DataTable` filled by the `Fill` method. The third checkbox instructs the wizard to create the `Insert`, `Update`, and `Delete` methods you'll need to update the

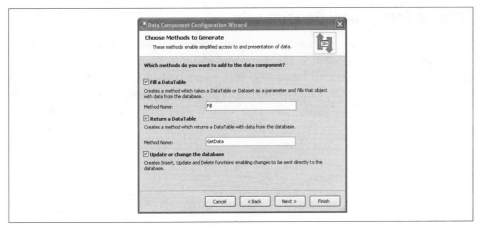

Figure 2-14. Choose Methods to Generate

database with changes to these tables. Accept all these defaults and click Next and then Finish.

Once the Suppliers table is added, repeat these steps to add the Products table. Notice that the one-to-many relationship between the Suppliers and Products is recognized in the XSD designer, as shown in Figure 2-15.

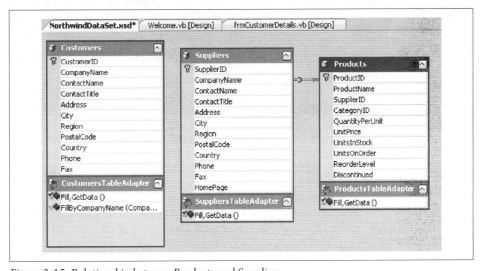

Figure 2-15. Relationship between Products and Suppliers

Also notice that the NorthWindDataSet now has three tables listed under it: Customers, Suppliers, and Products.

Create a Details View Declaratively

Create a new form to display the Suppliers and their Products, name it frmSuppliers. Set the size of the new form to 886,450 and add the details of the Suppliers to the form. Previously, you created labels and text boxes by hand, and then linked them up to the columns in the table. This time, open the Data Sources window, and click on the Suppliers table. Notice that one of the choices is Details, as shown in Figure 2-16.

Figure 2-16. Suppliers details

Choose Details and then let the drop-down box close. Now drag the Suppliers table onto your form. Hey! Presto! Four controls are added to the tray, and a set of labels and bound text boxes are added to the form, as shown in Figure 2-17.

Delete the SuppliersBindingNavigator (you won't be navigating through suppliers from here) and rearrange the labels and text boxes on the upper portion of the form, as shown in Figure 2-18.

We want to reserve the lower portion of the form to display a supplier's product information. We do not want the user to edit the supplier ID so change the enabled property of SupplierID to False.

Declare Master/Detail Relationship

The Suppliers and their Products are in a master/detail relationship. You can reflect this on your Suppliers form by clicking on the Products table and choosing DataGridView. Drag the products table onto your form, and then click on its smart tag. Change the data source, as shown in Figure 2-19.

Click on the smart tag again and choose EditColumns to pick the columns you want to display. This opens the Edit Columns dialog, as shown in Figure 2-20. Delete the SupplierID, UnitsOnOrder, and ReorderLevel columns.

Resize both the grid and the form to make it look as you'd like it to, as shown in Figure 2-21.

Feeding the Suppliers to the Suppliers Page

Your next task is to reproduce the logic used in the previous example to find the Suppliers, and to feed the supplier to this page.

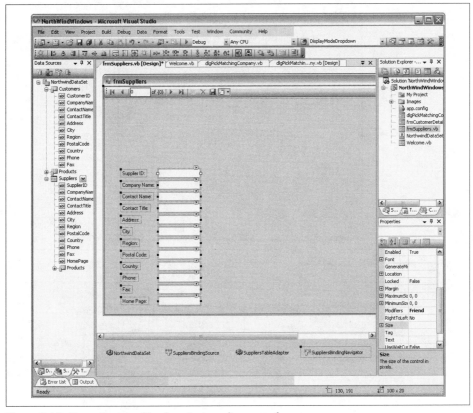

Figure 2-17. Controls created by dragging suppliers onto form

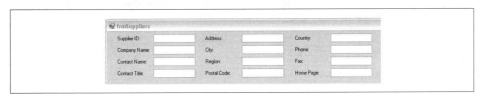

Figure 2-18. Rearrange Suppliers form control

Figure 2-19. Creating master detail

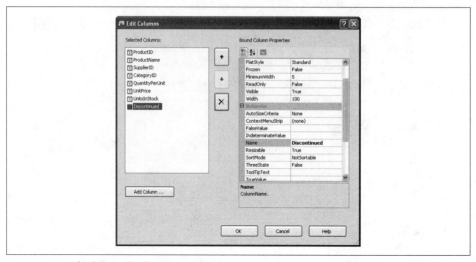

Figure 2-20. Edit data grid columns

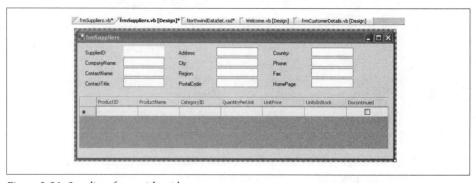

Figure 2-21. Suppliers form with grid

As you did last time, return to the Welcome page, and drag the Suppliers table onto the Welcome page. Immediately delete all the controls it places on the form. You are left with a SuppliersBindingSource and SuppliersTableAdapter in the tray, which is just what you want.

Click on the SuppliersBindingSource and create the parameterized query, as shown in Figure 2-22.

Open *frmSuppliers.vb* and copy the member variable and property from frmCustomerDetails.

Open the handler for the SuppliersFind button click event. The logic is very similar to the Customers Find dialog so copy and paste and then edit, as shown in Example 2-4.

Figure 2-22. Suppliers parameterized query

Example 2-4. Suppliers form Find button Click event handler

```
Dim filteredView As Data.DataView = _
    New Data.DataView(NorthwindDataSet.Suppliers)
filteredView.RowFilter = "CompanyName Like '%" + txtSupplierName.Text + "%'"
Dim rowsFound As Int32 = filteredView.Count

Select Case rowsFound
    Case 0  ' no records found
        MessageBox.Show( _
        "No matching records found", _
        "No records found", _
        MessageBoxButtons.OK, _
        MessageBoxIcon.Exclamation)
    Case 1
        frmSuppliers.CompanyNameParameter = filteredView.Item(0)("CompanyName")
        frmSuppliers.Show( )
    Case Else
        dlgPickMatchingCompany.FilteredView = filteredView
        Dim result As DialogResult
        result = dlgPickMatchingCompany.ShowDialog( )
        If result = DialogResult.OK Then
            Dim rowView As Data.DataRowView
            rowView = dlgPickMatchingCompany.lbMatching.SelectedItem
            Dim companyName As String = rowView.Row.Item("CompanyName")
            frmSuppliers.CompanyNameParameter = companyName
            frmSuppliers.Show( )
        End If
End Select
```

Modify the Load event handler to use the FillByCompanyName method you created for the Suppliers table, as shown in Example 2-5.

Example 2-5. Suppliers form Load event handler

```
Private Sub frmSuppliers_Load( _
  ByVal sender As System.Object, _
  ByVal e As System.EventArgs) _
  Handles MyBase.Load
    Me.SuppliersTableAdapter.FillByCompanyName( _
      Me.NorthwindDataSet.Suppliers, Me.m_CompanyNameParameter)
    Me.ProductsTableAdapter.Fill(Me.NorthwindDataSet.Products)
End Sub
```

When you enter a supplier company name, it is resolved just as the customer name was, and then the detail page is displayed, as shown in Figure 2-23.

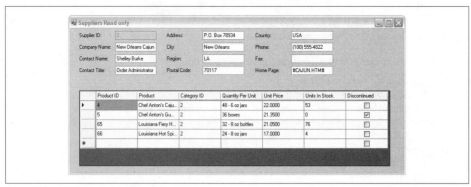

Figure 2-23. Suppliers detail form

Factor Out Common Code

The idea of having nearly duplicate code in two methods should send a shudder down your spine. Let's combine the btnSuppliersFind_Click method and the btnCustomersFind_Click methods into a single method named btnFind_Click, as shown in Example 2-6.

Example 2-6. Common Find button Click event handler

```
''' <summary>
''' Common find button event handler
''' </summary>
''' <param name="sender">the find button itself</param>
''' <param name="e">place holder for event args</param>
Private Sub btnFind_Click( _
    ByVal sender As System.Object, _
    ByVal e As System.EventArgs) _
    Handles btnSuppliersFind.Click, btnCustomersFind.Click

    ' cast the sender to be of type button and get its name
    Dim btn As Button = CType(sender, Button)
    Dim btnName As String = btn.Name
```

Example 2-6. Common Find button Click event handler (continued)

```
' common code

' determine which text field to draw from
' based on the button name
Dim text As String = String.Empty
Dim table As System.Data.DataTable = Nothing

' which text box to get the name from
' which data table to filter
Select Case btnName
   Case "btnSuppliersFind"
      text = txtSupplierName.Text
      table = NorthwindDataSet.Suppliers
   Case "btnCustomersFind"
      text = txtCustomerName.Text
      table = NorthwindDataSet.Customers
End Select

Dim filteredView As Data.DataView = _
      New Data.DataView(table)

' this row filter can now be generalized
filteredView.RowFilter = "CompanyName Like '%" + text + "%'"

Dim rowsFound As Int32 = filteredView.Count

Select Case rowsFound
   Case 0  ' no records found
      MessageBox.Show( _
      "No matching records found", _
      "No records found", _
      MessageBoxButtons.OK, _
      MessageBoxIcon.Exclamation)
   Case 1
      'which form you show depends on the button name
      Select Case btnName
         Case "btnSuppliersFind"
            frmSuppliers.CompanyNameParameter = _
               filteredView.Item(0)("CompanyName")
            frmSuppliers.Show( )
         Case "btnCustomersFind"
            frmCustomerDetails.CompanyNameParameter = _
               filteredView.Item(0)("CompanyName")
            frmCustomerDetails.Show( )
      End Select
   Case Else
      dlgPickMatchingCompany.FilteredView = filteredView
      Dim result As DialogResult
      result = dlgPickMatchingCompany.ShowDialog( )
      If result = DialogResult.OK Then
         Dim rowView As Data.DataRowView
         rowView = dlgPickMatchingCompany.lbMatching.SelectedItem
         Dim companyName As String = rowView.Row.Item("CompanyName")
```

Example 2-6. Common Find button Click event handler (continued)

```
            ' which form you show depends on the button name
            Select Case btnName
                Case "btnSuppliersFind"
                    frmSuppliers.CompanyNameParameter = _
                        filteredView.Item(0)("CompanyName")
                    frmSuppliers.Show( )
                Case "btnCustomersFind"
                    frmCustomerDetails.CompanyNameParameter = _
                        filteredView.Item(0)("CompanyName")
                    frmCustomerDetails.Show( )
            End Select
        End If
    End Select
End Sub
```

> **VB6 NOTE:** The use of the Handles keyword to define an event handler gives you much greater flexibility than you had when defining event handlers in VB6 and earlier versions. In VB6, the names of event handlers are invariable. And you can only define a single event handler for the events raised by multiple controls by using a control array (which is no longer supported in .NET). In contrast, the Handles keyword allows you to name the event handler whatever you'd like, and to handle events from multiple controls.

This common event handler can now replace the two previous event handlers. While this may be slightly more complex than either was individually, it is easier to maintain, because changes have to be made only in one place (cutting down the likelihood of error).

> The triple comment marks at the top of the new method are XML comments used to generate XML documentation (and help file documentation) for the new method. This technique is covered later in the book.

Updating Data

The data on your customer form is bound to the underlying data through the CustomerTableAdapter and the CustomerBindingSource. To allow the user to update the data, drag a button onto the tab and change its Text property to Update. Name it btnUpdate, as shown in Figure 2-24.

Double-click on the button to go to the defaultClick event handler. We'll want some feedback when the update is done. Add a label to the top of the tab named lblTitle. Set its font to blue, size 24, and set its text to Company Name Here.

Update the load method to set the label's text to the name of the company, as shown in Example 2-7.

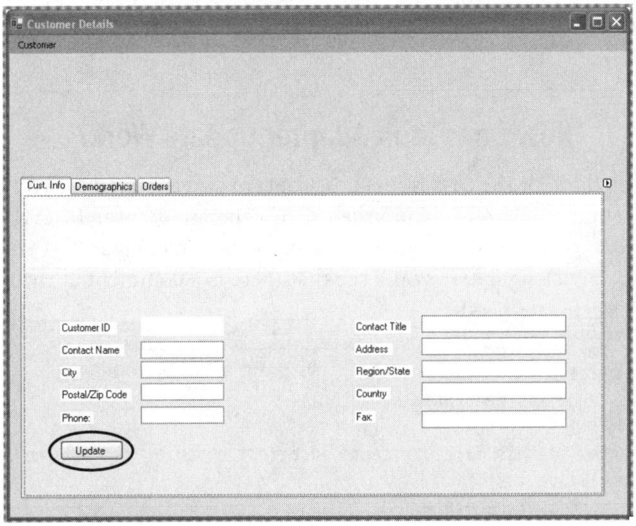

Figure 2-24. Adding the Update button

Example 2-7. Customer details form Load event handler

```
Private Sub frmCustomerDetails_Load( _
ByVal sender As System.Object, _
ByVal e As System.EventArgs) _
Handles MyBase.Load
    CustomersTableAdapter.FillByCompanyName( _
    NorthwindDataSet.Customers, m_CompanyNameParameter)
    lblTitle.Text = m_CompanyNameParameter
End Sub
```

You need to tell the DataConnector that you are done editing the data (so that the updates will be written back to the table in the Dataset). You also need to tell the CustomersTableAdapter to Update, passing in the changes in the Customers table. Example 2-8 shows how to code the Click event handler for the Update button on the Customer Details page.

Example 2-8. Customer Details Update button Click event handler

```
Private Sub btnUpdate_Click( _
ByVal sender As System.Object, _
ByVal e As System.EventArgs)
Handles btnUpdate.Click
    Me.CustomersBindingSource.EndEdit( )
    If NorthwindDataSet.Customers.GetChanges( ) IsNot Nothing Then
        Me.CustomersTableAdapter.Update(NorthwindDataSet.Customers.GetChanges( ))
        Label1.Text = "Updated!"
    End If
End Sub
```

EndEdit applies the changes in the bound fields to the underlying data source (the table in the Dataset).

How Does TableAdapter.Update Work?

The Update method for the `CustomersTableAdapter` was generated for you by the Data Source Configuration Wizard. You asked it to generate `Update`, `Insert`, and `Delete` statements based on the `Select` statement (see, for example, Figure 2-14). If you open *NorthwindDataSet.Designer.vb*, you'll see that there is a comment at the top warning you that this is generated code:

```
'----------------------------------------------------------
' <autogenerated>
'     This code was generated by a tool.
'
'     Changes to this file may cause incorrect behavior
'     and will be lost if
'     the code is regenerated.
' </autogenerated>
'----------------------------------------------------------
```

Scroll down to (or search for) the Update method and you'll find that it tells its Adapter to update, given a data table:

```
Public Overloads Overridable Function Update(
ByVal dataTable As NorthwindDataSet.CustomersDataTable) _
As Integer Implements ICustomersTableAdapter.Update
    Return Me.Adapter.Update(dataTable)
End Function
```

Adapter is a public property providing access to the internal member `m_Adapter`, which is a `SqlDataAdapter` with all the appropriate table and column mappings created for you:

```
Private WithEvents m_adapter As System.Data.SqlClient.SqlDataAdapter
```

Calling `Update` on the `SqlDataAdapter` updates the table that is mapped to the underlying database.

That's it. Make your changes, click update, and hey! Presto! The database is updated, as shown in Figure 2-25.

Modify the Display with Events

Let's modify the spec to say that the `Suppliers` form will come up in display mode (with editing disabled), and the user will have the ability to make a menu choice to edit the form, and then save or cancel the edits.

Figure 2-25. Customer Details updated

To accomplish this, you'll want to add a menu to the form, and an indication (perhaps in the form title bar) as to which mode you are in: Read, Edit, or Unsaved. In Read mode, the text boxes and grid will be disabled. In Edit mode the controls will be enabled. Once you've made changes to the form, but not yet saved them, you'll be in Unsaved mode. The advantage of distinguishing between Edit and Unsaved mode is that if Cancel is selected or there is an attempt to close the form, you can put up a reminder that the changes have not been saved.

To begin, add a menu strip control to *frmSuppliers.vb*, as shown in Figure 2-26.

Figure 2-26. Add Editing Menu to frmSuppliers

The code in the frmSuppliers_Load event handler, as it now stands, loads the data from the database. You need to change it to first disable the text boxes and the data-grid, and then add event handlers to detect when the user makes changes.

The new implementation of frmSuppliers_Load is shown in Example 2-9.

Example 2-9. New Suppliers form Load event handler

```
Private Sub frmSuppliers_Load( _
ByVal sender As System.Object, _
ByVal e As System.EventArgs) Handles MyBase.Load

    Me.SuppliersTableAdapter.FillByCompanyName( _
    Me.NorthwindDataSet.Suppliers, Me.m_CompanyNameParameter)
    Me.ProductsTableAdapter.Fill(Me.NorthwindDataSet.Products)
```

Example 2-9. New Suppliers form Load event handler (continued)

```
   Dim ctrl As Control
   Dim txtbox As TextBox = Nothing
   Dim dgv As DataGridView = Nothing
   For Each ctrl In Me.Controls
       If TypeOf ctrl Is TextBox Then
           txtbox = CType(ctrl, TextBox)
           txtbox.Enabled = False
           AddHandler txtbox.ModifiedChanged, AddressOf TextBoxChanged
       ElseIf TypeOf ctrl Is DataGridView Then
           dgv = CType(ctrl, DataGridView)
           dgv.Enabled = False
           AddHandler dgv.CellValueChanged, AddressOf DataGridChanged
       End If
   Next
   Me.Text = formName + " Read only"
End Sub
```

 You can't set every control to be disabled because you don't want to disable the menu!

Add a class member named `formName` and set that to the invariant text for the form title.

```
   Public Class frmSuppliers
       Private ReadOnly formName As String = "Suppliers"
```

The last line of Example 2-9 sets the form's title to *Suppliers Read only*. When the mode changes, you'll modify this string to keep the user up to date on the current mode.

Let's examine the For Each loop in Example 2-9 a bit more closely. You start by iterating through all of the controls in the form's Controls collection. You can't know what type of control you have, so you define your variable to be of type `Control`:

```
   Dim ctrl As Control
```

You are looking for `TextBox` and `DataGridView` controls (the two types of controls you want to modify) so you create references to those types, which you will use if you determine that the actual type of the control is one of these two types:

```
   Dim txtbox As TextBox
   Dim dgv As DataGridView
```

As you examine each control in turn, you check to see if it is of type `Textbox` If so, it is safe to cast that object to a `TextBox` and then set the `Enabled` property.

```
   If TypeOf ctrl Is TextBox Then
       txtbox = CType(ctrl, TextBox)
       txtbox.Enabled = False
```

The next step is to set the method that you want all text boxes to invoke when their contents are changed:

```
AddHandler txtbox.ModifiedChanged, AddressOf TextBoxChanged
```

AddHandler adds an event handler to the text box. It takes two arguments: the event you want to handle (in this case, ModifiedChanged which is fired whenever the modified state of the text box is changed) and the address of the method to invoke. The net effect is that whenever the text box is changed, then the TextBoxChanged method will be called.

If the control is not a Text box, you test to see if it is a DataGridView, and if so, you disable it and set its event handler:

```
ElseIf TypeOf ctrl Is DataGridView Then
    dgv = CType(ctrl, DataGridView)
    dgv.Enabled = False
    AddHandler dgv.CellValueChanged, AddressOf DataGridChanged
End If
```

Notice that with a DataGridView you are responding to a different event: CellValueChanged. You'll come back to these methods in a moment.

 At this point Visual Studio 2005 may be complaining because you have not yet added the event handler methods, though you have referred to them. You can ignore this complaint for now.

Add the Click event handler for the Edit menu item. To do so, click on Edit, then in the Properties window, click on the lightening bolt and then double-click next to the Click event. Visual Studio 2005 will create a skeleton for your event handler that you will fill in, as shown in Example 2-10.

Example 2-10. Edit item Click event handler

```
Private Sub EditToolStripMenuItemEdit_Click( _
ByVal sender As System.Object, ByVal e As System.EventArgs) _
Handles EditToolStripMenuItemEdit.Click

    Dim ctrl As Control
    For Each ctrl In Me.Controls
        ctrl.Enabled = True
    Next
    Me.Text = formName + " Ready to edit"

End Sub
```

When the user clicks Editing → Edit, the event handler iterates through the controls and enables every control. This is safe, because you don't mind enabling the menu items and labels and other controls you previously ignored. You also change the title of the form to "Ready to edit."

When the user makes a change to any of the text boxes, the ModifiedChanged event fires, and as you saw earlier, the TextBoxChanged method is invoked. The job of this method is to keep track of changes in the data, and to set the title to "Edited, not saved."

To track whether any value has been changed, create a member variable:

```
Private m_Dirty As Boolean = False
```

This will be useful later, when the user clicks Cancel: you can test if any values have been changed just by checking this one Boolean value.

Next, create event handlers so that when either the TextBoxChanged or the DataGridChanged events fire, a helper method DataChanged, will be called that sets the m_Dirty flag to True, and sets the text for the form to "Edited, not saved." You need to type in the code for these, as shown in Example 2-11, rather than using Visual Basic to create event handlers. You associate them with the event at runtime by calling AddHandler, as you saw above.

Example 2-11. DataGrid and TextBox changed event handlers and the DataChanged helper method

```
'event handler
Private Sub DataGridChanged( _
ByVal sender As System.Object, _
ByVal e As System.Windows.Forms.DataGridViewCellEventArgs)
    DataChanged( )
End Sub

'event handler
Private Sub TextBoxChanged( _
ByVal sender As System.Object, _
ByVal e As System.EventArgs)
    DataChanged( )
End Sub
'helper method
Private Sub DataChanged( )
    Me.m_Dirty = True
    Me.Text = formName + " Edited, not saved."
End Sub
```

Using the DataChanged helper method "factors out" common code from both event handlers, so that you do not have the same code in two places. This makes maintaining the program much easier.

 You may wonder why you didn't just set DataChanged as the event handler method for the two events. The answer is that the two events require methods with different signatures. The ModifiedChanged event requires a method that takes as its second argument an object of type System.EventArgs, while CellValueChanged takes as its second argument an object of type DataGridViewCellEventArgs

All that is left is to handle the Save and Cancel events. If the user clicks Cancel, you want to check and see if the m_Dirty flag has been set true (indicating that the user has made some changes that might be lost). If so, you'll show a warning dialog box. If the user insists on the Cancel (saying yes at the warning), then you'll reload the original data (just as you did in Form_Load), disable the appropriate controls, and set the form title back to read only (ReadOnly).

Because resetting the data is done both in Form_Load and in Cancel, it's useful to factor that code out to a common method that can be called from either event handler, as shown in Example 2-12.

Example 2-12. LoadFromDB helper method

```
Private Sub LoadFromDB( )
    Me.SuppliersTableAdapter.FillByCompanyName( _
    Me.NorthwindDataSet.Suppliers, Me.m_CompanyNameParameter)
    Me.ProductsTableAdapter.Fill(Me.NorthwindDataSet.Products)
End Sub
```

Thus, the start of the frmSuppliers_Load event handler goes from:

```
Private Sub frmSuppliers_Load( _
ByVal sender As System.Object, _
ByVal e As System.EventArgs) Handles MyBase.Load
    Me.SuppliersTableAdapter.FillByCompanyName( _
    Me.NorthwindDataSet.Suppliers, Me.m_CompanyNameParameter)
    Me.ProductsTableAdapter.Fill(Me.NorthwindDataSet.Products)
```

to the simpler:

```
Private Sub frmSuppliers_Load( _
ByVal sender As System.Object, _
ByVal e As System.EventArgs) Handles MyBase.Load
    LoadFromDB( )
```

Because you want to take the same action of disabling the controls and setting the form title back to read only whether the user clicks Cancel or Save, you'll factor *that* work out to a common method as well, as shown in Example 2-13.

Example 2-13. StopEditing helper method

```
Private Sub StopEditing( )
    Dim ctrl As Control
    For Each ctrl In Me.Controls
        If TypeOf ctrl Is DataGridView Or TypeOf ctrl Is TextBox Then
            ctrl.Enabled = False
        End If
    Next
    Me.Text = formName + " Read only"
End Sub
```

Example 2-14 shows the the source code for the Cancel button event handler.

Example 2-14. Cancel button Click event handler

```
Private Sub CancelToolStripMenuItemCancel_Click( _
ByVal sender As System.Object, ByVal e As System.EventArgs) _
Handles CancelToolStripMenuItemCancel.Click

    Dim doCancel As Boolean = True
    If Me.m_Dirty = True Then
        Dim result As DialogResult = _
            MessageBox.Show( _
                "You have unsaved work. Are you sure you want to cancel?", _
                "Risk of losing unsaved changes", _
                MessageBoxButtons.YesNo, _
                MessageBoxIcon.Warning)
        If result = DialogResult.No Then
            doCancel = False
        End If
    End If

    If doCancel = True Then
        LoadFromDB( )
        StopEditing( )
        m_Dirty = False
    End If

End Sub
```

You first test to see if the m_Dirty flag is true. If so, you show a message box with the warning text and the Yes and No buttons. The result is stored in a DialogResult variable, which you can then test against the enumerated constant DialogResult.No. Assuming this test fails (and the user clicked Yes), or if the m_Dirty flag was not true, you are now ready to reload the original data (by calling LoadFromDB) and disable the controls (by calling StopEditing).

Finally, if the user clicks Save, you will call EndEdit on the DataConnector, and Update on the TableAdapter (as shown earlier in this chapter). Finally, you will call StopEditing to return to read only mode. Code for handling the Save item on the menu is shown in Example 2-15.

Example 2-15. Save menu item Click event handler

```
Private Sub SaveToolStripMenuItem_Click( _
ByVal sender As System.Object, _
ByVal e As System.EventArgs) Handles SaveToolStripMenuItem.Click
    Me.SuppliersBindingSource.EndEdit( )

    If m_Dirty = True Then
        Dim tbChanges As Data.DataTable = _
            Me.NorthwindDataSet.Suppliers.GetChanges( )

        If Not tbChanges Is Nothing Then
            Me.SuppliersTableAdapter.Update(tbChanges)
        End If
```

Example 2-15. Save menu item Click event handler (continued)

```
      tbChanges = Me.NorthwindDataSet.Products.GetChanges( )
      If Not tbChanges Is Nothing Then
         Me.ProductsTableAdapter.Update(tbChanges)
      End If
   End If

   StopEditing( )

End Sub
```

The complete source for this form is shown in Example 2-16.

Example 2-16. Complete source code for frmSuppliers

```
Public Class frmSuppliers
   Private m_CompanyNameParameter As String
   Private m_Dirty As Boolean = False
   Private ReadOnly formName As String = "Suppliers"

   Public WriteOnly Property CompanyNameParameter( ) As String
      Set(ByVal value As String)
         m_CompanyNameParameter = value
      End Set
   End Property

   Private Sub frmSuppliers_Load( _
   ByVal sender As System.Object, _
   ByVal e As System.EventArgs) Handles MyBase.Load
      LoadFromDB( )
      Dim ctrl As Control
      Dim txtbox As TextBox
      Dim dgv As DataGridView
      For Each ctrl In Me.Controls
         If TypeOf ctrl Is TextBox Then
            txtbox = CType(ctrl, TextBox)
            txtbox.Enabled = False
            AddHandler txtbox.ModifiedChanged, AddressOf TextBoxChanged
         ElseIf TypeOf ctrl Is DataGridView Then
            dgv = CType(ctrl, DataGridView)
            dgv.Enabled = False
            AddHandler dgv.CellValueChanged, AddressOf DataGridChanged
         End If
      Next
      Me.Text = formName + " Read only"
   End Sub

   Private Sub StopEditing( )
      Dim ctrl As Control
      For Each ctrl In Me.Controls
         If TypeOf ctrl Is DataGridView Or TypeOf ctrl Is TextBox Then
            ctrl.Enabled = False
         End If
```

Example 2-16. Complete source code for frmSuppliers (continued)

```
      Next
      Me.Text = formName + " Read only"
   End Sub

   Private Sub LoadFromDB()
      Me.SuppliersTableAdapter.FillByCompanyName( _
      Me.NorthwindDataSet.Suppliers, Me.m_CompanyNameParameter)
      Me.ProductsTableAdapter.Fill(Me.NorthwindDataSet.Products)
   End Sub

   Private Sub EditToolStripMenuItem_Click( _
   ByVal sender As System.Object, _
   ByVal e As System.EventArgs) Handles EditToolStripMenuItem.Click
      Dim ctrl As Control
      For Each ctrl In Me.Controls
         ctrl.Enabled = True
      Next
      Me.Text = formName + " Ready to edit"
   End Sub

   'event handler
   Private Sub DataGridChanged( _
   ByVal sender As System.Object, _
   ByVal e As System.Windows.Forms.DataGridViewCellEventArgs)
      DataChanged()
   End Sub

   'event handler
   Private Sub TextBoxChanged( _
   ByVal sender As System.Object, _
   ByVal e As System.EventArgs)
      DataChanged()
   End Sub

   'helper method
   Private Sub DataChanged()
      Me.m_Dirty = True
      Me.Text = formName + " Edited, not saved."
   End Sub

   Private Sub CancelToolStripMenuItem_Click( _
   ByVal sender As System.Object, _
   ByVal e As System.EventArgs) Handles CancelToolStripMenuItem.Click

      Dim doCancel As Boolean = True
      If Me.m_Dirty = True Then
         Dim result As DialogResult = _
            MessageBox.Show( _
               "You have unsaved work. Are you sure you want to cancel?", _
               "Risk of losing unsaved changes", _
               MessageBoxButtons.YesNo, _
               MessageBoxIcon.Warning)
```

Example 2-16. Complete source code for frmSuppliers (continued)

```
        If result = DialogResult.No Then
            doCancel = False
        End If
    End If

    If doCancel = True Then
        LoadFromDB()
        StopEditing()
        m_Dirty = False
    End If

End Sub

Private Sub SaveToolStripMenuItem_Click( _
ByVal sender As System.Object, _
ByVal e As System.EventArgs) Handles SaveToolStripMenuItem.Click
    Me.SuppliersBindingSource.EndEdit()

    If m_Dirty = True Then
        Dim tbChanges As Data.DataTable = _
            Me.NorthwindDataSet.Suppliers.GetChanges()

        If Not tbChanges Is Nothing Then
            Me.SuppliersTableAdapter.Update(tbChanges)
        End If

        tbChanges = Me.NorthwindDataSet.Products.GetChanges()
        If Not tbChanges Is Nothing Then
            Me.ProductsTableAdapter.Update(tbChanges)
        End If
    End If

    StopEditing()

End Sub
End Class
```

When you run this application, and find a Supplier, the controls are initially disabled, as shown in Figure 2-27.

If you click on Editing → Edit, you enter Edit mode, and the title changes to "Ready to edit," as shown in Figure 2-28.

If you change any field the Title changes again to "Edited, not saved," as shown in Figure 2-29.

If you click on Cancel, because you have made changes, the warning dialog will come up, as shown in Figure 2-30.

If you click Yes here, the changes will be undone and you'll be returned to the original read only mode. If you click No, you'll remain in "Edited, not saved" mode.

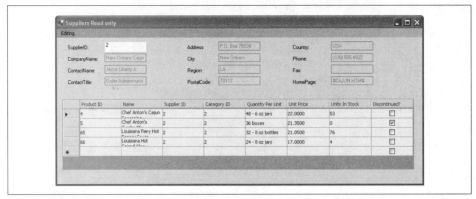

Figure 2-27. Suppliers form opens in read only mode

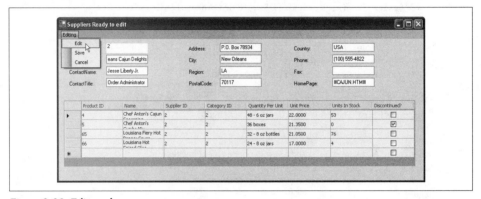

Figure 2-28. Edit mode

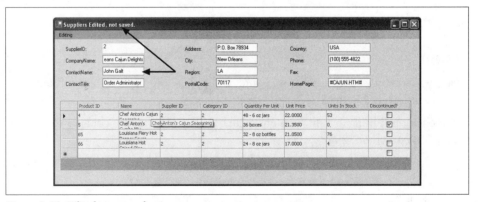

Figure 2-29. Edited, not saved

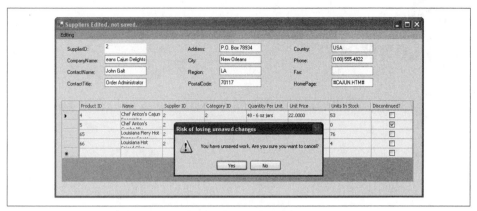

Figure 2-30. Warning dialog for canceling with unsaved work

Finally, if you click Save, the changes are saved, the database is updated, and you are returned to read only mode, with the new data reflected.

Mission accomplished.

CHAPTER 3

Cool Controls

In this chapter you'll explore the tools available for building advanced forms with Visual Basic 2005.

Start by changing the title displayed on the Welcome Form you created in Chapter 2. Click on the form, and set the Text property (in the Properties Windows) to Welcome.

Okay, that was pretty easy. Have a cookie and let's move on.

Adding a Menu and Toolbar

To navigate to the new pages that you'll be adding to the application in this chapter, you'll need to add a menu to the Welcome page. Lengthen the form and drag all the controls down (including the images) to make room for the menu. To do so, click in the form, click Control-A to mark all the images, then grab a move-handle and drag them in unison.

Drag a menu strip control from the Toolbox to the top of the Welcome page. Notice that "MenuStrip1" is added. Rename this to mnuWelcome. Click on the Menu, and add four top-level menus: Employees, Customers, Orders, and Suppliers. For each, create two sub-menu choices: Show All and Find.

 To move from one top-level menu item to the next, use tab. Within a menu, to move from one sub-item to the next, use Enter.

You can now move all the other controls back up into position below the menu.

Rename All the Menu Choices

Before proceeding, rename the various menu choices by clicking on each and setting its Name property in the Properties window. For example, click on Employees →

Show All and set its name to `mnuEmployeesShowAll`, and set its Find sub-menu to `mnuEmployeeFind`, as shown in Figure 3-1.

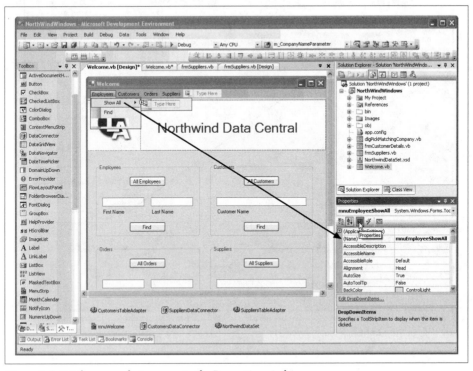

Figure 3-1. *Set the menu choice name in the Properties window*

Setting the event handlers for the menu choices is also pretty easy, as you want them to do the same thing their related buttons specify. Thus, click on the All Employees button, and in the Properties window, click the Events button (the lightning bolt) to see the names of the predefined event handlers for this control. Copy the button's Click event handler (`btnAllClick`).

Now click on the Employees menu to open it, and select Show All. In the Properties window, click on the Event button (the one with the lightning bolt) to reveal the events for this menu choice, and in the Click event, paste the `btnAllClick` event handler name, as shown in Figure 3-2.

 As an alternative, you can click in the Click event and choose `btnAllClick` from the drop-down menu.

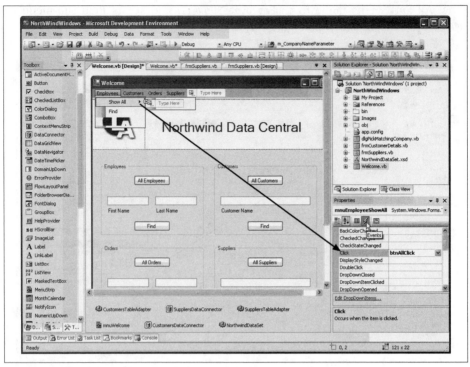

Figure 3-2. Setting the Click event handler

Do the same for the Show All for each of the other menu choices. Next, click on the Find button for Customers, and pick up btnFind_Click, which you can add to the Find menu choices for Customers and Suppliers.

Before you choose the Show All menu choice, you'll need to make some changes to the btnAllClick menu choice, because that event handler, as written, assumes it was clicked by a Button control. The modified event handler for the All buttons on the Welcome page is shown in Example 3-1.

Example 3-1. All buttons Click event handler

```
Private Sub btnAllClick( _
ByVal sender As System.Object, _
ByVal e As System.EventArgs) _
Handles btnAllCustomers.Click, _
btnAllSuppliers.Click, _
btnAllEmployees.Click, _
btnAllOrders.Click, _
mnuEmployeeShowAll.Click, _
ShowAllToolStripMenuItem1.Click, _
ShowAllToolStripMenuItem2.Click, _
ShowAllToolStripMenuItem3.Click
    MessageBox.Show(CType(sender, Button).Text + _
```

Example 3-1. All buttons Click event handler (continued)

```
    " not yet implemented", "Not Yet Implemented", _
        MessageBoxButtons.OK, MessageBoxIcon.Exclamation)
End Sub
```

Because a `ToolStripMenuItem` does not inherit from `Control`, you'll need to test the type of the *sender* and then cast accordingly. Thus, replace the body of Example 3-1 with the code shown in Example 3-2.

Example 3-2. Testing for sender type

```
Dim txt As String = String.Empty

If TypeOf sender Is Button Then
    txt = CType(sender, Button).Text
ElseIf TypeOf sender Is ToolStripMenuItem Then
    txt = CType(sender, ToolStripMenuItem).Text
End If

MessageBox.Show(txt + _
" not yet implemented", "Not Yet Implemented", _
    MessageBoxButtons.OK, MessageBoxIcon.Exclamation)
```

 You'll need to jump through even more hoops to make the Find Menu Choice and the Find buttons work with common code, but that is left as an exercise for the reader.

Other Cool Controls

Before we continue with this application, let's explore some other cool controls that don't quite fit with our immediate business requirements but are still very handy. To get started, you'll add a Web Browser menu command and, in fact, you'll make it the first menu item. No problem, click on the end of the menu bar and choose the smart tab's Edit Items... link. This opens the Items Collection Editor. You have the opportunity to edit the names of the items and to insert a new item by clicking the Add button, as shown in Figure 3-3.

Add a new menu item and rename it `mnuWebBrowser`. Set its Text to `Web Browser`. Click the Up button to raise it to the first position in the menu and click OK. Set the event handler for the Click event of this menu item, as shown in Example 3-3.

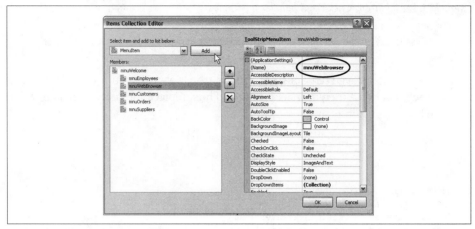

Figure 3-3. Adding menu items

Example 3-3. Web Browser menu item Click event handler

```
Private Sub mnuWebBrowser_Click( _
   ByVal sender As System.Object, _
   ByVal e As System.EventArgs) Handles mnuWebBrowser.Click
   frmWeb.Show( )
End Sub
```

Displaying Web Documents

Create a new form and name it frmWeb.

Resize the form to 800,700 and drag a Web Browser from the Toolbox onto the new form. You'll find that it fills the form. Click on the smart tab and click on the "Undock in parent container" link, as shown in Figure 3-4.

Figure 3-4. Undock the web form

Shrink the web form down just enough to add a text box (which you'll name txtURL) and four buttons (btnGo, btnHome, btnPrevious, and btnNext), as shown in Figure 3-5.

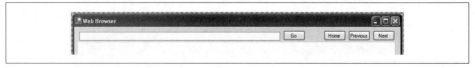

Figure 3-5. Designing the web browser

Setting Web Browser Event Handlers

It would be useful to disable the Previous button when it is not possible to go back any further, and to disable the Next button when there is no next page. The Web Browser has two properties (CanGoBack and CanGoForward) that you can test. Rather than testing these every time the form is navigated, it's more efficient to respond to the events that fire when these properties change—CanGoBackChanged and CanGoForwardChanged—as shown in Example 3-4.

Example 3-4. CanGoBackChanged and CanGoForward event handlers

```
Private Sub WebBrowser1_CanGoBackChanged( _
ByVal sender As System.Object, _
ByVal e As System.EventArgs) Handles WebBrowser1.CanGoBackChanged
    btnPrevious.Enabled = WebBrowser1.CanGoBack
End Sub

Private Sub WebBrowser1_CanGoForwardChanged( _
ByVal sender As System.Object, _
ByVal e As System.EventArgs) Handles WebBrowser1.CanGoForwardChanged
    btnNext.Enabled = WebBrowser1.CanGoForward
End Sub
```

In addition, you'll handle the Navigating event from the browser to set the cursor to a Wait cursor while the page is loading (see Example 3-5).

Example 3-5. Navigating event handler

```
Private Sub WebBrowser1_Navigating( _
ByVal sender As System.Object, _
ByVal e As System.Windows.Forms.WebBrowserNavigatingEventArgs) _
Handles WebBrowser1.Navigating
    Me.Cursor = Cursors.WaitCursor
End Sub
```

Finally, you'll handle the Navigated event, which fires once the new page is loaded, as shown in Example 3-6.

Example 3-6. Navigated event handler

```
Private Sub WebBrowser1_Navigated( _
ByVal sender As System.Object, _
ByVal e As System.Windows.Forms.WebBrowserNavigatedEventArgs) _
Handles WebBrowser1.Navigated
    Me.txtURL.Text = Me.WebBrowser1.Url.ToString( )
    Me.Cursor = Cursors.Default
End Sub
```

As you can see, once the page is loaded, you load its URL into txtURL and you reset the cursor to the default. You change the URL in the Navigated event in case the user has navigated through hyperlinks (so that the text box is kept up to date).

There are a number of ways to set the initial URL for the browser. You can set the URL property of the browser, or you can set the initial URL programmatically. You'll choose the latter, because you want to use the same address for the Home button. To make this work, you'll add a constant member of the frmWeb class that was declared for you by Visual Studio 2005 in the code file for the form:

```
Const home As String = "http://www.libertyassociates.com"
```

Next, navigate to that location in the form's Load event handler, as shown in Example 3-7.

Example 3-7. Web form Load event handler

```
Private Sub frmWeb_Load( _
 ByVal sender As System.Object, _
 ByVal e As System.EventArgs) _
 Handles MyBase.Load
    Me.WebBrowser1.Navigate(home)
    Me.btnNext.Enabled = False
    Me.btnPrev.Enabled = False
End Sub
```

The bold code, which calls the Navigate( ) method on the WebBrowser control, causes the web browser to open to the home page (and to disable the Next and Previous buttons), as shown in Figure 3-6.

Figure 3-6. Web browser home page

The Navigate method is overloaded with eight variations. We are using the simplest in which you just pass in a string representing the URL you wish to navigate to.

A number of event handlers will all do the same thing: tell the web browser to navigate to whatever URL is in the text box. So factor that logic out to a helper method of the frmWeb class, as shown in Example 3-8.

Example 3-8. GoToURL helper class

```
Private Sub GoToURL()
    If Not Me.txtURL.Text.Equals("") Then
        Me.WebBrowser1.Navigate(Me.txtURL.Text)
    End If
End Sub
```

Notice that if the URL text is blank, the method does nothing, but if the user navigates to a new page, that new page is shown in the text box.

If the user enters a URL in the text box and then hits tab (to leave the URL text box), you'll want to invoke the GoToURL method. The same logic will apply if the user presses the Go button, so you'll want to handle both events in the Leave event handler shown in Example 3-9.

Example 3-9. Leave event handler

```
Private Sub TextBox1_Leave( _
ByVal sender As System.Object, _
ByVal e As System.EventArgs) _
Handles txtURL.Leave, btnGo.Click
    GoToURL()
End Sub
```

 Notice that this one event handler handles two different events: txtURL.Leave and btnGo.Click

Finally, if the user enters a URL and presses the Enter key, you'll want to take that as a signal to go to the URL as well. To do so, you'll examine each key pressed in the TextBox to see if it is the enter key in the KeyUp event handler shown in Example 3-10.

Example 3-10. KeyUp event handler

```
Private Sub TextBox1_KeyUp( _
ByVal sender As System.Object, _
ByVal e As System.Windows.Forms.KeyEventArgs) Handles txtURL.KeyUp
    If e.KeyCode = Keys.Enter Then
        GoToURL()
```

Example 3-10. KeyUp event handler (continued)

```
    End If
End Sub
```

Adding an Auto-Complete Text Box to Navigate URLs

The text box should display all the URLs that match the text you've begun to type (this is how Internet Explorer behaves, why not you?) That turns out to be easy, thanks to two properties of the text box control: `AutoCompleteMode` and `AutoCompleteSource`, as shown in Figure 3-7.

Figure 3-7. Text box properties

The `AutoCompleteMode` may be `Suggest`, `Append`, or `SuggestAppend` (or none). `Suggest` provides a drop down (see Figure 3-8), `Append` attempts to complete the listing for you. Whatever mode you choose, you must also tell the text box where to get the data to use to try to complete your entry. Your choices are shown in Figure 3-7. For this example, select `Suggest` for `AutoCompleteMode`, and `AllUrl` for `AutoCompleteSource`. As the user enters text, the auto-complete box provides suggested matches, as shown in Figure 3-8

Figure 3-8. Text box with URL history

Clicking on a choice in the text box causes the browser to navigate to the selected page, as shown in Figure 3-9.*

As the user follows links, the `txtURL` text box is updated and the Next and Previous buttons will be enabled or disabled as appropriate. The `WebBrowser` control keeps track of its own history, so implementing the Next and Previous buttons' event handlers is fairly trivial, as shown in Example 3-11.

---

* This article is licensed under the GNU Free Documentation License (*http://www.gnu.org/copyleft/fdl.html*).

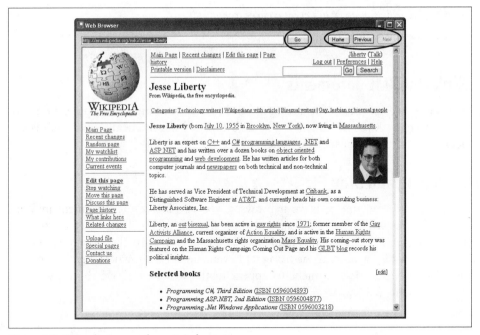

Figure 3-9. Using buttons and events in browsing

Example 3-11. Next and Previous button Click event handlers

```
Private Sub btnPrev_Click( _
ByVal sender As System.Object, _
ByVal e As System.EventArgs) _
Handles btnPrev.Click
    Me.WebBrowser1.GoBack( )
End Sub

Private Sub btnNext_Click( _
ByVal sender As System.Object, _
ByVal e As System.EventArgs) _
Handles btnNext.Click
    Me.WebBrowser1.GoForward( )
End Sub
```

You can now navigate from page to page, and move back and forth through the pages you've seen. Finally, the browser has a method GoHome that takes you to the URL marked as Home in Internet Explorer. Example 3-12 shows the implementation for the Home button Click event.

Example 3-12. Home button Click event handler

```
Private Sub btnHome_Click( _
ByVal sender As System.Object, _
ByVal e As System.EventArgs) Handles btnHome.Click
```

Example 3-12. Home button Click event handler (continued)

```
    Me.WebBrowser1.GoHome( )
End Sub
```

Displaying XML documents

One very powerful reason for having a web browser built into your application is to enable users to XML documents. The web browser automatically understands the hierarchical structure of such documents.

Using Drag and Drop

To see an XML document in your browser, you can locate the document in Windows Explorer and then just drag and drop it onto the Web Browser control (as shown in the circled area in Figure 3-10). When you drop the document in the browser, it is displayed and the Navigated event fires. As shown earlier, this causes the URL of the XML document to appear in the text box above the browser, as shown in Figure 3-10.

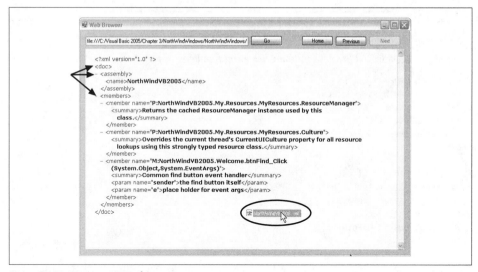

Figure 3-10. Viewing XML documents

 The browser automatically displays the indentation, and you can collapse and expand sections of the XML document (see the arrows in the figure).

Masked Text Box

A very handy advanced control provided by Visual Basic 2005 is the MaskedTextBox control. A Masked Text Box only allows data to be entered if it matches a particular pattern. For example, you might provide a telephone mask, if the user enters 6175551212, the mask will render the input as (617) 555-1212.

The mask can block invalid characters (such as the % sign) and can signal to the user what is expected (e.g., the parentheses indicate that an area code is required).

To see this at work, return to frmSuppliers and delete the txtPhone text box. Drag into its place a MaskedTextBox control, and name it mtbPhone. Click on its smart tag and click the Set Mask link, bringing up the Input Mask dialog that allows you to pick one of the existing masks for your control, as shown in Figure 3-11.

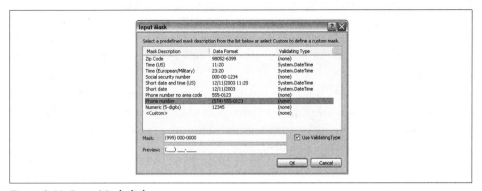

Figure 3-11. Input Mask dialog

While it is possible to create a custom mask, in this case, the Phone number mask is just what you want. The mask itself is shown at the bottom of the dialog, and you have a chance to "try" the mask before accepting it. Click OK to accept the mask.

Hooking the Masked Control to the Data

What you want, however, is a MaskedTextBox that is bound to your data. There are many ways to accomplish this, but the easiest is to drag one from the Suppliers table.

Delete the MaskedTextBox on your form and its associated label, and open the Data Source View (Data → Show Data Sources). Expand the Suppliers table and click on the drop down next to phone. Click on Customize. This opens the Options Dialog, as shown in Figure 3-12.

In the left window, pick Windows Forms Designer and under that Data UI Customization. The Associated Controls window will show the default list of controls associated with the Data type String. Check MaskedTextBox.

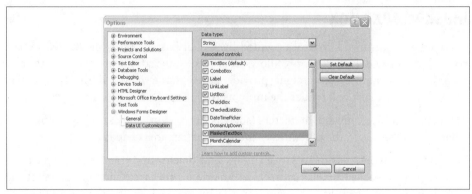

Figure 3-12. Options dialog for customizing data controls

You may click Set Default if you want this control to be available in the list for other controls that manage strings. In either case, click OK. Return to the Phone field and drop down the list of controls and choose Masked Text Box. You can now drag the MaskedTextBox onto your form, align its label, and then click on its smart tag to choose the mask you want.

You will have to change your code slightly to enable and disable the MaskedTextBox and to set up its event handler. In the Load method handler for the form, add a variable to hold the MaskedTextBox immediately following the definition of the txtbox variable in the existing code, like this:

```
Dim txtbox As TextBox = Nothing
Dim masked As MaskedTextBox = Nothing
```

In the For Each loop of the same method, add an if statement for MaskedTextBox, just as you have for TextBox, as shown in Example 3-13.

Example 3-13. Testing for a MaskedTextBox

```
For Each ctrl In Me.Controls
    If TypeOf ctrl Is MaskedTextBox Then
        masked = CType(ctrl, MaskedTextBox)
        masked.Enabled = False
        AddHandler masked.TextChanged, AddressOf TextBoxChanged
    ElseIf TypeOf ctrl Is TextBox Then
        txtbox = CType(ctrl, TextBox)
        txtbox.Enabled = False
        AddHandler txtbox.ModifiedChanged, AddressOf TextBoxChanged
    ElseIf TypeOf ctrl Is DataGridView Then
        dgv = CType(ctrl, DataGridView)
        dgv.Enabled = False
        AddHandler dgv.CellValueChanged, AddressOf DataGridChanged
    End If
Next
```

Notice that the event you will handle (TextChanged) is different from the event you handle for TextBox (ModifiedChanged), but you will share event handlers nonetheless.

Modify StopEditing to test for the MaskedTextBox type as well, as shown in Example 3-14.

Example 3-14. Testing for MaskedTextBox in the StopEditing event handler

```
Private Sub StopEditing()
    Dim ctrl As Control
    For Each ctrl In Me.Controls
        If TypeOf ctrl Is DataGridView _
        Or TypeOf ctrl Is TextBox _
        Or TypeOf ctrl Is MaskedTextBox Then
            ctrl.Enabled = False
        End If
    Next
    Me.Text = formName + " Read only"
End Sub
```

You're all set. When you run the program, the phone number is now in the mask. If you enter edit mode, you will not be able to enter illegitimate characters into the phone number and the mask will indicate the area code and the number of digits expected, as shown in Figure 3-13.

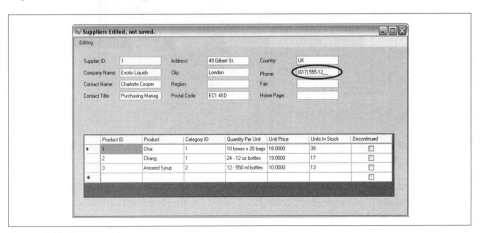

Figure 3-13. Input mask

Printing a Document

One of the key features of any full-fledged desktop application is the ability to print. Let's add another choice to the Welcome Form menu, mnuFile with the text File. While creating the menu choice, use the Properties window to create mnuFile_Click and add a single line:

```
Private Sub mnuFile_Click( _
ByVal sender As System.Object, _
```

```
      ByVal e As System.EventArgs) Handles mnuFile.Click
         frmText.Show( )
      End Sub
```

As you can guess, you'll now want to add a new form, frmText to the project. Resize the new form to 700,600 and set its text attribute to "Text Form."

This form will have two controls, a RichTextBox and a menu. The menu name will be "File" (mnuFile) and will have sub-menu items of Open, Save, and Print, as shown in Figure 3-14.

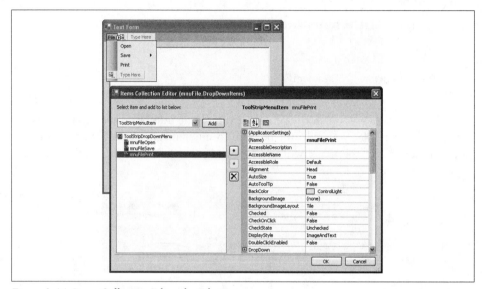

Figure 3-14. Items Collection Editor for File Menu

After your menu is set up, drag a RichTextBox control onto the form and set its size to 668,512 and its location to 12,42.

Drag an OpenFileDialog and a SaveFileDialog onto your tool strip, along with a PrintDocument and a PrintDialog control, leaving their default names as they are. Implement the mnuFileOpen_Click event handler first, as shown in Example 3-15.

Example 3-15. File menu Open item Click event handler

```
Private Sub mnuFileOpen_Click( _
ByVal sender As System.Object, _
ByVal e As System.EventArgs) _
Handles mnuFileOpen.Click
    ' set the initial directory in which to look for files
    Me.OpenFileDialog1.InitialDirectory = "C:\Temp"

    'set the file filter
    Me.OpenFileDialog1.Filter = "Text files (*.txt) | *.txt"
```

Example 3-15. File menu Open item Click event handler (continued)

```
    ' check to see if the user clicked ok, if so, load the
    ' file into the rich text box, setting the file type to
    ' plain text, and set the font
    Dim result As DialogResult = Me.OpenFileDialog1.ShowDialog( )
    If result = Windows.Forms.DialogResult.OK Then
        RichTextBox1.LoadFile( _
            OpenFileDialog1.FileName, _
            RichTextBoxStreamType.PlainText)
        RichTextBox1.SelectionFont = New Font("Verdana", 10)
    End If

End Sub
```

The File Save dialog box works just like the file save you saw for the Active Document example. When the user clicks save on the menu, the `mnuFilesSave_Click` event is raised. The event handler displays the `SaveFileDialog`, as shown in Example 3-16.

Example 3-16. Save menu item Click event handler

```
Private Sub mnuFilesSave_Click( _
ByVal sender As System.Object, _
ByVal e As System.EventArgs) _
Handles mnuFilesSave.Click
    Me.SaveFileDialog1.FileName = _
        Me.OpenFileDialog1.FileName
    Me.SaveFileDialog1.Filter = _
        Me.OpenFileDialog1.Filter
    Me.SaveFileDialog1.ShowDialog( )
End Sub
```

When the user clicks OK in the dialog, the `SaveFileDialog`'s `FileOK` event is raised, and handled in your handler by writing the file to disk, as shown in Example 3-17. Notice that the `RichTextBox` control knows how to do this.

Example 3-17. File dialog OK event handler

```
Private Sub SaveFileDialog1_FileOk( _
ByVal sender As System.Object, _
ByVal e As System.ComponentModel.CancelEventArgs) _
Handles SaveFileDialog1.FileOk

    Me.RichTextBox1.SaveFile( _
        Me.SaveFileDialog1.FileName, _
        RichTextBoxStreamType.RichText)
End Sub
```

Handling the Print Click Event

The print `Click` event handler is a bit more complicated. You will break the logic into two methods: the event handler for the menu choice, and the event handler for the

PrintDocument object you've added to your page. Because you will need to create the Stream object for the document in the Print event handler, and you'll need to reference that stream in the PrintDocument's PrintPage event handler, you'll create a member variable for the class to hold that stream.

```
Public Class frmText
    Private streamToPrint As StringReader
```

To *identify* the string reader, you'll add the following to the top of the file:

```
Imports System.IO
```

When the user clicks on the Print menu choice, the event handler initializes streamToPrint by creating a new StringReader with the text from the RichTextBox:

```
streamToPrint = New StringReader(Me.RichTextBox1.Text)
```

The PrintDialog is shown, allowing the user to pick a printer and set its characteristics:

```
Me.PrintDialog1.Document = PrintDocument1
Dim dlgResult As DialogResult = Me.PrintDialog1.ShowDialog()
```

If the user clicks OK, the PrintDocument's Print method is called, which raises the PrintPage event on that object, as shown in Example 3-18.

Example 3-18. Raising the PrintPage event

```
If dlgResult = Windows.Forms.DialogResult.OK Then
    Try
        PrintDocument1.Print()
    Catch ex As Exception
        MessageBox.Show("error printing " + ex.Message)
    Finally
        streamToPrint.Close()
    End Try
End If
```

When the PrintPage event is raised, the PrintDocument's event handler is called, as shown in Example 3-19.

Example 3-19. Print menu item PrintPage event handler

```
' called from mnuFilePrint_Click
Private Sub PrintDocument1_PrintPage( _
ByVal sender As System.Object, _
ByVal e As System.Drawing.Printing.PrintPageEventArgs) _
Handles PrintDocument1.PrintPage

    Dim printFont As Font = New Font("Verdana", 10)

    Dim linesPerPage As Single = 0
    Dim yPosition As Single = 0
    Dim ctr As Integer = 0
    Dim left As Single = e.MarginBounds.Left
    Dim top As Single = e.MarginBounds.Top
    Dim line As String = Nothing
```

Example 3-19. Print menu item PrintPage event handler (continued)

```
' Calculate the number of lines per page.
linesPerPage = e.MarginBounds.Height / _
    printFont.GetHeight(e.Graphics)

While ctr < linesPerPage
    line = streamToPrint.ReadLine( )
    If line Is Nothing Then
        Exit While
    End If
    yPosition = top + ctr * _
        printFont.GetHeight(e.Graphics)

    e.Graphics.DrawString( _
    line, _
    printFont, _
    Brushes.Black, _
    left, _
    yPosition, _
    New StringFormat( ))

    ctr += 1
End While

If line IsNot Nothing Then
    e.HasMorePages = True
Else
    e.HasMorePages = False
End If

End Sub
```

The second argument passed in is of type `PrintPageEventArgs`, which contains vital information about how to print the page.

For simplicity you'll hardcode a font (Verdana, 10 point) to print with, using the following declaration:

```
Dim printFont As Font = New Font("Verdana", 10)
```

With that font in hand, you can compute the number of lines per page:

```
linesPerPage = e.MarginBounds.Height / _
    printFont.GetHeight(e.Graphics)
```

That done, you can begin reading lines from the stream. As long as you have a valid line, you can compute its position on the page, then call the `DrawString` method on the `Graphics` object you get from the `PrintPageEventArgs` parameter, e.

This method is overloaded. The version you'll use takes six parameters, as shown in Example 3-20.

Example 3-20. Calling the DrawString method

```
yPosition = top + ctr * _
    printFont.GetHeight(e.Graphics)

printPageEventArgs.Graphics.DrawString( _
line, _
printFont, _
Brushes.Black, _
left, _
yPosition, _
New StringFormat( ))
```

In Example 3-20:

line
> Is the string to draw on the page

printFont
> Is the font to use to print the text

Brushes.Black
> Is a standard enumeration for the black color to draw the text

left
> Is the x coordinate at which to begin drawing

yPosition
> Is the y coordinate at which to begin drawing

StringFormat
> Is an object that specifies the formatting attributes, such as line spacing and alignment; here, you are using the default provided by the StringFormat class

Copying Files Using Tree Views

Let's try something a bit fancier. Add a menu choice to the Welcome form's menu named mnuFilesFileCopier. Set its Text to File Copier. The event handler for that menu choice will open the frmFilesCopier form that you'll create to copy files from a group of directories selected by the user to a single target directory or device, such as a floppy or backup hard drive.

Although you won't implement every possible feature, you can imagine programming this form so that you can mark dozens of files and have them copied to multiple disks.

Begin by creating the frmFilesCopier form, then extending it to a size of 570,740. Next, drag on three labels, a text box, two tree view controls, four buttons, and a checkbox, as shown in Figure 3-15.

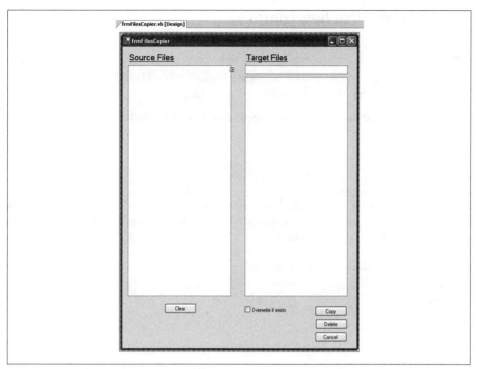

Figure 3-15. File Copier design

Drag a StatusStrip on to the form at the bottom. Click on the status strip's drop down (on the form) and chose StatusLabel. Set the label's name to lblStatus and set its Text to Ready.

You want checkboxes next to the directories and files in the source selection window but not in the target (where only one directory will be chosen). Set the Check-Boxes property on twwSource to true, and on twwTarget to false.

Once you've done this, double-click the Cancel button to create its event handler. The entire implementation for this event handler is to close the form without taking further action, as shown in Example 3-21.

Example 3-21. Cancel button Click event handler

```
Private Sub btnCancel_Click( _
ByVal sender As System.Object, _
ByVal e As System.EventArgs) Handles btnCancel.Click
    Me.Close( )
End Sub
```

Populating the TreeView Controls

The two TreeView controls work identically, except that the left control, tvwSource, lists the directories and files, whereas the right control, tvwTarget, lists only directories. Also, although tvwSource will allow multiselect, which is the default for TreeView controls, you will enforce single selection for tvwTarget.

Before you begin, please add these three Imports statements to the top of your code file:

```
Imports System.Collections.Generic
Imports System.Collections
Imports System.IO
```

Factor the common code for both TreeView controls into a shared method FillDirectoryTree, passing in the target tree view and a flag indicating whether to get the files, as shown in Example 3-22.

Example 3-22. FillDirectoryTree helper method

```
Private Sub FillDirectoryTree( _
ByVal tvw As TreeView, _
ByVal getFiles As Boolean)

End Sub
```

You'll call this method from the Form's Load event handler, once for each of the two controls, as shown in Example 3-23.

Example 3-23. FilesCopier form Load event handler

```
Private Sub frmFilesCopier_Load( _
ByVal sender As System.Object, _
ByVal e As System.EventArgs) Handles MyBase.Load

    Me.Cursor = Cursors.WaitCursor
    Me.FillDirectoryTree(Me.tvwSource, True)
    Me.FillDirectoryTree(Me.tvwTarget, False)
    Me.Cursor = Cursors.Default
End Sub
```

Because filling the Directory Trees will take a few seconds, you change the cursor to the WaitCursor mode until the work is complete.

TreeNode objects

The TreeView control has a property, Nodes, which gets a TreeNodeCollection object. The TreeNodeCollection is a collection of TreeNode objects, each of which represents a node in the tree. The first thing you'll do in FillDirectoryTree is empty that collection:

```
tvw.Nodes.Clear( )
```

You are ready to fill the TreeView's Nodes collection by recursing through the directories of all the drives. You'll implement a method called GetSubDirectoryNodes that does exactly that.

Recursion

A method can call any method. It can also call itself. Thus, the GetSubDirectoryNodes method may, in fact, call GetSubDirectoryNodes. This can be a powerful way to solve a problem, and it can be an effective way to crash your system. The trick is to avoid "infinite recursion" in which you recurse repeatedly and without end.

Each time your method recurses, a section of memory is allocated on the stack to hold the information about each call to the method (complete with the parameters passed in). If you recurse too many times you run out of stack and <poof> your program goes up in (virtual) smoke.

The answer to this problem is to have a terminal condition: a condition under which the method returns without further recursion.

The first time GetSubDirectoryNodes is called, the level parameter is passed in (let's say that value is 1). When you recurse, you increase that level by one:

```
GetSubDirectoryNodes(subNode, _
  dirsub.FullName, getFileNames, level + 1)
```

Processing of the current GetSubDirectoryNodes method stops and the new version runs. The value that is passed in is the original value (1) plus 1 = 2.

Each time through the loop that value is checked against the constant MaxLevel, which you previously set to 2:

```
Private Const MaxLevel As Integer = 2
If level < MaxLevel Then
```

Since level (2) is now no longer less than MaxLevel, you do not recurse again; you do your remaining work and then you return. What you return to is the original version of GetSubDirectoryNodes, which then completes its run and returns. This is illustrated in Figure 3-16.

Displaying the Directories

Before calling GetSubDirectoryNodes, FillDirectoryTree needs to get all the logical drives on the system. To do so, call a shared method of the Environment object, GetLogicalDrives. The Environment class provides information about and access to the current platform environment. You can use the Environment object to get the

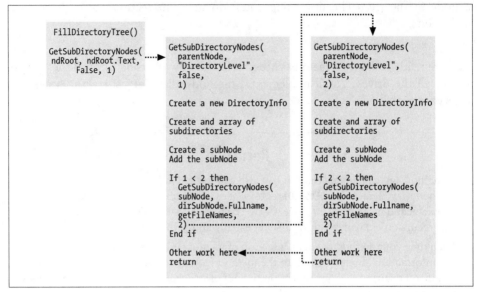

Figure 3-16. Recursion

machine name, OS version, system directory, and so forth, from the computer on which you are running your program.

```
Dim strDrives As String() = Environment.GetLogicalDrives()
```

GetLogicalDrives returns an array of strings, each of which represents the root directory of one of the logical drives. You will iterate over that collection, adding nodes to the TreeView control as you go.

```
For Each rootDirectoryName As String In strDrives
```

You process each drive within the For Each loop.

The very first thing you need to determine is whether the drive is ready. One hack for doing that is to get the list of top-level directories from the drive by calling GetDirectories on a DirectoryInfo object you create for the root directory, like this:

```
Try
    Dim dir As DirectoryInfo = New DirectoryInfo(rootDirectoryName)
    dir.GetDirectories()
```

The DirectoryInfo class exposes instance methods for creating, moving, and enumerating through directories, their files, and their subdirectories. The GetDirectories method throws an exception if the drive is not ready (e.g., the A: drive does not have a floppy in it). Your goal here is just to skip over those drives; you don't actually care about the directories returned.

Wrap the call in a try block and take no action in the catch block. The effect is that if an exception is thrown, the drive is skipped.

Continuing in the try block (if you're still there, the drive is ready), create a TreeNode to hold the root directory of the drive and add that node to the TreeView control, like this:

```
Dim ndRoot As TreeNode = New TreeNode(rootDirectoryName)
tvw.Nodes.Add(ndRoot)
```

To get the plus signs right in the TreeView, you must find at least two levels of directories (so the TreeView knows which directories have subdirectories and can write the plus sign next to them). You do not want to recurse through all the subdirectories, however, because that would be too slow.

The job of the GetSubDirectoryNodes method is to recurse two levels deep, as shown schematically in Figure 3-16. You pass it:

- The root node (ndRoot)
- The name of the root directory (ndRoot.Text)
- A flag indicating whether you want files (True) or just directories (False)
- The current level (you always start at level 1)

Here's the code for doing these steps:

```
If (getFiles = True) Then
    GetSubDirectoryNodes(ndRoot, ndRoot.Text, True, 1)
Else
    GetSubDirectoryNodes(ndRoot, ndRoot.Text, False, 1)
End If
```

You will see why you need to pass in ndRoot.Text when you recurse back into GetSubDirectoryNodes.

Recursing through the subdirectories

GetSubDirectoryNodes begins by once again calling GetDirectories, this time stashing away the resulting array of DirectoryInfo objects:

```
Private Sub GetSubDirectoryNodes( _
ByVal parentNode As TreeNode, _
ByVal fullName As String, _
ByVal getFileNames As Boolean, _
ByVal level As Int32)

    Dim dir As DirectoryInfo = New DirectoryInfo(fullName)
```

Notice that the node passed in is named parentNode. The current level of nodes will be considered children to the node passed in. This is how you map the directory structure to the hierarchy of the tree view.

Iterate over each subdirectory within a try block (forbidden files and directories will throw an exception that you can safely ignore). Here's some code for doing that:

```
Try
    Dim dirSubs As DirectoryInfo() = dir.GetDirectories()
```

```
        For Each dirsub As DirectoryInfo In dirSubs
        ' ' …
    Catch ex As Exception
        ' ignore exceptions
    End Try
```

Create a TreeNode with the directory name and add it to the Nodes collection of the node passed in to the method (parentNode), like this:

```
    Dim subNode As TreeNode = New TreeNode(dirsub.Name)
    parentNode.Nodes.Add(subNode)
```

Now you check the current level (passed in by the calling method) against a constant defined for the class:

```
    Private Const MaxLevel As Integer = 2
```

so as to recurse only two levels deep:

```
    If level < MaxLevel Then
        'recursion
        GetSubDirectoryNodes( _
            subNode, _
            dirsub.FullName, _
            getFileNames, _
            level + 1)
    End If
```

You pass in the node you just created as the new parent, the full path as the full name of the parent, and the flag you received (getFileNames), along with one greater than the current level (thus, if you started at level 1, this next call will set the level to 2).

> Notice that the call to the TreeNode constructor uses the Name property of the DirectoryInfo object, while the call to GetSubDirectoryNodes uses the FullName property. If your directory is *C:\WinNT\Media\ Sounds*, the FullName property will return the full path, while the Name property will return just Sounds. Pass in only the name to the node, because that is what you want displayed in the tree view. Pass in the full name with path to the GetSubDirectoryNodes method so that the method can locate all the subdirectories on the disk. This is why you need to pass in the root node's name the first time you call this method: what is passed in is not the name of the node, it is the full path to the directory represented by the node!

Getting the files in the directory

Once you've recursed through the subdirectories, it's time to get the files for the directory if the getFileNames flag is true. To do so, call the GetFiles method on the DirectoryInfo object. An array of FileInfo objects is returned:

```
    If getFileNames = True Then
        Dim files As FileInfo() = dir.GetFiles()
```

The FileInfo class provides instance methods for manipulating files. You can now iterate over this collection, accessing the Name property of the FileInfo object and passing that name to the constructor of a TreeNode, which you then add to the parent node's Nodes collection (thus creating a child node). There is no recursion this time because files do not have subdirectories:

```
For Each file As FileInfo In files
    Dim fileNode As TreeNode = New TreeNode(file.Name)
    parentNode.Nodes.Add(fileNode)
Next
```

That's all it takes to fill the two tree views. Run the program and see how it works so far.

 If you found any of this confusing, I highly recommend putting the code into your debugger and stepping through the recursion; you can watch the TreeView build its nodes.

Handling TreeView Events

You must handle a number of events for this page to work properly. For example, the user might click Cancel, Copy, Clear, or Delete. She might click one of the checkboxes in the left TreeView, one of the nodes in the right TreeView, or one of the plus signs in either view.

Let's consider the clicks on the TreeViews first, as they are the most interesting, and potentially the most challenging.

Clicking the source TreeView

There are two TreeView objects, each with its own event handlers. Consider the source TreeView object first. The user checks the files and directories he wants to copy from. Each time the user clicks the checkbox indicating a file or directory, a number of events are raised. The event you must handle is AfterCheck.

Your implementation of AfterCheck will delegate the work to a recursive method named SetCheck that you'll also write. The SetCheck method will recursively set the check mark for all the contained folders.

To add the AfterCheck event, select the tvwSource control, click the Events icon in the Properties window, then double-click AfterCheck. This will add the event, wire it, and place you in the code editor where you can add the body of the method, shown in Example 3-24.

Example 3-24. AfterCheck event handler

```
Private Sub tvwSource_AfterCheck( _
ByVal sender As System.Object, _
ByVal e As System.Windows.Forms.TreeViewEventArgs) _
```

Example 3-24. AfterCheck event handler (continued)

```
Handles tvwSource.AfterCheck
    SetCheck(e.Node, e.Node.Checked)
End Sub
```

The event handler passes in the sender object and an object of type TreeView-
EventArgs. It turns out that you can get the node from this TreeViewEventArgs object
(e). Call SetCheck, passing in the node and its checked state.

Each node has a Nodes property, which gets a TreeNodeCollection containing all the
subnodes. Your SetCheck method recurses through the current node's Nodes collection, setting each subnode's check mark to match that of the node that was
checked. In other words, when you check a directory, all its files and subdirectories
are checked, recursively, all the way down.

For each TreeNode in the Nodes collection, set the checked property to the Boolean
value passed in. A node is a leaf if its own Nodes collection has a count of zero; if the
current node is not a leaf, recurse. Code for the SetCheck method is shown in
Example 3-25.

Example 3-25. SetCheck method

```
Private Sub SetCheck( _
ByVal node As TreeNode, _
ByVal check As Boolean)
    For Each n As TreeNode In node.Nodes
        n.Checked = check
        If n.Nodes.Count <> 0 Then
            SetCheck(n, check)
        End If
    Next
End Sub
```

This propagates the check mark (or clears the check mark) down through the entire
structure. In this way, the user can indicate that he wants to select all the files in all
the subdirectories by clicking a single directory.

Expanding a directory

Each time you click on a plus sign next to a directory in the source (or in the target)
you want to expand that directory. To do so, you'll need an event handler for the
BeforeExpand event. Since the event handlers will be identical for both the source and
the target tree views, you'll create a shared event handler (assigning the same event
handler to both), as shown in Example 3-26.

Example 3-26. BeforeExpand event handler for source and target tree views

```
Private Sub tvwExpand( _
ByVal sender As System.Object, _
ByVal e As System.Windows.Forms.TreeViewCancelEventArgs) _
```

Example 3-26. BeforeExpand event handler for source and target tree views (continued)

```
Handles tvwSource.BeforeExpand, tvwTarget.BeforeExpand
    Dim tvw As TreeView = CType(sender, TreeView)
    Dim getFiles As Boolean = (tvw.Name = "tvwSource")
    Dim currentNode As TreeNode = e.Node
    Dim fullName As String = currentNode.FullPath
    currentNode.Nodes.Clear()
    GetSubDirectoryNodes(currentNode, fullName, getFiles, 1)
End Sub
```

 There are two schools of thought on how terse to make your code. For example, many programmers would argue that the declaration of getFiles should be written as:

```
Dim getFiles As Boolean = False
If tvw.Name = "tvwSource" Then
    getFiles = True
End If
```

The significant advantage to the longer style is that you can examine the interim values in the debugger if your results are not what you expect.

The first line of tvwExpand casts sender from System.Object to TreeView, which is safe since you know that only a TreeView can trigger this event.

You must determine whether you want to get the files in the directory you are opening. You want to get the files only if the name of the TreeView that triggered the event is tvwSource.

You determine which node's plus mark was checked by getting the Node property from the TreeViewCancelEventArgs that is passed in as the second argument.

```
Dim currentNode As TreeNode = e.Node
```

Once you have the current node, you get its full path name (which you will need as a parameter to GetSubDirectoryNodes). You then clear its collection of subnodes; you are going to refill that collection by calling GetSubDirectoryNodes.

```
currentNode.Nodes.Clear()
```

Why do you clear the subnodes and then refill them? Because this time you will go another level deep so that the subnodes know if *they*, in turn, have subnodes, and thus will know if they should draw a plus mark next to their subdirectories.

Clicking the target TreeView

The second event handler for the target TreeView (in addition to BeforeExpand) is somewhat trickier. The event itself is AfterSelect. (Remember that the target TreeView does not have checkboxes.) This time, you want to take the one directory chosen and put its full path into the text box at the upper-left corner of the form.

To do so, you must work your way up through the nodes, finding the name of each parent directory and building the full path. An event handler for AfterSelect that does all this is shown in Example 3-27.

Example 3-27. AfterSelect event handler for target tree

```
Private Sub tvwTarget_AfterSelect( _
ByVal sender As System.Object, _
ByVal e As System.Windows.Forms.TreeViewEventArgs) _
Handles tvwTarget.AfterSelect
    Dim theFullPath As String = GetParentString(e.Node)
```

(You'll see GetParentString in just a moment.)

Once you have the full path, you must lop off the backslash (if any) on the end, and then you can fill the text box, like this:

```
    If theFullPath.EndsWith("\") Then
        theFullPath = theFullPath.Substring(0, theFullPath.Length - 1)
    End If
    Me.txtTarget.Text = theFullPath
```

The GetParentString method takes a node and returns a string with the full path. To do so, it recurses upward through the path, adding the backslash after any node that is not a leaf, as shown in Example 3-28.

Example 3-28. GetParentString method

```
Private Function GetParentString(ByVal node As TreeNode) As String
    If node.Parent Is Nothing Then
        Return node.Text
    Else
        Dim endString As String = String.Empty
        If node.Nodes.Count <> 0 Then endString = "\"
        Return GetParentString(node.Parent) + node.Text + endString
    End If
End Function
```

The recursion stops when there is no parent; that is, when you hit the root directory.

Handling the Clear button event

Given the SetCheck method developed earlier, handling the Clear button's Click event is trivial, as shown in Example 3-29.

Example 3-29. Clear button Click event handler

```
Private Sub btnClear_Click( _
ByVal sender As System.Object, _
ByVal e As System.EventArgs) _
Handles btnClear.Click
    For Each node As TreeNode In tvwSource.Nodes
        SetCheck(node, False)
```

Example 3-29. Clear button Click event handler (continued)

```
    Next
End Sub
```

Just call the SetCheck method on the root nodes and tell them to recursively uncheck all their contained nodes.

Implementing the Copy Button Event

Now that you can check the files and pick the target directory, you're ready to handle the Copy button's Click event. The very first thing you need to do is to get a list of which files were selected. This will be represented as a collection of FileInfo objects. Delegate responsibility for filling the list to a method called GetFileList as the first step executed by the event handler:

```
Private Sub btnCopy_Click( _
ByVal sender As System.Object, _
ByVal e As System.EventArgs) _
Handles btnCopy.Click
    Dim fileList As List(Of FileInfo) = GetFileList()
```

Let's examine the GetFileList method before returning to the event handler.

Getting the selected files

Start by instantiating a new List(Of string) object to hold the strings representing the names of all the files selected:

```
Private Function GetFileList() As List(Of FileInfo)
    Dim fileNames As List(Of String) = New List(Of String)
```

To get the selected filenames, you can walk through the source TreeView control:

```
For Each theNode As TreeNode In tvwSource.Nodes
    GetCheckedFiles(theNode, fileNames)
Next
```

To see how this works, look at the GetCheckedFiles method, shown in Example 3-30. This method is pretty simple: it examines the node it was handed. If that node has no children, it is a leaf. If that leaf is checked, get the full path (by calling GetParentString on the node) and add it to the List(Of String) passed in as a parameter.

Example 3-30. GetCheckedFiles method

```
Private Sub GetCheckedFiles( _
ByVal node As TreeNode, _
ByVal fileNames As List(Of String))
    If node.Nodes.Count = 0 Then
        If node.Checked Then
            fileNames.Add(GetParentString(node))
        End If
    Else
```

Example 3-30. GetCheckedFiles method (continued)

```
        For Each n As TreeNode In node.Nodes
            GetCheckedFiles(n, fileNames)
        Next
    End If

End Sub
```

Notice that if the node is *not* a leaf, you recurse down the tree, finding the child nodes.

This will return the `List` filled with all the filenames. Back in `GetFileList`, create a second `List`, this time to hold the actual `FileInfo` objects:

```
    Dim fileList As List(Of FileInfo) = New List(Of FileInfo)
```

Notice the use of type-safe `List` objects to ensure that the compiler will flag any objects added to the collection that are not of type `FileInfo`.

You can now iterate through the filenames in `fileNames`, picking out each name and instantiating a `FileInfo` object with it. You can detect if it is a file or a directory by calling the `Exists` property, which will return `False` if the `File` object you created is actually a directory. If it is a `File`, you can add it to the new `List(Of FileInfo)`, as shown in the following snippet:

```
    For Each fileName As String In fileNames
        Dim file As FileInfo = New FileInfo(fileName)
        If file.Exists Then
            fileList.Add(file)
        End If
    Next
```

That done, you can return `fileList` to the calling method:

```
    Return fileList
```

The calling method was `btnCopy_Click`. Remember, you went off to `GetFileList` in the first line of the event handler! At this point, you've returned with a list of `FileInfo` objects, each representing a file selected in the source `TreeView`. You can now iterate through the list, copying the files and updating the UI, as shown in the completed Click event handler in Example 3-31.

Example 3-31. Copy button Click event handler

```
Private Sub btnCopy_Click( _
ByVal sender As System.Object, _
ByVal e As System.EventArgs) Handles btnCopy.Click

    Dim fileList As List(Of FileInfo) = GetFileList( )

    For Each file As FileInfo In fileList
        Try
            lblStatus.Text = "Copying " + txtTarget.Text + "\" + file.Name + "..."
```

Example 3-31. Copy button Click event handler (continued)

```
            Application.DoEvents( )
            file.CopyTo(txtTarget.Text + "\" + file.Name, cbOverwrite.Checked)
        Catch ex As Exception
            MessageBox.Show(ex.Message)
        End Try
    Next
    lblStatus.Text = "Done"
    Application.DoEvents( )
End Sub
```

As you go, write the progress to the `lblStatus` label and call `Application.DoEvents` to give the UI an opportunity to redraw. Then call `CopyTo` on the file, passing in the target directory obtained from the text field, and a Boolean flag indicating whether the file should be overwritten if it already exists.

You'll notice that the flag you pass in is the value of the `cbOverwrite` checkbox. The `Checked` property evaluates to `True` if the checkbox is checked and `False` if not.

The copy is wrapped in a `Try` block because you can anticipate any number of things going wrong when copying files. For now, handle all exceptions by popping up a dialog box with the error; you might want to take corrective action in a commercial application.

That's it; you've implemented file copying!

Handling the Delete Button Event

The code to handle the delete event is even simpler. The very first thing you do is make sure the user really wants to delete the files. You can use the `MessageBox` static `Show` method, passing in the message you want to display, the title "Delete Files" as a string, and flags:

`MessageBox.YesNo`
: Asks for two buttons: Yes and No

`MessageBox.IconExclamation`
: Indicates that you want to display an exclamation mark icon

`MessageBox.DefaultButton.Button2`
: Sets the second button (No) as the default choice

When the user chooses Yes or No, the result is passed back as a `System.Windows.Forms.DialogResult` enumerated value. You can test this value to see if the user selected Yes, as shown in the following code snippet:

```
    Private Sub btnDelete_Click( _
        ByVal sender As System.Object, _
        ByVal e As System.EventArgs) Handles btnDelete.Click
        Dim result As DialogResult = _
            MessageBox.Show( _
```

```
                    "Are you quite sure?", _
                    "Delete Files", _
                    MessageBoxButtons.YesNo, _
                    MessageBoxIcon.Exclamation, _
                    MessageBoxDefaultButton.Button2)
        If result = Windows.Forms.DialogResult.Yes Then
            Dim fileNames As List(Of FileInfo) = GetFileList()
            For Each file As FileInfo In fileNames
                Try
                    lblStatus.Text = "Deleting " + txtTarget.Text + "\" +
                    file.Name + "..."
                    Application.DoEvents()
                    file.Delete()
                Catch ex As Exception
                    MessageBox.Show(ex.Message)
                End Try
            Next
            lblStatus.Text = "Done."
            Application.DoEvents()
        End If
    End Sub
```

Assuming the value you get back from the DialogResult is Yes, you get the list of fileNames and iterate through it, deleting each as you go:

The final working version of FilesCopier window is shown in Figure 3-17.

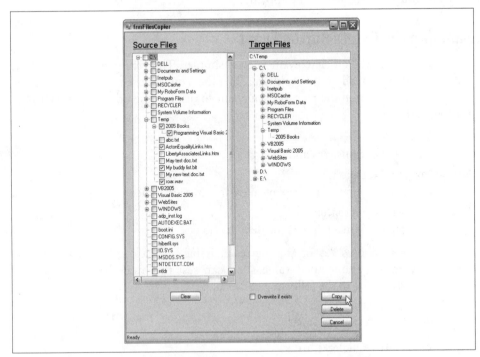

Figure 3-17. Working version of the FilesCopier

CHAPTER 4

Custom Controls

When the user clicks on the All Customers button of the Welcome page you've been building in previous chapters, a Rolodex of all the customers is displayed, as shown in Figure 4-1.

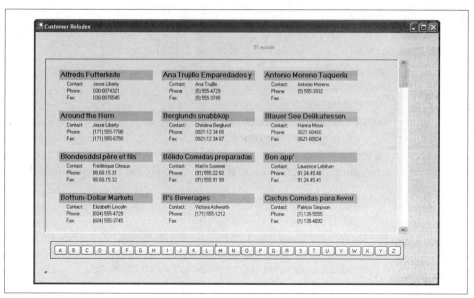

Figure 4-1. Complete Customer Rolodex

Unfortunately, Microsoft neglected to include a Rolodex control in Visual Studio 2005. No problem, though; in this chapter, you'll implement your own as a custom control.

This code builds on the project started in the previous chapter. You can download the source code completed in Chapter 3 if you would like to start here.

Custom Controls

Custom controls come in three flavors:

A derived control
> With a derived control, you take an existing control (e.g., a button) and give it new capabilities. For example, you might create a button that knows how many times it has been clicked.

A composite control
> In a composite control, you take existing controls (whether provided by the Framework, or ones you've created) and you package them together into a single control.

A from-scratch control
> Creating a custom control from scratch requires that you draw the control yourself using the GDI+ capabilities covered in the next chapter.

Design

There are two ways to approach a custom control of the complexity of the Rolodex. One is to build it incrementally; the other is to design it up front. I typically build incrementally, factoring out common code as I go. However, to present all the myriad iterations as functionality is added one step at a time would be a book in itself.

Thus, as an expedient, I'm going to build this as if I were omniscient, anticipating in advance a complete design that I can then implement.[*]

Your Rolodex will be housed in forms. You will have a Rolodex form for Customers, a second Rolodex form for Suppliers, and one each for Employees and Orders (you'll only implement Customers here; the others will be left as an exercise).

These four forms will all derive from a common base form, frmRolodex. The job of frmRolodex will be to hold the code and design common to all the derived forms.

---

[*] The design and code for the applications in this book, especially the Rolodex custom controls, are based on work done by Liberty Associates, Inc. on behalf of and owned by Catalyst, Inc. (*http://catalystwomen.org/*), and are used with their generous permission.

Within each of these forms will be a Rolodex panel. The job of the panel will be to:

- Display all the buttons (a–z)
- Display twelve Rolodex entries at a time
- Display the scrollbars

The Rolodex panel is shown in Figure 4-2.

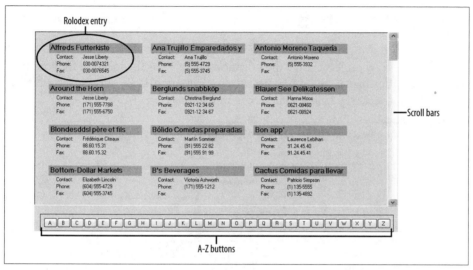

Figure 4-2. Rolodex panel

Within the panel are Rolodex entries. You'll design a MustInherit base class, RolodexEntry, and then you'll derive classes (like RolodexCustomerEntry) from it. These classes will specialize what information goes in the entry. For Customers, you want the customer name, contract, phone, and fax. For suppliers, Employees, and Orders, you'll want different information.

In summary, for this chapter, you'll build the following:

frmRolodex
    The base class for all forms using a Rolodex

frmCustomerRolodex
    Derives from frmRolodex, holds the customer Rolodex

RolodexPanel
    Holds Rolodex entries, scrollbar, and A–Z buttons

RolodexEntry
    The base class for all entries in the Rolodex panel

RolodexCustomerEntry
    Derived from RolodexEntry, specialized for customers

To simplify project management, the forms will be kept in the NorthWindWindows project, but the custom controls (RolodexPanel, RolodexEntry, and RolodexCustomerEntry) will be in a new project named NorthWindControls. Both the NorthWindWindows project and the NorthWindControls project will be housed within the NorthWindWindows solution, thus making it easy for the projects to be kept together and managed as a single development effort.

Building the Controls

Add a new project to your existing solution. To do so, right-click on the solution and choose Add → New project. Leave the Location the same as the location for your previous project, but name the new project NorthWindControls. Be sure to set the template to Windows Control Library, as shown in Figure 4-3.

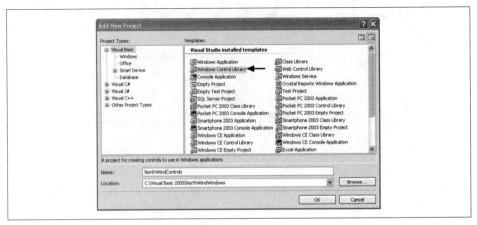

Figure 4-3. Create the new Windows Control Library project

Visual Studio 2005 creates a new project (NorthWindControls) and within that project adds a UserControl, which it names UserControl1. Begin by renaming its file to *RolodexPanel.vb*.

To use the Rolodex panel, however, you need Rolodex entries. Therefore, you need to create a couple of additional custom controls.

To start, right-click on the new project and choose Add → New User Control and name it *RolodexEntry.vb*. This will serve as the base class for all the specialized RolodexEntry controls. You will create a derived RolodexEntry type for customers (RolodexCustomerEntry), on which the discussion in this chapter will focus. If you like, you can also create RolodexEntry types for Suppliers, Employees, and Orders.

RolodexEntry will have a Boolean member: chosen.

```
Public MustInherit Class RolodexEntry
    Protected chosen As Boolean
```

In addition, you will define an event for this user control. As you remember, all controls can publish events. The controls you've used so far have had such events as Click. You can create your own custom event for your new control just by declaring it with the Event keyword. In this case, you'll want to define an EntrySelected event, as follows:

```
Public Event EntrySelected(ByVal sender As Object, ByVal e As EventArgs)
```

 You read this line of code as follows: EntrySelected is a public event that will be handled by a method that takes two parameters: one of type Object and the other of type EventArgs.

Provide a public property for the chosen member variable:

```
Public Property Selected( ) As Boolean
    Get
        Return Me.chosen
    End Get
    Set(ByVal value As Boolean)
        Me.chosen = value
        SetSelectedProperties( )
    End Set
End Property
```

Notice that the Set accessor not only sets the value of chosen but also calls the method SetSelectedProperties:

```
Protected Overridable Sub SetSelectedProperties( )
End Sub
```

SetSelectedProperties has no implementation, but it is marked Overridable. This indicates that the derived class (e.g., RolodexCustomerEntry) will override this method to do some work when the Selected property is set.

Finally, add a method, InternalClick, that raises the EntrySelected event, as shown in Example 4-1.

Example 4-1. InternalClick method
```
Public Overridable Sub InternalClick( _
ByVal sender As Object, _
ByVal e As EventArgs)
    RaiseEvent EntrySelected(sender, e)
End Sub
```

This method looks suspiciously like an event handler, except that it does not have the keyword Handles to indicate what events it does handle. This will be explained in time, but keep an eye on this method!

Before proceeding, build the project to ensure that the RolodexEntry exists so you can derive from it. Next, create the derived RolodexCustomerEntry.

To do so, right-click on the NorthWindControls project and choose Add → New Item. In the Add New Item dialog, choose Inherited User Control and name the new control RolodexCustomerEntry.vb. Clicking Add will bring up the Inheritance Picker so that you can select which control you are inheriting from, as shown in Figure 4-4.

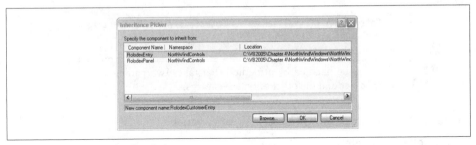

Figure 4-4. Inheritance Picker dialog

Click OK and your third custom control (RolodexCustomerEntry) is created. You want each RolodexCustomerEntry to have a fixed size, large enough to accommodate the information for a customer, as shown in Figure 4-5.

Figure 4-5. RolodexCustomerEntry design

Set the size of the control to 225,75. Open the Toolbox and add the seven labels shown: lblCompanyName, lblContactPrompt, lblContactName, lblPhonePrompt, lblPhone, lblFaxPrompt, and lblFax.

The top label lblCompanyName has a BackColor of Silver and a font of Microsoft Sans Serif, 12pt, style = Bold. Set its AutoSize property to False, and set its size to 225,21. This will cause it to fill the top of the control. Set its TextAlign to TopLeft.

For the other six labels (which you can drag on to the control and then select all at once), set their font to Sans Serif, 8.25 and their BackColor property to Control. Set the TextAlign property to MiddleLeft, and set AutoSize to False. Set the size for the three labels in the left column to 56,16, and for the three in the right column to 145,16.

The name, text, and location of each of the seven labels are shown in Table 4-1.

Table 4-1. Label name, text, and location

Name	Text	Location
lblCompanyName	Liberty Associates, Inc.	0,0
lblContactPrompt	Contact:	17,28

Table 4-1. Label name, text, and location (continued)

Name	Text	Location
lblContactName	Jesse Liberty	80,28
lblPhonePrompt	Phone:	17,44
lblPhone	617-555-1212	80,44
lblFaxPrompt	Fax:	17,60
lblFax	617-555-2121	80,60

Now open the code for RolodexCustomerEntry. You should see that it is already marked as Inherits NorthWindControls.RolodexEntry and that there is a collapsed region Windows Form Designer generated code. You may expand and examine that region, but do not edit the code.

It is time to override the overridable methods from the base class. Start by overriding SetSelectedProperties, as shown in Example 4-2.

Example 4-2. Overriding the SetSelectedProperties method

```
Protected Overrides Sub SetSelectedProperties( )
    If Me.Selected Then
        Me.lblCompanyName.BackColor = Color.Red
    Else
        Me.lblCompanyName.BackColor = Color.Silver
    End If
End Sub
```

Remember that when the Selected property is set, this method is called. For the selected RolodexCustomerEntry, it sets the background color of its lblCompanyName label to Red. For any RolodexCustomerEntrys that are not selected, it sets the background color of lblCompanyName to Silver.

You will also override the InternalClick method, setting it to handle a click on any of the labels on the RolodexCustomerEntry form (or on the form itself), as shown in Example 4-3.

Example 4-3. Overriding the InternalClick method

```
Public Overrides Sub InternalClick( _
ByVal sender As Object, _
ByVal e As System.EventArgs) _
Handles lblCompanyName.Click, lblFax.Click, _
lblPhone.Click, lblContactName.Click, _
lblFaxPrompt.Click, lblPhonePrompt.Click, _
lblContactPrompt.Click, MyBase.Click
    MyBase.InternalClick(Me, e)
End Sub
```

Notice that it calls the base class's `InternalClick` method (which, you remember, looked a lot like an event handler), passing a reference to itself (the selected `RolodexCustomerEntry`) and the `eventArgs` object it receives.

This effectively channels all responses to clicking anywhere in the `RolodexCustomerEntry` to the base class's `InternalClick` method. It, in turn, raises the `EntrySelected` event, broadcasting a reference to the specific entry that was clicked.

Finally, you will add a method (`LoadValues`) to load the values for the `lblCompanyName`, `lblContactName`, `lblPhone`, and `lblFax` labels, as shown in Example 4-4.

Example 4-4. LoadValues method

```
Public Sub LoadValues( _
 ByVal companyName As String, _
 ByVal contactName As String, _
 ByVal phone As String, _
 ByVal fax As String)
     Me.lblCompanyName.Text = companyName
     Me.lblContactName.Text = contactName
     Me.lblPhone.Text = phone
     Me.lblFax.Text = fax
 End Sub
```

You'll see how this method is invoked later.

Building the Rolodex Panel

Return to the `RolodexPanel` that was created when you first created this new project. You are ready to give this panel (which will host any type of `RolodexEntry`) some substance.

First, set its size to 875,510.

Second, add a panel (from the toolbox). Name that panel `pnlRolodex` and set its size to 872,440, and place it near the upper left of the Rolodex Panel (location 4,4). Set its `BorderStyle` to `Fixed3D`.

Next, add a second, smaller panel to hold the buttons. Name it `pnlNavigationButtons`, then set its size to 848,40 and its location to 14,451. Within the `pnlNavigationButtons` panel, add 26 buttons, each of the same size: 32,23, each with a white background and a single capital letter as its text. Name the buttons `btnA`, `btnB`, ..., `btnZ`.

Set the Click event handler for all 26 buttons to `LetterButton_Click` (which you'll implement shortly).

Now open the code for the Rolodex Panel and add these constants:

```
Public Const StartX As Integer = 32
Public Const StartY As Integer = 24
Public Const BufferSpace As Integer = 20
Public Const ScrollBarWidth As Integer = 25
```

```
Public Const RowsPerPage As Integer = 4
Public Const ColsPerRow As Integer = 3
Public Const NumEntriesPerPage As Integer = RowsPerPage * ColsPerRow
```

Add two events to the panel:

```
Public Event RowFillEvent(ByVal sender As Object, ByVal e As EventArgs)
Public Event ButtonSelectedEvent(ByVal sender As Object, ByVal e As EventArgs)
```

Add the following protected members:

```
Protected chosenLtr As Char
Protected xIncr As Integer
Protected yIncr As Integer
Protected vsb As VScrollBar = New VScrollBar( )
Protected entry As RolodexEntry = Nothing
```

Create ReadOnly properties for all of these, (except for vsb, for which you will create a Read/Write property.) For example:

```
ReadOnly Property ChosenLetter( ) As Char
    Get
        Return chosenLtr
    End Get
End Property
```

When the panel is first loaded, it is important to set the size of the panels and to add a vertical scrollbar (along with an event handler for when that scrollbar is clicked). The Load event handler for the Rolodex panel form is shown in Example 4-5.

Example 4-5. Rolodex Panel form Load event handler

```
Private Sub RolodexPanel_Load( _
    ByVal sender As System.Object, _
    ByVal e As System.EventArgs) Handles MyBase.Load
    Dim entry As RolodexCustomerEntry = New RolodexCustomerEntry( )
    xIncr = entry.Width + Me.BufferSpace
    yIncr = entry.Height + Me.BufferSpace
    Me.pnlRolodex.Height = RowsPerPage * _yIncrement + StartY
    Me.pnlNavigationButtons.Top = Me.pnlRolodex.Bottom + BufferSpace
    Me.pnlRolodex.Width = Me.pnlRolodex.Width - ScrollBarWidth
    Me.pnlRolodex.AutoScroll = False
    vsb.SmallChange = ColsPerRow
    vsb.LargeChange = NumEntriesPerPage
    vsb.Parent = Me
    vsb.Location = New Point(pnlrolodex.Right, pnlrolodex.Top)
    vsb.Size = New Size(ScrollBarWidth, pnlrolodex.Height)
    vsb.Minimum = 0
    AddHandler vsb.ValueChanged, AddressOf vbar_ValueChanged
End Sub
```

Note that the handler for the ValueChanged event of the vertical scrollbar has been set to vbar_ValueChanged. Example 4-6 shows how you implement this method.

Example 4-6. Vertical scrollbar ValueChanged event handler method

```
Protected Sub vbar_ValueChanged( _
ByVal sender As Object, ByVal e As EventArgs)
    RaiseEvent RowFillEvent(Me, New EventArgs())
End Sub
```

Each time the scrollbar is clicked, the RowFillEvent is called (which will cause the rows to be refilled with the newly visible rows).

Example 4-7 shows the event hander called when any of the A–Z buttons are pressed.

Example 4-7. Letter button Click event handler

```
Private Sub LetterButton_Click( _
ByVal sender As System.Object, _
ByVal e As System.EventArgs) _
Handles btnZ.Click, btnY.Click, btnX.Click, btnW.Click, btnV.Click, btnU.Click, _
btnT.Click, btnS.Click, btnR.Click, btnQ.Click, btnP.Click, btnO.Click, btnN.Click, _
btnM.Click, btnL.Click, btnK.Click, btnJ.Click, btnI.Click, btnH.Click, btnG.Click, _
btnF.Click, btnE.Click, btnD.Click, btnC.Click, btnB.Click, btnA.Click
    Me.entry = Nothing
    Dim oldCursor As Cursor = Me.Cursor
    Me.Cursor = Cursors.WaitCursor
    Dim btn As Button = CType(sender, Button)
    If btn IsNot Nothing Then
    Dim letter as char = CChar(btn.Text.ToUpper())
       Me.LoadRolodex(letter)
    End If
    Me.Cursor = oldCursor
    RaiseEvent ButtonSelectedEvent(sender, e)

End Sub
```

This event handler sets the cursor to the wait cursor, casts the sender to a button, and then invokes LoadRolodex, passing in the letter. After doing that, it raises the ButtonSelectedEvent, passing in the sender.

The LoadRolodex method is overloaded. One version sets the Rolodex to start with the letter A. The other sets it to begin with the letter you pass it, as shown in Example 4-8.

Example 4-8. Two version of the overloaded Rolodex form Load event handler

```
Protected Sub LoadRolodex()
    LoadRolodex(CType("A", Char))
End Sub


Protected Sub LoadRolodex(ByVal letter As Char)
    Me._currentLetter = letter
End Sub
```

You need a method to add an entry to the panel and one to clear all the entries out of the panel. The former is accomplished by passing in the entry as a Control (it is a custom control) and adding it to the pnlRolodex's Controls collection, as shown in Example 4-9.

Example 4-9. Add method for adding an entry to the Rolodex panel

```
Public Sub Add(ByVal c As Control)
    Me.pnlRolodex.Controls.Add(c)
End Sub
```

The latter method (to clear all the entries in the panel) is accomplished by calling the Clear method within the Controls collection of pnlRolodex, as shown in Example 4-10.

Example 4-10. Clear method for clearing all entries in the Rolodex panel

```
Public Sub Clear()
    Me.pnlRolodex.Controls.Clear()
End Sub
```

Finally, you need a method to handle what occurs when an entry is clicked. The entry that was clicked will be passed in as sender. You'll cast it to type RolodexEntry, then iterate through each of the controls in the panel's Controls collection, casting each of them to RolodexEntry and setting its Selected property to False. Finally, the selected control has *its* Selected property set to True (see Example 4-11).

Example 4-11. entry_click method

```
Public Sub entry_click( _
ByVal sender As System.Object, _
ByVal e As System.EventArgs)
    chosenEntry = CType(sender, RolodexEntry)
    For Each c As Control In Me.pnlRolodex.Controls
        Try
            Dim re As RolodexEntry = CType(c, RolodexEntry)
            re.Selected = False
        Catch ex As Exception
            Continue For
        End Try
    Next
    chosenEntry.Selected = True

End Sub
```

Note that as you iterate through the controls in the Controls collection it is possible that you'll come across controls that are not RolodexEntry controls. If so, the attempt at the cast (using CType) will throw an exception. That is why you wrap the cast in a Try/Catch block. The action of the Catch block is to go to the next iteration of the For loop.

The astute reader will note that in the case shown, the Continue For statement is redundant; had you just done nothing in the Catch statement, you'd fall through to the Next statement restarting the loop.

The Continue For statement is added as a precaution. (practice safe programming!) If you modify this loop later and add new code after the Catch statement but before the Next statement, the Continue For ensures that the new code will not be executed if an exception was raised on the cast.

Further, the incredibly perceptive and meticulous reader will also notice that this event handler has no Handles keyword. This event handler must be linked to the EntrySelected event of the entry object. That will be done by the associated form, as shown later.

Using the Custom Controls

Your custom control (RolodexPanel) will be housed within a form. The base form will be frmRolodex, whose job will be to provide common code for all the specialized forms (e.g., frmCustomerRolodex).

Back in the NorthWindWindows project, add a new form, frmRolodex. Set its size to 976,615. Open the Toolbox and expand the NorthWindControls Components section. Drag a RolodexPanel onto the new form, and drag a label named lblDisplay above it, as shown in Figure 4-6.

Everything in frmRolodex will be shared by all its derived types. You want to factor all the elements common to the derived forms into this form, so they will be as simple (and maintainable) as possible.

You need two members:

```
Protected orderedBy As String
Protected infoTable As Data.DataTable
```

The first, orderedBy, will keep track of the sort order for the data table. The second, infoTable, will hold a reference to a DataTable (e.g., the Customers table).

There are three event handlers you must create: one for when the form is loaded, the second for when the RowFillEvent is fired by the RolodexPanel, and the third for when the ButtonSelectedEvent is fired by the RolodexPanel.

When the form is loaded, you'll call LoadRolodex, a helper method, as shown in Example 4-12.

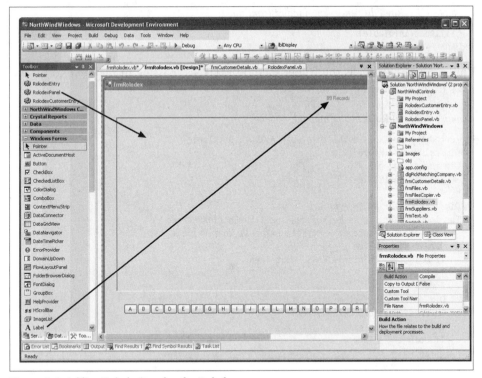

Figure 4-6. Adding RolodexPanel to frmRolodex

Example 4-12. Rolodex form Load event handler

```
Private Sub frmRolodex_Load( _
ByVal sender As System.Object, _
ByVal e As System.EventArgs) Handles MyBase.Load
    LoadRolodex( )
End Sub
```

This method will not be implemented in the base class, but will be implemented in the derived forms:

```
Protected Overridable Sub LoadRolodex( )
End Sub
Protected Overridable Sub LoadRolodex(ByVal letter As Char)
End Sub
```

The second event handler responds to the RowFillEvent of the RolodexPanel, as shown in Example 4-13.

Example 4-13. RowFillEvent event handler

```
Private Sub OnFillRows( _
ByVal sender As Object, _
 ByVal e As EventArgs) _
 Handles RolodexPanel1.RowFillEvent
```

Example 4-13. RowFillEvent event handler (continued)

```
    FillRows(infoTable)
End Sub
```

This event handler calls the helper method `FillRows`, passing in the table to fill the rows from, as shown in Example 4-14.

Example 4-14. FillRows helper method

```
Protected Sub FillRows(ByVal infoTable As Data.DataTable)
   Dim column As Integer = 0
   Dim row As Integer = 0
   Me.RolodexPanel1.Clear()

   Dim loopcounter As Integer
   For loopcounter = 0 To Me.RolodexPanel1.NumEntriesPerPage -1
      Dim offset As Integer = Me.RolodexPanel1.Vbar.Value + _
      (row * 3) + column
      If offset >= infoTable.Rows.Count Then
         Exit For
      End If
      Dim dataRow As System.Data.DataRow = infoTable.Rows(offset)
      AddEntry(dataRow, column, row)
      column = column + 1
      If column = 3 Then
         column = 0
         row = row + 1
      End If
   Next
End Sub
```

The effect is to fill the Rolodex Panel with three rows of `RolodexEntry` objects.

The `FillRows` method is overloaded. The second version is called by the event handler that responds to an A–Z button being pressed.

```
    Private Sub OnButtonSelected( _
    ByVal sender As Object, _
    ByVal e As EventArgs) _
    Handles RolodexPanel1.ButtonSelectedEvent
        FillRows(Me.RolodexPanel1.CurrentLetter, Me.infoTable)
    End Sub
```

This version of `FillRows` takes the letter to search for within the data (as well as the `DataTable` containing the data), as shown in Example 4-15.

Example 4-15. Overloaded version of FillRows helper method

```
Protected Sub FillRows( _
ByVal letter As Char, _
ByVal infoTable As Data.DataTable)
   Dim offset As Integer = 0
   Dim orderByName As Char = CType("A", Char)
   For Each dr As Data.DataRow In infoTable.Rows
```

Example 4-15. Overloaded version of FillRows helper method (continued)

```
      orderByName = dr(orderedby).ToString( ).ToUpper( )(0)
      If orderByName >= letter Then
          Exit For
      End If
      offset = offset + 1
   Next
   Me.RolodexPanel1.Vbar.Value = offset

End Sub
```

 For a description of how the If statement statement works in this code, please see the step-by-step description of clicking on a letter, later in this chapter.

Finally, the code that will be shared by the LoadRolodex override of all the derived forms is factored into the DoLoad method of the base class, shown in Example 4-16.

Example 4-16. DoLoad method of the Rolodex form base class

```
Protected Sub DoLoad( _
ByVal count As Integer, _
ByVal letter As Char, _
ByVal infoTable As Data.DataTable)
    Me.RolodexPanel1.Vbar.Maximum = count
    Me.lblDisplay.Text = count.ToString() + " records "
    Me.RolodexPanel1.Vbar.Value = 0
    FillRows(infoTable)
End Sub
```

Building the Specialized Forms

With the base form in place, you're ready to derive a specialized form: frmCustomerRolodex.

Right-click on the NorthWindWindows project and choose Add → New Item and select Inherited Form. Name the new form frmCustomerRolodex.vb. You are then presented with the InheritancePicker. Select frmRolodex and press OK. A new form is created that inherits from frmRolodex named frmCustomerRolodex.

Notice that the panel and label are already in place (though the label may be invisible because we set its text to blank). You need access to the CustomersTableAdapter that you created earlier. Look in the toolbox and open the section marked NorthWind-Windows Components. Drag the CustomersTableAdapter and the NorthwindDataSet to your form. Rename the dataset instance from NorthwindDataSet1 to NorthwindDataSet and CustomerTableAdapter1 to CustomerTableAdapter.

You want this form shown when the user clicks All Customers from the Welcome page. Go to btnAllClick in *Welcome.vb* and modify the btnAllClick method to invoke this method if the button's text is All Customers or if the menu contains the word Customers in the text, as shown in the bold code in Example 4-17.

Example 4-17. Modifying the AllClick event handler

```
Private Sub btnAllClick( _
ByVal sender As System.Object, ByVal e As System.EventArgs) _
Handles btnAllCustomers.Click, btnAllSuppliers.Click, _
btnAllEmployees.Click, btnAllOrders.Click, mnuEmployeesShowAll.Click, _
mnuCustomersShowAll.Click, mnuOrdersShowAll.Click
Dim txt As String = String.Empty

If TypeOf sender Is Button Then
    txt = CType(sender, Button).Text
ElseIf TypeOf sender Is ToolStripMenuItem Then
    txt = CType(sender, ToolStripMenuItem).Name
End If
Dim oldCursor As Cursor = Me.Cursor
Me.Cursor = Cursors.WaitCursor
If txt.Contains("Customers") Then
    Dim rolodex As frmRolodex = New frmCustomerRolodex( )
    rolodex.Show( )
Else
    MessageBox.Show(txt + _
    " not yet implemented", "Not Yet Implemented", _
        MessageBoxButtons.OK, MessageBoxIcon.Exclamation)
End If
Me.Cursor = oldCursor
End Sub
```

Now you can go back to `frmCustomerRolodex` and override the three overridable methods from the base form. The first is `LoadRolodex`, which is overloaded. The code is shown in Example 4-18.

Example 4-18. Overriding the Rolodex form Load event handler

```
Protected Overrides Sub LoadRolodex( )
    LoadRolodex(CChar("A"))
End Sub
Protected Overrides Sub LoadRolodex(ByVal letter As Char)
    CustomersTableAdapter.Fill( _
    CType(Me.NorthwindDataSet.Tables("Customers"), _
    NorthWindWindows.NorthwindDataSet.CustomersDataTable))

    Dim dataTable As NorthwindDataSet.CustomersDataTable = _
        CustomersTableAdapter.GetData( )
    Dim count As Integer = dataTable.Rows.Count
    Me.infoTable = dataTable
    Me.orderedby = "CompanyName"
    DoLoad(count, letter, infoTable)
End Sub
```

In the second overload (the one that takes a letter), you call the Fill method on the CustomersTableAdapter, passing in the Customers table you extract from the NorthwindDataSet variable you just added to the form.

Your only other override is of AddEntry, shown in Example 4-19. This method is very specific to customers. It is also tightly coupled with the Customers table (it knows what values to extract) and with the RolodexCustomerEntry (it knows what values to set). It is, in many ways, the bridge between the RolodexCustomerEntry and its underlying table.

Example 4-19. Overriding the AddEntry method

```
Protected Overrides Sub AddEntry( _
ByVal dataRow As System.Data.DataRow, _
ByVal column As Integer, _
ByVal row As Integer)

   Dim entry As NorthWindControls.RolodexCustomerEntry = _
      New NorthWindControls.RolodexCustomerEntry( )

   Dim companyName As String = String.Empty
   Dim contactName As String = String.Empty
   Dim phone As String = String.Empty
   Dim fax As String = String.Empty

   If IsDBNull(dataRow("CompanyName")) = False Then
      companyName = CStr(dataRow("CompanyName"))
   End If
   If IsDBNull(dataRow("ContactName")) = False Then
      contactName = CStr(dataRow("ContactName"))
   End If
   If IsDBNull(dataRow("Phone")) = False Then
      phone = CStr(dataRow("Phone"))
   End If
   If IsDBNull(dataRow("Fax")) = False Then
      fax = CStr(dataRow("Fax"))
   End If

   entry.LoadValues(companyName, contactName, phone, fax)
   entry.Left = Me.RolodexPanel1.StartX + _
      (column * Me.RolodexPanel1.XIncrement)
   entry.Top = Me.RolodexPanel1.StartY + _
      (row * Me.RolodexPanel1.YIncrement)
   AddHandler entry.EntrySelected, _
      AddressOf Me.RolodexPanel1.entry_click
   Me.RolodexPanel1.Add(entry)

End Sub
```

Displaying the Rolodex, Step by Step

The order of operations is critical here. The very best way to see this in action is to use your debugger and to set break points on the following methods:

- *Welcome.vb*: btnAllClick
- frmCustomerRolodex: all three methods
- frmRolodex: frmRolodex_Load, FillRows (both overloads), and DoLoad
- RolodexPanel: RolodexPanel_Load
- RolodexCustomerEntry: Load_Values

When you ask to see all the customers by clicking on the All Customers button, the btnAllClick method is called in *Welcome.vb*. The button is examined and since its text is All Customers, the frmCustomerRolodex is created and shown.

When frmCustomerRolodex is loaded, the LoadRolodex method runs, fills the CustomersDataTable in the NorthWindDataSet, and then sets the member variable infoTable to the CustomersDataTable. The DoLoad method is then called in the base class, frmRolodex.

DoLoad sets the vertical scrollbar maximum and minimum values, sets lblDisplay.Text, then calls FillRows, passing in the CustomersDataTable. FillRows populates the three columns by extracting one row from the data table (Customers) and calling AddEntry.

AddEntry creates a new RolodexCustomerEntry object and sets its lblCompanyName, lblContactName, lblPhone, and lblFax based on the data in the DataRow.

It then sets the position (the column and row) of the entry and, most importantly, it adds an event handler for that entry. When the entry fires its EntrySelected event, you want the event to be handled by the entry_click method of the Rolodex Panel.

```
AddHandler entry.EntrySelected, _
    AddressOf Me.RolodexPanel1.entry_click
```

The entry is then added to the panel. This process repeats for as many entries as will fit in the form (defined as RolodexPanel.NumPageEntries). Once completed, FillRows is finished and the form is displayed.

Clicking on an Entry

When you click on an entry, it is lit up as red. The best way to see how this works is to put break points on:

- RolodexCustomerEntry: InternalClick, SetSelectedProperties
- RolodexEntry: InternalClick, Selected Set Accessor
- RolodexPanel: entry_click

When the user clicks on an entry, that click is captured by RolodexCustomerEntry. InternalClick. It invokes MyBase.InternalClick, passing in a reference to itself. The base method raises the EntrySelected event, placing a reference to the RolodexEntry that was clicked into the sender argument.

RolodexPanel.entry_click handles that event and deselects every one of its controls. It then sets Selected to True on the one RolodexEntry that was passed in as sender. This invokes the Selected accessor on that Rolodex entry, which calls SetSelectedProperties.

SetSelectedProperties is overridden in RolodexCustomerEntry. When the item is not selected, its lblCompanyName background is set to Silver. When it is selected, the background is set to Red.

Walking Through a Letter Button Click

To see what happens when a Letter button is clicked, set break points in:

- RolodexPanel: LetterButtonClick, LoadRolodex, and vBar_valueChanged
- frmRolodex: OnButtonSelected, FillRows

Click on the letter T. The LetterButton_Click method is invoked. The result of this is to invoke LoadRolodex (passing in the letter), which sets the current letter, and then to raise the event ButtonSelectedEvent.

That event is caught by frmRolodex, which invokes the FillRows method, passing in the current letter and the data table. FillRows iterates through the rows until it finds a name that begins with a letter equal to or greater than the requested name, at which time it sets the vertical scrollbar value to the offset.

Setting the vertical scrollbar's value causes the vbar to raise the ValueChanged event, which you set in RolodexPanel1_Load to be handled by vbar_ValueChanged. That, in turn, raises the RowFillEvent, passing in the Rolodex Panel itself).

The RowFillEvent is handled by OnFillRows in frmRolodex, which calls the other FillRows method, passing in the DataTable. FillRows extracts the offset from the vertical scrollbar and creates the entries, as you saw earlier, filling in the panel, as shown in Figure 4-7.

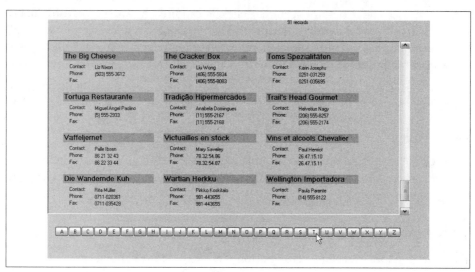

Figure 4-7. Running the completed Rolodex

CHAPTER 5

GDI+ and Drawing

In the previous chapter, you created custom controls by combining already existing controls. As noted in that chapter, there are times when you want to take over the entire responsibility of drawing a custom control. In fact, there are times when you want to take over the entire display on a form.

To do so, you'll need the tools made available through GDI+ and the Graphics class.

 The GDI+-managed class interface is part of the Microsoft .NET Framework and is implemented as a set of wrappers over Windows objects.

The control you will create is shown in Figure 5-1.

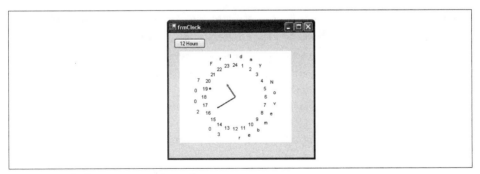

Figure 5-1. Clock Face Custom Control

To begin, right-click on NorthWindControls and choose Add → New Item. In the Add New Item dialog box, choose Custom Control and name your new Custom Control ClockFaceCtrl.vb. Switch to code view, since you'll be creating this control entirely through code, from scratch.

To create this control, you will be responsible for every aspect of drawing the clock and animating it. To simplify your coding, you'll want to add an `Imports` statement for the `Drawing` namespace:

```
Imports System.Drawing
```

The `Drawing` namespace includes a number of classes and structures that we'll use in this program. Some of the most important members of this class are summarized briefly in Table 5-1.

Table 5-1. Members of the Drawing class

Class	Description
Bitmap	Encapsulates a GDI+ bitmap—i.e., pixel data representing an image.
Brush	Abstract base class. Used to fill the interiors of graphical shapes.
Brushes	Provides static brush definitions for all the standard colors.
Font	Defines a format for text, including font face and size.
FontFamily	Group of type faces with the same basic design.
Graphics	Encapsulates a GDI+ drawing surface.
Icon	Transparent bitmaps used for Windows icons.
Image	Abstract base class common to the Bitmap, Icon, and Metafile classes.
Pen	Defines an object used to draw lines and curves.
Pens	Provides static Pen definitions for all the standard colors.
Color	Structure representing colors—e.g., Color.Green.
Point	Structure used to represent an ordered pair of integers. Typically used to specify two-dimensional Cartesian coordinates.
PointF	Same as Point, but uses floating-point numbers (float in C#, single in VB .NET) rather than integers.
Rectangle	Structure that represents the location and size of a rectangular region.
RectangleF	Same as Rectangle, but uses floating-point values (float in C#, single in VB .NET) rather than integers.
Size	Structure that represents the size of a rectangular region as an ordered pair representing width and height.
SizeF	Same as Size; stores an ordered pair of floating-point values.

Arguably the most important class for graphics programming is (surprise!) the `Graphics` class. The other classes will be described as they are encountered, but before proceeding it is worth taking a moment to examine the `Graphics` class in some detail.

The Graphics Class

The `Graphics` class represents a GDI+ drawing surface. A `Graphics` object maintains the state of the drawing surface, including the scale and units, as well as its orientation.

The Graphics class provides a great many properties. The most commonly used ones are listed in Table 5-2.

Table 5-2. Graphics class members

Property	Type	Description
Clip	Region	Read/write. Specifies the area available for drawing.
DpiX DpiY	Float/single	Read/write. The horizontal and vertical resolution (respectively) of the Graphics object in dots per inch.
PageScale	Float/single	Read/write. The scaling between world units and page units for this Graphics object.
PageUnit	GraphicsUnit	Read/write. The unit of measure for page coordinates. Valid values are members of the GraphicsUnit enumeration, listed in Table 5-3.

The PageScale sets the scaling between the world units and the page units. To understand these, you must first understand coordinates.

Coordinates

The French philosopher Rene Descartes (1596–1650) is best known today for stating that while he may doubt, he cannot doubt that he exists. This is summarized in his oft-quoted statement *Cogito Ergo Sum* ("I think; therefore, I am"). Among mathematicians, however, Descartes is known for inventing Analytical Geometry and what are now called Cartesian coordinates. In a classic Cartesian coordinate system, you envision an x-axis and a y-axis, as shown in Figure 5-2, with the origin (0,0) at the center. The values to the right of the origin and above the origin are positive, and the values to the left and below the origin are negative.

The coordinates you pass to the various drawing methods of the Graphics class are said to be *World Coordinates*. Unlike traditional Cartesian coordinates, World Coordinates have their origin at the upper lefthand corner, rather than in the center, and you count upward to the right and *down*, as shown in Figure 5-3.

Transforms introduced

These World Coordinates are transformed into *page coordinates* by *world transformations*. You'll use these world transformations (e.g., TranslateTransform, ScaleTransform, and RotateTransform) to set the center and the orientation of your coordinate system. When drawing a clock face, for example, it will be more convenient to set the origin (0,0) to the center of the clock.

Page transforms convert page coordinates into device coordinates: that is, pixels relative to the upper lefthand corner of the client area on your monitor. The page transforms are the PageUnit and PageScale properties of the Graphics object.

The PageUnit property chooses the unit you'll use to make your transformations and to scale your drawings. These units are one of the GraphicsUnit enumerated values shown in Table 5-3.

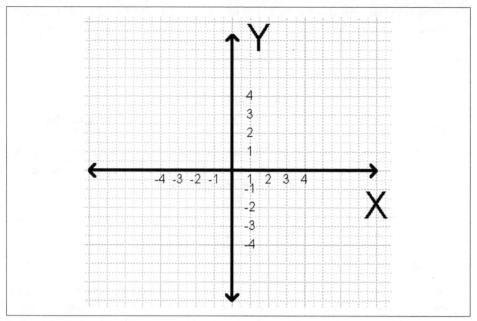

Figure 5-2. Cartesian coordinates

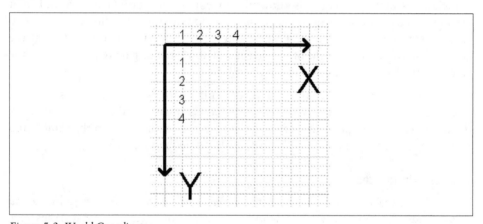

Figure 5-3. World Coordinates

Table 5-3. GraphicsUnit enumeration

Enumerated value	Unit of measure
Display	1/75 of an inch
Document	1/300 of an inch
Inch	1 inch
Millimeter	1 millimeter
Pixel	1 Pixel

Table 5-3. GraphicsUnit enumeration (continued)

Enumerated value	Unit of measure
Point	1/72 of an inch
World	World unit

Using the unit described by the PageUnit you can set the PageScale, which specifies the value for scaling between world units and page units. You'll see this at work later in this chapter when you'll create a scale of 2,000 units by 2,000 units—that is, rather than working in pixels or inches, you'll create a logical unit that is 1/2,000 of the width (or height) of your screen.

Implementing the Control

Now, you are ready to create your control. First, add the following members to the ClockFaceCtrl class. (You'll implement the StringDraw class shortly.)

```
Private Shared offset As Integer = 0
Private b24Hours As Boolean = False
Private Const FaceRadius As Integer = 700
Private Const DateRadius As Integer = 900
Private currentTime As DateTime
Private myFont As New Font("Arial", 80)
Private sdToday As StringDraw
Private bForceDraw As Boolean = True
```

Second, you'll need a timer to drive the automatic updating of the clock. Drag a Timer control onto the ClockFaceCtrl window. Visual Basic automatically creates an object of the System.Windows.Forms.Timer class, and names it Timer1. You don't need to do anything else with it for now; you'll set its Elapsed event in the initialization code.

Third, there are two helper methods you'll need to handle some trigonometry for you, GetCos and GetSin. I'll explain what they do later; for now, you can just type them in.

```
Private Shared Function _
   GetCos(ByVal degAngle As Single) As Single
     Return CSng(Math.Cos((Math.PI * degAngle / 180.0F)))
End Function 'GetCos

Private Shared Function _
   GetSin(ByVal degAngle As Single) As Single
     Return CSng(Math.Sin((Math.PI * degAngle / 180.0F)))
End Function 'GetSin
```

Add a constructor to the ClockFaceCtrl class. The easiest way to do so is to click on the class in the upper-left drop down, and to click on the method you want to override (New) in the upper-right drop down, as shown in Figure 5-4.

Partial Classes

The definition of a class in two files is an example of using *partial classes* that allow you, as the developer of the class, to divide the definition of the class into more than one file.

The keyword `Partial` is not required in each part of the class, although it does make for good documentation.

You'll notice that just about every class generated by the designer is split into two files: the Designer file and the file you see when you right-click on the form and choose "View Code." Partial classes allow for a clean separation of tool-generated code from programmer-created code, and are a great advantage in creating maintainable code.

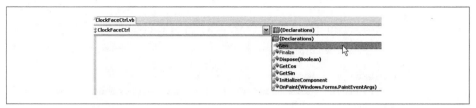

Figure 5-4. Overriding the constructor

This creates a default constructor (one with no arguments). The first two lines of your new constructor must invoke the base class' constructor and also call `InitializeComponent`.

```
MyBase.New( )

InitializeComponent( )
```

 A default constructor is any constructor (`Sub New`) that has no arguments. If you don't create a constructor in your own code, the compiler will create a default constructor for you. Just because it is created by the compiler does *not* make it the default constructor; it is because the constructor takes no arguments (no parameters) that makes it a default constructor. This is, alas, the source of endless confusion, because the compiler creates a default constructor for you, by default!

The next two lines set the `BackColor` and `ForeColor` for your control. When you draw the clock face you'll need to tell the CLR what color to use for the numbers. You might be tempted to use black, which is perfectly appropriate, but it does raise a problem. The user may have changed the color scheme to a very dark background (even to black) which would make your clock face invisible.

A better alternative is to set the BackColor and ForeColor for ClockFaceCtrl to the Window and WindowText colors the user has chosen:

```
BackColor = SystemColors.Window
ForeColor = SystemColors.WindowText
```

You can now create a brush that uses the foreground color and feel comfortable that this is a good choice.

Here are the next several lines in the constructor:

```
Dim today As String = System.DateTime.Now.ToLongDateString( )
today = " " + today.Replace(",","") // remove commas
sdToday = New StringDraw(today, Me)

currentTime = DateTime.Now
AddHandler Timer1.Elapsed AddressOf OnTimer
```

Because these lines require you to implement the StringDraw class and the OnTimer method, and those will need quite a few pages of explanation, the complete listing of the constructor is shown in Example 5-1. (You can finish typing it in now, but it won't compile until StringDraw and OnTimer are complete.) We'll later pick up our discussion of the constructor beginning with the currentTime assignment statement.

Example 5-1. Constructor for ClockFaceCtrl custom control (from ClockFaceCtrl.vb)

```
Public Sub New( )
   MyBase.New( )

   ' This call is required by the Component Designer.
   InitializeComponent( )

   BackColor = SystemColors.Window
   ForeColor = SystemColors.WindowText

   Dim today As String = System.DateTime.Now.ToLongDateString( )
   today = " " + today.Replace(",", "") // remove commas
   sdToday = New StringDraw(today, Me)


   currentTime = DateTime.Now
   Dim timer As New System.Timers.Timer( )
   AddHandler timer.Elapsed, AddressOf OnTimer
   timer.Interval = 50
   timer.Enabled = True
End Sub 'New
```

The StringDraw class

Now let's implement the StringDraw class. Its job will be to draw the date and time in a circle around the clock. The date and time will turn upside down if you don't make a special effort to prevent the letters from rotating, so you will use letters that act like a Ferris-wheel car, remaining upright as they rotate around the clock.

You're going to nest StringDraw within the ClockFaceCtrl class. Add the class declaration to ClockFaceCtrl, as follows:

```
Public Class ClockFaceCtrl
    …
    Private Class StringDraw
    End Class
End Class
```

The StringDraw class has three members: a list of LtrDraw objects (described in a moment), an instance of LtrDraw, and an instance of a ClockFaceCtrl:

```
Private myLtrDrawList As Generic.List(Of LtrDraw) = _
    New Generic.List(Of LtrDraw)
Private myLtrDraw As LtrDraw
Private theControl As ClockFaceCtrl
```

The StringDraw constructor takes two parameters: a string and a ClockFaceCtrl object. For each character in the string, it initializes a LtrDraw object, which it then adds to the myLtrDrawList collection, as shown in Example 5-2.

Example 5-2. StringDraw constructor

```
Public Sub New(ByVal s As String, _
  ByVal theControl As ClockFaceCtrl)
    Me.theControl = theControl
    Dim c As Char
    For Each c In s
        myLtrDraw = New LtrDraw(c)
        myLtrDrawList.Add(myLtrDraw)
    Next c
End Sub 'New
```

When the constructor of the ClockFaceCtrl creates a StringDraw (represented by the variable sdToday), it passes in its Me reference, which refers to the custom control you are creating. For the string, it passes in the current date from which all commas have been removed. (See Example 5-1.)

The code still won't compile even after you enter the StringDraw constructor. To complete the implementation, you still need the LtrDraw class and the ClockFaceCtrl.OnTimer method. (You'll also return to StringDraw to add its most important method, DrawTheString.)

The LtrDraw class

The LtrDraw class is responsible for drawing an individual letter. Like the StringDraw class, it is defined as a private nested class within ClockFaceCtrl (see the sidebar "Nested Classes").

Add the class declaration for LtrDraw:

```
Public Class ClockFaceCtrl
...

        Private Class LtrDraw
        End Class
End Class
```

LtrDraw has five members: the character it holds (myChar), and the current and old x,y coordinates. It remembers the old x and y coordinates so it can erase the character from its previous position before drawing it in its new one.

```
Private myChar As Char
Private _x As Single
Private _y As Single
Private oldx As Single
Private oldy As Single
```

Nested Classes

In Visual Basic 2005 you may nest one class within another, as we've done here with the LtrDraw and StringDraw classes. These classes are "scoped" within the outer class (ClockFaceCtrl) and if you were to refer to the GetWidth( ) method of the LtrDraw class, you would refer to it as ClockFaceCtrl.LtrDraw.GetWidth.

However, because we've defined LtrDraw to be a private nested class, none of its methods are available to outside classes (that is, classes other than the outer class (ClockFaceCtrl) and classes nested within ClockFaceCtrl (such as StringDraw).

Nested classes help hide these "helper" classes from other classes and avoid cluttering up your namespace with class names that are not relevant to other classes.

The constructor for this class takes a char and sets its myChar member variable:

```
Public Sub New(ByVal c As Char)
    myChar = c
End Sub
```

The class also provides read/write properties named X and Y. The Set accessor for X remembers the current value of _x in oldx, then sets the value of _x to the value passed in:

```
Public Property X() As Single
    Get
        Return _x
    End Get
    Set(ByVal Value As Single)
        oldx = _x
        _x = Value
    End Set
End Property
```

The Y property does the same work for the _y member.

The LtrDraw class has three methods: GetWidth, GetHeight, and DrawLetter.

GetWidth is passed an instance of a Graphics object and an instance of a Font object. It calls the MeasureString method on the Graphics object, passing in the character the class is holding and the font in which that character will be rendered, to get the width of the character as it will be displayed in the application. The GetWidth method is shown in Example 5-3.

Example 5-3. GetWidth method

```
Public Function GetWidth( _
  ByVal g As Graphics, ByVal theFont As Font) _
  As Single
    Dim stringSize As SizeF = _
      g.MeasureString(myChar.ToString(), theFont)
    Return stringSize.Width
End Function 'GetWidth
```

GetHeight works the same way, returning the rendered height, as shown in Example 5-4.

Example 5-4. GetHeight method

```
Public Function GetHeight( _
  ByVal g As Graphics, ByVal theFont As Font) _
  As Single
    Dim stringSize As SizeF = _
      g.MeasureString(myChar.ToString(), theFont)
    Return stringSize.Height
End Function 'GetHeight
```

DrawLetter's job is to actually draw the string in the appropriate location. It is passed a Graphics object as well as a Brush (to determine the color for the letters) and the control itself.

```
Public Sub DrawLetter( _
    ByVal g As Graphics, ByVal brush As Brush, _
    ByVal ctrl As ClockFaceCtrl)
```

There are two steps to drawing a letter. First, you set the brush to the background color and draw the character at its old location. The effect is to erase the character.

```
' get a blanking brush to blank out the old letter
Dim blankBrush As SolidBrush = New SolidBrush(ctrl.BackColor)
' draw over the old location (erasing the letter)
g.DrawString(myChar.ToString( ), theFont, _
    blankBrush, oldx, oldy)
```

Second, you change to the brush you were given and redraw the character at its new location:

```
' draw the letter in the new location using the
' brush that was passed in
g.DrawString(myChar.ToString( ), _
    theFont, brush, X, Y)
```

Example 5-5 combines these two steps, and shows the full listing of DrawLetter.

Example 5-5. LtrDraw.DrawLetter method

```
Public Sub DrawLetter( _
    ByVal g As Graphics, ByVal brush As Brush, _
    ByVal ctrl As ClockFaceCtrl)

    'get the font to draw
    Dim theFont As Font = ctrl.myFont

    ' get a blanking brush to blank out the old letter
    Dim blankBrush As SolidBrush = New SolidBrush(ctrl.BackColor)

    ' draw over the old location (erasing the letter)
    g.DrawString(myChar.ToString( ), theFont, _
        blankBrush, oldx, oldy)

    ' draw the letter in the new location using the
    ' brush that was passed in
    g.DrawString(myChar.ToString( ), _
        theFont, brush, X, Y)
End Sub 'DrawLetter
```

The version of Graphics.DrawString you use in this example takes five parameters:

- The string to draw (myChar.ToString)
- The font to draw in (e.g., Arial 8)
- A brush to determine the color and texture of the text
- The x coordinate of the upper lefthand corner of the text
- The y coordinate of the upper lefthand corner of the text

The DrawString.DrawTheString( ) method

As mentioned above, the DrawString class is still missing one method, DrawTheString. Now that you've finished implementing LtrDraw.DrawLetter, you have the key piece.

The first job of this method is to compute the angle by which each letter will be separated. You ask the string for the count of characters, and you use that value to divide the 360 degrees of the circle into equal increments.

```
Dim angle As Integer = 360 \ theString.Count
```

Now you iterate through the members of myLtrDrawList. For each LtrDraw object you'll want to compute the new x and y coordinates.

You do so by multiplying the angle value computed above by what amounts to the index of the letter (that is, 0 for the first letter, 1 for the second letter, 2 for the third, and so forth), represented by the variable counter. You then add 90 to start the string at 12 o'clock (this is not strictly necessary, since the string will rotate around the clock face!). To make the date string rotate, you must also subtract the value of the shared member variable ClockFaceCtrl.offset. The full computation of the angle is:

```
angle * counter + 90 - ClockFaceCtrl.offset
```

You take the cosine of this value using the helper method GetCos, which I presented earlier without explanation. GetCos makes use of the Math class's Cos method, which expects an angle in radians rather than degrees. To convert the angle to radians, you multiply it by the value of pi (3.14159265358979..., represented as Math.PI) and divide by 180.

```
Private Shared Function _
    GetCos(ByVal degAngle As Single) As Single
       Return CSng(Math.Cos((Math.PI * degAngle / 180.0F)))
End Function 'GetCos
```

To get the x coordinate, you multiply the cosine by the constant ClockFaceCtrl. DateRadius (defined as 900), as shown in Example 5-6.

Example 5-6. GetCos method

```
Dim newX As Single = _
  GetCos((angle * counter + _
  90 - ClockFaceCtrl.offset)) _
  * ClockFaceCtrl.DateRadius
```

 ClockFaceCtrl.DateRadius was defined as the private constant value 700.

Returning to DrawTheString, you compute newY the same way as newX, except that you use the GetSin helper method. Like GetCos, it takes an angle in degrees, converts it to radians, and calls Math.Sin to return its sine, as shown in Example 5-7.

Computing the X, Y Coordinates

You compute the x coordinate of a point on a circle by multiplying the cosine of the angle by the radius and you compute the y coordinate of a point on a circle by multiplying the sine of the angle by the radius (see *PreCalculus with Unit Circle Trigonometry* by David Cohn, [Brooks Cole]).

But this formula (cosine of the angle multiplied by radius) assumes that the center of the circle is the origin of your coordinate system, and that the angle you are multiplying is in radians, measured counter clockwise from the positive x-axis. It also assumes that the y-axis is positive above the origin and negative below.

The first issue is radians versus degrees. A circle is 360 degrees, so if you want to place 12 numbers around the face, each number is 30 degrees from the previous number. You'll need to convert degrees to radians using a simple formula:

> radians equal degrees times pi, divided by 180

When creating a clock face, it is convenient to measure the degrees offset from the y-axis (aligned with 12 o'clock) rather than the x-axis. And it is convenient to increase the angle as you move clockwise (hence the name) rather than the traditional counter-clockwise. In addition, the coordinate system you'll be using has y values that are negative above the origin, rather than positive.

You solve all three problems (using the y-axis as the zero angle, moving clockwise, and the coordinate system) by taking advantage of the fact that the cosine of 90 plus an angle is equal to the opposite of the cosine of 90 minus the angle. This gives us a way to implement a fairly straightforward computation. For example, to compute 2 o'clock in this system, you compute that 2 is 60 degrees *clockwise from 12*, add 90, and convert the resulting angle (150) to radians and take the cosine of that value. You can then multiply the result times the radius of the circle and you'll get x,y coordinates that match your coordinate system.

Example 5-7. GetSin method

```
Private Shared Function _
   GetSin(ByVal degAngle As Single) As Single
   Return CSng(Math.Sin((Math.PI * degAngle / 180.0F)))
End Function 'GetSin
```

Unfortunately, what you've computed is the upper lefthand corner of the bounding rectangle for the character you are going to draw. To center the character at this location, you must compute the width and height of the character, and adjust your coordinates accordingly:

```
theLtr.X = newX - theLtr.GetWidth( _
   g, theControl.myFont) / 2

theLtr.Y = newY - theLtr.GetHeight( _
   g, theControl.myFont) / 2
```

That accomplished, you increment the counter:

```
counter += 1
```

Now, you tell the LtrDraw object to draw itself, then you move to the next letter in the string:

```
    theLtr.DrawLetter(g, brush, theControl)
Next theLtr
```

Once the loop is completed, you increment the shared offset member of the ClockFace. This will cause you to draw the letter at a slightly different angle the next time around (i.e., the next time the OnTimer event fires), thereby rotating the date string around the perimeter of the clock.

```
ClockFaceCtrl.offset += 1
```

When you draw each letter, you'll compute the angle as:

```
angle * counter + 90 - ClockFaceCtrl.offset
```

If the date string has 30 characters, angle will be 12 (360° / 30). counter starts at zero, and ClockFaceCtrl.offset is initialized to 0, so you'll get 12 * 0 + 90 – 0, or 90°. For the second character, counter will be 1, and you'll compute its angle as 12 * 1 + 90 – 0, or 102°.

The next time OnTimer fires, ClockFaceCtrl.offset will be 1. Therefore, you'll compute an angle of 89° for the first character, 101° for the second, etc. Because OnTimer is called 20 times a second, this creates the illusion of the string marching around the outside of the clock face.

The complete listing of StringDraw.DrawTheString is shown in Example 5-8.

Example 5-8. StringDraw.DrawTheString method

```
Public Sub DrawTheString( _
  ByVal g As Graphics, ByVal brush As Brush)
    Dim angle As Integer = 360 \ myLtrDrawList.Count
    Dim counter As Integer = 0

    Dim theLtr As LtrDraw
    For Each theLtr In myLtrDrawList
        Dim newX As Single = _
          GetCos((angle * counter + 90 - _
          ClockFaceCtrl.offset)) * _
          ClockFaceCtrl.DateRadius

        Dim newY As Single = _
          GetSin((angle * counter + 90 - _
          ClockFaceCtrl.offset)) * _
          ClockFaceCtrl.DateRadius
        theLtr.X = newX - theLtr.GetWidth( _
          g, theControl.myFont) / 2
        theLtr.Y = newY - theLtr.GetHeight( _
          g, theControl.myFont) / 2
```

Example 5-8. StringDraw.DrawTheString method (continued)

```
        counter += 1
        theLtr.DrawLetter(g, brush, theControl)
    Next theLtr
    ClockFaceCtrl.offset += 1
End Sub 'DrawString
```

Drawing the clock face

All of the above has been a digression from the middle of the `ClockFaceCtrl` constructor. The next part of the constructor gets the current time:

```
currentTime = DateTime.Now
```

As you saw earlier, when you dragged the `Timer` control onto the `ClockFaceCtrl`, Visual Basic created a `System.Windows.Forms.Timer` object for you and named it `Timer1`. It has a property, `Interval`, that sets how long the timer should tick (in milliseconds) before its time elapses. You will want to set that property and also enable the timer so that it begins ticking down.

```
Timer1.Interval = 50   // milliseconds
Timer1.Enabled = True
```

When the `Interval` has elapsed the timer will fire its `Elapsed` event. You want to handle that event in the `OnTimer` method, and you can set that relationship programmatically using the `AddHandler` statement, passing in the `Event` and the address of the method that will respond to the event:

```
AddHandler timer.Elapsed, AddressOf OnTimer
```

The `OnTimer` method is where things get interesting. Once you've implemented it, you'll be able to build and run the project and see the custom control in action. The stub for `OnTimer` is shown in Example 5-9, with the various methods to be implemented marked by comments.

Example 5-9. Stub for OnTimer method

```
Public Sub OnTimer( _
ByVal source As Object, _
ByVal e As Timers.ElapsedEventArgs)

    Using g As Graphics = Me.CreateGraphics
        'SetScale(g)
        'DrawFace(g)
        'DrawTime(g, False)
        'DrawDate(g)
    End Using
End Sub 'OnTimer
```

This method runs every 50 milliseconds (when the timer interval elapses). It gets a Graphics object, then takes four steps before deleting it. To ensure that the Graphics object itself is deleted as soon as you are done with it, you acquire the device in a Using statement. When the End Using statement is reached, the Graphics object is disposed.

Within the Using block you call four methods: SetScale, DrawDate, DrawFace, and DrawTime. (DrawFace and DrawTime are commented out for now; you'll get to them soon.)

The first step is to set the scale for the clock; the SetScale method takes care of this. To do so, you need to move the origin of the x,y axis from its normal position at the upper left to the center of the clock. You do that by calling TranslateTransform on the Graphics object, passing in the x,y coordinates of the center (that is, x is half the width and y is half the height).

The TranslateTransform method is overloaded; the version you'll use takes two Singles as parameters: the x component of the translation and the y component. You want to move the origin from the upper left halfway across the form in the x direction and halfway down the form in the y direction.

 World translations are implemented with Matrices. This mathematical concept is beyond the scope of this book, and you do not need to understand matrices to use the transformations.

The form inherits two properties from Control that you'll put to use: Width and Height. Each of these returns its value in pixels.

```
g.TranslateTransform(CSng(Width / 2), CSng(Height / 2))
```

The effect is to transform the origin (0,0) to the center both horizontally and vertically.

You are now set to transform the scale from its current units (pixels by default) to an arbitrary unit. You don't care how large each unit is, but you do want 1,000 units in each direction from the origin, no matter what the screen resolution. The size of the units must be equal in both the horizontal and the vertical direction, so you'll need to choose a size. You thus compute which size is smaller in inches: the width or the height of the device.

```
Dim inches As Single = Math.Min(Width / g.DpiX, Height / g.DpiY)
```

You'll next multiply inches by the dots per inch on the x-axis to get the number of dots in the width, and divide by 2,000 to create a unit that is 1/2,000 of the width of the screen. You'll then do the same for the y-axis. If you pass these values to ScaleTransform( ), you'll create a logical scale 2,000 units on the x-axis and 2,000 units on the y-axis, or 1,000 units in each direction from the center.

```
g.ScaleTransform(
    inches * g.DpiX / 2000, inches * g.DpiY / 2000)
```

The complete listing for the SetScale method appears in Example 5-10.

Example 5-10. ClockFaceCtrl.SetScale( )

```
Private Sub SetScale(ByVal g As Graphics)
    If Width = 0 Or Height = 0 Then
        ' User has made the clock invisible
        Return
    End If
    ' set the origin at the center
    g.TranslateTransform(CSng(Width / 2), CSng(Height / 2))

    Dim inches As Single = _
        Math.Min(Width / g.DpiX, Height / g.DpiY)

    g.ScaleTransform( _
        inches * g.DpiX / 2000, inches * g.DpiY / 2000)
End Sub 'SetScale
```

Drawing the date

After you set the scale of the clock in OnTimer, you call DrawDate:

```
Private Sub DrawDate(ByVal g As Graphics)
    Dim brush As SolidBrush = New SolidBrush(ForeColor)
    sdToday.DrawTheString(g, brush)
End Sub 'DrawDate
```

This code invokes the DrawTheString method on the member variable sdToday (which is of type DrawString). As you saw earlier, DrawTheString draws the date around the clock by calling DrawLetter on each letter in the string, passing in the Graphics object, the brush created here in DrawDate, and the ClockFaceCtrl object itself. DrawLetter erases the letter from its old position and draws the letter in its new position, thus "animating" the string to move around the clock face.

Adding the Control to a Form

Before you can use the ClockFaceCtrl that you just created, you'll need to build the NorthWindControls project. After you've done that, create a form named *frmClock.vb* in the NorthWindWindows project so you can test the control as you add functionality to it. Set the form's size to 520,470.

Drag two controls onto the form: a button (which you'll name btn1224) and a ClockFaceCtrl (which you'll find in the toolbox in the NorthWindControlsComponents tab). Set the clock face control's location to 60,60 and its size to 350,350.

Modify the Welcome form to add a menu choice, Clock. In its Click event handler, show the frmClock form.

```
Private Sub ClockToolStripMenuItem_Click( _
  ByVal sender As System.Object, _
  ByVal e As System.EventArgs) _
  Handles ClockToolStripMenuItem.Click
    frmClock.Show( )
End Sub
```

Run the application. When you click on the Clock item on the main menu, you should see frmClock with the ClockFaceCtrl displaying the date around the perimeter of the clock, as shown in Figure 5-5.

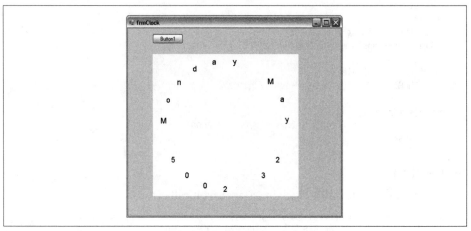

Figure 5-5. Clock custom control displaying date

Drawing the numbers

The work of drawing the clock face is done by the DrawFace method. (As you may recall, we've commented out the call to it in the OnTimer procedure.) To draw this clock, you must write the strings 1 through 12 (or 1 through 24 if the Boolean value b24Hours is set to True) in the appropriate location. You will specify the location as x,y coordinates, and these coordinates must be on the circumference of an imaginary circle.

The formula is to get the degrees by dividing the entire circle (360) by the number of hours (12 or 24). Once again, you get the coordinates by using GetCos and GetSin, passing in the number multiplied by the degrees plus 90, and all of that in turn multiplied by the value in FaceRadius (a member constant defined as 700), which represents the radius of the clock face.

However, these x,y coordinates will be the location of the upper lefthand corner of the numbers you draw. This will make for a slightly lopsided clock.

To fix this, you must center the string around the point determined by your location formula. There are two ways to do so. The first is to measure the string, then subtract half the width and height from the location. You begin by calling the MeasureString method on the Graphics object, passing in the string (the number you want to display) and the font in which you want to display it.

```
Dim stringSize As SizeF = _
    g.MeasureString(i.ToString(), font)
```

You get back an object of type SizeF, a Structure that has two properties: Width and Height. You can now compute the coordinates of the number you're going to draw, then offset the x location by half the width and the y location by half the height.

```
x = GetCos(i*deg + 90) * FaceRadius;
x += stringSize.Width / 2;
y = GetSin(i*deg + 90) * FaceRadius;
y += stringSize.Height / 2;
```

This works perfectly well, but .NET is willing to do a lot of the work for you. The trick is to call an overloaded version of the DrawString method that takes an additional (sixth) parameter: an object of type StringFormat.

```
Dim format As New StringFormat( )
```

You set its Alignment and LineAlignment properties to control the horizontal and vertical alignment of the text you want to display. These properties take one of the StringAlignment enumerated values: Center, Far, and Near. Center will center the text, as you'd expect. The Near value specifies that the text is aligned near the origin, while the Far value specifies that the text is displayed far from the origin. In a left-to-right layout, the Near position is left and the Far position is right.

```
format.Alignment = StringAlignment.Center
format.LineAlignment = StringAlignment.Center
```

You are now ready to display the string:

```
g.DrawString(
    i.ToString( ), font, brush, -x, -y,format);
```

 Notice that the x and y values represent how much you must back off the upper lefthand corner of location of the letter so that the character is centered. Thus, these values must be negative.

The StringFormat object takes care of aligning your characters, and your clock face is no longer lopsided. As a nice added feature, if the second hand is pointing to one of the numbers, you'll paint that number green.

```
If currentTime.Second = i * 5 Then
    g.DrawString(i.ToString( ), myFont, _
      greenBrush, -x, -y, format)
Else
    g.DrawString(i.ToString( ), myFont, _
      brush, -x, -y, format)
End If
```

Example 5-11 shows the complete listing.

Example 5-11. ClockFaceCtrl.DrawFace( )

```
Private Sub DrawFace(ByVal g As Graphics)

    Dim brush As SolidBrush = New SolidBrush(ForeColor)
    Dim greenBrush As SolidBrush = New SolidBrush(Color.Green)
```

Example 5-11. ClockFaceCtrl.DrawFace() (continued)

```
    Dim x, y As Single

    Dim numHours As Integer
    If b24Hours Then
        numHours = 24
    Else
        numHours = 12
    End If

    Dim deg As Integer = 360 \ numHours

    Dim i As Integer
    For i = 1 To numHours
        x = GetCos((i * deg + 90)) * FaceRadius
        y = GetSin((i * deg + 90)) * FaceRadius

        Dim format As New StringFormat()
        format.Alignment = StringAlignment.Center
        format.LineAlignment = StringAlignment.Center

        If currentTime.Second = i * 5 Then
            g.DrawString(i.ToString(), myFont, _
                greenBrush, -x, -y, format)
        Else
            g.DrawString(i.ToString(), myFont, _
                brush, -x, -y, format)
        End If
    Next i
End Sub 'DrawFace
```

You can now rebuild the project and run it, but first you need to make one small change: return to the OnTimer method and uncomment the call to DrawFace. You can do this quickly by selecting the line and pressing Ctrl-T U.

When you run it, the form now looks like Figure 5-6.

Drawing the time

After drawing the face of the clock, you are ready to draw the hour and minute hands and the second dot (the dot moves around the clock face, indicating the seconds).

Now things get really interesting. The complete listing for the DrawTime method is shown in Example 5-12, and is analyzed line by line afterward.

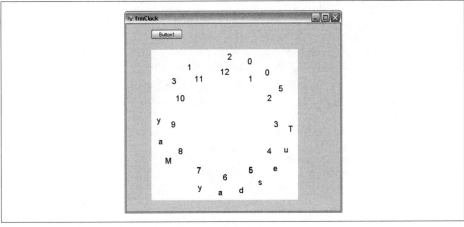

Figure 5-6. ClockFaceCtrl with date display and clock face

Example 5-12. DrawTime method

```
Private Sub DrawTime( _
      ByVal g As Graphics, ByVal forceDraw As Boolean)

        Dim hourLength As Single = FaceRadius * 0.5F
        Dim minuteLength As Single = FaceRadius * 0.7F
        Dim secondLength As Single = FaceRadius * 0.9F

        Dim hourPen As New Pen(BackColor)
        Dim minutePen As New Pen(BackColor)
        Dim secondPen As New Pen(BackColor)

        hourPen.EndCap = Drawing2D.LineCap.ArrowAnchor
        minutePen.EndCap = Drawing2D.LineCap.ArrowAnchor

        hourPen.Width = 30
        minutePen.Width = 20

        Dim secondBrush As SolidBrush = New SolidBrush(Color.Green)
        Dim blankBrush As SolidBrush = New SolidBrush(BackColor)


        Dim rotation As Single
        Dim state As Drawing2D.GraphicsState

        Dim newTime As DateTime = DateTime.Now
        Dim newMin As Boolean = False

        If newTime.Minute <> currentTime.Minute Then
            newMin = True
        End If
```

Example 5-12. DrawTime method (continued)

```
        rotation = GetSecondRotation( )
        state = g.Save( )
        g.RotateTransform(rotation)
        g.FillEllipse(blankBrush, -25, -secondLength, 50, 50)
        g.Restore(state)

        If newMin Or forceDraw Then

            rotation = GetMinuteRotation( )
            state = g.Save( )
            g.RotateTransform(rotation)
            g.DrawLine(minutePen, 0, 0, 0, -minuteLength)
            g.Restore(state)

            rotation = GetHourRotation( )
            state = g.Save( )
            g.RotateTransform(rotation)
            g.DrawLine(hourPen, 0, 0, 0, -hourLength)
            g.Restore(state)
        End If

        currentTime = newTime

        hourPen.Color = Color.Red
        minutePen.Color = Color.Blue
        secondPen.Color = Color.Green

        state = g.Save( )
        rotation = GetSecondRotation( )
        g.RotateTransform(rotation)
        g.FillEllipse(secondBrush, -25, -secondLength, 50, 50)
        g.Restore(state)

        If newMin Or forceDraw Then

            state = g.Save( )
            rotation = GetMinuteRotation( )
            g.RotateTransform(rotation)
            g.DrawLine(minutePen, 0, 0, 0, -minuteLength)
            g.Restore(state)

            state = g.Save( )
            rotation = GetHourRotation( )
            g.RotateTransform(rotation)
            g.DrawLine(hourPen, 0, 0, 0, -hourLength)
            g.Restore(state)
        End If
    End Sub 'DrawTime
```

In the DrawTime method, you first delete the hands from their current positions, then draw them in their new positions. You draw the hands as lines, and put an arrow at the end of the line to simulate an old-fashioned clock's hand. Deleting the hands is accomplished by drawing the hands with a brush set to the color of the background (thus making them invisible).

Drawing the hands

You draw the hands of the clock with a set of Pen objects:

```
Dim hourPen As New Pen(BackColor)
Dim minutePen As New Pen(BackColor)
Dim secondPen As New Pen(BackColor)
```

The length of the pens is set based on the size of the clock itself, with the hour hand shorter than the minute hand, and the second dot moving at the outer edge of the clock face (just inside the numbers):

```
Dim hourLength As Single = FaceRadius * 0.5F
Dim minuteLength As Single = FaceRadius * 0.7F
Dim secondLength As Single = FaceRadius * 0.9F
```

The F's in 0.5F, 0.7F, and 0.9F force the values to be treated as Singles rather than Doubles.

The hour and minute hands will have arrows on their ends, like an old-fashioned clock. You accomplish that by setting the pen's EndCap property to ArrowAnchor. This is a value defined in the LineCap enumeration of the Drawing2D namespace.

```
hourPen.EndCap = Drawing2D.LineCap.ArrowAnchor
minutePen.EndCap = Drawing2D.LineCap.ArrowAnchor
```

Having computed the length for the hands, you must set the width of the line that will be drawn, by setting properties on the pen:

```
hourPen.Width = 30
minutePen.Width = 20
```

You now need two brushes for the second hand, one to erase (using the BackColor) and one to draw the second hand (dot) as green:

```
Dim secondBrush As SolidBrush = New SolidBrush(Color.Green)
Dim blankBrush As SolidBrush = New SolidBrush(BackColor)
```

With the pens created, you are ready to draw the hands, but you must determine where to position the lines for the hour and minute hands, and where to put the second-hand dot. And here you're going to use an interesting approach. Rather than computing the x,y location of the second hand, you will assume that the second hand is always at 12 o'clock. How can this work? The answer is to rotate the world around the center of the clock face.

Picture a simple clock face, with an x,y grid superimposed on it, as shown in Figure 5-7.

One way to draw a second hand at 2 o'clock is to compute the x,y coordinates of 2 o'clock (as you did when drawing the clock face). An alternative approach is to

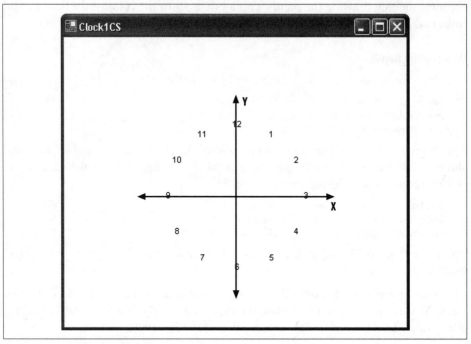

Figure 5-7. Drawing the clock face

rotate the clock the appropriate number of degrees, and then draw the second hand straight up, which is what you'll do now.

Picture the clock face and a ruler, as shown in Figure 5-8. You can move the ruler to the right angle, or you can keep the ruler straight up and down, and rotate the clock face under it.

To keep your code clean, you'll factor out the computation of how much to rotate the clock into a helper method, ClockFaceCtrl.GetSecondRotation, which will return a Single.

```
Private Function GetSecondRotation( ) As Single
    Return 360.0F * currentTime.Second / 60.0F
End Function 'GetSecondRotation
```

GetSecondRotation uses the currentTime member field. You multiply the current second by 360.0F (360 degrees in a circle), then divide by 60.0F (60 seconds per minute). For example, at 15 seconds past the minute, GetSecondRotation will return 90, because 360 * 15 / 60 = 90.

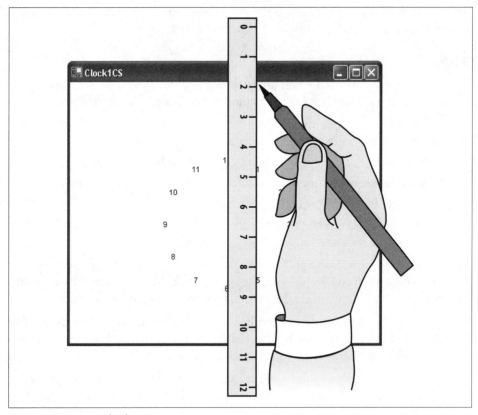

Figure 5-8. Paper and ruler

RotateTransform( )

You now know how much you want to rotate the world (i.e., rotate the paper under the ruler), so you can erase the second hand (by drawing an ellipse over it using the background color). The steps you will take will be:

1. Save the current state of the Graphics object.

2. Rotate the world.

3. Draw the second hand.

4. Restore the state of the Graphics object.

It is as if you spin your paper, draw the dot, and then spin it back to the way it was. The code snippet to accomplish this is:

```
rotation = GetSecondRotation( )
Dim state As Drawing2D.GraphicsState = g.Save( )
g.RotateTransform(rotation)
'' erase the second hand dot here
g.Restore(state)
```

The transform method for rotating the world is called `RotateTransform()`, and it takes a single argument: the number of degrees to rotate.

FillEllipse

The `Graphics` Object method you'll use to draw the dot that will "erase" the existing second-hand dot is `FillEllipse`. This method is overloaded; the version you will use takes five parameters:

- The brush that will determine the color and texture of the ellipse
- The x coordinate of the upper lefthand corner of the bounding rectangle
- The y coordinate of the upper lefthand corner of the bounding rectangle
- The width of the bounding rectangle
- The height of the bounding rectangle:

```
g.FillEllipse(blankBrush, -25, -secondLength, 50, 50)
```

You pass in `blankBrush` (later you'll pass in `secondBrush` to draw the ellipse in its new position). Thus, when you are deleting the second hand, `blankBrush` will be set to the background color. When you are drawing it, `secondBrush` will be set to green.

The x and y coordinates of the second hand will be determined so that the second hand is straight up from the origin, centered on the y-axis (remember, you've turned the paper under the ruler, you now want to draw along the ruler).

The y coordinate is easy: you'll use the constant you've defined for the length of the second hand. Remember, however, that in this world, the y coordinates are negative above the origin, and since you want to draw straight up to 12 o'clock you must use a negative value.

The x coordinate is just a bit trickier. The premise was that you'd just draw straight up, along the y axis. Unfortunately, this will place the upper lefthand corner of the bounding rectangle along the y-axis, and what you want is to center the ellipse on the y-axis. You thus pass an x coordinate that is half of the size of the bounding rectangle (e.g., 25), and you set that to negative, so that the ball will be centered right on the y-axis.

Since you want your ellipse to be circular*, the bounding rectangle will be square, with each side set to 50.

Having drawn the second hand, you go on to draw the hour and minute hands. If you redraw them both every second, however, the clock face flickers annoyingly. You will therefore only redraw these two hands if the minute has changed. To test

---

* A circle is just a special kind of ellipse.

this, you will compare the new time with the old time and determine if the minute value has changed:

```
If newTime.Minute <> currentTime.Minute Then
    newMin = True
End If
```

If the time has changed or if you are in a situation where drawing is forced (e.g., the user has moved or resized the control), then you will redraw the hour and minute hands.

```
If newMin Or forceDraw Then
'' draw minute and hour
End If
```

Notice that the If statement tests that *either* the minute has changed or the forceDraw parameter passed into the DrawTime method is True. This allows ClockFaceCtrl_Paint to redraw the hands on a repaint by just setting bForceDraw to True, as shown in Example 5-13.

Example 5-13. ClockFaceCtrl_Paint method

```
Private Sub ClockFaceCtrl_Paint(ByVal sender As System.Object, _
        ByVal e As System.Windows.Forms.PaintEventArgs) _
    Handles MyBase.Paint
    bForceDraw = True
End Sub
```

(Go ahead and add this Paint event handler to the ClockFaceCtrl class.)

The implementation of drawing the hour and minute hands is nearly identical to that for drawing the second hand. This time, however, rather than drawing an ellipse, you actually draw a line. You do so with the DrawLine method of the Graphics object, passing in a pen and four integer values.

The first two values represent the x,y coordinates of the origin of the line, and the second set of two values represent the x,y coordinates of the end of the line. In each case, the origin of the line will be the center of the clock face, 0,0. The x coordinate of the end of the line will be 0, because you'll be drawing along the y-axis. The y-coordinate of the end of the line will be the length of the hour hand. Once again, because the y coordinates are negative above the origin, you'll pass this as a negative number.

For this to work, you must rotate the clock to the appropriate positions for the hour and the minute hand, which you do with the helper methods GetMinuteRotation and GetHourRotation, respectively. GetMinuteRotation is very similar to GetSecondRotation.

```
Private Function GetMinuteRotation( ) As Single
    Return 360.0F * currentTime.Minute / 60.0F
End Function 'GetMinuteRotation
```

GetHourRotation is made more complicated only because you may have a 12-hour clock or a 24-hour clock. With the former, six o'clock is halfway around the circle, while with the latter it is only one quarter of the way around. In addition, the hour hand moves between the hours based on how many minutes it is past the hour. Code for the method is shown in Example 5-14.

Example 5-14. GetHourRotation method

```
Private Function GetHourRotation() As Single
    ' degrees depend on 24 vs. 12 hour clock
    Dim deg As Single
    Dim numHours As Single
    If b24Hours Then
        deg = 15
        numHours = 24
    Else
        deg = 30
        numHours = 12
    End If

    Return 360.0F * currentTime.Hour / numHours + _
            deg * currentTime.Minute / 60.0F
End Function 'GetHourRotation
```

After the three hands are erased by redrawing them with the background color, the currentTime member variable is updated with the new time (newTime), and the second, minute, and hour hands are redrawn with the appropriate colors.

```
currentTime = newTime
hourPen.Color = Color.Red
minutePen.Color = Color.Blue
secondPen.Color = Color.Green
```

Refactor

Notice that the code for erasing the seconds, minute, and hour are repeated within DrawTime (see Example 5-12). It just pains me to write the same code in more than one place, so let's factor the common code into two helper methods: DoDrawSecond and DoDrawTime. The job of DoDrawSecond is to draw the second ellipse with whatever brush it is given. Code for the method is shown in Example 5-15.

Example 5-15. DoDrawSecond method

```
Private Sub DoDrawSecond( _
    ByVal g As Graphics, _
    ByVal secondBrush As SolidBrush)
    Dim secondLength As Single = FaceRadius * 0.9F
    Dim state As Drawing2D.GraphicsState = g.Save()
    Dim rotation As Single = GetSecondRotation()
    g.RotateTransform(rotation)
```

Example 5-15. DoDrawSecond method (continued)

```
    g.FillEllipse(secondBrush, -25, -secondLength, 50, 50)
    g.Restore(state)
End Sub
```

The first time this is called, secondBrush will represent a brush with the background color. On the second call, it will be a green brush.

The DoDrawTime method works much the same way, but its job is to first erase, and then to draw, the hour and minute hands, as shown in Example 5-16.

Example 5-16. DoDrawTime method

```
Private Sub DoDrawTime( _
    ByVal g As Graphics, _
    ByVal hourPen As Pen, _
    ByVal minutePen As Pen)

    Dim minuteLength As Single = FaceRadius * 0.7F
    Dim state As Drawing2D.GraphicsState = g.Save()
    Dim rotation As Single = GetMinuteRotation()
    g.RotateTransform(rotation)
    g.DrawLine(minutePen, 0, 0, 0, -minuteLength)
    g.Restore(state)

    Dim hourLength As Single = FaceRadius * 0.5F
    state = g.Save()
    rotation = GetHourRotation()
    g.RotateTransform(rotation)
    g.DrawLine(hourPen, 0, 0, 0, -hourLength)
    g.Restore(state)

End Sub
```

Factoring out this code allows us to greatly simplify the DrawTime method, whose complete code can now be shown in Example 5-17.

Example 5-17. DrawTime method

```
Private Sub DrawTime( _
    ByVal g As Graphics, ByVal forceDraw As Boolean)

    ' hold the old time
    Dim oldTime As DateTime = currentTime

    Dim secondBrush As SolidBrush = New SolidBrush(Color.Green)
    Dim blankBrush As SolidBrush = New SolidBrush(BackColor)
    DoDrawSecond(g, New SolidBrush(BackColor))
```

Example 5-17. DrawTime method (continued)

```
    Dim newTime As DateTime = DateTime.Now
    currentTime = newTime    ' set the new time and update the seconds
    DoDrawSecond(g, New SolidBrush(Color.Green))

    ' if we've advanced a minute
    If newTime.Minute <> oldTime.Minute Or forceDraw Then
        currentTime = oldTime ' to erase
        Dim hourPen As New Pen(BackColor)
        Dim minutePen As New Pen(BackColor)
        hourPen.EndCap = Drawing2D.LineCap.ArrowAnchor
        minutePen.EndCap = Drawing2D.LineCap.ArrowAnchor
        hourPen.Width = 30
        minutePen.Width = 20
        DoDrawTime(g, hourPen, minutePen) ' erase
        currentTime = newTime    ' to draw new time
        hourPen.Color = Color.Red
        minutePen.Color = Color.Blue
        DoDrawTime(g, hourPen, minutePen) ' redraw
    End If

End Sub 'DrawTime
```

Your custom control is now complete. Go back to `ClockFaceCtrl.OnTimer` and uncomment the call to `DrawTime`. Rebuild and run the application. You should see something like Figure 5-9.

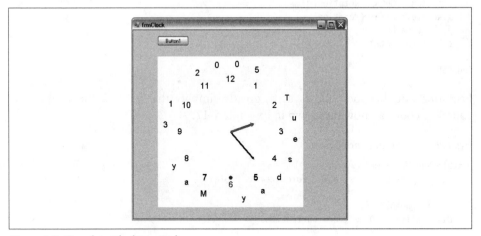

Figure 5-9. Complete ClockFaceCtrl

Switching from 12-Hour to 24-Hour Display

You've placed a button on the frmClock screen, but so far you haven't done anything with it. The control has a Boolean that tells it which clock face to draw (b24Hours). So the form can get and set that value, the ClockFaceCtrl class will need to expose a public property, TwentyFourHours, as coded in Example 5-18.

Example 5-18. TwentyFourHours property

```
Public Property TwentyFourHours() As Boolean
    Get
        Return b24Hours
    End Get
    Set(ByVal Value As Boolean)
        b24Hours = Value
        Me.Invalidate()
    End Set
End Property
```

Notice that the Set accessor not only sets the Boolean value, but it invalidates the control, causing it to be redrawn with the appropriate clock face.

Your only remaining task is to get the 24-hour button to work. First, open *frmClock. vb* in Design view and change the button's Text to "24 Hours." Then double-click on the button to add a Click event handler. Implement it as shown in Example 5-19.

Example 5-19. 24-hour button Click event handler

```
Private Sub btn1224_Click( _
    ByVal sender As System.Object, _
    ByVal e As System.EventArgs) _
      Handles btn1224.Click
    If Me.ClockFaceCtrl1.TwentyFourHours = True Then
        Me.btn1224.Text = "24 Hours"
        Me.ClockFaceCtrl1.TwentyFourHours = False
    Else
        Me.btn1224.Text = "12 Hours"
        Me.ClockFaceCtrl1.TwentyFourHours = True
    End If
End Sub
```

Run the application and click on the 24-hour button. The clock changes to 24-hour display, and the button changes to say "12 Hours," as shown in Figure 5-10.

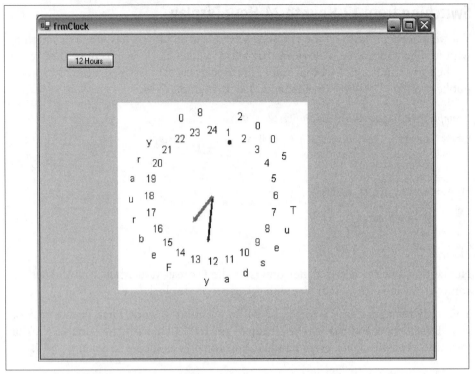

Figure 5-10. Clock Control in 24-hour mode (2:32:06 p.m. Feb. 8, 2005)

CHAPTER 6

Mice and Fonts

In the previous chapter, you created a custom control from scratch, and placed it in a form. In this chapter, you'll have the clock control that you created respond to mouse events and you'll allow the user to set the clock's fonts.

Every control supports several mouse events, including MouseClick, DoubleClick, MouseEnter, MouseHover, MouseLeave, MouseDown, MouseMove, MouseWheel, and MouseUp.

> The base Control class supports two related events: Click and MouseClick. Click will be fired any time the control is clicked (e.g., by tabbing to it and pressing spacebar or by clicking with the mouse) while MouseClick will only fire if the control is clicked with the mouse.

To test these, we'll add the following behavior:

- When the user clicks in the control, we'll center the clock on that click point.
- When the user presses the mouse button, we'll change the cursor to a hand, at the click point.
- When the user drags the clock (with the mouse button down), we'll move the clock, centered on the mouse location.
- When the user lets up the mouse button, we'll change the cursor back to default and leave the clock at the location of the MouseUp.
- When the mouse enters our control, we'll set the background color to light blue.
- When the mouse leaves our control, we'll restore its default background color.

The net effect is that the user can click on a new location to move the clock, or the user can drag the clock to the new location.

Click the Mouse

To get started, you'll need to change how you set the center of the clock within the control. To do so, add two new member variables to the ClockFaceCtrl class:

```
Private xCenter As Integer = 0
Private yCenter As Integer = 0
```

In the SetScale( ) method, see if these members are still zero (meaning that the user has not moved the clock). If so, set the center to the middle of the control, as you did previously:

```
If Me.xCenter = 0 And Me.yCenter = 0 Then
    Me.xCenter = Width \ 2
    Me.yCenter = Height \ 2
End If
```

g.TranslateTransform(xCenter, yCenter)

Notice that if you do change the xCenter and yCenter values, the effect will be to recenter the clock. That's just what you'll do in the mouse events.

Click on the ClockFace control to put it in designer mode. You will not see a typical designer; in fact, the message tells you to drag components from the server explorer or toolbox and to use the Properties window. Fortunately, as shown in Figure 6-1, you are still free to set event handlers through the Properties window.

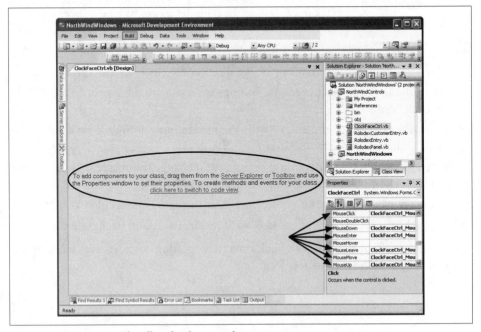

Figure 6-1. Setting event handlers for the control

The simplest event to code is the MouseClick event, shown in Example 6-1.

Example 6-1. MouseClick event handler

```
Private Sub ClockFaceCtrl_MouseClick( _
 ByVal sender As System.Object, _
 ByVal e As System.Windows.Forms.MouseEventArgs) _
 Handles MyBase.MouseClick
    Me.xCenter = e.X
    Me.yCenter = e.Y
    Me.Invalidate( )
End Sub
```

In this code, you extract the x and y location of the mouse click from the MouseEventArgs object passed in as a parameter. You use these values to set the xCenter and yCenter member variables and then you invalidate the control, forcing a complete redraw using the new values as the center of the clock. The result is that clicking on the control makes the clock jump to wherever the control was clicked.

You can verify this by rebuilding and running the application. When you click the mouse in the ClockFace control, you should see something like Figure 6-2.

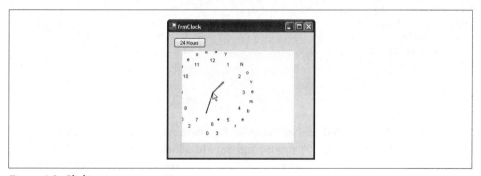

Figure 6-2. Clicking to a new position

Using MouseDown, MouseUp, and MouseMove

It would be nice to allow the user to drag the clock around in the control. You can capture the MouseDown event to know when you have begun dragging (and set the cursor to a hand to indicate that you are dragging). The MouseUp event tells you that you are done. MouseMove is a bit of a problem, because you don't want to move the clock every time you move the mouse, but only if you are dragging (signaled by the mouse button being down).

To accomplish this, you'll add a member variable:

```
    Private isMoving As Boolean = False
```

You are now ready to implement your three event handlers, as shown in Example 6-2.

Example 6-2. MouseDown, MouseUp, and MouseMove event handlers

```
Private Sub ClockFaceCtrl_MouseDown( _
ByVal sender As System.Object, _
ByVal e As System.Windows.Forms.MouseEventArgs) _
Handles MyBase.MouseDown
    Me.Cursor = Cursors.Hand
    Me.isMoving = True
End Sub

Private Sub ClockFaceCtrl_MouseUp( _
ByVal sender As System.Object, _
ByVal e As System.Windows.Forms.MouseEventArgs) _
Handles MyBase.MouseUp
    Me.xCenter = e.X
    Me.yCenter = e.Y
    Me.Invalidate( )
    Me.Cursor = Cursors.Default
    Me.isMoving = False
End Sub

Private Sub ClockFaceCtrl_MouseMove( _
ByVal sender As System.Object, _
ByVal e As System.Windows.Forms.MouseEventArgs) _
Handles MyBase.MouseMove
    If isMoving = True Then
        Me.xCenter = e.X
        Me.yCenter = e.Y
        Me.Invalidate( )
    End If
End Sub
```

When the mouse is pressed down, the isMoving member is set to True, and the cursor is set to a hand. When the mouse moves, the clock is moved. When the user releases the mouse button the isMoving member is set back to False and the cursor is returned to the default.

Note that the three lines of logic to move the clock in MouseMove, MouseUp, and MouseClick are identical. Let's factor those out to a helper method, Relocate, shown in Example 6-3.

Example 6-3. Relocate helper method

```
Private Sub Relocate(ByVal e As System.Windows.Forms.MouseEventArgs)
    Me.xCenter = e.X
    Me.yCenter = e.Y
    Me.Invalidate( )
End Sub
```

You can now simplify the previous methods, as shown in Example 6-4.

Example 6-4. Simplified versions of the MouseClick, MouseUp, and MouseMove event handlers

```
Private Sub ClockFaceCtrl_MouseClick( _
ByVal sender As System.Object, _
ByVal e As System.Windows.Forms.MouseEventArgs) _
Handles MyBase.MouseClick
    Relocate(e)
End Sub

Private Sub ClockFaceCtrl_MouseUp( _
ByVal sender As System.Object, _
ByVal e As System.Windows.Forms.MouseEventArgs) _
Handles MyBase.MouseUp
    Relocate(e)
    Me.Cursor = Cursors.Default
    Me.isMoving = False
End Sub

Private Sub ClockFaceCtrl_MouseMove( _
ByVal sender As System.Object, _
ByVal e As System.Windows.Forms.MouseEventArgs) _
Handles MyBase.MouseMove
    If isMoving = True Then Relocate(e)
End Sub
```

To see the effect of what you've done, rebuild and run the application. You should be able to drag the clock face around using the mouse. Notice also how the center of the clock face follows the mouse; the hands of the clock radiate from this point.

Using MouseEnter and MouseLeave

Finally, just for fun, we'll set the background color when the user's mouse enters the control, and reset it when the mouse leaves. Add a new member variable to ClockFaceCtrl:

```
Private currentColor As Color
```

Add handlers for the MouseEnter and MouseLeave events and implement them, as shown in Example 6-5.

Example 6-5. MouseEnter and MouseLeave event handlers

```
Private Sub ClockFaceCtrl_MouseEnter( _
ByVal sender As System.Object, _
ByVal e As System.EventArgs) Handles MyBase.MouseEnter
    Me.currentColor = Me.BackColor
    Me.BackColor = Color.Aqua
End Sub
```

Example 6-5. MouseEnter and MouseLeave event handlers (continued)

```
Private Sub ClockFaceCtrl_MouseLeave( _
ByVal sender As System.Object, _
ByVal e As System.EventArgs) Handles MyBase.MouseLeave
    Me.BackColor = Me.currentColor
End Sub
```

Rebuild and Run the Application

Not only is the background color set to light blue when you move the mouse over the clock, but when you drag the mouse within the control, the clock is moved against the new color background until you release the mouse button, as shown in Figure 6-3.

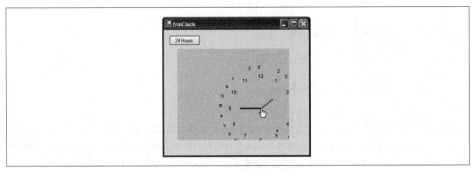

Figure 6-3. Dragging the mouse

Setting Fonts

As you saw in the earlier versions of this program, the text was drawn, one letter at a time, by using an instance of the Font class:

```
Public Sub DrawLetter( _
    ByVal g As Graphics, ByVal brush As Brush, _
    ByVal ctrl As ClockFaceCtrl)

    'get the font to draw
    Dim theFont As Font = ctrl.myFont
```

The myFont instance was initialized as a member of the ClockFaceCtrl class:

```
Dim myFont as new Font("Arial",80)
```

To add some flexibility (and make things look nicer) we'll set the font to Verdana, and provide a public accessor:

```
Private myFont As Font = New Font("Verdana", 80)
Private myFontFamily As String = "Verdana"
Public Property FontFamily( ) As String
    Get
        Return myFontFamily
    End Get
    Set(ByVal value As String)
        myFontFamily = value
    End Set
End Property
```

We also want to allow the user to set the Font size and other font characteristics. To do so we'll need to provide public properties that allow the client class to set these values within the clock itself, as shown in Example 6-6.

Example 6-6. Adding FontSize, bold, and italic properties

```
Private myFontSize As Single = 80
Private isBold As Boolean = False
Private isItalic As Boolean = False
Public Property FontSize( ) As Single
    Get
        Return myFontSize
    End Get
    Set(ByVal value As Single)
        myFontSize = value
    End Set
End Property
Public WriteOnly Property Bold( ) As Boolean
    Set(ByVal value As Boolean)
        isBold = value
    End Set
End Property
Public WriteOnly Property Italic( ) As Boolean
    Set(ByVal value As Boolean)
        isItalic = value
    End Set
End Property
```

Add new controls to the form, as shown in Figure 6-4.

Resize the Clock Face Control within the form to 267,212 and set it location to 13,43. Place the other controls under the clock and realign the 24 Hours button. Open frmClock and populate its font list box in the Load event handler, setting "Verdana" as the default font, as shown in Example 6-7.

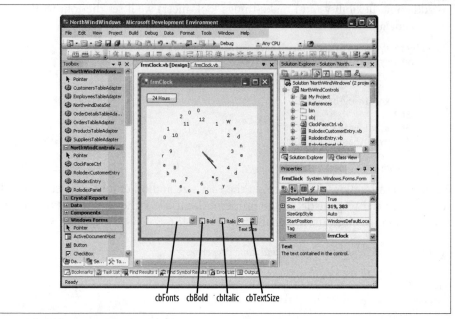

Figure 6-4. Adding new controls to the form

Example 6-7. Clock form Load event handler

```
Private Sub frmClock_Load( _
ByVal sender As System.Object, _
ByVal e As System.EventArgs) Handles MyBase.Load
    For Each aFontFamily As FontFamily In FontFamily.Families
        Me.cbbFonts.Items.Add(aFontFamily.Name)
        If aFontFamily.Name = "Verdana" Then
            cbbFonts.SelectedIndex = Me.cbbFonts.Items.Count - 1
        End If
    Next
    ChangeClockFont( )
End Sub
```

Set the event handlers for all the controls to the same event handler, as shown in Example 6-8.

Example 6-8. OnFontHasChanged event handler

```
Private Sub OnFontHasChanged( _
ByVal sender As System.Object, _
ByVal e As System.EventArgs) _
Handles cbbFonts.SelectedIndexChanged, _
cbBold.CheckedChanged, _
cbItalic.CheckedChanged, _
numFontSize.ValueChanged
    ChangeClockFont( )
End Sub
```

Factor out the code to set the new font to create the `ChangeClockFont` method shown in Example 6-9.

Example 6-9. ChangeClockFont method

```
Private Sub ChangeClockFont( )

    If Me.cbbFonts.SelectedItem Is Nothing Then Return

    Me.ClockFaceCtrl1.FontFamily = Me.cbbFonts.SelectedItem
    Me.ClockFaceCtrl1.Bold = Me.cbBold.Checked
    Me.ClockFaceCtrl1.Italic = Me.cbItalic.Checked
    Me.ClockFaceCtrl1.FontSize = Me.numFontSize.Value

    Me.ClockFaceCtrl1.Invalidate( )

End Sub
```

Return to the Clock control and update its `OnTimer` method, shown in Example 6-10.

Example 6-10. Revised OnTimer method

```
Public Sub OnTimer( _
  ByVal source As Object, _
  ByVal e As System.EventArgs)

    Using g As Graphics = Me.CreateGraphics( )
        SetScale(g)
        CreateFont( )
        DrawDate(g)
        DrawFace(g)
        DrawTime(g, bForceDraw)
        bForceDraw = False
    End Using
End Sub 'OnTimer
```

Create the helper method `CreateFont`, shown in Example 6-11.

Example 6-11. CreateFont helper method

```
Public Sub CreateFont( )
    ' get font family as set by form.ChangeClockFont
    Dim fntFamily As New FontFamily(Me.myFontFamily)

    ' initialize style to regular, then modify if set by ChangeClockFont
    Dim fntStyle As FontStyle = FontStyle.Regular
    If Me.isBold Then fntStyle = FontStyle.Bold
    If Me.isItalic Then fntStyle = FontStyle.Italic
    If Me.isBold And Me.isItalic Then fntStyle = FontStyle.Bold Or FontStyle.Italic

    ' check that font exists on this machine
    ' if so, set my font to the new font
    ' otherwise, put up msg. box
    If fntFamily.IsStyleAvailable(fntStyle) Then
```

Example 6-11. CreateFont helper method (continued)

```
        Me.myFont = New Font(fntFamily, Me.FontSize, fntStyle)
    Else
        MessageBox.Show("That is not a legal font on this machine. Resetting...", _
            "Illegal Font", MessageBoxButtons.OK, MessageBoxIcon.Error)
    End If
End Sub
```

Now run the application and you should see the results shown in Figure 6-5.

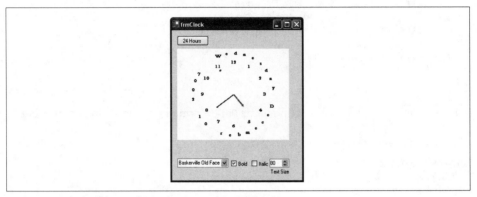

Figure 6-5. Clock with new font set

As the user changes the font (or turns on and off bold and italics) the various events
checkedChanged, etc.) are fired. Your event handler calls the factored out method
OnFontHasChanged which sets all the font characteristics and invalidates the clock
(forcing it to be redrawn with the new settings).

Every time the clock is updated due to a timer event, the clock's font is set as well,
ensuring that the clock continues with the new font settings until the user changes
them again.

Finally, I'm not sure why you would want to, but you can change the font to
WingDings2 and make a very entertaining (if not very informative) clock, as shown
in Figure 6-6.

 Actually, this does makes for an interesting game. Ask your kid to
crack the code and tell you the time and date shown on the clock. Feel
free to send in your guesses for Figure 6-6. Void in sectors E and 12,
and where otherwise prohibited. Your mileage may vary. This is not
an offering, which can only be made by prospectus. Contents are hot,
exercise caution. Batteries not included.

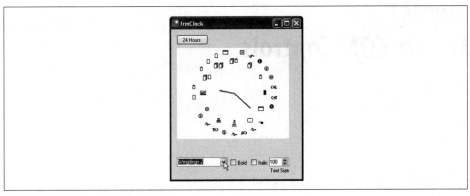

Figure 6-6. Wing ding clock

By taking responsibility for drawing your own object, you can achieve precisely the look and feel you want, at the expense of writing a bit more code. As Microsoft adds more controls to the Toolbox, you'll find yourself doing this less often, but when you do need to draw figures dynamically, there is no substitute for doing so programmatically.

CHAPTER 7

Legacy COM Controls

Most Visual Basic 6 programmers have developed a library of COM controls, and are rightly concerned that when they move to .NET all this work will be lost.

Microsoft has made a commitment to ensure that these legacy components are usable from within .NET applications, and (perhaps less importantly) that .NET components are easily callable from COM.

In this chapter, you will add a relatively simple COM control to the NorthWindWindows application.

Importing ActiveX Controls

ActiveX controls are COM components that you can drop into a form. They may or may not have a user interface. When Microsoft developed the OCX standard, which allowed developers to build ActiveX controls in Visual Basic and use them with C++ (and vice versa), the ActiveX control revolution began. Over the past decade, thousands of such controls have been developed, sold, and used. They are small, easy to work with, and an effective example of binary reuse.

Importing ActiveX controls into .NET is surprisingly easy, considering how different COM objects are from .NET objects. Visual Studio 2005 is able to import ActiveX controls automatically.

 As an alternative to using Visual Studio, Microsoft has developed a command-line utility, AxImp, that will create the assemblies necessary for the control to be used in a .NET application.

Creating an ActiveX Control

To demonstrate the ability to use classic ActiveX controls in a .NET application, you'll first develop a simple four-function calculator as an ActiveX control. You'll build the control in VB6, then import it into your Windows Forms application.

If you do not have VB6, you can download the completed project from O'Reilly's site or from *http://www.LibertyAssociates.com* (click on Books, navigate to this book, and click on thesource code). Once you have the control, you can run Regsvr32 to register it.

To create the control, open VB6 and create a new project, choosing ActiveX Control as the project type. Make the project form as small as possible, because this control will not have a user interface. Right-click `UserControl1` and choose Properties. Rename it `Calculator` in the Properties window. Click the Project in the project explorer, and in the Properties window, rename it `CalcControl`. Immediately save the project and name both the file and the project `CalcControl`, as shown in Figure 7-1.

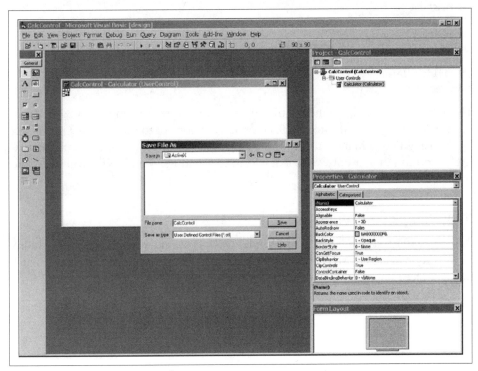

Figure 7-1. Creating a VB6 control

Now, you can add the four calculator functions by right-clicking the `CalcControl` form, selecting View Code from the pop-up menu, and typing in the VB code shown in Example 7-1.

Example 7-1. Implementing the ActiveX control in VB6

```
Public Function _
Add(left As Double, right As Double) _
As Double
```

Example 7-1. Implementing the ActiveX control in VB6 (continued)

```
    Add = left + right
End Function

Public Function _
Subtract(left As Double, right As Double) _
As Double
    Subtract = left - right
End Function

Public Function _
Multiply(left As Double, right As Double) _
As Double
    Multiply = left * right
End Function

Public Function _
Divide(left As Double, right As Double) _
As Double
    Divide = left / right
End Function
```

This is the entire code for the control. If you want to test this in your VB6 environment before importing it into .NET, compile your control to the file *CalcControl.ocx* by choosing File → Make CalcControl.ocx on the Visual Basic 6 menu bar. Alternatively, you can drag it onto your .NET form (covered next) and .NET will build and register the control for you.

Importing a Control in .NET

Add a new form to the NorthWindWindows application named `frmActiveX`. Modify the menu on Welcome so that Clock and ActiveX are sub-menu choices under a new menu choice Fun, as shown in Figure 7-2.

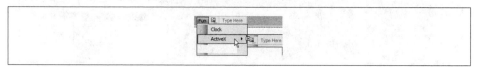

Figure 7-2. Adding ActiveX menu choice

Go back to `frmActiveX` and add the necessary controls to test the ActiveX Control (two text boxes, four buttons, and a label), as shown in Figure 7-3.

Importing a control

To import the control, choose Tools → Choose Toolbox Items…. When the Choose Toolbox Items menu opens, select the COM Components tab and find the `CalcControl.Calculator` object you just registered, as shown in Figure 7-4.

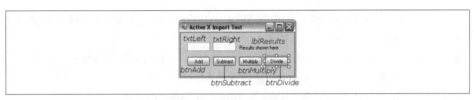

Figure 7-3. Test form for ActiveX Control

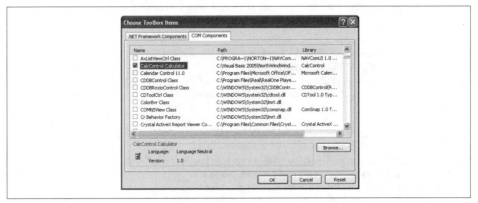

Figure 7-4. Choose Toolbox Items dialog

Because `CalcControl` is registered on your .NET machine, the Visual Studio 2005 Customize Toolbox is able to find it. When you select the control from this dialog box, it is imported into your application; Visual Studio takes care of the details, including adding it to your toolbar, as shown in Figure 7-5.

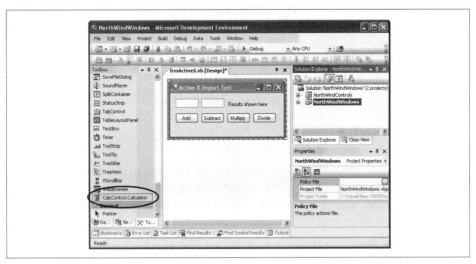

Figure 7-5. CalcControl added to toolbar

Now you can drag this control onto your Windows Form and make use of its functions.

Add event handlers for each of the four buttons. The event handlers will delegate their work to the ActiveX Control you wrote in VB6 and imported into .NET.

The source code for the event handlers is shown in Example 7-2.

Example 7-2. Implementing handlers that use the CalcControl ActiveX Control

```
Private Sub btnAdd_Click( _
ByVal sender As System.Object, _
ByVal e As System.EventArgs) Handles btnAdd.Click
    Dim left As Double = Double.Parse(txtLeft.Text)
    Dim right As Double = Double.Parse(txtRight.Text)
    lblResults.Text = Me.AxCalculator1.Add(left, right)
End Sub

Private Sub btnSubtract_Click( _
ByVal sender As System.Object, _
ByVal e As System.EventArgs) Handles btnSubtract.Click
    Dim left As Double = Double.Parse(txtLeft.Text)
    Dim right As Double = Double.Parse(txtRight.Text)
    lblResults.Text = Me.AxCalculator1.Subtract(left, right)
End Sub

Private Sub btnMultiply_Click( _
ByVal sender As System.Object, _
ByVal e As System.EventArgs) Handles btnMultiply.Click
    Dim left As Double = Double.Parse(txtLeft.Text)
    Dim right As Double = Double.Parse(txtRight.Text)
    lblResults.Text = Me.AxCalculator1.Multiply(left, right)

End Sub

Private Sub btnDivide_Click( _
ByVal sender As System.Object, _
ByVal e As System.EventArgs) Handles btnDivide.Click
    Dim left As Double = Double.Parse(txtLeft.Text)
    Dim right As Double = Double.Parse(txtRight.Text)
    lblResults.Text = Me.AxCalculator1.Divide(left, right)
End Sub
```

Each implementing method obtains the values in the text fields, converts them to Double using the shared method Double.Parse, and passes those values to the calculator's methods. The results are cast back to a string and inserted in the label, as shown in Figure 7-6.

Figure 7-6. Running the ActiveX Control

Importing COM Components

Many of the COM components that companies develop are not ActiveX Controls; they are standard COM dynamic link library (DLL) files. To see how to use these with .NET, return to VB6 and create a COM business object that will act exactly as the component from the previous section did.

 Once again, if you don't have VB6, you can download the DLL as explained earlier.

The first step is to create a new ActiveX DLL project. This is how VB6 creates standard COM DLLs. Name the class ComCalc and name the project ComCalculator. Save the file and project. Copy the methods from Example 7-1 (shown here for your convenience in Example 7-3) into the code window.

Example 7-3. Methods for VB6 COM DLL ComCalc

```
Public Function _
Add(left As Double, right As Double) _
As Double
    Add = left + right
End Function

Public Function _
Subtract(left As Double, right As Double) _
As Double
    Subtract = left - right
End Function

Public Function _
Multiply(left As Double, right As Double) _
As Double
    Multiply = left * right
End Function

Public Function _
Divide(left As Double, right As Double) _
As Double
    Divide = left / right
End Function
```

Integrating the COM DLL into .NET

Create a new form called `frmCOMDLL`. Add a menu choice to the Fun menu on the Welcome form that invokes that form.

Now that you have created the `ComCalc` DLL, you can import it into .NET. Before you can import it, however, you must choose between early and late binding. When the client calls a method on the server, the address of the server's method in memory must be resolved. That process is called *binding*.

With *early binding*, the resolution of the address of a method on the server occurs when the client project is compiled and metadata is added to the client .NET module. With *late binding*, the resolution does not happen until runtime, when COM explores the server to see if it supports the method.

Early binding has many advantages. The most significant is performance. Early-bound methods are invoked more quickly than late-bound methods. For the compiler to perform early binding, it must interrogate the COM object. If the compiler is going to interrogate the server's type library, it must first be imported into .NET.

Importing the Type Library

TheVB6-created COM DLL has a type library within it, but the format of a COM type library cannot be used by a .NET application. To solve this problem, you must import the COM type library into an assembly. Once again, you have two ways of doing this: you can allow the Integrated Development Environment (IDE) to import the class by adding a reference to the component, or you can import the type library manually by using the standalone program *TlbImp.exe*.

> *TlbImp.exe* will produce an interop assembly. The .NET object that wraps the COM object is called a *Runtime Callable Wrapper* (RCW). The .NET client will use the RCW to bind to the methods in the COM object, as shown in the following section.

Select the COM tab on the Add Reference dialog box and select the registered COM object, as shown in Figure 7-7.

This will invoke *TlbImp* for you and will copy the resulting RCW to *C:\Documents and Settings\Administrator\Application Data\Microsoft\VisualStudio\RCW*.

> The exact directory in which the RCW will be placed will vary with how you've set up your machine.

You'll have to be careful, however, because the DLL it produces has the same name as the COM DLL.

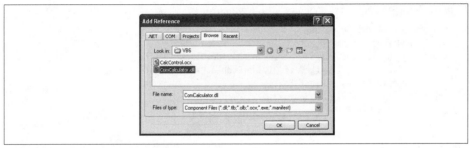

Figure 7-7. Add Reference to ComCalculator.dll

Creating a Test Program

Return to frmActiveX and select all the controls (except the ActiveX Control), then copy them to the clipboard. Switch to frmCOMDLL and paste the controls to the new form. Move them into position. Note that they have all retained their names and their event handler names.

Add the following member variable to the frmCOMDLL class:

```
Private theCalc As New ComCalculator.ComCalc
```

Click on the event handlers and add the code in Example 7-4 to call the methods of the ComCalc object.

Example 7-4. Using the ComCalculator DLL

```
Public Class frmCOMDLL
    Private theCalc As New ComCalculator.ComCalc

    Private Sub btnAdd_Click( _
    ByVal sender As System.Object, _
    ByVal e As System.EventArgs) Handles btnAdd.Click
        Me.lblResults.Text = theCalc.Add(Double.Parse(txtLeft.Text), _
            Double.Parse(txtRight.Text))
    End Sub

    Private Sub btnSubtract_Click( _
    ByVal sender As System.Object, _
    ByVal e As System.EventArgs) Handles btnSubtract.Click
        Me.lblResults.Text = theCalc.Subtract(Double.Parse(txtLeft.Text), _
            Double.Parse(txtRight.Text))
    End Sub

    Private Sub btnMultiply_Click( _
    ByVal sender As System.Object, _
    ByVal e As System.EventArgs) Handles btnMultiply.Click
        Me.lblResults.Text = theCalc.Multiply(Double.Parse(txtLeft.Text), _
            Double.Parse(txtRight.Text))
    End Sub
```

Example 7-4. Using the ComCalculator DLL (continued)

```
    Private Sub btnDivide_Click( _
    ByVal sender As System.Object, _
    ByVal e As System.EventArgs) Handles btnDivide.Click
        Me.lblResults.Text = theCalc.Divide(Double.Parse(txtLeft.Text), _
            Double.Parse(txtRight.Text))
    End Sub
End Class
```

Late Binding

To invoke a COM object with late binding in Visual Basic 2005 you must use *Reflection* (see the sidebar "Reflection"), though this is an unusual requirement, and hence an advanced topic (i.e., feel free to skip this section, I won't be offended).

Reflection

Reflection is how a program sits up and looks at itself, or at the internal metadata of another program. Reflection is generally used for any of four tasks:

Viewing metadata

Metadata is data that is captured with a program, but is not part of the running of the program. Metadata might include version information, special attributes that tell tools like Visual Studio 2005 how to display a control and so forth. In COM, metadata is captured in a type library. In .NET, metadata is stored with the program itself.

Performing type discovery

This allows you to examine the types in an assembly and interact with or instantiate those types. This can be useful when you want to allow your users to interact with your program using a scripting language, such as JavaScript, or a scripting language you create yourself.

Late binding to methods and properties

This allows the programmer to invoke properties and methods on objects dynamically instantiated, based on type discovery. This is also known as *dynamic invocation*; it's what we'll use reflection for in this chapter.

Creating types at Runtime

This is called Reflection-emit, and is a very obscure and advanced use of reflection that actually allows you to create and run programs dynamically.

To see how to use late binding, remove the reference to the imported com library. The four button handlers must now be rewritten. You can no longer instantiate a ComCalculator.comCalc object, so instead you must invoke its methods dynamically.

Because all four event handlers must replicate this work of reflecting on the object, differing only in the method they call, you'll factor the common code to a private helper method named DoInvoke. Each button-click event handler calls this method with the name of the appropriate target method (Add, Subtract, Multiply, or Divide), as shown in Example 7-5.

Example 7-5. Late binding code for the Add, Subtract, Multiply, and Divide button Click event handlers

```
Private Sub btnAdd_Click( _
ByVal sender As System.Object, _
ByVal e As System.EventArgs) Handles btnAdd.Click
    DoInvoke("Add")
End Sub

Private Sub btnSubtract_Click( _
ByVal sender As System.Object, _
ByVal e As System.EventArgs) Handles btnSubtract.Click
    DoInvoke("Subtract")
End Sub

Private Sub btnMultiply_Click( _
ByVal sender As System.Object, _
ByVal e As System.EventArgs) Handles btnMultiply.Click
    DoInvoke("Multiply")
End Sub

Private Sub btnDivide_Click( _
ByVal sender As System.Object, _
ByVal e As System.EventArgs) Handles btnDivide.Click
    DoInvoke("Divide")
End Sub
```

Before you implement DoInvoke, you'll need to add two member variables to the frmCOMDLL class. One of these will be a Type object that will hold information about the comCalc type. You also need a generic Object to represent the COM object you'll instantiate.

```
Private comCalcType As Type = Type.GetTypeFromProgID("ComCalculator.ComCalc")
Private comCalcObject As Object
```

The call to GetTypeFromProgID instructs the .NET Framework to open the registered COM DLL and retrieve the necessary type information for the specified object.

Next, add a handler for the Load event on frmCOMDLL. In this method, call CreateInstance to get back an instance of the comCalc object, as shown in Example 7-6.

Example 7-6. COMDLL form Load event handler

```
Private Sub frmCOMDLL_Load(ByVal sender As System.Object, _
                           ByVal e As System.EventArgs) Handles MyBase.Load
```

Example 7-6. COMDLL form Load event handler (continued)

```
        comCalcObject = Activator.CreateInstance(comCalcType)
End Sub
```

Now that you have the type metadata for the COM object, and have instantiated an object of that type, you can implement DoInvoke. It will invoke the methods of the COM object (Add, Subtract, Multiply, and Divide) indirectly, by calling the InvokeMember method of the Type class. This is exactly what you would do if you were invoking methods through reflection on a class described in a .NET assembly.

In DoInvoke, first create an array to hold the arguments to your method:

```
        Dim left As Double = Double.Parse(txtLeft.Text)
        Dim right As Double = Double.Parse(txtRight.Text)
        Dim inputArguments As Object = New Object(1) {left, right}
```

 Note that the constructor for the array of objects takes the upper bound (1), indicating that this array will hold two objects.

Type.InvokeMember expects several arguments:

- The method you want to invoke as a string (Add, Subtract, Multiply, or Divide)
- A binder flag (set to Reflection.BindingFlags.InvokeMethod)
- A binder (set to Nothing)
- The object returned by CreateInstance( )
- The input argument array

The results of this invocation are cast to Double and stored in the local variable result:

```
        result = Double.Parse(comCalcType.InvokeMember( _
                                whichMethod, _
                                Reflection.BindingFlags.InvokeMethod, _
                                Nothing, _
                                comCalcObject, _
                                inputArguments))
```

You can then display this result in the user interface, as shown in Figure 7-8.

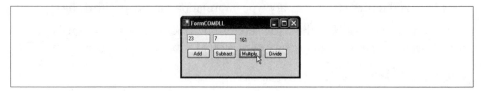

Figure 7-8. Running with late binding

The complete implementation of DoInvoke is shown in Example 7-7.

Example 7-7. Implementation of DoInvoke() Method

```
Public Sub DoInvoke(ByVal whichMethod As String)
    Dim left As Double = Double.Parse(txtLeft.Text)
    Dim right As Double = Double.Parse(txtRight.Text)
    Dim result As Double = Nothing

    Dim inputArguments As Object = New Object(1) {left, right}
    result = Double.Parse(comCalcType.InvokeMember( _
                              whichMethod, _
                              Reflection.BindingFlags.InvokeMethod, _
                              Nothing, _
                              comCalcObject, _
                              inputArguments))

    Me.lblResults.Text = result.ToString( )

End Sub
```

PART II

Building Web Applications

Web Application, Desig
and First Forms

In this chapter, you will begin to create a web application. As in Part I, you will find that we get down to business quickly, but this time a bit of introduction is absolutely necessary before we can start creating applications. The introductory comments are intended to set the stage for everything else we're doing. I'll keep them as short as possible.

There are five essential, overlapping stages in the development of any application: *Analysis*, *Design*, *Implementation*, *Testing*, and *Deployment*. These are described in Chapter 1, and except for *Deployment*, are no different for web applications than for Windows applications.

The key difference between a Windows application and a web application is in *deployment*. Applications deployed to the Web do not need to be distributed to your clients; you simply deploy to the "production server" (the machine your clients connect to) and your application is instantly available.

 Parts I and II are relatively independent. You do not need to have read Part I to understand the material in Part II, but, where they are relevant, I'll refer you to topics already covered in earlier chapters, rather than duplicating the material for web applications.

The requirements for a meaningful web application will be spelled out in this chapter, and the rest of the section will focus on implementation. We will explore design decisions as we go, and our general approach, once again, will be to get it working and keep it working.

Note that the requirements for the web application are similar to, but not the same as, those shown for the Windows application in the first part of the book. The goal is to demonstrate how the Web both enhances and constrains what is realistic in an application. As you'll see, the implementation is strikingly similar in some areas, and drastically different in others.

This is not a book on HTML nor on clean web design. (For a good book on using HTML to create web pages, see *HTML: The Definitive Guide* [O'Reilly]).

Rather than taking the time to show you the skills necessary to lay out clean, usable, impressive web pages with HTML, the pages in this application are *intentionally* sparse—almost placeholders for the professional user interface that you'll want to design but that goes beyond the scope of this book. Our focus is not on the layout, it is on the functionality.

Understanding Web Forms

Before we build the application, it really is essential to provide a quick overview of the ASP.NET application architecture. Please bear with me, we'll be writing real code in no time.

The key to ASP.NET is the creation and interaction of web forms, which implement a programming model in which web pages are dynamically generated on a web server for delivery to a browser over the Internet. With ASP.NET Web Forms, you create an ASPX page with more or less static content consisting of HTML and web controls, and you write Visual Basic 2005 code to add additional dynamic content. The Visual Basic 2005 code *runs on the server*, and the data produced is integrated with the declared objects on your page to create an HTML page that is sent to the browser.

There are three critical points to pick up from the previous paragraph. Keep them in mind throughout this chapter.

- Web pages can contain both HTML and web controls (described later).
- All processing is done on the server (you can have client-side processing with scripting languages, but that is not part of ASP.NET and is not covered in this book).
- If you use ASP.NET web controls, what the browser sees is just HTML (there is an exception to this; with some modern browsers, script may be sent as well). That is, even though ASP.NET web controls provide a new way to create web applications, by the time the page is sent to the browser, it is vanilla HTML.

ASP.NET 2.0 Web Forms are the successor to the enormously successful ASP.NET 1.x Web Forms, which, in turn, were the successor to ASP pages. The goal of ASP.NET 2.0 was to reduce the amount of coding by 70% compared to ASP 1.x. This means that web programming is increasingly *declarative* rather than *programmatic*—that is, you declare controls on your web form rather than writing (and rewriting) boiler-plate code.

You still have the option of writing code (you can always write code) but for the vast majority of the web programming you do, you'll write a lot less code with ASP.NET 2.0 than you did with 1.x.

Web forms are designed to be viewed through any browser, with the server generating the correct browser-compliant HTML. You can do the programming for the logic of the web form in any .NET language. We will, of course, use Visual Basic 2005. Since Visual Studio makes the process of designing and testing web forms *much* easier, this book will use nothing but Visual Studio 2005 to develop web applications.

Web forms divide the user interface into two parts: the visual part or user interface (UI); and the logic that lies behind it. This is very similar to developing Windows Forms. The division between the file that contains the user interface, and the corresponding file that contains the code, is called code separation, and all the examples in this book will use code separation, though it is possible to write the Visual Basic 2005 code in the same file with the user interface content (e.g., HTML).

In Version 2.0 of ASP.NET, Visual Studio takes advantage of partial classes, allowing the code-separation page to be far simpler than it was in 1.x. Because the code-separation and the declarative page are part of the same class, Visual Studio can hide its initialization code in a separate file.

The UI page is stored in a file with the extension *.aspx*. When you access the page through your browser, the server runs any associated code and then generates HTML that is sent to the client browser. Your ASP.NET application makes use of the rich web controls found in the System.Web and System.Web.UI namespaces of the .NET Framework Class Library (FCL).

With Visual Studio 2005, web forms programming couldn't be simpler: open a form, drag some controls onto it, and write the code to handle events. Presto! You've written a web application.

On the other hand, even with Visual Studio 2005, writing a robust and complete web application can be a daunting task. Web forms offer a very rich UI and there are a great many web controls available to you to simplify your work, yet the very variety can be overwhelming at first.

Web Form Events

Much like the Windows Forms you built in Part I, web forms are event-driven. An *event* represents the idea that "something happened."

An event is generated (or *raised*) when the user presses a button, selects from a list box, or otherwise interacts with the UI. Events can also be generated by the system starting or finishing work. For example, open a file for reading, and the system raises an event when the file has been read into memory.

The method that responds to the event is called the *event handler*. Event handlers are written in Visual Basic 2005 and are associated with controls in the HTML page through control attributes.

By convention, ASP.NET event handlers are subs (not functions) and take two parameters. The first parameter represents the object raising the event. The second, called the *event argument*, contains any information specific to the event. For most events, the event argument is of type EventArgs, which does not expose any properties and is really just a placeholder. For some controls, however, the event argument might be of a type derived from EventArgs that can expose properties specific to that event type.

For example, when you bind a row to a GridView (see Chapter 10), an event fires that passes in a GridViewRowEventArgs object that derives from EventArgs. The GridViewRowEventArgs object has a Rows property, which returns a collection of GridViewRow objects. These, in turn, provide access to all the attributes of the corresponding rows, including the underlying data object (DataItem) that is being used to populate that row.

 In web applications, with the exception of client-side script event handling, which is not covered in this book, events are handled on the server and, therefore, require a roundtrip. ASP.NET only supports a limited set of events, such as button clicks and text changes. These are the events that the user might expect to cause a significant change, as opposed to the myriad events handled in Windows Forms applications (see Part I), such as mouse events that might happen many times during a single user-driven task.

Event Model

The two models of program execution (which are not necessarily mutually exclusive) are *linear* and *event-driven*.

Linear programs move from step 1, to step 2, to the end of all the steps. Flow control structures within the code (such as loops, If statements, function or subroutine calls) may redirect the flow of the program, but essentially, once program execution begins, it runs its course unaffected by anything the user or system may do. Prior to the advent of GUI environments, most computer programs were linear.

In contrast, event-driven programming responds to something happening (such as a button being pressed). Most often, events are generated by user action, but events can also be raised by the system starting or finishing work. For example, the system might raise an event when a file that you open for reading has been read into memory or when your battery's power is running low.

In ASP.NET, objects may raise events and other objects may have assigned event handlers. For example, a button may raise the Click event and the page may have a method to handle the button's click event (e.g., Button1_Click). The event handler responds to the button's being clicked in whatever way is appropriate for your application.

ASP.NET Events

Classic ASP had just six events, of which only four were commonly used. These were:

Application_OnStart
> Fired when the application started

Application_OnEnd
> Fired when the application terminated

Session_OnStart
> Fired at the beginning of each session

Session_OnEnd
> Raised when the session ended

ASP.NET, on the other hand, has literally thousands of events. The application raises events, each session raises events, and the page and most of the server controls can also raise events. All ASP.NET event handlers are executed on the server. Some events cause an immediate posting to the server, while other events are simply stored until the next time the page is posted back to the server, to be executed at that time.

Because they are executed on the server, ASP.NET events are somewhat different from events in traditional client applications, in which both the event itself and the event handler are on the client. In ASP.NET applications, an event is typically raised on the client (e.g., by the user clicking a button displayed in the browser), but handled on the server.

Consider a classic ASP web page with a button control on it. A Click event is raised when the button is clicked. This event is handled by the client (that is, the browser), which responds by posting the form to the server. No event handling occurs server-side.

Now consider an ASP.NET web page with a similar button control. The difference between an ASP.NET button control and a classic HTML button control is primarily that the ASP.NET button has an attribute, runat=server, that allows the developer to add server-side processing to all the normal functionality of an HTML button.

When the Click event is raised, the browser handles the client-side event by posting the page to the server. This time, however, an event message is also transmitted to the server. The server determines if the Click event has an event handler associated with it, and, if so, the event handler is executed on the server.

An event message is transmitted to the server via an HTTP POST. ASP.NET automagically (that's a technical term) handles all the mechanics of capturing the event, transmitting it to the server, and processing the event. As the programmer, all you have to do is create your event handlers.

Many events, such as MouseOver, are not eligible for server-side processing because they kill performance. All server-side processing requires a postback (a roundtrip to the server and back), and you do not want to post the page every time there is a MouseOver event. If these events are handled at all, it is on the client side (using script) and outside the scope of ASP.NET.

Application and Session Events

ASP.NET supports the Application and Session events familiar to ASP programmers. An Application_Start event is raised when the application first starts. This is a good time to initialize resources that will be used throughout the application, such as database connection strings (but not the database connection itself). An Application_End event is raised when the application ends. This is the time to close resources and do any other housekeeping that may be necessary. Note that garbage collection will automatically take care of freeing up memory, but if you allocated unmanaged resources, such as components created with languages that are not compliant with the .NET Framework, you must clean them up yourself.

Likewise there are session events. A session starts when a user first requests a page from your application and ends when the application closes the session or the session times out. A Session_Start event is raised when the session starts, at which time you can initialize resources that will be specific to the session, such as opening a database connection. When the session ends, there will be a Session_End event.

Page events are wired automatically to methods with the following names:

- Page_AbortTransaction
- Page_CommitTransaction
- Page_DataBinding
- Page_Disposed

- Page_Error
- Page_Init
- Page_InitComplete
- Page_Load
- Page_LoadComplete
- Page_PreInit
- Page_PreLoad
- Page_PreRender
- Page_PreRenderComplete
- Page_SaveStateComplete
- Page_Unload

Events in Visual Studio .NET

The Visual Studio .NET IDE can automatically handle much of the work required to implement events in ASP.NET. For example, Visual Studio offers a list of all the possible events for each control and if you choose to implement an event, you can type in a name for the event handler. The IDE will create the boilerplate code necessary and will wire up the associated delegate.

As you add controls, they will have their own events that you may handle as well. When you add the control, you can see its events by clicking on the control and then clicking on the events button (the lightning bolt) in the Properties window. For example, the events for a button are shown in Figure 8-1.

Figure 8-1. Button events

You may type the name of a method in the space next to any event or you may double-click in that space and an event handler will be created for you. You'll be placed in the event handler itself, ready to implement the event.

Every control has a default event, presumably the event most commonly implemented for that control. Not surprisingly, the default event for the button class is the Click Event. You can create the default event handler just by double-clicking on the control. Thus, had you not created the Button1_Click event handler as shown earlier, you could open Design view and double-click on the button. The effect would be identical: an event handler named Button1_Click would be created, and you'd be placed in the event handler ready to implement the method.

The default events for some of the most common web controls are listed in Table 8-1.

Table 8-1. Default events for some ASP.NET controls

Control	Default event
Button	Click
Calendar	SelectionChanged
CheckBox	CheckedChanged
CheckBoxList	SelectedIndexChanged
DataGrid	SelectedIndexChanged
DataList	SelectedIndexChanged
DropDownList	SelectedIndexChanged
HyperLink	Click
ImageButton	Click
Label	None
LinkButton	Click
ListBox	SelectedIndexChanged
RadioButton	CheckedChanged
RadioButtonList	SelectedIndexChanged
Repeater	ItemCommand

Multiple Controls to One Event Handler

It is possible for a single event handler to handle events from several different controls. For example, you may have a generic button-click event handler that handles all the buttons on your form. The button that raised the event can be determined by testing the sender parameter. In the following code snippet, a button-click event handler casts the sender object (that is, the control that raised the event) to the Button type, then assigns the ID property of that button to a string variable.

```
Protected Sub GenericButton_Click( _
ByVal sender As Object, _
ByVal e As System.EventArgs) Handles btnOrder.Click
        Dim b As Button = CType(sender, Button) 'cast object to button
        Dim buttonID As String = b.ID            'save the button ID properly
End Sub
```

This can eliminate a great deal of duplicate code and make your program easier to read and maintain.

Postback Versus Non-Postback Events

Postback events are those that cause the form to be posted back to the server immediately. These include click-type events, such as the button-click event. In contrast, many events (typically change events) are considered *non-postback* in that the form is not posted back to the server immediately. Instead, these events are cached by the control until the next time a postback event occurs.

> You can force controls with non-postback events to behave in a postback manner by setting their AutoPostBack property to True.

State

A web application's *state* is the current value of all the controls and variables for the current user in the current session. The Web however, is inherently a "stateless" environment. This means that normally every post to the server loses the state from previous posts, unless the developer takes the trouble to preserve this session knowledge. ASP.NET, however, provides support for maintaining the state of a user's session.

Whenever a page is posted to the server, the server recreates it from scratch before returning it to the browser. ASP.NET provides a mechanism that automatically maintains state for server controls (the ViewState property) independent of the HTTP session. Thus, if you provide a list and the user has made a selection, that selection is preserved after the page is posted back to the server and redrawn on the client.

> The state of other objects (that are not controls) is not automatically maintained in ViewState and must be stored by the developer, either in ViewState or in Session State, described in later sections.
>
> The HTTP Session maintains the illusion of a connection between the user and the web application, despite the web being a stateless, connectionless environment.

Getting Started

To get started, let's create a web application named WebNorthWind. Open Visual Studio 2005. Click on New Web Site and in the drop-down menus, choose FileSystem, filling in an appropriate file location. Make sure the language is set to Visual Basic, as shown in Figure 8-2.

Visual Studio 2005 will create a filesystem-based web site (you will not find the web site listed under IIS Management) and will create a file, *Default.aspx*, that represents the first ASP.NET form. The editor will open, and the web Toolbox will be visible (if

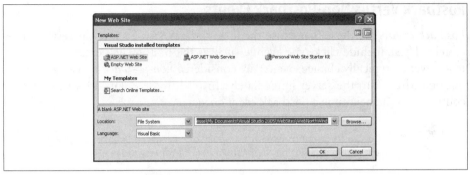

Figure 8-2. Creating a new web site

not, you can make it visible through the View window). The toolbox, like all windows, can be "pinned" in place by clicking on the thumbtack.

Depending on how you've configured your system, you'll probably find yourself in the Source view, with a tabbed window allowing you to switch to WYSIWYG (What You See Is What You Get) Design view, as shown in Figure 8-3.

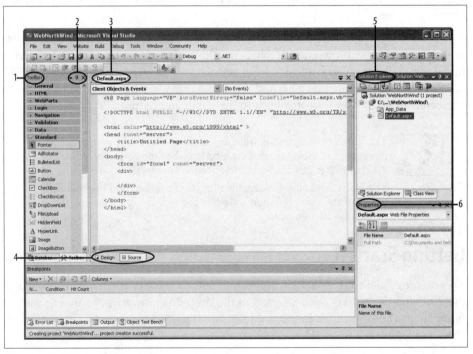

Figure 8-3. Web development editor

I've circled and numbered six areas of this screen:

1. The Toolbox, which consists of multiple drop-down collections of controls you can add to your application (the standard collection is visible). You can right-click in any one of these collections to pick a menu choice that will sort them alphabetically, as has been done here.

2. The window manipulation controls. Clicking on the down arrow allows you to change the window placement, as shown in Figure 8-4. Clicking on the thumb-tack the window open in place, or, if it is already tacked open auto-hides the window and creates a tab on the side of the editing window. Hover over that tab and the Toolbox reemerges, move away from the Toolbox and it hides again, as shown in Figure 8-5. (Reclicking on the thumbtack pins the window back into place.) Finally, clicking on the "X" closes the Toolbox (you can reopen it from the View menu).

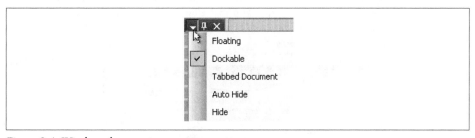

Figure 8-4. Window placement

Figure 8-5. Auto-hiding the Toolbox

3. The tab indicating the form you are working on (you may have many open at once, and use the tabs to move among them).

4. The tab that allows you to switch between Source and Design view. You can drag controls from the Toolbox directly onto either view.

5. The Solution explorer shows you the name and files for each project in your web solution. A solution is just a collection of projects, with each project typically compiled into an assembly.

6. The Properties window. As you click on controls (or your form), the Properties window will change to reflect the properties (and if appropriate, the events) of that control.

Visual Studio creates a folder named *WebNorthWind* in the directory you've indicated, and within that directory it creates your *Default.aspx* page (for the User interface), *Default.aspx.vb* (for your code) and an *App_Data* directory (currently empty but often used to hold mdb files or other data-specific files).

While Visual Studio no longer uses projects for web applications, it does keep solution files to allow you to return quickly to a web site or Desktop application you've been developing. The solution files are kept together in a directory you may designate through the Tools → Options window, as shown in Figure 8-6.

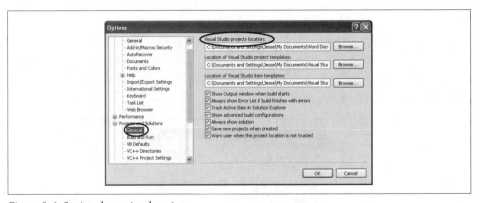

Figure 8-6. Setting the project location

Code-Behind Files

Let's take a closer look at the *.aspx* and code-behind files that Visual Studio creates. Start by renaming *Default.aspx* to *Welcome.aspx*. To do this, click on the name in the Solution explorer and rename the file.

Note to ASP.NET 1.1 programmers: the code-behind model for ASP. NET has changed.

In Versions 1.x, the code-behind file defined a class that derived from Page. This code-behind class contained instance variables for all the controls on the page, with explicit event binding using delegates and the *.aspx* page derived from the code-behind class.

In Version 2.0, ASP.NET generates a single class from the combined *.aspx* page and partial class definitions in the code-behind file.

ASP.NET can infer the control instances and derive event bindings from the markup during compilation; thus, the new code-behind file includes only the application code you need, such as event handlers, and does not need to include instance variables or explicit event binding. The new code-behind files are simpler, easier to maintain, and always in sync with the *.aspx* page.

Rename the class, which you do by right-clicking on the *.aspx* page and choosing View Code in the code page. Rename the class Welcome_aspx. You'll see a small line next to the name. Click on it and you'll open the smart tag that allows you to rename the class wherever it is used. Rename Default_aspx as Welcome_aspx, and Visual Studio will do the work of ensuring that every occurrence of Default_aspx is replaced with its new name, as shown in Figure 8-7.

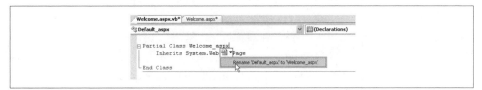

Figure 8-7. Renaming the class

Unfortunately, the name of the class is not changed in the page directive in *Welcome.aspx,* so go back to the *Welcome.aspx* file and change the page directive's Inherits attribute to *Welcome_aspx*.

```
<%@ Page Language="VB" AutoEventWireup="false" CodeFile="Welcome.aspx.vb"
Inherits="Welcome_aspx" %>
```

Within the HTML view of *Welcome.aspx*, you see that a form has been specified in the body of the page using the standard HTML form tag:

```
<form id="Form1" runat="server">
```

ASP.NET assumes that you need at least one form to manage the user interaction, and creates one when you open a project. The attribute runat="server" is the key to the server-side magic. Any tag that includes this attribute is considered a server-side control to be executed by the ASP.NET framework on the server. Within the form, Visual Studio has added div tags to facilitate placing your controls and text.

Put a Toe in the Water

Having created an empty web form, the first thing you might want to do is add some text to the page. By switching to Source view, you can add script and HTML directly to the file (just as you could with classic ASP.) Adding the following line to the <body> segment of the HTML page will cause it to display a greeting and the current local time:

```
Hello World! It is now <% = DateTime.Now.ToString( ) %>
```

The <% and %> marks indicate that code falls between them (in this case, Visual Basic 2005). The = sign immediately following the opening tag causes ASP.NET to display the value, just like a call to Response.Write. You could just as easily write the line as:

```
Hello World! It is now
<% Response.Write(DateTime.Now.ToString( ))%>
```

Run the page by pressing F5. Visual Studio 2005 will notice that you have not enabled debugging for this application, and a dialog box will appear, offering to enable debugging for you, as shown in Figure 8-8. Click OK. You should see the string printed to the browser, as in Figure 8-9.

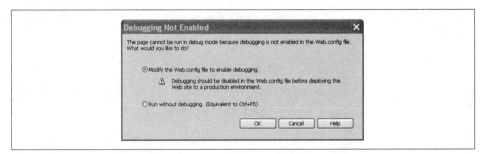

Figure 8-8. Enabling debugging

Figure 8-9. Hello World from ASP.NET

Adding Controls

Before proceeding, delete the line that tells the time from your aspx page, so that you can start the next part clean. In fact, that is the last time you'll mix HTML and code;

from now on you'll add controls to the aspx page, and code in the code-behind (*aspx.vb*) page.

You can add server-side controls to a web form in three ways: by dragging controls from the Toolbox to the Design page, by writing HTML into the source page, or by programmatically adding them at runtime. For example, suppose you want to use buttons to let the user choose one of three shippers provided in the Northwind database. To do so, click on Design view, and drag a RadioButtonList control onto the form, as shown in Figure 8-10.

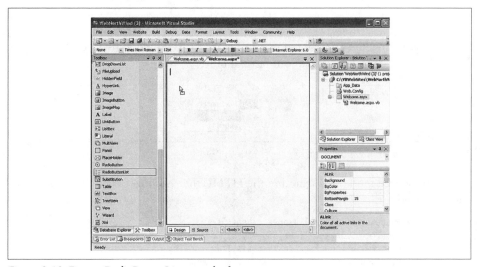

Figure 8-10. Drag a RadioButtonList onto the form

Once the RadioButtonList control is on your form, click its smart tag and choose Edit Items to add items to the list, as shown in Figure 8-11.

Figure 8-11. Edit items in RadioButtonList

The ListItem Collection Editor opens. Click the Add button to add a List Item. Type in Text (e.g., "Speedy Express") and for the first item set Selected to True (to select the first radio button in the list). Add entries for "United Package" and for "Federal Shipping," as shown in Figure 8-12.

When you click OK, the three buttons appear in the group. Click on the group and go to the Properties window. Name the group *rblShipper* (by setting the ID property) and examine the other properties you can set for the group. Pay particular attention

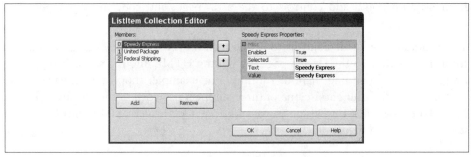

Figure 8-12. List Item Collection Editor

to the *RepeatDirection* control (shown in Figure 8-13) which allows you to have the buttons stacked vertically or laid out horizontally.

Figure 8-13. RepeatDirection property

Switch to Source mode and examine the HTML that has been generated for you by the Design editor:

```
<asp:RadioButtonList ID="rblShipper" runat="server">
    <asp:ListItem Selected="True">Speedy Express</asp:ListItem>
    <asp:ListItem>United Package</asp:ListItem>
    <asp:ListItem>Federal Shipping</asp:ListItem>
</asp:RadioButtonList></div>
```

You could, of course, have hand-coded this, but the designer is easier and less prone to typos. Feel free, however, to add additional ListItem controls by hand if you prefer; the changes will be reflected back in the designer.

> You can add controls to a page in one of two modes. The default mode is FlowLayout. With FlowLayout, the controls are added to the form from top to bottom, as in a standard html document. The alternative is GridLayout, in which the controls are arranged in the browser using absolute positioning (x and y coordinates).
>
> To change from Flow to Grid or back, change the PageLayout property of the document in Visual Studio .NET. In this book, we will always use the Flow mode, as the Grid mode clutters the code with positioning information and has pretty much fallen out of favor with many developers.

Return to Design mode and click on the RadioButtonList. In the Properties window, set the BackColor to a pale blue and set the BorderColor to red, as shown in Figure 8-14.

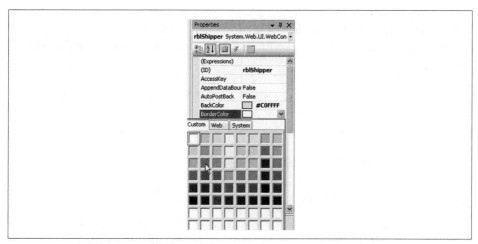

Figure 8-14. Setting radio button controls

Notice that you can type in the hex code for the color you want, or you can simply drop down the color picker. You can even type the word **Red** into the Border color property, and the standard red color will be chosen. (If you want to see the border, change the BorderStyle from its default setting of none to something like Solid). Switch back to Source mode and notice that your HTML has been updated appropriately:

```
<asp:RadioButtonList
ID="rblShipper"
runat="server"
BackColor="#C0FFFF"
BorderColor="Red"
BorderStyle="Solid">
```

Server Controls

Web forms offer two types of server-side controls. The first is server-side HTML controls. These are HTML controls that you tag with the attribute runat="Server".

The alternative to marking HTML controls as server-side controls is to use ASP.NET web controls, also called ASP controls. Web controls have been designed to augment and replace the standard HTML controls. Web controls provide a more consistent object model and more consistently named attributes. For example, with HTML controls, there are myriad different ways to handle input:

```
<input type="radio">
<input type="checkbox">
<input type="button">
<input type="text">
<textarea>
```

Each of these behaves differently and takes different attributes. The web controls try to normalize the set of controls, using attributes consistently throughout the ASP control object model. The web controls that correspond to the preceding HTML server-side controls are:

```
<asp:RadioButton>
<asp:CheckBox>
<asp:Button>
<asp:TextBox rows="1">
<asp:TextBox rows="5">
```

The remainder of this book focuses on web controls.

Adding Controls and Events

Before proceeding, let's start a new application that will build on what you already have. To do so, create a new web application, and name this one *NorthWindASP*.

To copy the existing web site's files into your new web site, click on WebSite → Copy Web Site. The Copy Web Site page will open. In the upper left is the Connect to: drop down with a blue button next to it. Click on the button to display the Open Web Site Dialog, as shown in Figure 8-15.

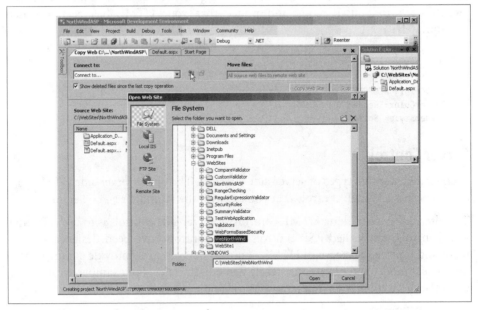

Figure 8-15. Opening the web site to copy from

Select the web site you want to copy from and click *Open*. Your dialog is now set up to transfer the files. Highlight all the files in the remote web site, and click the transfer arrow, as shown in Figure 8-16.

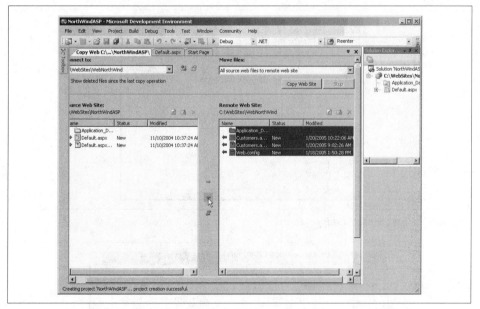

Figure 8-16. Copy all target web site files to new web site

You can now close the Copy Web page (big X in upper righthand corner). Delete the *Default.aspx* web page (right-click on it in Solution explorer and choose Delete) and set the *Welcome.aspx* page to be the start page for your application (right-click on it in Solution explorer and choose Select As Start Page). Your new web site should be a duplicate of your old. Run it to make sure all is working properly.

Adding the Shipper Page

By adding just a few more controls, you can create a complete form with which users can interact. You will do this by adding a more appropriate greeting ("Welcome to NorthWind"), a text box to accept the name of the user, two new buttons (Order and Cancel), and text that provides feedback to the user. Figure 8-17 shows the finished form.

Right-click on the application and choose Add New Item. From the Add New Item dialog click on web form and name the new web form *Shipper.aspx*, as shown in Figure 8-18.

You'll want to lay out your new controls in a table, and the easiest way to do so is to drag a table from the Toolbox into the Source view (within the `<div>` tags in the form). Once the table is in place, you can easily add rows by typing the open angle bracket within the table: IntelliSense springs into action to help you create an `ASP:TableRow` tag (and its closing tag), as shown in Figure 8-19.

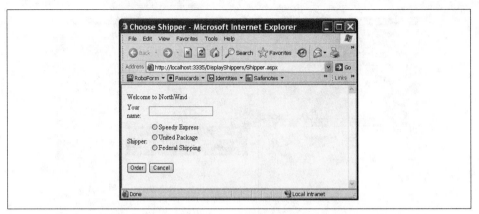

Figure 8-17. The completed shipper form

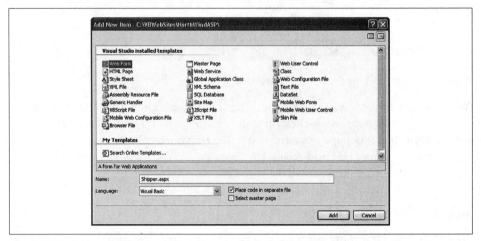

Figure 8-18. Add new web page

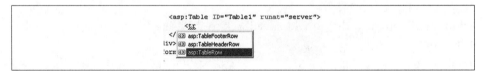

Figure 8-19. Adding a table row

Within the first row you'll add a table cell. Again IntelliSense makes this very easy. After adding the cell, click space, and all the attributes for the cell are displayed. You'll want to set its ColumnSpan attribute to 2, as shown in Figure 8-20.

Within the TableCell declaration, you can then type the welcome statement:

```
<asp:TableCell ColumnSpan="2">Welcome to NorthWind</asp:TableCell>
```

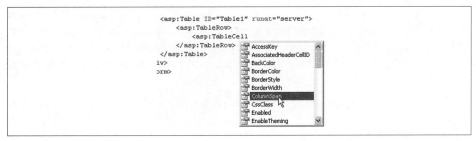

Figure 8-20. Setting the ColumnSpan attribute

 XHTML-compliant HTML requires that the attribute values be in double quotes. Visual Studio 2005 can help you with that. Open the menu item Tools → Options, open the Text editor section, and then open the HTML section. Within HTML click on the Format choice, and check the box under Automatic formatting options that says Insert attribute value quotes when typing, as shown in Figure 8-21.

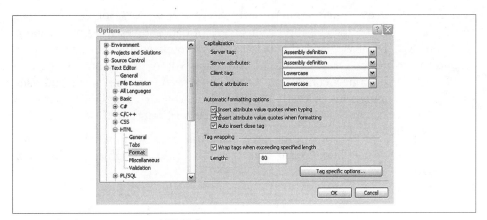

Figure 8-21. Setting automatic HTML formatting

Create a second row with two columns. The first column will contain a text prompt. Drag a text box into the second column from the Toolbox, as shown in Figure 8-22.

```
<asp:TableRow>
    <asp:TableCell>Your name:</asp:TableCell>
    <asp:TableCell></asp:TableCell>
</asp:TableRow>
p:Table>
```

Figure 8-22. Dragging a TextBox into a table cell

Your next step is to create a third row with the RadioButtonList that you created earlier on the welcome page. First, create the row and two columns (the first with the prompt Shipper).

The second column will be for a new `RadioButtonList`, but you'll create it first, and then add it to the table once you have it set the way you want. Click on Design view, and drag a `RadioButtonList` onto your form, below the table. Note that it is marked *Unbound*. Rather than populating this list with hard-coded list items (as you did previously), you'll bind this list to data from the database.

To do so, click on the smart tag, and then click Choose Data Source, as shown in Figure 8-23.

Figure 8-23. Choose data source for RadioButtonList

In the Data Source Configuration Wizard, choose <New Data Source...>. When you do, the Wizard brings up the various types of data sources you might choose. Click on SQL Database, and the Wizard offers to name the new data source *SqlDataSource1*. Click OK. The Wizard now wants you to choose an existing connection or to make a new connection. Create a connection to the Northwind database, as shown in previous chapters, and click Next. You are offered the opportunity to save this connection. Save it as *NorthWindConnectionString* and click Next.

The next step in the Wizard is to pick the fields you want from the table you want. You'll pick `ShipperID` and `CompanyName` from the `Shippers` table, as shown in Figure 8-24.

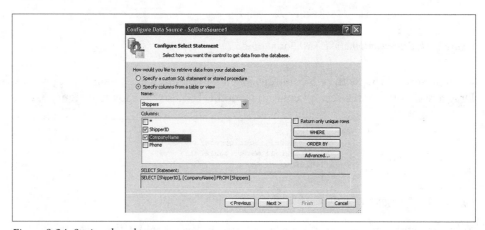

Figure 8-24. Setting the select statement

Click Next and you have an opportunity to test your query, as shown in Figure 8-25.

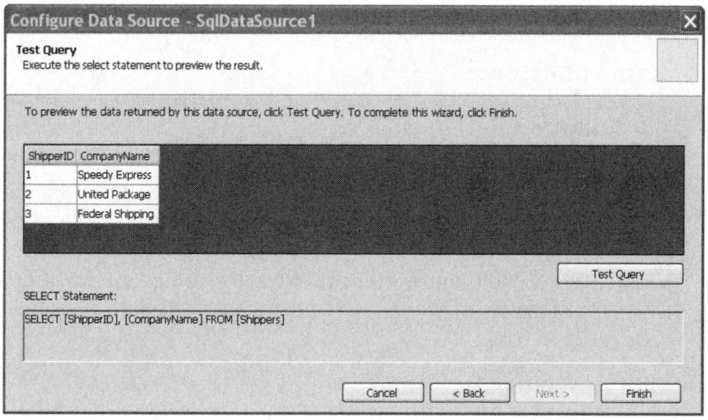

Figure 8-25. Testing the query

Notice that the CompanyName field has the data you wish to display. You'll want the ShipperID in the Value field for the list item so you can uniquely identify the chosen shipper.

Click Finish and you are returned to the Data Source Configuration Wizard. Now you can indicate which field to display and which to set as the value field for the RadioButtonList, as shown in Figure 8-26.

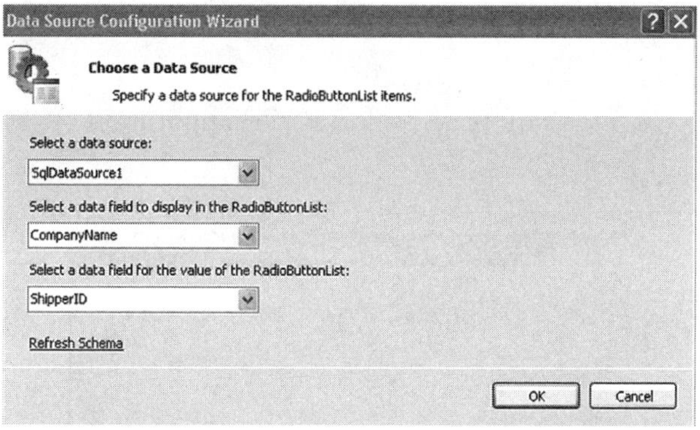

Figure 8-26. Setting the Display and Value fields

Once the RadioButtonList and its associated SqlDataSource are configured, return to source view, and move them into the table cell you held ready for them.

```
<asp:TableRow runat="server">
    <asp:TableCell runat="server">Shipper: </asp:TableCell>
    <asp:TableCell runat="server">
        <asp:RadioButtonList
        DataSourceID="SqlDataSource1"
        DataTextField="CompanyName"
```

```
                DataValueField="ShipperID"
                ID="RadioButtonList1" runat="server" />

                <asp:SqlDataSource
                ConnectionString="<%$ ConnectionStrings:NorthwindConnectionString %>"
                ID="SqlDataSource1" runat="server"
                SelectCommand="SELECT [ShipperID], [CompanyName] FROM [Shippers]" />
        </asp:TableCell>
    </asp:TableRow>
```

 Visual Studio 2005 will not create the self-closing tags for the controls, I've done so to save space and because I believe it makes the code easier to read.

Finally, add two more rows, one with two buttons, and one with a label that has no text:

```
<asp:TableRow>
    <asp:TableCell>
        <asp:Button ID="btnOrder" runat="server" Text="Order"/>
    </asp:TableCell>
    <asp:TableCell>
        <asp:Button ID="btnCancel" runat="server" Text="Cancel"/>
    </asp:TableCell>
</asp:TableRow>
<asp:TableRow>
    <asp:TableCell ColumnSpan="2">
        <asp:Label ID="lblMsg" runat="server"></asp:Label>
    </asp:TableCell>
</asp:TableRow>
```

Set *Shipper.aspx* as the start page and run the application. It should look like Figure 8-27.

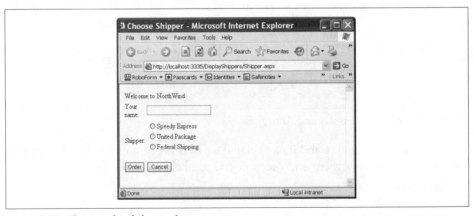

Figure 8-27. The completed shipper form

This form will not win any awards for design, but it illustrates a number of key points about web forms. When the user clicks on the Order button, you'll check that the user has filled in his or her name, and you'll also provide feedback on which shipper was chosen. Remember, at design time you can't know the name of the shipper (this is obtained from the database) so you'll have to ask the RadioButtonList for the chosen name (and ID).

To accomplish all of this, switch to Design mode and double-click on the Order button. Visual Studio will put you in the code-behind page, and will create an event handler for the button's Click event.

You add the event-handling code, setting the text of the label to pick up the text from the text box and the text and value from the RadioButtonList, as shown in Example 8-1.

Example 8-1. Order button Click event handler

```
Protected Sub btnOrder_Click( _
ByVal sender As Object, _
ByVal e As System.EventArgs) Handles btnOrder.Click
    lblMsg.Text = "Thank you " + TextBox1.Text.Trim( ) + ".  You chose " + _
        RadioButtonList1.SelectedItem.Text.ToString( ) + " whose ID is " + _
        RadioButtonList1.SelectedValue.ToString( )
End Sub
```

Run the program, click on one of the radio buttons, fill in the text box, and click Order. The label is filled in, as shown in Figure 8-28.

Figure 8-28. Testing the Shipper page

Stop and rerun the program; notice that none of the radio buttons is selected. Binding the list did not specify which one is the default. There are a number of ways around this, but the simplest is to override the OnLoad event and select the first radio button.

Return to *Shipper.aspx.vb* and place the cursor within the class, but not within the existing Sub. Type **Protected Overrides**. You will see a scrolling list of all the overrideable methods, properties, etc., as shown in Figure 8-29.

Figure 8-29. Overriding OnLoad

 Note that I do not use the proper capitalization, but once I pick a method, Visual Studio 2005 will fix the capitalization for me, capitalizing the P in protected and the O in overrides.

You can scroll to OnLoad or you can start typing **OnLoad**; when it is highlighted, press Tab. The stub for the overridden method is created. A single line of code is inserted for you. Add a second line of code so that the entire Sub looks like this:

```
Protected Overrides Sub OnLoad(ByVal e As System.EventArgs)
    MyBase.OnLoad(e)
    RadioButtonList1.SelectedIndex = 0
End Sub
```

The first line calls the base class (System.Web.UI.Page) OnLoad( ) method, so that the Page can do whatever it needs to do to load, and then it executes your additional line of code to select the first button in the RadioButtonList.

The problem with this solution is subtle. If you run the application, you'll see that the first button is selected, but if you choose the second (or third) button and press Order, you'll find that the first button is reset. You can't seem to choose any but the first selection. This is because each time the page is loaded, the OnLoad event fires, and in that event handler you are (re)setting the selected index.

You only want to set this button the first time the page is loaded, not when it is posted back to the browser as a result of the Order button being clicked.

To solve this, wrap the setting in an If statement that tests if the page has been posted back.

```
If IsPostBack = False Then RadioButtonList1.SelectedIndex = 0
```

If you put an if statement all on one line you do not need the end if statement.

When you run the page, the `IsPostBack` property is checked. The first time the page is posted, this value is `False` and the radio button is set. If you click on a radio button and then press Order, the page is sent to the server for processing (where the `btnOrder_Click` handler is run) and then the page is posted back to the user. This time the `IsPostBack` property is `True`, and thus the code within the `If` statement is not run, and the user's choice is preserved, as shown in Figure 8-30.

Figure 8-30. The user's choice is preserved on postback

The new page knows what button was clicked, even though the Web itself is stateless. This is accomplished, in this case, through view state, as described in the next section.

State

State is the current value of all the controls and variables for the current user in the current session. The Web is inherently a *stateless* environment, which means that every time a page is posted to the server and then sent back to the browser, the page is recreated from scratch. Unless you explicitly preserve the state of all the controls before the page is posted, the state is lost and all the controls are created with default values. One of the great strengths of ASP.NET is that it automatically maintains state for server controls—both HTML and ASP. This section will explore how that is done and how you can use the ASP.NET state management capabilities.

ASP.NET manages three types of state:

- View state (which is saved in the state bag)
- Application state
- Session state

Table 8-2 compares the different kinds of state.

Table 8-2. State types

Variables	View state	Application state	Session state
Uses server resources	No	Yes	Yes
Uses bandwidth	Yes	No	Depends
Times out	No	No	Yes
Security exposure	Yes	No	Depends
Optimized for nonprimitive types	No	Yes	Yes
Available for arbitrary data	Yes	Yes	Yes
Programmatically accessible	Yes	Yes	Yes
Scope	Page	Application	Session
Survives restart	Yes	No	Depends

The following sections will examine each type of state.

View State

The *view state* is the state of the page and all its controls. The view state is automatically maintained across posts by the ASP.NET Framework. When a page is posted to the server, the view state is read. Just before the page is sent back to the browser the view state is restored.

The view state is saved in the state bag (described in the next section) via hidden fields on the page that contain the state encoded in a string variable. Since the view state is maintained in standard html form fields, it works with all browsers.

If you don't need to maintain the view state for a page, you can boost performance by disabling view state for that page. For example, if the page does not post back to itself, or if the only control that needs to have its state maintained is populated from a database with every trip to the server, there is no need to maintain the view state for that page. To disable view state for a page, add the EnableViewState attribute with a value of False to the Page directive:

```
<%@ Page Language="VB"  EnableViewState="false" %>
```

The default value for EnableViewState is True.

The view state can be disabled for an entire application by setting the EnableViewState property to False in the <pages> section of the *machine.config* or *Web.config* configuration file.

It is also possible to maintain or disable view state for specific controls. This is done with the Control.EnableViewState property, which is a Boolean value with a default of True. Disabling view state for a control, just as for the page, will improve performance slightly. This would be appropriate, for example, in the situation where a control is populated from a database every time the page is loaded. In this case, the contents of the control would simply be overridden by the database query, so there is no point in maintaining view state for that control, especially if a lot of data is involved.

There are some situations where view state is not the best place to store data. If there is a large amount of data to be stored, then view state is not an efficient mechanism, since the data is transferred back and forth to the server with every page post. If there are security concerns about the data and it is not otherwise being displayed on the page, then including the data in view state increases the security exposure. Finally, view state is optimized only for strings, integers, Booleans, arrays, lists, and dictionaries. Other .NET types may be serialized and persisted in view state, but will result in degraded performance and a larger view-state footprint.

In some of these instances, session state might be a better alternative; on the other hand, view state does not consume any server resources and does not time out like session state.

State Bag

If there are values that are not associated with any control and you wish to preserve these values across roundtrips, you can store these values in the page's state bag. The *state bag* is a data structure containing attribute/value pairs, stored as strings associated with objects. The valid objects are the primitive data types—integers, bytes, strings, Booleans, and so on. The state bag is implemented using the StateBag class, which is a dictionary object. You add or remove items from the state bag as with any dictionary object assigning a value to a "key," as shown below.

The state bag is maintained using the same hidden fields as the view state. You can set and retrieve values of things in the state bag using the ViewState keyword. To experiment with this, add another page to your application (or create a new application with the new page) named *StateBagDemo.aspx*. In either case, set the new page as the start page.

Between the <div> tags, write the word **Counter:** and drag a label onto the form, setting its ID to lblCounter and removing any Text attribute (or setting the text to blank through the Properties window).

Drag a button onto the form, set its ID to btn and set its text to Increment Counter. When you are done, the HTML in the source window should look like that in Example 8-2.

Example 8-2. Counter source

```
<div>
   Counter:
   <asp:Label ID="lblCounter" runat="server"></asp:Label>
   <asp:Button ID="btn" runat="server" Text="Increment Counter" />
</div>
```

You'll track the Counter as a property by adding the code shown in Example 8-3 to the code-behind.

Example 8-3. Counter property

```
Public Property Counter() As Integer
    Get
        If (ViewState("intCounter") IsNot Nothing) Then
            Return CInt(ViewState("intCounter")) 'extract from view state
        Else
            Return 0
        End If
    End Get

    Set(ByVal value As Integer)
        ViewState("intCounter") = value 'Add to view state
    End Set
End Property
```

ViewState is the dictionary, "int Counter" is the key, and value is the value associated with that key. Override the OnLoad() method (as discussed above), adding the lines shown in bold in Example 8-4.

Example 8-4. Overriding the StateBagDemo form OnLoad event handler

```
Protected Overrides Sub OnLoad(ByVal e As System.EventArgs)
    MyBase.OnLoad(e)
    lblCounter.Text = Counter.ToString()
    Counter += 1
End
```

StateBagDemo.aspx sets up a Counter that is maintained as long as the session is active. Every time the Increment Counter button is clicked, the page is reloaded, which causes the Counter to increment.

To make this work, you need to maintain state between postbacks. One way to do so is to store the value of the counter in a state bag. ASP.NET provides that state bag in its ViewState collection, which you access by indexing into it by name. In this example, you access the ViewState collection through the Counter Property. The property's get accessor casts the value stored in the ViewState to an integer, because ViewState stores objects.

Each time the page is loaded, you display the value of the Counter property and then increment it by 1:

```
Protected Overrides Sub OnLoad(ByVal e As System.EventArgs)
    MyBase.OnLoad(e)
    lblCounter.Text = Counter.ToString()
    Counter += 1
End Sub
```

In the Get block of the Counter property, the contents of the statebag named intCounter are tested to see if anything is there:

```
If (ViewState("intCounter") IsNot Nothing) Then
```

If the intCounter state bag is not empty, the value stored is returned; otherwise, the value 0 is returned. To retrieve the value, you access it by name, but you must cast the object back to an integer to use it in your program.

```
If (ViewState("intCounter") IsNot Nothing) Then
    Return CInt(ViewState("intCounter"))
Else
    Return 0
End If
```

 In this and in all programs in this book Option Strict is always set to True. Unfortunately, the default is False, but good object-oriented, type-safe programming requires that you set this to True to enlist the compiler in helping you find type-cast errors.

Session State

While an application is running, there will be many *sessions*. A session is a series of requests coming from a single browser client in a more or less continuous manner. If there are no requests from that client within a specified period of time (the timeout period), then the session ends. The default timeout period is 20 minutes.

As noted above, the Web is an inherently stateless environment. The HTTP protocol has no means of identifying which requests should be grouped together in the same session. A session must be imposed on top of HTTP. ASP.NET provides session state with the following features:

- Works with browsers that have had cookies disabled.
- Identifies if a request is part of an existing session.
- Stores session-scoped data for use across multiple requests. This data persists across server restarts and works in multiprocessor (web garden) and multi-machine (web farm) environments, as well as in single-processor, single-server situations.
- Automatically releases session resources if the session ends or times out.

Session state is stored in server memory separately from the ASP.NET process. This means that if the ASP.NET process crashes or is restarted, the session state is not lost. Session state can also be stored on a dedicated and shared machine or even within a database.

Sessions are identified and tracked with a 120-bit SessionID that is passed from client to server and back using either an HTTP cookie or a modified URL, depending on how the application is configured. The SessionID is handled automatically by the .NET Framework; there is no need to manipulate it programmatically. The SessionID consists of URL-legal ASCII characters that have two important characteristics:

- They are unique, so there is no chance of two different sessions having the same SessionID.
- They are random, so it is difficult to guess the value of another session's SessionID after learning the value of an existing session's SessionID.

Session state is implemented using the Contents collection of the HttpSessionState class. This collection is a (key-value) dictionary containing all the session state dictionary objects that have been directly added using code.

To see session state at work, create a new page *SessionState.aspx* (either in this application or in a new application) and set it to be the start page.

Drag a RadioButtonList onto your page, set its ID to rbl and use the smart tag to edit the items. Add three items. The first has the text .NET and the value n, the second has the text Databases and the value d, and the third has the text Hardware and the value h, as shown in Figure 8-31.

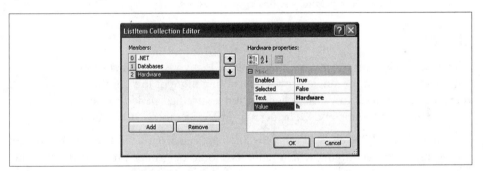

Figure 8-31. Adding three items to RadioButtonList

Also add a button, and set its ID to btn and its Text to Submit. Add a label control (id=lblMsg), and a drop-down list with the ID ddl. Set its Visible property to False.

You're all set. Now just change to Code view and implement a handler for the button's Click event, and one for the SelectedIndexChanged event in the RadioButtonList control. The complete source for these methods is shown in Example 8-5.

Example 8-5. SessionState.aspx.vb

```vb
Partial Class SessionState_aspx
    Inherits System.Web.UI.Page
    Protected Sub btn_Click( _
    ByVal sender As Object, _
    ByVal e As System.EventArgs) Handles btn.Click

        If (rbl.SelectedIndex = -1) Then
            lblMsg.Text = "You must select a book category."
        Else
            Dim sb As StringBuilder = New StringBuilder( )
            sb.Append("You have selected the category ")
            sb.Append(CStr(Session("cattext")))
            sb.Append(" with code """)
            sb.Append(CStr(Session("catcode")))
            sb.Append(""".")

            lblMsg.Text = sb.ToString( )

            ddl.Visible = True

            Dim CatBooks() As String = CType(Session("books"), String( ))

            '  Populate the DropDownList.
            Dim i As Integer
            ddl.Items.Clear( )
            For i = 0 To CatBooks.GetLength(0) - 1
                ddl.Items.Add(New ListItem(CatBooks(i)))
            Next
        End If
    End Sub


    Protected Sub rbl_SelectedIndexChanged( _
    ByVal sender As Object, _
    ByVal e As System.EventArgs) Handles rbl.SelectedIndexChanged
        If (rbl.SelectedIndex <> -1) Then

            Dim Books(3) As String

            Session("cattext") = rbl.SelectedItem.Text
            Session("catcode") = rbl.SelectedItem.Value

            Select Case (rbl.SelectedItem.Value)
                Case "n"
                    Books(0) = "Programming Visual Basic 2005"
                    Books(1) = "Programming ASP.NET"
                    Books(2) = "C#: A Developer's Notebook"
                Case "d"
                    Books(0) = "Oracle & Open Source"
                    Books(1) = "SQL in a Nutshell"
                    Books(2) = "Transact-SQL Programming"
                Case "h"
```

Example 8-5. SessionState.aspx.vb (continued)

```
                    Books(0) = "PC Hardware in a Nutshell"
                    Books(1) = "Dictionary of PC Hardware and " + _
                        "Data Communications Terms"
                    Books(2) = "Linux Device Drivers"

            End Select
            Session("books") = Books
        End If

    End Sub
End Class
```

Look first at `rbl_SelectedIndexChanged`, the `RadioButtonList` event handler. After testing to ensure that something is selected, `rbl_SelectedIndexChanged` defines a string array to hold the lists of books in each category. Then it assigns the selected item `Text` and `Value` properties to two `Session` dictionary objects.

```
    Session("cattext") = rbl.SelectedItem.Text
    Session("catcode") = rbl.SelectedItem.Value
```

The first line stores the text of the selected item in session state using the key "cattext."

`rblSelectedIndexChanged` next uses a `Select Case` statement to fill the previously declared string array (`Books`) with a list of books, depending on the book category selected. Finally, the method assigns the string array to a `Session` dictionary object.

```
    Session("books") = Books
```

This example stores only strings and an array in the `Session` dictionary objects. However, you can store any object that inherits from `ISerializable`. These include all the primitive data types and arrays comprising of primitive data types, as well as the `DataSet`, `DataTable`, `HashTable`, and `Image` objects. This allows you to store query results, for example, or a collection of items in session state to implement a user's shopping cart.

The other event-handler method, `btn_Click`, is called whenever the user clicks on the Submit button. It first tests to verify that a radio button has been selected. If not, then the Label is filled with a warning message.

```
    If (rbl.SelectedIndex = -1) Then
        lblMsg.Text = "You must select a book category."
```

The `Else` clause of the `If` statement is the meat of this page. It retrieves the `Session` dictionary objects and uses the `StringBuilder` class to concatenate the strings into a single string for display in the Label control.

```
    dim sb as StringBuilder = new StringBuilder(  )
    sb.Append("You have selected the category ")
    sb.Append(Cstr(Session("cattext")))
    sb.Append(" with code """)
```

```
sb.Append(Cstr(Session("catcode")))
sb.Append(""".")

lblMsg.Text = sb.ToString( )
```

The `btn_Click` method also unhides the `DropDownList` that was created and made invisible in the HTML portion of the page. The method then retrieves the string array from the `Session` dictionary object and populates the `DropDownList`.

```
ddl.Visible = true
dim CatBooks( ) as string= CType(Session("books"), string( ))

'  Populate the DropDownList.
dim i as integer
ddl.Items.Clear( )
for i = 0 to CatBooks.GetLength(0) - 1
   ddl.Items.Add(new ListItem(CatBooks(i)))
next
```

Because the `Page` directive in the VB.NET example sets `Strict="true"`, it is necessary to explicitly cast the `Session` dictionary object containing the string array from object to type string array using the `CType` function. The results are shown in Figure 8-32.

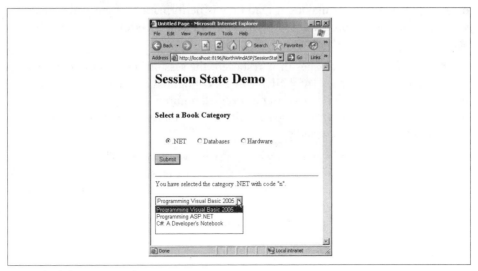

Figure 8-32. Session state demonstration

As you look at this example, you might wonder what advantage is gained here by using session state, rather than just using the programmatically accessible control values. The answer is that since this example is fairly trivial, no advantage is gained. However, in a real-life application with many different pages, session state provides an easy method for values and objects to be passed from one page to the next, with all the advantages listed at the beginning of this section.

Session-State Configuration

The configuration of session state is controlled on a page-by-page basis by entries in the Page directive at the top of the page. On an application-wide basis, it is controlled by a file called *Web.config*, typically located in the virtual root directory of the application.

Session state is enabled by default. You can enable session state for a specific page by adding the EnableSessionState attribute to the Page directive, as in the following VB Page directive:

```
<%@ Page Language="VB" Strict="true" EnableSessionState="true"%>
```

To disable session state for the page you would use:

```
<%@ Page Language="VB" Strict="true" EnableSessionState="false"%>
```

To enable session state in a read-only mode—that is, values can be read but not changed—use the ReadOnly value of EnableSessionState, as in:

```
<%@ Page Language="VB" Strict="true" EnableSessionState="ReadOnly"%>
```

(All of the values for EnableSessionState are case-insensitive.) The reason for either disabling session state or making it read-only is performance. If you know that you will not be using session state on a page, you can gain a performance boost by disabling it.

If the ASP.NET process crashes or is restarted, the session state is not lost. In addition to unplanned outages, ASP.NET can be configured to periodically perform a preventive restart of each process after a specified number of requests or after a specified length of time, improving availability and stability (this is configurable in *machine.config* and/or *Web.config*).

Web.config is an XML file and as such it must be well-formed. The values are case-sensitive, and the file consists of sections delimited by tags. The session-state configuration information is contained within the <system.web> section, which is contained within the <configuration> section. Thus, a typical session-state configuration snippet will look something like Example 8-6.

Example 8-6. Code excerpt from Web.config

```
<?xml version="1.0" encoding="utf-8" ?>
<configuration>

  <system.web>
.
.
.
  <sessionState
          mode="InProc"
          cookieless="false"
          timeout="20"
```

Example 8-6. Code excerpt from Web.config (continued)

```
            stateConnectionString="tcpip=127.0.0.1:42424"
            sqlConnectionString="data source=127.0.0.1;userid=sa;password="
    />
```

There are five possible attributes for the sessionState section:

mode

Specifies whether the session state is disabled for all the pages controlled by this copy of *Web.config*, and, if enabled, where the session state is stored. Table 8-3 lists the permissible values.

Table 8-3. Possible values for the mode attribute

Values	Description
Off	Session state is disabled.
Inproc	Session state is stored in-process on the local server. This is the default value.
StateServer	Session state is stored on a remote server. If this attribute is used, then there must also be an entry for stateConnectionString, specifying which server to use to store the Session state.
SqlServer	Session state is stored on a SQL Server. If this attribute is used, then there must also be an entry for sqlConnectionString, which specifies how to connect to the SQL Server. The SQL Server used can either be on a local or remote machine.

Storing the session state Inproc is the fastest and is well-suited to small amounts of volatile data. However, it is vulnerable to machine crashes and is not suitable for web farms (multiple servers) or web gardens (multiple processors on a single machine). For these cases, you should use either StateServer or SqlServer. SqlServer is the most robust for surviving crashes and restarts.

cookieless

Cookies are used with session state to store the SessionID so that the server knows which session it is connected to. The permissible values of cookieless are True and False, with False being the default. In other words, the default behavior is to use cookies. However, if the client browser either does not support cookies or has had cookie support turned off by the user, then any attempt at saving and retrieving session state will be lost. To prevent this, set cookieless to True.

If cookieless is set to True, then the SessionID is persisted by adding a value to the URL.

timeout

Specifies the number of minutes of inactivity before a session times out and is abandoned by the server. The default value is 20.

stateConnectionString

Specifies the server and port used to save the session state. It is required if mode is set to StateServer. Use of a specific server for saving state enables easy and effective session-state management in web-farm or web-garden scenarios. An example of a stateConnectionString is:

```
stateConnectionString="tcpip=127.0.0.1:42424"
```

In this example, a server with an IP address of 127.0.0.1 would be used. This happens to be localhost, or the local machine. The port is 42424. For this to work, the server being specified must have the ASP.NET State service started (accessible via Control Panel/Administrative Tools/Services) and must have the specified port available for communications (that is, not disabled or blocked by a firewall or other security measure).

sqlConnectionString

Specifies a connection string to a running instance of SQL Server. It must be set if mode is set to SqlServer. Similar to stateConnectionString in that it lends itself to use with web farms and gardens, it also will persist despite crashes and shutdowns. The session state is saved in SQL tables indexed by SessionID.

Session-Scoped Application Objects

One additional way of providing information across the session is through the use of static objects, which are declared in the *global.asax* file. Once declared with the Scope attribute set to Session, the objects are accessible to the session by name anywhere within the application code.

Lifecycle

A user sits at her browser and types in a URL. A web page appears, with text, images, buttons, and so forth. She fills in a text box and clicks on a button. What is going on behind the scenes?

Every request made of the web server initiates a sequence of steps. These steps, from beginning to end, constitute the *lifecycle* of the page.

When a page is requested, it is loaded, processed, sent to the user, and unloaded. From one end of the lifecycle to the other, the goal of the page is to render appropriate HTML and other output back to the requesting browser. At each step, there are methods and events available to let you override the default behavior or add your own programmatic enhancements.

To fully understand the lifecycle of the page and its controls, it is necessary to recognize that the Page class creates a hierarchical tree of all the controls on the page. All the components on the page, except for any Page directives (described shortly), are part of this *control tree*. You can see the control tree for any page by adding trace="True" to the Page directive.

The page itself is at the root of the tree. All the named controls are included in the tree, referenced by control ID. Static text, including whitespace, NewLines, and

HTML tags, are represented in the tree as Literal controls. The order of controls in the tree is strictly hierarchical. Within a given hierarchy level, the controls are ordered in the tree using the same sequence in which they appear in the page file.

Web components, including the Page, go through the entire lifecycle every time the page is loaded. Events fire first on the Page, then recursively on every object in the control tree.

The following is a detailed description of each of the phases of the component lifecycle in a web form. There are two slightly different sequences of events in the lifecycle: on the first loading of the page and on subsequent postbacks. This lifecycle is shown schematically in Figure 8-33.

During the first page load, the lifecycle is composed of the following steps:

Initialization

> The *initialization* phase is the first phase in the lifecycle for any page or control. The control tree is built during the initialization phase. In this phase, you can initialize any values needed for the duration of the request.
>
> The initialize phase is modified by handling the `Init` event with the `OnInit` method.

Load

> User code runs and the form controls show client-side data.
>
> The load phase can be modified by handling the `Load` event with the `OnLoad` method.

PreRender

> This is the phase just before the output is rendered. `CreateChildControls` is called, if necessary, to create and initialize server controls in the control tree. Modifications are made via the `PreRender` event, using the `OnPreRender` method.

Save ViewState

> The view state is saved to a hidden variable on the page, persisting as a string object that will complete the roundtrip to the client. This can be overridden using the `SaveViewState` method.

Render

> The page and its controls are rendered as HTML. You can override using the `Render` method. Within `Render`, `CreateChildControls` is called, if necessary, to create and initialize server controls in the control tree.

Dispose

> This is the last phase of the lifecycle. It gives you an opportunity to do any final cleanup and release references to any expensive resources, such as database connections. This is important for scalability. It can be modified using the `Dispose` method.

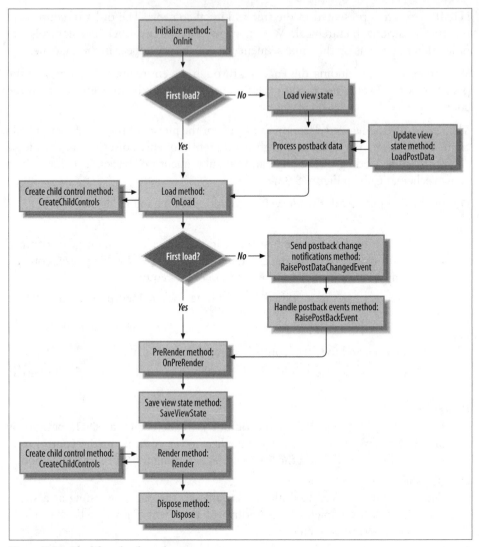

Figure 8-33. The lifecycle of a web page

During postback, the lifecycle is:

Initialization

Same as on first load.

Load ViewState

The ViewState property of the control is loaded from a hidden variable on the page, as described in "View State" earlier in this chapter. You can modify this behavior by overriding the LoadViewState method.

Postback Data is loaded
> During this phase, the data sent to the server via the POST method is processed. Any updates to the view state necessitated by the postback are performed via the `LoadPostData` method.

Load
> Same as on first load.

Change events are raised
> If there are any state changes between the current state and the previous state, change events are raised via the `RaisePostDataChangedEvent` method. Again, the events are raised for the controls in the order in which the controls appear in the control tree.

Handle postback events
> Exactly one user action caused the postback. That user action is handled now, after all the change events have been handled. The original client-side event that instigated the postback is handled in the `RaisePostBackEvent` method.

Directives

Directives are used to pass optional settings to the ASP.NET pages and compilers. They typically have the following syntax:

```
<%@ directive attribute=value [attribute=value] %>
```

There are many valid types of directives, which will be described in detail in the following sections. Each directive can have one or more attribute/value pairs, unless otherwise noted. Attribute/value pairs are separated by a space character. Be careful *not* to have any space characters surrounding the equal sign (=) between the attribute and its value.

Directives are typically located at the top of the appropriate file, although that is not a strict requirement. For example, `Application` directives are at the top of the *global.asax* file, and `Page` directives are at the top of the *.aspx* files.

Application Directive

The `Application` directive is used to define application-specific attributes. It is typically the first line in the *global.asax* file.

Here is a sample `Application` directive:

```
<%@ Application Language="VB" %>
```

There are three possible attributes for use in the `Application` directive, which are outlined in Table 8-4.

Table 8-4. Possible attributes for the Application directive

Attribute	Description
Inherits	The name of the class to inherit from.
Description	Text description of the application. This is ignored by the parser and compiler.
Language	Identifies the language used in any code blocks. Valid values are C#, VB, and VJ#. As other languages adopt support for the .NET Framework, this list will be expanded.

IntelliSense will help you with choosing the enumerated value, as shown in Figure 8-34.

Figure 8-34. Setting the Application Language directive

Assembly Directive

The Assembly directive links an assembly to the application or page at parse time. It is analogous to the /reference: command-line switch used by the VB.NET command-line compilers.

The Assembly directive is contained in either the *global.asax* file, for application-wide linking, or in a page (*.aspx*) or user control (*.ascx*) file, for linking to a specific page or user control. There can be multiple Assembly directives in any file. Each Assembly directive can have multiple attribute/value pairs.

Assemblies located in the *bin* subdirectory under the application's virtual root are automatically linked to the application and do not need to be included in an Assembly directive. There are two permissible attributes, listed in Table 8-5 and shown in Figure 8-35.

Table 8-5. Attributes for the Assembly directive

Attribute	Description
Name	The name of the assembly to link to the application or page. Does not include a filename extension. Assemblies usually have a dll extension (they can also have .*exe* extensions).
Src	Path to a source file to dynamically compile and link.

Figure 8-35. Setting the Assembly directive

Other directives will be covered later in the book as their use becomes relevant.

CHAPTER 9

Validation Controls

Almost every web application requires some kind of user input. The sad fact is, however, that users make mistakes: they skip required fields, they put in six-digit phone numbers, and they return all manner of incorrectly formatted data to your application. Your database routines can choke on corrupted data, and orders can be lost if, for example, a credit card number is entered incorrectly or an address is omitted. So it is imperative that user input be validated, and it is much more efficient to validate the data *before* it is submitted to the database or to a third-party vendor.

Traditionally, it has taken a great deal of time and effort to validate user input. Each field must be checked and routines must be created for ensuring data integrity. In the event that bad data is found, error messages must be displayed so that the user knows how to correct the problem.

In a given application, you may choose to validate that certain fields have a value, that the values fall within a given range, or that the data is formatted correctly. For example, when processing an order, you may need to ensure that the user has input an address and phone number, that the phone number has the right number of digits (and no letters), and that the social security number entered is in the appropriate form of nine digits separated by hyphens.

Some applications require more complex validation, in which one field is validated to be within a range established by two other fields. For example, you might ask in one field what date the customer wishes to arrive at your hotel, and in a second field you might ask for the departure date. When the user books dinner, you'll want to ensure that the date is between the arrival and departure dates.

There is no limit to the complexity of the validation routines you may need to write. Credit cards have checksums built into their values, as do ISBN numbers. ZIP and postal codes follow complex patterns, as do international phone numbers. You may need to validate passwords, membership numbers, dollar amounts, dates, runway choices, and launch codes.

In addition, it is very desirable for all of this validation to happen client-side so that you avoid the delay of repeated roundtrips to the server while the user tinkers with his input. In the past, this was solved by writing client-side JavaScript to validate the input, and then server-side script to handle input from browsers that don't support client-side programming. Traditionally, this involved writing your validation code twice.

For these reasons, traditional Internet programming requires extensive custom programming for data validation. The ASP.NET 2.0 Framework greatly simplifies this process by providing rich controls for validating user input. They allow you to manage the validation routine very precisely, while requiring far less custom coding. The validation controls also let you specify exactly how and where the error messages will be displayed: either inline with the input controls, aggregated together in a summary report, or both. These controls can be used to validate input for both HTML and ASP controls.

You add validation controls to your ASP document just as you would add any other control. Within the declaration of the validation control, you specify which control is being validated. You may freely combine the various validation controls, and you may write your own, as you'll see later in this chapter.

Sometimes you don't want any validation to occur, such as when a Cancel button is clicked. To allow this, many postback controls, such as Button, ImageButton, LinkButton, ListControl, and TextBox, have a CausesValidation property, which dictates if validation is performed on the page when the control's default event is raised.

If CausesValidation is set to True, the default value, the postback will *not* occur if any control on the page fails validation. If CausesValidation is set to False, however, no validation will occur when that button is used to post the page.

ASP.NET supports the following validation controls:

RequiredFieldValidator *control*
> The simplest validation control, it ensures that the user does not skip over your input control. A RequiredFieldValidator can be tied to a text box to force input into the text box. With selection controls, such as a drop-down menus or radio buttons, the RequiredFieldValidator ensures that the user makes a selection other than the default. The RequiredFieldValidator does not examine the validity of the data, but only makes sure that some data is entered or chosen.

RangeValidator *control*
> Ensures that the value entered is within a specified lower and upper boundary. You can check the range within a pair of numbers (e.g., greater than 10 and less than 100), a pair of characters (e.g., greater than D and less than K) and a pair of dates (e.g., after 1/1/01 and before 2/28/01). The values you check can be constants that you create at design time, or they can be derived from other controls

on your page (greater than the value in `textBox1` and less than the value in `textBox2`).

CompareValidator *control*

Compares the user's entry (greater than, less than, etc.) against another value. It can compare against a constant that you specify at design time, or against another control's property value. It can also compare against a database value.

RegularExpressionValidator *control*

One of the most powerful validators, it compares the user's entry with a regular expression that you provide. You can use this validator to check for valid social security numbers, phone numbers, passwords, and so forth.

CustomValidator *control*

If none of these controls meets your needs, you can use the `CustomValidator`. This checks the user's entry against whatever algorithm you provide in a custom method.

In the remainder of this chapter, we'll examine how to use each of these controls to validate data in ASP.NET applications.

The RequiredFieldValidator

Let's start with one the simplest validator: the `RequiredFieldValidator`, which ensures that the user provides a value for your control.

To begin, start by creating a new web application named `Validators`. Select the *Default.aspx* page in Design view, and set its `Title` property to `Validation Page`. While still in Design view, type in **Please enter bug reports here**, then press Enter.

Next, you'll create the simple bug reporting form shown in Figure 9-1. (Detailed instructions follow shortly.)

When the user presses the Submit Bug button, the form is validated to ensure that each field has been modified. If not, the offending field is marked. You might mark it with a red asterisk, or with a meaningful prompt indicating what is wrong, as shown in Figure 9-2.

If you switch to Source view, you'll see the Visual Studio created a default `<form>` tag for you already, with an `ID` of `form1`. Change the `ID` to `frmBugs`.

To create this form, you'll put the controls inside a three-column table, with the first column containing right-aligned text (or labels). The easiest way to do this is to open the HTML section of the toolbar and drag an HTML table onto the form. You can then expand that table (which will initially be three rows by three cells) so that each cell is large enough to type in or to drag a control into.

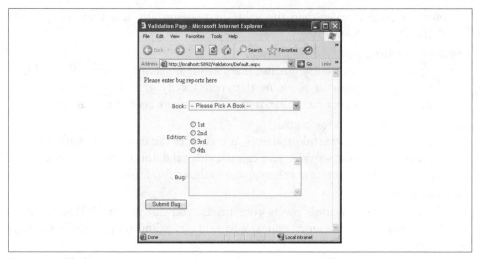

Figure 9-1. The bug report

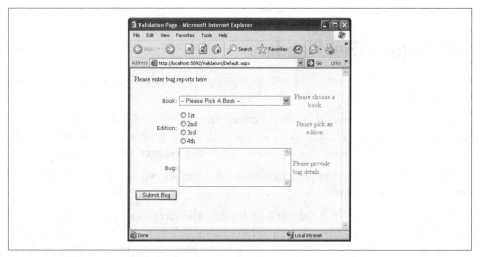

Figure 9-2. Bug report with error prompts

 If you put the cursor in the bottom-right cell and press TAB, the table will add a new row and place the cursor in the bottom-left cell.

Click on the arrow above the left-most column and set its `align` property to `right`—or just set the property by hand in Source view:

```
<td align="right">
</td>
```

Type the prompt **Book:** in either Source or Design view. In Source view, the new `<td>` section should look like this:

```
<td align="right">
Book:
</td>
```

Next, drag a drop-down list into the center column. Set its `ID` to `ddlBooks`. Click on its smart tag, then choose Edit Items... to add book titles to the list. Set book 0 (zero) to `-- Please Pick A Book --`. Then add the other books shown in Figure 9-3 (or as many as you feel like entering).

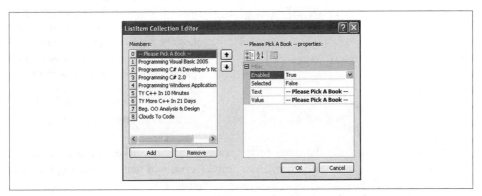

Figure 9-3. Using the ListItem Collection Editor to populate the drop-down list

The Toolbox is divided into sections. Open the Validation section, as shown in Figure 9-4.

Figure 9-4. Validation controls

Drag a `RequiredFieldValidator` into the third column. This validator is designed to ensure that a given control (in this case, the drop-down list) has a valid entry (in this case, any entry except the very first)—that is, that the user has made a choice.

After you drop the control into its column, click on the control and then set its properties in the Properties windows, as shown in Table 9-1.

Table 9-1. Attributes for first validator

Property	Value	Explanation
(ID)	reqFieldBooks	The ID of the validation control itself.
ControlToValidate	ddlBooks	The ID of the control to be validated (in this case, the drop-down list).
Display	Static	See the description later in this chapter.
InitialValue	--Please Pick A Book --	If this value is set, the user must choose a value that does not match this value for the control to be valid (useful for drop-down lists, as shown here).
SetFocusOnError	True	If this is true, and if this is the first control on the page that is not valid, focus will be placed here. There is almost never a reason to set this false, which is why, of course, false is the default!
Text	"You did not pick a book"	The text to show if the control is not valid.

The Display element can take one of three values: Dynamic, None, and Static. If you type this property into the Source window, IntelliSense will help by offering the valid values when you hit the equal sign, as shown in Figure 9-5.

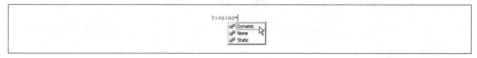

Figure 9-5. Choosing the Display value

If you choose Dynamic, no room will be allocated in the table for the error message; if you choose Static, then the room will be allocated even if no error message is visible. Which you choose will be decided by how you want your page to look before and after an error (dynamically allocated error messages may shift the controls around to make room for the error message). If you do not enter the property, it defaults to Static. Set the property value to Static, or accept the default.

You are now ready to set up your second row. Set the prompt to *Edition:*. In the second column add a RadioButtonList and call it rblEdition. Use the Edit Items... option to add four items: *1st*, *2nd*, *3rd*, and *4th*. Set its RepeatLayout property to Flow.

Next, drag a RequiredFieldValidator into the third column. The attributes for this second RequiredFieldValidator are shown in Table 9-2.

Table 9-2. Attributes for second validator

Property	Value	Explanation
(ID)	reqFieldEdition	
ControlToValidate	rblEdition	Notice that you can set this through a drop-down list in the Property window (nifty).
Display	Static	
InitialValue	(blank)	Leave this field blank; not needed for validation of the radio buttons.
SetFocusOnError	True	See Table 9-1.
Text	Please pick an edition to validate	

Set up the third row. The prompt in the first column is *Bug:*. Drop a TextBox into the second column, and give it an ID of txtBug. Set its TextMode property to MultiLine. These are the only significant elements in this control (besides the requisite *runat=server*, of course).

Drag a RequiredFieldValidator into the third column. Its attributes are shown in Table 9-3.

Table 9-3. Attributes for third validation control

Property	Value	Explanation
(ID)	reqFieldBug	
ControlToValidate	txtBug	
Display	Static	
InitialValue	(blank)	Leave this field blank. You could give the text field an initial (must change) value, but, in this case, we'll start out with an empty text box.
SetFocusOnError	True	See Table 9-1.
Text	Please provide bug details	

The fourth row of the table will be occupied by the Submit button, which triggers the page validation. Add a Button control to the first column of this row, and give it an ID of btnSubmit. Set its Text property to Submit Bug.

Go to Source view and examine the HTML that has been produced, shown in Example 9-1.

Example 9-1. Validation controls

```
<%@ Page Language="VB" AutoEventWireup="false" CodeFile="Default.aspx.vb"
Inherits="Default_aspx" %>

<!DOCTYPE html PUBLIC "-//W3C//DTD XHTML 1.1//EN" "http://www.w3.org/TR/xhtml11/DTD/
xhtml11.dtd">
```

Example 9-1. Validation controls (continued)

```
<html xmlns="http://www.w3.org/1999/xhtml" >
<head runat="server">
   <title>Validation Page</title>
</head>
<body>
   <form id="frmBugs" runat="server">
      Please enter bug reports here<br />
      <br />
      <table id="TABLE1">
         <tr>
            <td align="right">
               Book:
            </td>
            <td>
               <asp:DropDownList ID="ddlBooks" runat="server">
                  <asp:ListItem>
                     -- Please Pick A Book --
                  </asp:ListItem>
                  <asp:ListItem>
                      Programming Visual Basic 2005
                  </asp:ListItem>
                  <asp:ListItem>
                     Programming C# A Developer's Notebook
                  </asp:ListItem>
                  <asp:ListItem>Programming C# 2.0</asp:ListItem>
                  <asp:ListItem>
                     Programming Windows Applications
                  </asp:ListItem>
                  <asp:ListItem>
                     Teach Yourself C++ In 21 Days
                  </asp:ListItem>
                  <asp:ListItem>
                     Teach Yourself C++ In 24 Hours
                  </asp:ListItem>
                  <asp:ListItem>TY C++ In 10 Minutes</asp:ListItem>
                  <asp:ListItem>TY More C++ In 21 Days</asp:ListItem>
                  <asp:ListItem>Beg. OO Analysis &amp; Design</asp:ListItem>
                  <asp:ListItem>Clouds To Code</asp:ListItem>
               </asp:DropDownList>
            </td>
            <!-- Validator for the drop-down -->
            <td align=center rowspan=1>
               <asp:RequiredFieldValidator
               id="reqFieldBooks"
               ControlToValidate="ddlBooks"
               Display="Static"
               InitialValue="-- Please Pick A Book --"
               Width="100%" runat=server>
               You did not pick a book
               </asp:RequiredFieldValidator>
            </td>
```

Example 9-1. Validation controls (continued)

```
        </tr>
        <tr>
          <td align=right>
            Edition:
          </td>
          <td>
                <ASP:RadioButtonList id=rblEdition
                RepeatLayout="Flow" runat=server>
                    <asp:ListItem>1st</asp:ListItem>
                    <asp:ListItem>2nd</asp:ListItem>
                    <asp:ListItem>3rd</asp:ListItem>
                    <asp:ListItem>4th</asp:ListItem>
                </ASP:RadioButtonList>
          </td>
          <!-- Validator for editions -->
          <td align=center rowspan=1>
            <asp:RequiredFieldValidator
            id="reqFieldEdition"
            ControlToValidate="rblEdition"
            Display="Static"
            InitialValue=""
            Width="100%" runat=server>
                Please pick an edition
            </asp:RequiredFieldValidator>
          </td>
        </tr>
        <tr>
          <td align=right style="HEIGHT: 97px">
            Bug:
          </td>
          <!-- Multi-line text for the bug entry -->
          <td style="HEIGHT: 97px">
            <ASP:TextBox id=txtBug runat=server width="262px"
            textmode="MultiLine" height="84px"/>
          </td>
          <!-- Validator for the text box-->
          <td style="HEIGHT: 97px">
            <asp:RequiredFieldValidator
            id="reqFieldBug"
            ControlToValidate="txtBug"
            Display=dynamic
            Width="100%" runat=server>
              Please provide bug details
            </asp:RequiredFieldValidator>
          </td>
        </tr>
        <tr>
          <td align="right">
            <ASP:Button id=btnSubmit
            text="Submit Bug" runat=server />
          </td>
        </tr>
    </table>
```

Example 9-1. Validation controls (continued)

```
    </form>
</body>
</html>
<
```

Now build and run the application. Your web page should look like Figure 9-6 (which is the same as Figure 9-2, and is shown again here for your convenience).

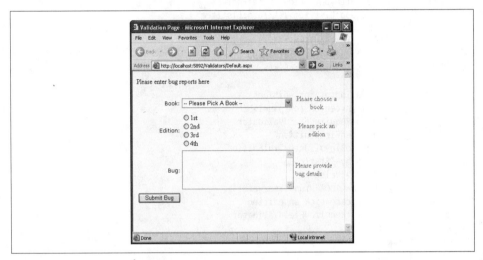

Figure 9-6. Bug report with prompts

Client-Side Evaluation

When you run this application, you will find that the error messages will not show as you move from field to field unless you either submit the page, or you set a value and then set it back to the original (e.g., you pick a book and then set the drop-down list back to the initial prompt). In either case, if you are using IE 4 or better, the form is *not* submitted. You can see this by opening the generated source code for the page, shown in Example 9-2.

Example 9-2. Validation page generated source code

```
<script src="/Validators/WebResource.axd?a=s&amp;r=WebUIValidation.
js&amp;t=632413796581225376" type="text/javascript"></script>
<script type="text/javascript">
<!--
function WebForm_OnSubmit() {
if (ValidatorOnSubmit() == false) return false;
return true;
}
// -->
</script>
```

Example 9-2. Validation page generated source code (continued)

```html
<script type="text/javascript">
<!--
var Page_Validators =  new Array(document.all["reqFieldBooks"], document.
all["reqFieldEdition"], document.all["reqFieldBug"]);
// -->
</script>

<script type="text/javascript">
<!--
var reqFieldBooks = document.all["reqFieldBooks"];
reqFieldBooks.controltovalidate = "ddlBooks";
reqFieldBooks.evaluationfunction = "RequiredFieldValidatorEvaluateIsValid";
reqFieldBooks.initialvalue = "-- Please Pick A Book --";
var reqFieldEdition = document.all["reqFieldEdition"];
reqFieldEdition.controltovalidate = "rblEdition";
reqFieldEdition.evaluationfunction = "RequiredFieldValidatorEvaluateIsValid";
reqFieldEdition.initialvalue = "";
var reqFieldBug = document.all["reqFieldBug"];
reqFieldBug.controltovalidate = "txtBug";
reqFieldBug.display = "Dynamic";
reqFieldBug.evaluationfunction = "RequiredFieldValidatorEvaluateIsValid";
reqFieldBug.initialvalue = "";
// -->
</script>
```

You don't need to fully understand JavaScript to see that this auto-generated code is the client-side routines needed to validate the controls. If the controls fail validation, the page is never submitted, the error messages are displayed, and the user has another chance to correct the errors, as shown in Figure 9-7.

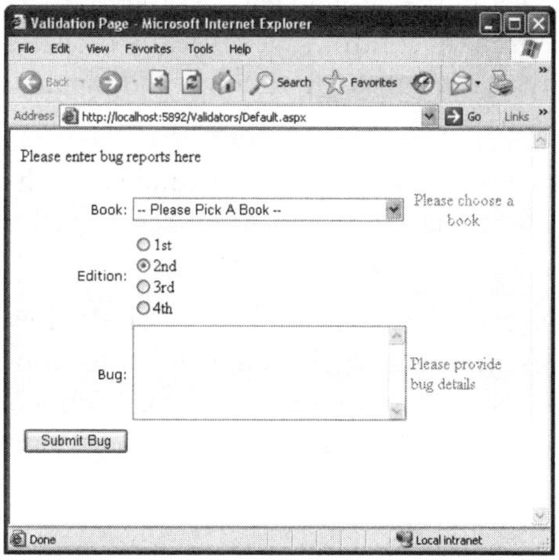

Figure 9-7. Client-side validation

This client-side validation saves you a roundtrip if the user has not entered valid data. If the data is valid on the source, the form will be submitted, and the validators will be checked again (to protect against spoofing on the client).

With downlevel browsers *your* code is unchanged, but the code sent to the client does not include the JavaScript. Because client-side validation will prevent your server-side event handlers from ever running if the control is not valid, you may want to force server-side validation. In that case, set a page attribute at the top of *Default.aspx*:

```
<%@ Page Language="VB"
AutoEventWireup="false"
ClientTarget="downlevel"
CodeFile="Default.aspx.vb"
Inherits="Default_aspx" %>
```

The ClientTarget="downlevel" directive will prevent the JavaScript from being sent to the client, even if your browser would have otherwise supported DHTML and client-side validation.

The Summary Validator

You have great control over how validation errors are reported. For example, rather than putting error messages alongside the control, you can summarize all the validation failures with a ValidationSummary control. This control can place a summary of the errors in a bulleted list, a simple list, or a paragraph that appears on the web page or in a pop-up message box.

Add a ValidationSummary control at the bottom of the page (after the table). There are a few properties to set in the design view. Set the id to valSum (that becomes the ID of the validation summary control). Next set the DisplayMode by clicking on the Display Mode property. Notice that the various valid display modes are displayed in a drop-down list, as shown in Figure 9-8.

Interestingly, if you choose to set these attributes by hand, in Source Mode, IntelliSense helps you with the valid Display Modes as well, as shown in Figure 9-9. You can leave the default, BulletList, for now.

In addition to choosing among a BulletList, List, or SingleParagraph format for displaying the list of errors, you must decide on whether to show a summary at the bottom of the page and/or a pop-up message box. You configure this using the ShowMessageBox and ShowSummary properties, as shown in Figure 9-10.

Set ShowMessageBox to True and ShowSummary to False for now.

The HeaderText property holds the header that will be displayed if there are errors to report. Set it to The following errors were found:.

From ASPX Back to Drag and Drop

At times, you will start out with *.aspx* code (either reading it in a book or using existing aspx pages) and you'll want to recreate the page in your form. You can certainly just retype the aspx, but it is a great skill to be able to "see" aspx and "do" drag and drop. Here's how. Suppose you were given Example 9-1 as a starting point, with no image of what the page is to look like.

Rather than hand-coding the page, you'll read the code but use drag and drop to choose the controls. You'll read the attributes of the controls, but set the attributes in the Properties window.

Open a new web site and name it ValidatorsFromAspx keep Example 9-1 handy. Open that web site's *Default.aspx* page.

Notice in Example 9-1 that the title is set (Validation Page) as is the form ID (frmBugs). Click on Design view and scroll down in the document's properties to Title. Set the title. You'll have to switch back to Source mode to set the form's ID by hand.

Next, looking at the source, notice that there is a table, whose ID is Table1. Here you have a few choices. You can type the table in by hand (IntelliSense will help), or you can drag a table onto your form from the HTML controls tab and then fix it up. Finally, you can decide to use an ASP:Table control instead, which will use slightly more server resources, but is easier to set up.

Once your table is in place (with at least one row and one column) your next step is to add the DropDownList, which you can do by dragging a DropDownList from the Standard tab of the Toolbox, into the appropriate table cell (<TD>) in Source view, or into the cell in Design view if the cell is expanded enough and you have good aim.

After you drag the drop-down list into place, make sure you are in Design view and click on your new drop-down list. Its properties come up in the Properties window. The first property to set is its ID: ddlBooks. The second property to set is the collection of ASPListItem members. The easiest way to do so is to click on the Items property (click on the button with the ellipsis) and open the ListItem Collection Editor, as you have done before (of course, you are free to type these directly into the Source window, but that is more work).

In the ListItems Collection Editor, click Add to add a new member, and set its text to -- Please Pick A Book --. Click Add to add a second item. Referring to the example, you see that the text for the second example should be Programming Visual Basic 2005, so type that into the Text field.

Also notice that when you dragged the RequiredFieldValidator into place, the ErrorMessage field was automatically set. You can remove that from the HTML, or just set the ErrorMessage property to blank in the Properties window.

You add the RadioButtonList and its validator in much the same way.

—continued—

Keep adding one item for each item shown in the source code. When you are done, click OK and then switch to Source view; you'll find that your source closely matches the source shown in the example.

Drag a RequiredFieldValidator into the next column. Switch back to Design view to set the properties using the Property window, or stay in HTML and set them by hand. In either case, the properties you need are shown in the source:

```
<asp:RequiredFieldValidator
id="reqFieldBooks"
ControlToValidate="ddlBooks"
Display="Static"
InitialValue="-- Please Pick A Book --"
Width="100%" runat=server>
    You did not pick a book
</asp:RequiredFieldValidator>
```

Set the ID property to reqFieldBooks, set the ControlToValidate property to ddlBooks (in the Properties window you can use the drop-down list to pick the control you want), leave the Display as Static (the default) and type in the Initial value.

If you do use the Properties window, the only tricky part is to realize that the innerHTML (that is, the text between the open tag and the close tag) is set in the Text property. (You did not pick a book.)

Figure 9-8. Set the Summary Display Mode

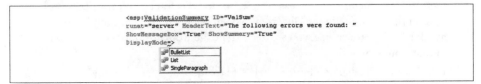

Figure 9-9. Set the Summary Display Mode in source

To make the summary validator work as expected, you'll need to add an ErrorMessage attribute to the other validation controls.

Click on the first validation control (reqFieldBooks) and in its properties, set its ErrorMessage to You did not pick a book. This value will now be displayed in the summary, and need not be displayed next to the incorrect value. Thus you can change the Text property from You did not pick a book to an asterisk: "*".

You'll want to do the equivalent for the other three validators.

Figure 9-10. Show Summary property

Rather than choose which of the three types of summary reports (bulleted list, list, or summary paragraph) to provide, for this example you'll let the user choose from a drop-down list. To do so, add a row to the table, right above the Submit Bug button. In the first column, add the title *Display Report*. Set its `align` property to `right`.

In the second column, drag in a DropDownList (id=ddlFormat) and set its `AutoPostBack` property to `True`. Finally, add three items to the drop down's items list: `List`, `BulletList`, and `SingleParagraph`.

Set the event handler for `SelectedIndexChanged` by clicking on the lightning bolt in the Properties window, then double-clicking on the space next to the `SelectedIndexChanged` event. When you double-click on the event handler, it is given a name, and you are placed in the code editor to implement the event handler. It just sets the `DisplayMode` of the summary validator.

```
Protected Sub ddlFormat_SelectedIndexChanged( _
    ByVal sender As System.Object, _
    ByVal e As System.EventArgs)

    ValSum.DisplayMode = _
      CType(ddlFormat.SelectedIndex, _
        ValidationSummaryDisplayMode)

End Sub
```

> The validation summary object (`ValSum`) has its `DisplayMode` set to the index of the selected item. This is a bit of a cheat. The ValidationSummary Display Mode is controlled by the `ValidationSummaryDisplayMode` enumeration, in which `BulletList = 0`, `List = 1`, and `SingleParagraph = 2`. You take advantage of this and order your list so that the index of the selected item will equal the choice you want.

Similarly, you'll add a second drop-down list to allow the user to control whether the error report appears in the page or in a pop-up menu. Add another row to the table, right above the row you just created. In the first column, type the prompt **Display Errors**. Set its align property to right.

Drag a drop-down list into the second column. Set its ID to ddlDisplay. Populate it with the two choices, Summary and Message Box. Remember to set its AutoPostback property to True, and implement its SelectedIndexChanged handler as follows:

```
Protected Sub ddlDisplay_SelectedIndexChanged( _
    ByVal sender As System.Object, _
    ByVal e As System.EventArgs)
    If ddlDisplay.SelectedIndex = 0 Then
        ValSum.ShowSummary = True
        ValSum.ShowMessageBox = False
    Else
        ValSum.ShowSummary = False
        ValSum.ShowMessageBox = True
    End If
End Sub
```

Note that the decision to use a summary or a message box and the display mode, are set in event handlers. If the user clicks the button before changing either of these drop-down settings, default values will be used. There are many ways to solve this problem, including using member variables to hold the state, but a simple solution is to invoke these event handlers programmatically when the page is loaded.

```
Protected Sub Page_Load( _
ByVal sender As Object, _
ByVal e As System.EventArgs) Handles Me.Load
    ddlFormat_SelectedIndexChanged(sender, e)
    ddlDisplay_SelectedIndexChanged(sender, e)
End Sub
```

Build and run the application. If you click on Submit Bug without setting anything, the default values of BulletList and summary will be used, as shown in Figure 9-11.

If you change Summary to Message Box and BulletList to List, a message box is shown rather than the summary, as shown in Figure 9-12.

The Compare Validator

While ensuring that the user has made an entry is very useful, you will often want to validate that the content of the entry is within certain guidelines. One of the most common requirements for validation is to compare the user's input to a constant, the value of another control, or a database value.

Add a new control to your bug-reporting dialog that will ask the user how many copies of the book he purchased. Manually type in a new row (using <tr><td> tags) above the Display Errors row, and set the prompt column to Number purchased:. The second column needs a text box (txtNumPurch), and the third column now takes *two* validators (just drag them both into the same column).

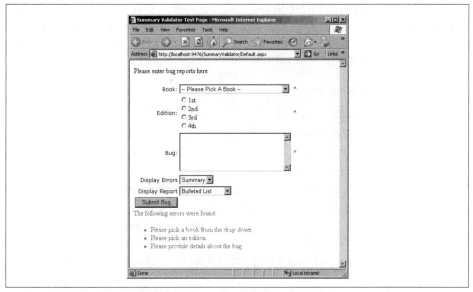

Figure 9-11. Summary and BulletList

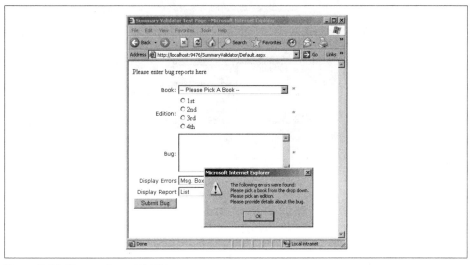

Figure 9-12. Message box with List

The validator first is a `RequiredFieldValidator` (ID = `reqFieldNumPurch` and `ControlToValidate=txtNumPurch`.

The `RequiredFieldValidator` ensures that the user does not leave the entry blank. Finally, set its `ErrorMessage` property to Please enter the number of books purchased, and its `Text` property to an asterisk.

The second validator is of type `CompareValidator` (which you also find in the Validation tab in the Toolbox). You'll use this validator to ensure that the user does not enter the value zero. The properties of the `CompareValidator` are the same as you've seen before, except as shown in Table 9-4.

Table 9-4. CompareValidator properties

Property	Value	Explanation
(ID)	CompareValidatorNumPurch	
ControlToValidate	txtNumPurch	
ErrorMessage	Invalid number purchased	
Operator	GreaterThan	See explanation below.
Text	*	
ValueToCompare	0	Value to compare the entered value with.

The `Operator` property is set with a drop-down list, as shown in Figure 9-13.

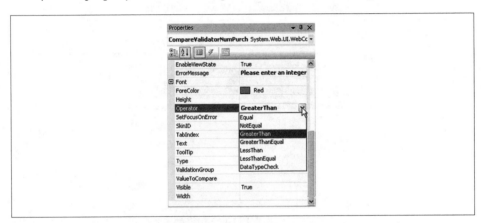

Figure 9-13. Compare Operator property

You can stipulate that the value entered must equal a value, or you can set an inequality, or you can even check the type of the data entered (see the next section, "Checking the Input Type").

For now, we're ensuring that a value greater than zero is chosen.

Build and run the application. When you enter **0** for the number of books purchased, your screen should look like Figure 9-14.

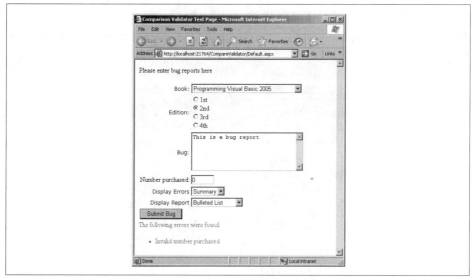

Figure 9-14. Comparing to zero

Checking the Input Type

Rather than checking that the number of books purchased is greater than zero, you might simply want to check that it is a number (rather than a letter or date). To do this, you make some minor changes to the CompareValidator, as shown in Table 9-5.

Table 9-5. CompareValidator data type check

Property	Value
(ID)	CompareValidatorNumPurch
ControlToValidate	txtNumPurch
ErrorMessage	Please enter an integer value
Operator	DataTypeCheck
Type	Integer

Once again, the Type value is a drop-down list, as shown in Figure 9-15.

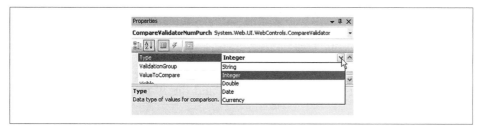

Figure 9-15. CompareOperator data type check

The validator will now test the type of the entry, rather than its value.

Build and run the application. Enter nonnumeric data for the number of books purchased. The screen should resemble Figure 9-16.

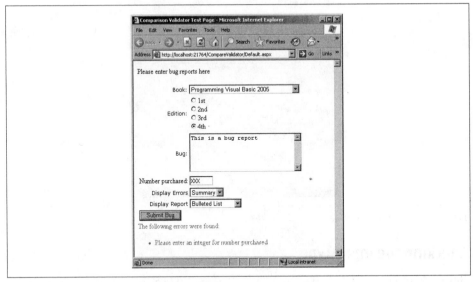

Figure 9-16. Comparing against type

Comparing to Another Control

It is possible to compare a value in one control to the value in another control rather than to a constant. A classic use of this might be to ask the user to enter her password twice, and then to validate that both entries are identical. The CompareValidator is perfect for this.

Add two rows to your design, each with a text box so that the password may be entered twice, as shown in Figure 9-17.

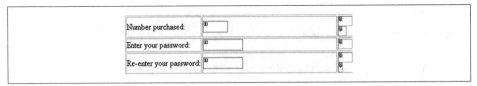

Figure 9-17. Adding the password rows

Set the TextMode property of the text fields to Password so the entries will be hidden. Set the ID property of the first to txtPasswd1 and the ID property of the second to txtPasswd2.

All validators other than the RequiredFieldValidator consider a blank field to be valid. In fact, if one field has a value and the other field is blank, the comparison validator will return valid! To avoid this problem, add RequiredFieldValidators for both passwords.

You are now ready to validate that the entries in both text fields are identical. Add a comparison validator for the second password field (in addition to the required field validator). Set its attributes as shown in Table 9-6.

Table 9-6. CompareValidator attributes

Property	Value
(ID)	CompValPasswords
ControlToValidate	txtPasswd2
ErrorMessage	Passwords do not match
Operator	Equal
Type	String
ControlToCompare	textPasswd1

In this case, you do not have a ValueToCompare attribute, but instead you have a ControlToCompare attribute, which takes the ID of the control against which you'll compare this value.

Set the Operator attribute to Equal, which indicates that the new value must be equal to the value in the control with which you're comparing it, and set the Type of the comparison to String.

Once again, build and run the application. If you enter two different passwords, the error is reported, as shown in Figure 9-18.

If the two passwords are identical, the ComparisonValidator is satisfied, and the second password field is marked as valid.

Range Checking

At times you'll want to validate that a user's entry falls within a range. That range can be within a pair of numbers, characters, or dates. In addition, you can express the boundaries for the range by using constants or by comparing its value with values found in other controls.

For example, you might add a RangeValidator to check that the number of books purchased is between 1 and 10 (the books are on sale!). To do so, you need only add another validator to the txtNumPurch text box of type RangeValidator. Drag it into the third column and set its properties, as shown in Table 9-7.

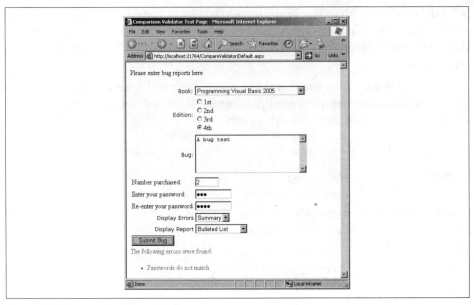

Figure 9-18. Passwords do not match

Table 9-7. RangeValidator attributes

Property	Value
ID	rangeValid
ControlToValidate	txtNumPurch
Type	Integer
MinimumValue	1
MaximumValue	10
ErrorMessage	Sorry, only 10 per customer
SetFocusOnError	True

The key new attributes are MinimumValue and MaximumValue (setting the range). Set the Type to tell the RangeValidator how to evaluate these values (e.g., as numbers rather than as dates). You can set this from a drop-down list of valid values, as shown in Figure 9-19.

Set the Text property to * to indicate that an asterisk should be displayed if the field is not valid.

Build and run the application again. If you enter a value out of range, an error is displayed, as shown in Figure 9-20.

Figure 9-19. RangeValidation types

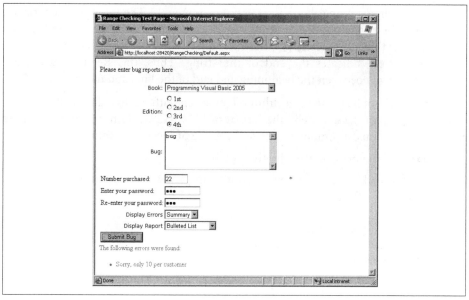

Figure 9-20. Out-of-range error

Regular Expressions

Often a simple value or range check is insufficient; you must check that the *form* of the data entered is correct. For example, you may need to ensure that a ZIP code is five digits, an email address is in the form *name@place.com*, a credit card matches the right format, and so forth.

A RegularExpressionValidator allows you to validate that a text field matches a *regular expression*. Regular expressions are a language for describing and manipulating text.

For more complete coverage of regular expressions, please see *Mastering Regular Expressions*, Second Edition, by Jeffrey Friedl (O'Reilly). For a wonderful tool that will help you create, understand, and master regular expressions, take a look at RegEx buddy available at *http://www.regexbuddy.com*.

A regular expression consists of two types of characters: literals and metacharacters. A literal is just a character you wish to match in the target string. A metacharacter is a special symbol that acts as a command to the regular expression parser. The parser is the engine responsible for understanding the regular expression. Consider this regular expression:

```
^\d{5}$
```

This will match any string that has exactly five numerals. The initial metacharacter, ^, indicates the beginning of the string. The second metacharacter, \d, indicates a digit. The third metacharacter, {5}, indicates exactly five of the digits, and the final metacharacter, $, indicates the end of the string. Thus, this Regular Expression matches five digits between the beginning and end of the line, and nothing else.

A slightly more sophisticated algorithm might accept either a five-digit ZIP code or a nine-digit (plus four) ZIP code in the format of 12345-1234. Rather than using the \d metacharacter, you can simply designate the range of acceptable values:

```
ValidationExpression="[0-9]{5}|[0-9]{5}-[0-9]{4}"
```

To see this at work, add a new row to your form (below the second password row), as shown in Figure 9-21.

Figure 9-21. Zip Code row

The middle column consists of a textbox control (txtZip) and the third column has a RegularExpressionValidator. Set its attributes as shown in Table 9-8.

Table 9-8. RegularExpressionValidator attributes

Property	Value
ID	regExVal
ControlToValidate	txtZip
ValidationExpression	^\d{5}$
ErrorMessage	Please enter a valid 5-digit zip code
Text	*

With this validator, your ZIP code is checked against the regular expression.

Build and run the application again. If you enter a zip code in an invalid format, then the validation fails, and you see the message shown in Figure 9-22.

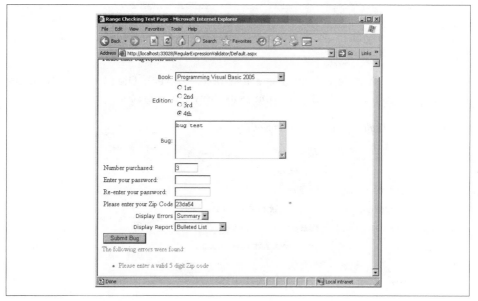

Figure 9-22. Regular expression validation

 When you use a RegularExpressionValidator control with client-side validation, the regular expressions are matched using JScript. This may differ in small details from the regular-expression checking done on the server.

Custom Validation

There are times when the validation of your data is so specific to your application that you will need to write your own validation method. The CustomValidator is designed to provide all the infrastructure support you need. You provide the name of your validation method and have it return a Boolean value: True or False. The CustomValidator control takes care of all the rest of the work.

Because validation can be done on the client or on the server, depending on the browser, the CustomValidator has attributes for specifying both a server-side and a client-side method for validation. The server-side method can be written in any .NET language, (we, of course will use Visual Basic 2005), while the client-side method must be written in a scripting language understood by the browser, such as VBScript or JavaScript.

Add one more row to your form (below the ZIP-code row), asking the user for an even number, as shown in Figure 9-23.

Figure 9-23. Even number row

Once again, the middle column has a text box (txtEven). Drag a CustomValidator into the third column and set its attributes as shown in Table 9-9.

Table 9-9. CustomValidator properties and events

Property	Value
ID	cvEven
ControlToValidate	txtEven
ClientValidationFunction	ClientEventValidator
ValidateEmptyText	False
ErrorMesssage	Your number is rather odd
Text	*
ServerValidate [EVENT]	ServerEventValidate

The CustomValidator takes three new elements. The first, OnServerValidate, points to the server method that will be called to perform validation. You'll add this to the code-behind page, as shown in Example 9-3.

Example 9-3. Server method to perform validation

```
Protected Sub ServerEvenValidate(ByVal source As Object, _
          ByVal e As ServerValidateEventArgs)
   Dim evenNumber As Int32 = Int32.Parse(e.Value)

   If evenNumber Mod 2 = 0 Then
      e.IsValid = True
   Else
      e.IsValid = False
   End If

End Sub
```

The second new element is the ClientValidationFunction. This is a script function that will be called to validate the user's entry, *client-side*, before your form is submitted, as shown in Example 9-4. Place this script in the header section of your content (*.aspx*) file.

Example 9-4. Client-side validation script

```
<script language="javascript">
   function ClientEvenValidator(source, args)
```

Example 9-4. Client-side validation script (continued)

```
  {
    if (args.Value % 2 == 0)
      args.IsValid=true;
    else
      args.IsValid=false;
    return;
  }
</script>
```

If the value is not even, the server-side method sets e.IsValid to False. Similarly, the client-side method sets args.IsValid to False. In either case, the error is displayed.

Build and run the application. Enter an odd number into this field. You should see the error message shown in Figure 9-24.

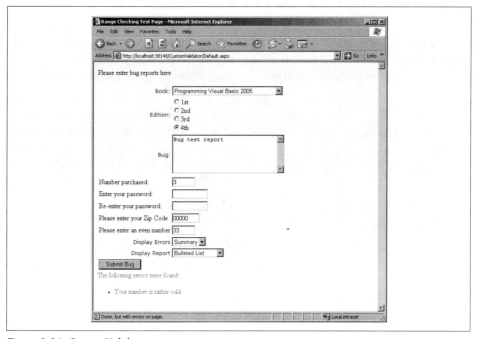

Figure 9-24. CustomValidator

The third new property, and one that can save you a lot of special coding, is ValidateEmptyTest:

```
ValidateEmptyText=false
```

The default is True, but by setting it to False, the text field will be considered invalid if it is empty.

Unfortunately, this only works on the `CustomValidator`.

`ValidateEmptyTest` avoids the need for a `RequiredFieldValidator` (and, boy, do I wish they added this attribute to the other validators as well!).

Validation Groups

The examples shown in this chapter have been kept intentionally simple. In a real application, however, you might have a form with a great many controls on it. In addition, the form may be divided into sections, with more than one button that can submit the form, depending on what the user is doing.

At times, it is convenient to be able to say "when I press the first button, I want to validate only these first five controls; but when I press the second button, I want to validate only the last four controls." This allows you to create forms in which you *expect* that some of the controls will be invalid, depending on how the form is submitted.

To accomplish this, you set the `ValidationGroup` property on all the controls (and the button that submits the form) to the same value for each group. In the example described earlier, the first five controls and the first button might all have `ValidationGroup` set to `GroupOne` while all the other controls would have `ValidationGroup` set to `GroupTwo`.

To try this out, create a new web site called ValidationGroup and copy the web site with the *CompareValidator.aspx* page as a starting point.

Make two changes. First, hand edit the ASP page to move the two rows for password entry *after* the row that holds the Submit Bug button. Then add an additional row, after the passwords, to hold a new button, with the ID of `btnPW` and the Text Login. Your form should look like Figure 9-25.

That done, you can add the `ValidationGroup` to each of your validation controls and to the buttons. For all the controls above the Submit Bug button, set the `ValidationGroup` property to `Bug`. For all the controls below the Submit Bug button, set the `ValidationGroup` property to `Login`.

 Note that the drop-down lists have their AutoPostBack property set to True. This will cause a postback (and thus validation) when the drop-down value changes. Be sure to set the `ValidationGroup` to `Bug` for these controls as well.

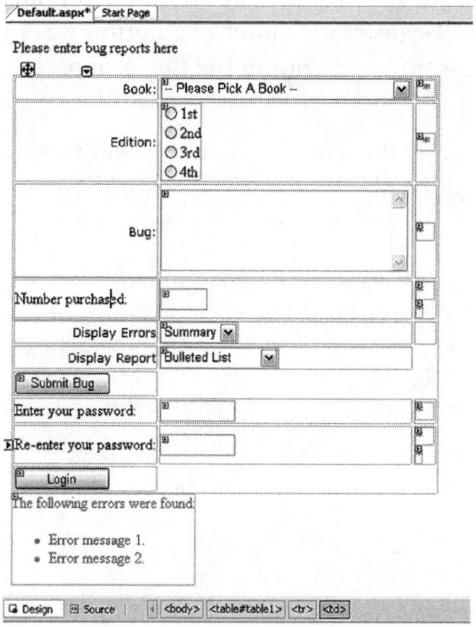

Figure 9-25. Validation Group design

Once again, build and run the application. Click the Submit Bug button. You should observe that only the controls in its group are validated, as shown in Figure 9-26.

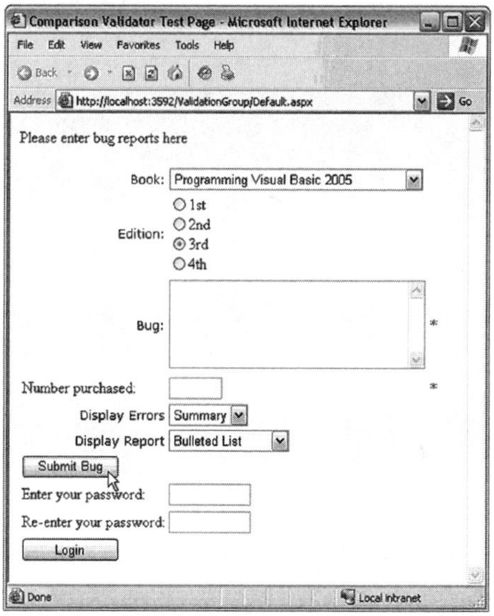

Figure 9-26. Validating only one group

Look carefully at Figure 9-26—the password fields are not filled in, though they have a RequiredFieldValidator. Because the Submit Bug button was pressed, and the validators for the password controls were not in the Bug group, they were not validated at all.

Now click Login. This time, the password controls will be validated, but none of the other controls will be validated.

CHAPTER 10

Master Pages and Navigation

Web sites look better and are less confusing to users when they have a consistent "look and feel" as you move from page to page. ASP.NET 2.0 facilitates creating consistency with *master pages*.

A master page provides shared HTML, controls, and code that can be used as a template for all of the pages of a site. The O'Reilly web site (*http://www.oreilly.com*) is a good example of a site that could be implemented using a master page. With a master page, the logo (the O'Reilly tarsier) and an image (the O'Reilly header) can be shared across multiple pages.

Creating Master Pages

To get started with master pages, you'll take the following steps:

1. Create a new web site.
2. Add a master page to the site.
3. Add content pages based on the master page.

To begin, create a new web site and call it `MasterPages`. Once the new site opens, right-click on the project and choose Add New Item. In the dialog box that opens, choose Master Page, and name your master page *SiteMasterPage.master*, as shown Figure 10-1.

An `asp:contentplaceholder` control has been added for you in the new page. It is this placeholder that will be filled by the content of each of the pages that use this master page.

Within the master page itself you may add anything you like surrounding the `contentplaceholder`. Whatever you add will be displayed on all pages that use the master page.

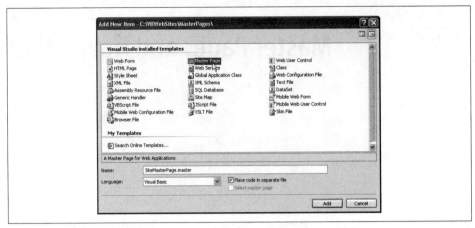

Figure 10-1. Add new master page

In this example, you'll use the O'Reilly logos, *Animal.gif* and *OReillyLogo.gif*, provided for your use in the download files at the download sites for this book (see the Preface for details).

Right-click on the application and choose Add → Regular Folder. Name the folder *Images*. Open Windows Explorer and navigate to that folder, into which you will copy *Animal.gif* and *OReillyLogo.gif*.

Return to the application and add the files to the project by right-clicking on the images folder and choosing Add → Existing item....

You'll place the logos and the `contentplaceholder` into a table within the SiteMasterPage.master file. To do so, drag `Image` controls into place, and set their `ID`, `ImageURL`, and `ImageAlign` properties. For example, for the *Animal.gif* file, set the `ID` to `animalLogo`, the `ImageURL` property to:

```
"~/Images/Animal.gif"
```

and the `ImageAlign` property to `Left`.

For the *OreillyLogo.gif* file, set the properties as follows:

```
ID="oreillyLogo" ImageUrl="~/Images/OreillyLogo.gif" ImageAlign="Bottom"
```

As always, you can set these in the Properties window in Design view, or you can manually type them into the control in Source view.

In Design view in Visual Studio, you'll see the master page with standard logos in place, and a `ContentPlaceHolder` displaying where content from other pages will be placed, as shown in Figure 10-2.

You can type directly into the placeholder area. (In Figure 10-2, I typed in the words, "If you see this content, then the master page content was not replaced.")

Figure 10-2. Master page in Display view

To see the master page at work, create two new *.aspx* pages. Name them *Page1.aspx* and *Page2.aspx*, respectively. Create these pages as normal web pages, but check the "Select master page" checkbox, as shown in Figure 10-3.

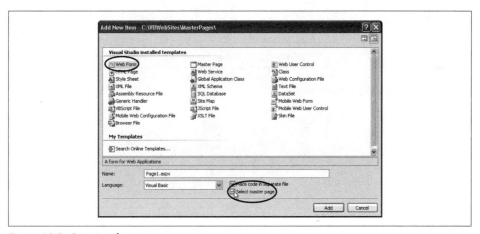

Figure 10-3. Creating the content pages

When you click OK, you'll be asked to pick which master page you want to use. In this case, there is only one choice: *SiteMasterPage.master*. Select it and press OK.

Open your new page in design mode. You'll see exactly how the content for this new page will fit within the master page you've chosen, as shown in Figure 10-4.

 Visual Studio 2005 assumes you want to use custom content. If you want to use the default content, click on the smart tag and choose Default to Master's Content.

Drag controls into the content area. Begin by dragging in a table (two columns wide, two rows high). In the left columns put labels and in the right column put text boxes. Below the table, add a link to page 2, so that your page looks like Figure 10-5.

Switch to *Page2.aspx*, and this time drag a Calendar control onto the Content area of the page. Add a hyperlink back to page 1, as shown in Figure 10-6.

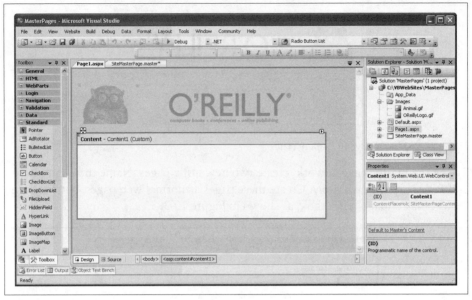

Figure 10-4. Content page within master page

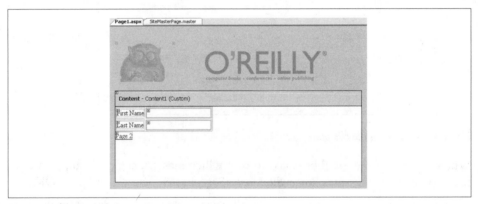

Figure 10-5. Page1.aspx

Run the application. The two pages share a common look and feel, although each page is made unique by the data and controls you placed within the ContentPlaceHolder, as shown in Figure 10-7.

Navigation

Web sites are becoming larger and more complex, and developers are called upon to provide navigational hints and menus to assist visitors avoid "getting lost" and to help visitors find all the features of the site.

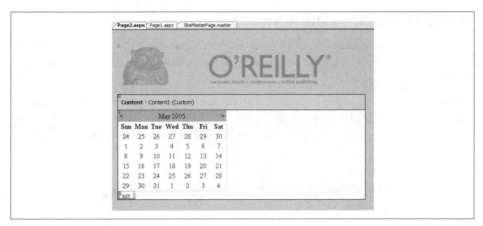

Figure 10-6. Page2.aspx

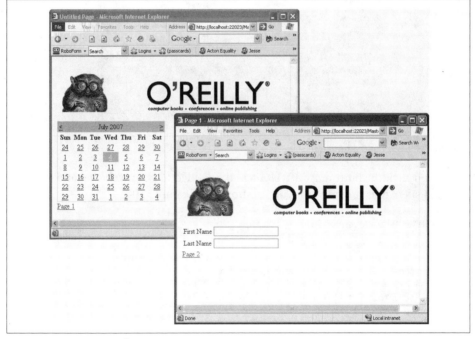

Figure 10-7. Two pages sharing a common master page

The ASP.NET toolset includes a number of controls that facilitate creating both "bread crumbs" (how did I get to this page?) and site maps (how do I find that other page?).

Most of the time, you will want all of these features to be present on every page, and thus master pages are a great asset. If you change the site map or the control, you only have to update the master, and all the other pages are "updated" automatically.

Getting Started with Site Navigation

The most common way to create a site navigation data source is to create an xml file. It is possible to use a database, multiple xml files, and other sources, but for now let's keep things simple.

To begin, create a new web site called SiteNavigation. Right-click on the web site in Solution explorer and choose Add New Item. The Add New Item dialog box appears. Choose Site map and verify that the name provided is *Web.sitemap*, as shown in Figure 10-8.

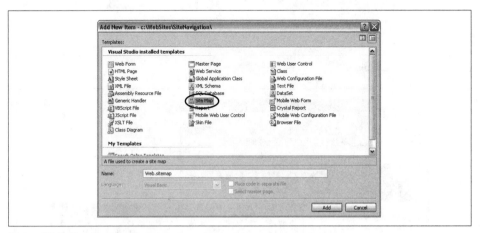

Figure 10-8. Creating the sitemap

When you click the button, Add *Web.sitemap* is added to your web site, and the skeleton of a sitemap is provided for you, as shown in Example 10-1.

Example 10-1. Web.sitemap skeleton

```xml
<?xml version="1.0" encoding="utf-8" ?>
<siteMap xmlns="http://schemas.microsoft.com/AspNet/SiteMap-File-1.0" >
    <siteMapNode url="" title=""  description="">
        <siteMapNode url="" title=""  description="" />
        <siteMapNode url="" title=""  description="" />
    </siteMapNode>
</siteMap>
```

The title attribute defines the text that will be used as the link, while the description attribute will be used in the tool tip.

Replace the contents of *Web.sitemap* with the sitemap XML shown in Example 10-2.

Example 10-2. Web.sitemap

```xml
<?xml version="1.0" encoding="utf-8" ?>
<siteMap xmlns="http://schemas.microsoft.com/AspNet/SiteMap-File-1.0" >
   <siteMapNode title="Welcome" description="Welcome" url="~/welcome.aspx">
```

Example 10-2. Web.sitemap (continued)

```
    <siteMapNode title="Writing" description="Writing"
       url="~/Writing.aspx">
       <siteMapNode title="Books" description="Books"
          url="~/Books.aspx">
          <siteMapNode title="In Print Books"
             description="Books in Print"
          url="~/BooksInPrint.aspx" />
          <siteMapNode title="Out Of Print Books"
             description="Books no longer in Print"
          url="~/OutOfPrintBooks.aspx" />
       </siteMapNode>
       <siteMapNode title="Articles" description="Articles"
          url="~/Articles.aspx" />
    </siteMapNode>
    <siteMapNode title="Programming"
       description="Contract Programming"
       url="~/Programming.aspx">
       <siteMapNode title="On-Site Programming"
          description="On-site contract programming"
          url="~/OnSiteProgramming.aspx" />
       <siteMapNode title="Off-Site Programming"
          description="Off-site contract programming"
          url="~/OffSiteProgramming.aspx" />
    </siteMapNode>
    <siteMapNode title="Training"
       description="On-Site Training"
       url="~/OnSiteTraining.aspx">
       <siteMapNode title="C# Training"
          description="C# Training"
          url="~/TrainCSharp.aspx" />
       <siteMapNode title="ASP.NET Training"
          description="ASP.NET Training"
          url="~/TrainASPNET.aspx" />
       <siteMapNode title="Windows Forms Training"
          description="Windows Forms Training"
          url="~/TrainWinForms.aspx" />
    </siteMapNode>
    <siteMapNode title="Consulting"
       description="Consulting"
       url="~/Consulting.aspx">
       <siteMapNode title="Application Analysis"
          description="Analysis"
          url="~/ApplicationAnalysis.aspx" />
       <siteMapNode title="Application Design"
          description="Design"
          url="~/ApplicationDesign.aspx" />
       <siteMapNode title="Mentoring"
          description="Team Mentoring"
          url="~/Mentoring.aspx" />
    </siteMapNode>
  </siteMapNode>
</siteMap>
```

The sitemap file has a single <sitemap> element that defines the namespace:

```
<siteMap xmlns="http://schemas.microsoft.com/AspNet/SiteMap-File-1.0" >
```

Only one SiteMapNode (in this case, Welcome) may be nested within the sitemap element. Nested within that SiteMapNode, however, can be any number of children SiteMapNode elements.

In Example 10-2, there are four such children: Writing, Programming, Training, and Consulting. Nested within each of these SiteMapNode elements may be more nodes. For example, Writing has both Books and Articles. You may nest arbitrarily deep. The Books node has nested within it nodes for books in print and books no longer in print.

 ASP.NET is configured to protect files with the extension *.sitemap* so that they can not be downloaded to a client (web browser). If you need to use a different extension, be sure to place your file in the protected *App_Data* folder.

Setting Up the Pages

To experiment with the sitemap, right-click on the project and choose Add New Item. Create a master page for this application named *MasterPage.master* (the default name offered by Visual Studio 2005), as shown in Figure 10-9.

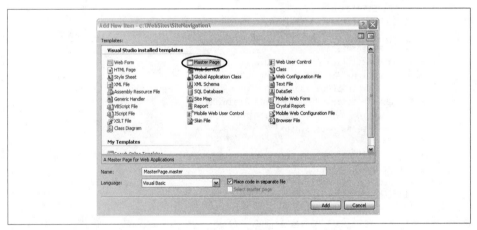

Figure 10-9. Adding a master page

From the Toolbox, drag a SiteMapDataSource control from the Data tab, onto the master page. By default, the SiteMapDataSource control will look for and use the file named *Web.sitemap*.

Add all the navigation controls to the master page *outside* the contentPlaceHolder because you want them to be displayed on every page.

Make sure you are in Design view and drag a TreeView control from the navigation panel onto the form, (again, outside of the Content area). Click on its smart tag and set the data source to the SiteMapDataSource control you just created, as shown in Figure 10-10.

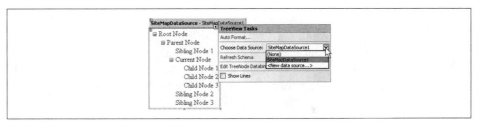

Figure 10-10. Creating the TreeView

To take control of the layout of the various elements on the master page, drag a table control into Source view and set its width to 100%. Drag the TreeView into the first cell, and drag a SiteMapPath control into a second cell. Add two `<br/>` elements after the SiteMapPath and then drag the contentplaceholder control already on the master page into the same cell, as shown in Example 10-3.

Example 10-3. MasterPage.master

```
<%@ Master Language="C#" AutoEventWireup="true" CodeFile="MasterPage.master.cs"
Inherits="MasterPage" %>

<!DOCTYPE html PUBLIC "-//W3C//DTD XHTML 1.1//EN" "http://www.w3.org/TR/xhtml11/DTD/
xhtml11.dtd">

<html xmlns="http://www.w3.org/1999/xhtml" >
<head runat="server">
    <title>Liberty Associates, Inc.</title>
</head>
<body>
    <form id="form1" runat="server">
    <div>
        <asp:SiteMapDataSource ID="SiteMapDataSource1" runat="server" />
        <asp:Table ID="Table1" runat="server" Width="100%" >
            <asp:TableRow>
                <asp:TableCell>
                    <asp:TreeView ID="TreeView1" runat="server"
                        DataSourceID="SiteMapDataSource1" />
                </asp:TableCell>
                <asp:TableCell VerticalAlign="Top">
                    <asp:SiteMapPath ID="SiteMapPath1" runat="server" />
```

Example 10-3. MasterPage.master (continued)

```
                        <br /><br />
                        <asp:contentplaceholder id="ContentPlaceHolder1"
                            runat="server">
                        </asp:contentplaceholder>
                    </asp:TableCell>
                </asp:TableRow>
            </asp:Table>
        </div>
    </form>
</body>
</html>
```

To test this master page, you'll need to create at least a few of the pages defined in the sitemap. Delete the default page and create a new page named *Welcome.aspx*. Be sure to check the Select master page checkbox and set the master page to *MasterPage.master*. Within the content control, add the line of code shown in bold below:

```
<asp:Content ID="Content1"
ContentPlaceHolderID="ContentPlaceHolder1"
Runat="Server">
    <h1>Welcome</h1>
</asp:Content>
```

Create each of the other pages, providing whatever stubbed out data you want, as long as you can tell what page you are on. When you are done, your Solution Explorer should look more or less like Figure 10-11.

Figure 10-11. Solution explorer

Start the application and navigate from the welcome page to another page, e.g., Programming, as shown in Figure 10-12.

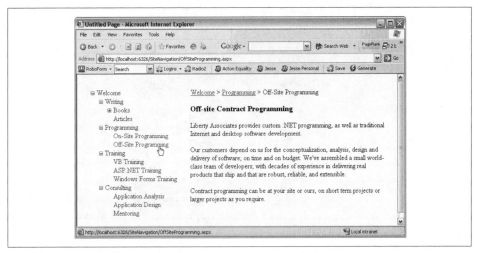

Figure 10-12. Off-Site Programming

There are a few things to notice about the Programming page. The TreeView was built for you (by reading the XML file through the SiteMapDataSource control, as shown in Figure 10-12). You can see that each node can be collapsed or expanded. When you click on a node (in this case Off-Site Programming), you are brought directly to that page. The bread crumbs, put in place by the SiteMapPath, show you how you got here and how to get back to home.

> It is uncommon in production applications to provide both a map and bread crumbs on the same page.

Customizing the Look and Feel

There are a number of properties that you can set for the TreeView. To begin with, you may click on the Smart Tag and choose Auto Format... to bring up the Auto Format dialog that offers a series of preset formats for the tree, as shown in Figure 10-13.

In addition, you can click on the TreeView control and then set its properties through the Properties window. Most of the TreeView's properties have to do with the styles used for the various nodes, as shown in Figure 10-14

Some of the most important properties are shown in Table 10-1.

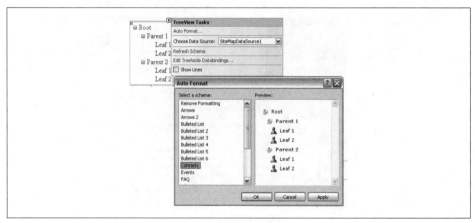

Figure 10-13. TreeView Auto Format

Figure 10-14. TreeView node styles

Table 10-1. TreeView properties

Property	Description
AutogenerateDataBindings	Defaults to true; lets you manually set the bindings between data and tree nodes.
CheckedNodes	Get back a collection of TreeNode objects that contains only those nodes whose checkbox was selected.
ExpandDepth	How many levels should the tree be expanded to.
PathSeparator	Change the character used to delimit the node values.
SelectedNode	Returns the selected TreeNode object.
ShowExpandCollapse	Should the expand/collapse indicators be displayed (default = true).

The TreeView has a number of public methods that allow you to poke into the control and pick out specific nodes, or to programmatically change, expand and contract nodes. The most important methods are shown in Table 10-2.

Table 10-2. TreeView methods

Method	Description
CollapseAll	Collapses the entire tree
ExpandAll	Expands the entire tree
FindNode	Retrieves the designated TreeNode

Finally, there are a number of events that the TreeView control raises that allow you to hook into the user's interaction with the TreeView and modify the results. The most important events are shown in Table 10-3.

Table 10-3. TreeView events

Event	Description
SelectedNodeChanged	When a node is selected in the TreeView
TreeNodeCollapsed	When a node is collapsed
TreeNodeExpanded	When a node is expanded
TreeNodePopulate	Fires when a node whose PopulateOnDemand property is set to true is expanded in the TreeView (gives you an opportunity to fill in the sub-nodes for that node)

Similarly, the SiteMapPath control can be modified either by using the smart tag to set Autoformatting or by setting properties on the control. Some common tasks include customizing the link *style* properties (such as RootNodeStyle-Font-Names and Root-NodeStyle-BorderWidth). These can be set in the declaration of the control itself. IntelliSense will help; when you press the spacebar while within the declaration of the control, a list of its properties, methods, and events will pop up, as shown in Figure 10-15.

Figure 10-15. Setting SiteMapPath properties

 In addition to setting styles for the RootNode you can also set separate styles for the ParentNode, the CurrentNode and the PathSeparator. You can also use the NodeTemplate to customize the style of all the links at once.

In the previous example, the bread crumbs separated the various pages with the greater-than symbol (>). It is easy to add the PathSeparator property to change that to, for example, an arrow:

```
<asp:SiteMapPath ID="SiteMapPath1" runat="server"  PathSeparator="->" />
```

The result is shown in Figure 10-16.

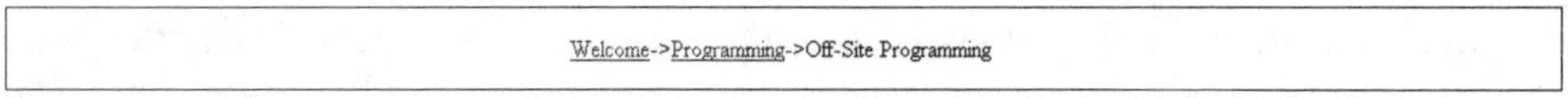

Welcome->Programming->Off-Site Programming

Figure 10-16. Arrow path separator

Limiting the number of links shown

For very "deep" ASP.NET sites, the bread crumbs may become unwieldy. You have the option to limit the number of levels shown by setting the ParentLevelDisplayed property:

```
<asp:SiteMapPath ID="SiteMapPath1" runat="server"  ParentLevelDisplayed="3" />
```

Populating on Demand

You may decide that you would like your TreeView to populate on demand. That is, rather than loading all the contents of each node when the tree is first shown, and displaying the full tree, you can display, for example, just the first node. As each node is clicked on, it will populate the next level.

To do this, you'll make some simple changes to the master page: First, modify the TreeView not to be a self-closing element (you'll be adding content between the opening and closing tags). Also add an attribute to TreeView *ExpandDepth* that you will set to 0 (or whatever zero-based level you want the tree to expand to when loaded).

Within the TreeView you'll add a DataBindings element and within *that* you'll add an ASP:TreeNodeBinding, as shown in Example 10-4.

Example 10-4. Adding Tree Node bindings for Populate On Demand

```
<asp:TreeView ID="TreeView1" runat="server"
 DataSourceID="SiteMapDataSource1" ExpandDepth="0">
    <DataBindings>
        <asp:TreeNodeBinding DataMember="SiteMapNode" NavigateUrlField="URL"
        PopulateOnDemand="true" TextField="Title" />
    </DataBindings>
</asp:TreeView>
```

Run the application with *Welcome.aspx* as the first page. The tree is fully closed. Expand it to choose Off-Site Programming. When you get to the page, once again the tree is fully closed, as shown in Figure 10-17.

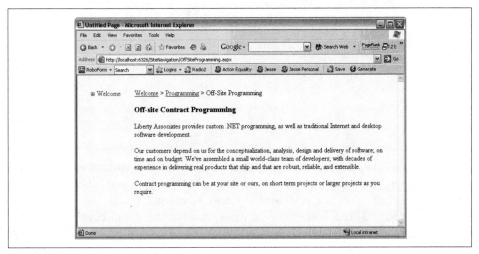

Figure 10-17. Menu fully closed

The nodes are loaded as you click on each level of the TreeView. With a large site map, this can save a bit of memory overhead.

CHAPTER 11

Web Data Access

In the previous chapter, you created forms, but they did not interact with real data. In this chapter, you'll begin to extract data from the database and fill in your forms. You'll do this incrementally, adding complexity as you go. You'll put a premium on using data controls and letting the controls manage the "plumbing" of database interaction.

Getting Data from a Database

To see how to interact with a database, begin by creating a new web application that can be used to display information about the Northwind database. Call it `WebNorthWind`, as shown in Figure 11-1.

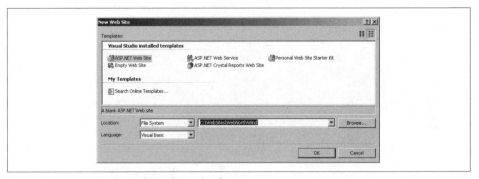

Figure 11-1. Creating the WebNorthWind web site

You'll be working with the Customers table in the Northwind database, so rename your *.aspx* file from *Default.aspx* to *Customers.aspx* (don't forget to change the class name both in the code file and in the page directive!).

Create a Data Connection

You need a connection to the database. You can explicitly create one, or you can use a control that depends on having a connection and one will be created for you. Let's start by explicitly creating one.

Drag a SqlDataSource control onto the form, as shown in Figure 11-2.

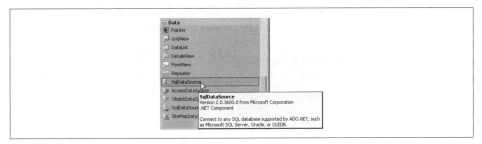

Figure 11-2. Data source control

The SqlDataSource control will appear on your form, as shown in Figure 11-3.

Figure 11-3. SqlDataSource control on form

 If you do not see the SqlDataSource control, choose View → Non-Visual Controls.

As you can see in Figure 11-3, the SqlDataSource control has a smart tag. Clicking on Configure Data Source... opens the Data Source Configuration wizard. Your first option is to choose an existing connection or to press the button to create a new connection.

When you create a new connection, you are first asked to choose the data source and data provider you'd like to use. For this book, you'll choose Microsoft SQL Server as the data source, and the .NET Framework Data Provider for SQL Server as the Data Provider, as shown in Figure 11-4.

Once you've chosen your data provider, you have the option to save the connection string in the application file (the alternative is to save the connection string in the page as a property of the control). Generally, you'll want to save the connection string in the application file where it is more secure and encrypted.

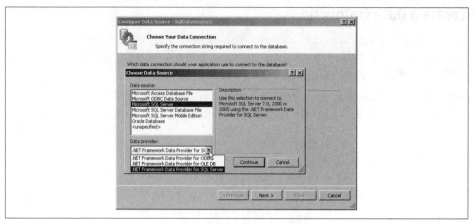

Figure 11-4. Choosing the SQL Data Provider

Step three is to specify your query or to pick the columns you want from a specific table. For this example, you'll choose all the columns from the Customers table, as shown in Figure 11-5.

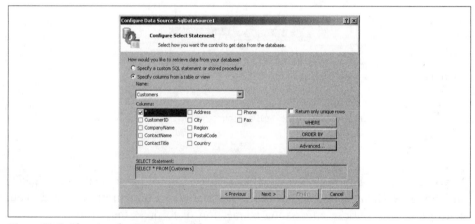

Figure 11-5. Choosing the Customers table

 While you are here, click the Advanced button to see that you can instruct the wizard to generate the update statements you'll need later in this chapter to update the database. For now, you can leave this unchecked.

The next step in the wizard allows you to test your query. Clicking Finish creates the connection.

Data Source Controls

In ASP.NET 2.0 database interaction is almost always through the DataSource controls.

 Visual Basic .NET users will be used to dealing with the ADO.NET object model; this has been abstracted into the DataSource control.

The DataSource control provides a single object that you can define either declaratively (in your web page) or programmatically (in your code-behind). It will own the connection information, the query information, the parameters, and the behavior (such as paging and caching). You can bind it to various UI objects for display on your web page.

There are a number of DataSource controls, including controls for accessing SQL from SQL Server, from ODBC or OLE DB servers, from XML files, and from business objects. All of these DataSource controls expose the same properties and methods, and all bind to UI objects (such as DataList and GridView) in the same way. You'll bind them to GridViews, DataLists, and some other controls later in this chapter.

Thus, you have a variety of UI controls all binding in the same way to a variety of underlying data sources, and the details are handled by the DataSource controls, greatly simplifying even complex data manipulation tasks in web applications.

Binding Data Controls with Drag and Drop

Now that you have a working DataSource control, let's hook it up to a data display control to examine the data you've retrieved. Drag a GridView onto the page. The GridView recognizes that there is already a SqlDataSource on the page, so it does not create its own. Instead, its smart tag opens and asks you to choose your data source, as shown in Figure 11-6.

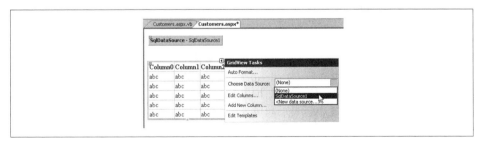

Figure 11-6. Choosing an existing data source

As soon as you set the data source, the data grid is redrawn, with a column for each field returned by the DataSource. Notice that the column headers have also been filled in for you. Switch to Source view, and examine the declaration of the data grid, as shown in Example 11-1.

Example 11-1. ASP GridView bound to DataSource

```
<asp:GridView
ID="GridView1"
PageSize="4"
runat="server"
DataSourceID="SqlDataSource1"
AutoGenerateColumns="False"
DataKeyNames="CustomerID">
    <Columns>
        <asp:BoundField ReadOnly="True" HeaderText="CustomerID"
        DataField="CustomerID" SortExpression="CustomerID">
        </asp:BoundField>
        <asp:BoundField HeaderText="CompanyName"
        DataField="CompanyName" SortExpression="CompanyName">
        </asp:BoundField>
        <asp:BoundField HeaderText="ContactName"
        DataField="ContactName" SortExpression="ContactName">
        </asp:BoundField>
        <asp:BoundField HeaderText="ContactTitle"
        DataField="ContactTitle" SortExpression="ContactTitle">
        </asp:BoundField>
        <asp:BoundField HeaderText="Address"
        DataField="Address" SortExpression="Address"></asp:BoundField>
        <asp:BoundField HeaderText="City"
        DataField="City" SortExpression="City"></asp:BoundField>
        <asp:BoundField HeaderText="Region"
        DataField="Region" SortExpression="Region"></asp:BoundField>
        <asp:BoundField HeaderText="PostalCode"
        DataField="PostalCode" SortExpression="PostalCode">
        </asp:BoundField>
        <asp:BoundField HeaderText="Country"
        DataField="Country" SortExpression="Country"></asp:BoundField>
        <asp:BoundField HeaderText="Phone"
        DataField="Phone" SortExpression="Phone"></asp:BoundField>
        <asp:BoundField HeaderText="Fax"
        DataField="Fax" SortExpression="Fax"></asp:BoundField>
    </Columns>
</asp:GridView>
```

Visual Studio 2005 has done a lot of work for you. It has examined the data source, and created a BoundField for each column in the data. Further, it has set the HeaderText to the name of the DataField. Finally, you'll notice on the third line of the declaration of the data grid that it has set AutoGenerateColumns to False.

If you were creating the GridView by hand, and if you were going to let the data grid create all the columns right from the retrieved data, you could greatly simplify the code by just setting AutoGenerateColumns to True. To see this at work, create, by hand, a second GridView below the one created for you, as shown in Example 11-2.

Example 11-2. Creating a GridView by hand

```
<asp:GridView
ID="GridView2"
PageSize="4"
runat="server"
DataSourceID="SqlDataSource1"
AutoGenerateColumns="True"
DataKeyNames="CustomerID"/>
```

Run the application. You should see two data grids, one above the other, as shown in Figure 11-7.

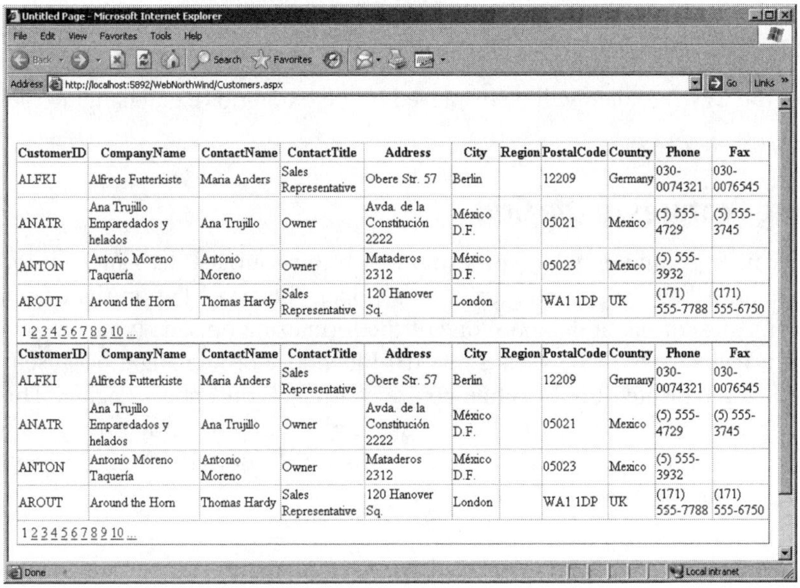

CustomerID	CompanyName	ContactName	ContactTitle	Address	City	Region	PostalCode	Country	Phone	Fax
ALFKI	Alfreds Futterkiste	Maria Anders	Sales Representative	Obere Str. 57	Berlin		12209	Germany	030-0074321	030-0076545
ANATR	Ana Trujillo Emparedados y helados	Ana Trujillo	Owner	Avda. de la Constitución 2222	México D.F.		05021	Mexico	(5) 555-4729	(5) 555-3745
ANTON	Antonio Moreno Taquería	Antonio Moreno	Owner	Mataderos 2312	México D.F.		05023	Mexico	(5) 555-3932	
AROUT	Around the Horn	Thomas Hardy	Sales Representative	120 Hanover Sq.	London		WA1 1DP	UK	(171) 555-7788	(171) 555-6750

1 2 3 4 5 6 7 8 9 10 ...

CustomerID	CompanyName	ContactName	ContactTitle	Address	City	Region	PostalCode	Country	Phone	Fax
ALFKI	Alfreds Futterkiste	Maria Anders	Sales Representative	Obere Str. 57	Berlin		12209	Germany	030-0074321	030-0076545
ANATR	Ana Trujillo Emparedados y helados	Ana Trujillo	Owner	Avda. de la Constitución 2222	México D.F.		05021	Mexico	(5) 555-4729	(5) 555-3745
ANTON	Antonio Moreno Taquería	Antonio Moreno	Owner	Mataderos 2312	México D.F.		05023	Mexico	(5) 555-3932	
AROUT	Around the Horn	Thomas Hardy	Sales Representative	120 Hanover Sq.	London		WA1 1DP	UK	(171) 555-7788	(171) 555-6750

1 2 3 4 5 6 7 8 9 10 ...

Figure 11-7. Comparing the two grids

They are indistinguishable. So why did Visual Studio 2005 bother with turning off `AutoGenerateColumns`? The answer is that doing so gives you much greater control. You can, for example, set the headings on the columns (e.g., changing ContactTitle to Title). You can remove columns you don't need, and you can add new columns for manipulating the rows.

You can make these changes by hand-coding the HTML in the Source view, or by clicking on the smart tag for the `GridView` and choosing Edit Columns. Doing so brings up the Fields dialog box, as shown in Figure 11-8.

The dialog box is divided into three main areas: the list of available fields, the list of selected fields (with buttons to remove or reorder the fields), and the Bound Field Properties window on the right. Click on a selected field (e.g., ContactTitle) and you

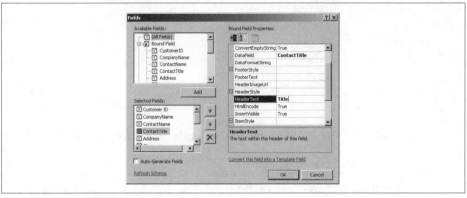

Figure 11-8. Fields dialog

can set the way that field will be displayed in the data grid (e.g., changing the header to Title).

Adding Features to the Grid

While you're examining what you can do with the `GridView`, let's make it look a bit nicer. First, delete the second grid. Second, open the smart tag on the original grid. Click on AutoFormat and choose one of the formatting options (you can, of course, format it by hand, but why work so hard?) I'll choose Brown Sugar because it shows up well in the printed book. While you're at it, click on Enable Paging. This keeps your application from trying to load every single record into the grid. Finally, click on Enable Sorting (Hey! Presto! The columns can be sorted). Run the application. The output should look like Figure 11-9.

Adding Insert, Update, and Delete Statements

The `DataSource` control that you've created currently has only a Select statement to extract data from the database,

```
<asp:SqlDataSource ID="SqlDataSource1"
    runat="server" SelectCommand="SELECT * FROM [Customers]"
    ConnectionString="<%$ ConnectionStrings:NorthwindConnectionString %>">
</asp:SqlDataSource>
```

You can, however, ask your `DataSource` control to create the remaining three CRUD (*C*reate, *R*etrieve, *U*pdate, and *D*elete) statements, using a wizard to make your work much easier. To do so, switch to design view, click on the `SqlDataSource`'s smart tag, and choose Configure Data Source.... The Configure Data Source wizard opens, displaying your current connection string. Click Next and the Configure Select Statement dialog is displayed. Click the Advanced button, as shown in Figure 11-10.

Figure 11-9. Running the formatted grid

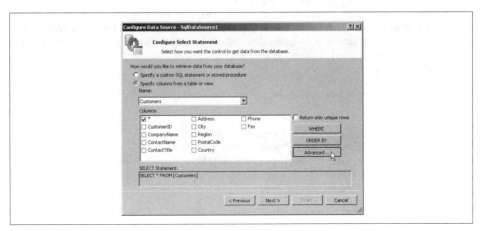

Figure 11-10. Click the Advanced button

This opens the Advanced SQL Generation Options dialog. Click the Generate Insert, Update and Delete statements checkbox, as shown in Figure 11-11.

Clicking this checkbox instructs the wizard to create the remaining three CRUD methods, and it also enables the second checkbox: Use Optimistic Concurrency. Do not check this yet. Click OK, Next, and Finish. You will be asked to update your grid, which, unfortunately, will wipe out all your careful work setting titles, etc., but the good news is that you are now bound to a DataSource control that provides all four CRUD methods. Take a look at the HTML generated for the DataSource control, shown in Example 11-3.

Figure 11-11. Add CRUD methods

Example 11-3. Source code for SQL DataSource with CRUD

```
<asp:SqlDataSource ID="SqlDataSource1"
    runat="server" SelectCommand="SELECT * FROM [Customers]"
    ConnectionString="<%$ ConnectionStrings:NorthwindConnectionString %>"
    DeleteCommand="DELETE FROM [Customers]
    WHERE [CustomerID] = @original_CustomerID"
    InsertCommand="INSERT INTO [Customers] ([CustomerID], [CompanyName], [ContactName],
    [ContactTitle], [Address], [City], [Region], [PostalCode], [Country], [Phone], [Fax])
    VALUES (@CustomerID, @CompanyName, @ContactName, @ContactTitle, @Address, @City,
    @Region, @PostalCode, @Country, @Phone, @Fax)"
    UpdateCommand="UPDATE [Customers] SET [CompanyName] = @CompanyName,
    [ContactName] = @ContactName, [ContactTitle] = @ContactTitle, [Address] = @Address,
    [City] = @City, [Region] = @Region, [PostalCode] = @PostalCode, [Country] = @Country,
    [Phone] = @Phone, [Fax] = @Fax
    WHERE [CustomerID] = @original_CustomerID">
    <DeleteParameters>
        <asp:Parameter Type="String" Name="original_CustomerID" />
    </DeleteParameters>
    <UpdateParameters>
        <asp:Parameter Type="String" Name="CompanyName" />
        <asp:Parameter Type="String" Name="ContactName" />
        <asp:Parameter Type="String" Name="ContactTitle" />
        <asp:Parameter Type="String" Name="Address" />
        <asp:Parameter Type="String" Name="City" />
        <asp:Parameter Type="String" Name="Region" />
        <asp:Parameter Type="String" Name="PostalCode" />
        <asp:Parameter Type="String" Name="Country" />
        <asp:Parameter Type="String" Name="Phone" />
        <asp:Parameter Type="String" Name="Fax" />
        <asp:Parameter Type="String" Name="original_CustomerID" />
    </UpdateParameters>
    <InsertParameters>
        <asp:Parameter Type="String" Name="CustomerID" />
        <asp:Parameter Type="String" Name="CompanyName" />
        <asp:Parameter Type="String" Name="ContactName" />
        <asp:Parameter Type="String" Name="ContactTitle" />
        <asp:Parameter Type="String" Name="Address" />
        <asp:Parameter Type="String" Name="City" />
        <asp:Parameter Type="String" Name="Region" />
        <asp:Parameter Type="String" Name="PostalCode" />
```

Example 11-3. Source code for SQL DataSource with CRUD (continued)

```
            <asp:Parameter Type="String" Name="Country" />
            <asp:Parameter Type="String" Name="Phone" />
            <asp:Parameter Type="String" Name="Fax" />
    </InsertParameters>
</asp:SqlDataSource>
```

Taking this apart, you see first the declaration for the SqlDataSource (and the closing tag at the very bottom). After the ID and the obligatory runat="server" you see four attributes: the SelectCommand (that was there previously) and the new DeleteCommand, InsertCommand, and UpdateCommand.

```
SelectCommand="SELECT * FROM [Customers]"
DeleteCommand="DELETE FROM [Customers]
WHERE [CustomerID] = @original_CustomerID"
InsertCommand="INSERT INTO [Customers] ([CustomerID], [CompanyName], [ContactName],
[ContactTitle], [Address], [City], [Region], [PostalCode], [Country], [Phone], [Fax])
VALUES (@CustomerID, @CompanyName, @ContactName, @ContactTitle, @Address, @City,
@Region, @PostalCode, @Country, @Phone, @Fax)"
UpdateCommand="UPDATE [Customers] SET [CompanyName] = @CompanyName,
[ContactName] = @ContactName, [ContactTitle] = @ContactTitle, [Address] = @Address,
[City] = @City, [Region] = @Region, [PostalCode] = @PostalCode, [Country] = @Country,
[Phone] = @Phone, [Fax] = @Fax
WHERE [CustomerID] = @original_CustomerID">
```

The DeleteCommand takes a single parameter (@original_CustomerID), specified in the DeleteParameters element:

```
<DeleteParameters>
    <asp:Parameter Type="String" Name="original_CustomerID" />
</DeleteParameters>
```

The UpdateCommand requires more parameters, one for each column you'll be updating, as well as a parameter for the original customer ID (to make sure the correct record is updated). Similarly, the InsertCommand takes parameters for each column for the new record. All of these parameters are within the definition of the SQLDataSource.

Multiuser Updates

You may have noticed that I did not ask you to turn on support for optimistic concurrency. You are now going to go back and check this box, but before you do, let's take a moment to put optimistic concurrency in context.

As things stand, you read data from the database and into your data grid through the SqlDataSource. You have now added the ability to update (or delete) that information. Of course, more than one person may be interacting with the database at the same time (few web applications support only single-user access).

You can easily imagine that this could cause tremendous problems of data corruption. Imagine, for example, that two people download a record:

```
Company: Liberty Associates, Inc. / City: Boston / Contact Name: Jesse Liberty
```

The first editor changes the City from Boston to New York. The second person changes the Contact Name from Jesse Liberty to Milo Liberty. Now things get interesting. The first editor writes back the data record, and the database has:

Company: Liberty Associates, Inc. / City: **New York** / Contact Name: Jesse Liberty

A moment later, the second person updates the database and the database now has:

Company: Liberty Associates, Inc. / City: **Boston** / Contact Name: **Milo Liberty**

These earlier updated values are overwritten and lost. The technical term for this is *bad*.

To prevent this kind of problem, you may use any of the following strategies:

Lock the records
> When one user is working with a record, other users can read the records but they cannot update them.

Update only the columns you change
> In the previous example the first editor would have changed only the city, while the second editor would have changed only the name

Update only the records you change
> Preview whether the database has changed before you make your updates. If so, notify the user and don't make the change

Handle the error
> Attempt the change and handle the error, if any.

The following sections explore each of these possible strategies.

Lock the Records

Many databases provide *pessimistic* record-locking. When a user opens a record, it is locked, and no other user may write to that record. For database efficiency, most databases also implement pessimistic page-locking; that is, not only is the particular record locked, but a number of surrounding records are locked as well.

While record and page locking are not uncommon in some database environments, they are generally undesirable, especially in large web applications. It's possible for a user to lock a record, and then never return to the database to unlock it. You would need to write monitoring processes that keep track of how long records have been locked, and unlock records after a time-out period. Yuck.

More important, a single query may touch many records in many tables. If you were to lock all those records for each user, it wouldn't take long before the entire database was locked. In addition, it often isn't necessary. While each user may look at dozens of records, typically each user will update only a very few. Locking is a very big, blunt weapon; what is needed in a web application is a small, delicate surgical tool.

Update Only the Records You Change

This is great in theory but it exposes you to the risk of having a database that is internally consistent but that no longer reflects reality. Here's an example. Suppose two salespeople each check the inventory for a given part. The NumberOnHand value returned to both is 1. The first person makes the sale and sets it to 0. The second person makes the sale and also sets it to zero. The database is perfectly happy, but one or the other customer is not going to get the part, because you can only sell a given part once. To prevent this, you are back to locking records, and we already saw that we don't like that solution.

Compare Original Against New

To understand how to compare the changed records against the database, you must keep in mind three possible values for each of your fields:

- The value currently in the database
- The value that was in the database when you first filled the DataSource
- The value that is now in the DataSource because you have changed it

You could decide that before you make an update, you'll check the record and make sure that it has not changed, and only if it has not changed will you make the update. Unfortunately, this still does not solve the problem. If you look at the database before updating it, there is still the (admittedly small) chance that someone will update the database between the time you peek at it and the time you write your changes. Given enough transactions over enough time, there is certain to be corrupted data.

Handle the Errors

Odd as it may seem at first, it turns out that the best approach to managing concurrency is to try the update with a Where clause that will only succeed if the rows you are updating have not changed since you read them. You then respond to errors as they arise. For this approach to be effective, you must craft your Update statement so that it will fail if someone else has updated the record in *any* way.

This approach has tremendous efficiency advantages. In the vast majority of cases, your update will succeed, and you will not have bothered with extra reads of the database. There is no lag between checking the data and the update, so there is no chance of someone sneaking in another write. Finally, if your update fails, you know why, and you can take corrective action.

For this approach to work, your updates must fail if the data has changed in the database since the time you retrieved the data. Since the DataSource can tell you the original values that it received from the database, you only need to pass those values back into the stored procedure as parameters, and then add them to the Where clause in your Update statement. That is, you must extend your Where statement to say "where each field still has its original value."

When you update the record, the original values are checked against the values in the database. If they are different, you will not update any records until you fix the problem.

Reopen the wizard, but this time makes sure to check both checkboxes, as shown in Figure 11-12.

Figure 11-12. Turn on Optimistic Concurrency

Click OK, Next, and Finish. Once more, examine the source code shown in Example 11-4.

Example 11-4. DataSource control with Optimistic Concurrency

```
<asp:SqlDataSource ID="SqlDataSource1"
    runat="server" SelectCommand="SELECT * FROM [Customers]"
    ConnectionString="<%$ ConnectionStrings:NorthwindConnectionString %>"
    DeleteCommand="DELETE FROM [Customers]
    WHERE [CustomerID] = @original_CustomerID
    AND [CompanyName] = @original_CompanyName
    AND [ContactName] = @original_ContactName
    AND [ContactTitle] = @original_ContactTitle
    AND [Address] = @original_Address
    AND [City] = @original_City
    AND [Region] = @original_Region
    AND [PostalCode] = @original_PostalCode
    AND [Country] = @original_Country
    AND [Phone] = @original_Phone
    AND [Fax] = @original_Fax"
    InsertCommand="INSERT INTO [Customers] ([CustomerID],
    [CompanyName], [ContactName], ContactTitle], [Address], [City], [Region],
    [PostalCode], [Country], [Phone], [Fax])
    VALUES (@CustomerID, @CompanyName, @ContactName, @ContactTitle,
    @Address, @City, @Region, @PostalCode, @Country, @Phone, @Fax)"
    UpdateCommand="UPDATE [Customers] SET [CompanyName] = @CompanyName,
    [ContactName] = @ContactName, [ContactTitle] = @ContactTitle,
    [Address] = @Address, [City] = @City, [Region] = @Region,
    [PostalCode] = @PostalCode, [Country] = @Country, [Phone] = @Phone,
    [Fax] = @Fax
```

Example 11-4. DataSource control with Optimistic Concurrency (continued)

```
    WHERE [CustomerID] = @original_CustomerID
    AND [CompanyName] = @original_CompanyName
    AND [ContactName] = @original_ContactName
    AND [ContactTitle] = @original_ContactTitle AND [Address] = @original_Address
    AND [City] = @original_City AND [Region] = @original_Region
    AND [PostalCode] = @original_PostalCode AND [Country] = @original_Country
    AND [Phone] = @original_Phone AND [Fax] = @original_Fax"
ConflictDetection="CompareAllValues">
    <DeleteParameters>
        <asp:Parameter Type="String" Name="original_CustomerID" />
        <asp:Parameter Type="String" Name="original_CompanyName" />
        <asp:Parameter Type="String" Name="original_ContactName" />
        <asp:Parameter Type="String" Name="original_ContactTitle" />
        <asp:Parameter Type="String" Name="original_Address" />
        <asp:Parameter Type="String" Name="original_City" />
        <asp:Parameter Type="String" Name="original_Region" />
        <asp:Parameter Type="String" Name="original_PostalCode" />
        <asp:Parameter Type="String" Name="original_Country" />
        <asp:Parameter Type="String" Name="original_Phone" />
        <asp:Parameter Type="String" Name="original_Fax" />
    </DeleteParameters>
    <UpdateParameters>
        <asp:Parameter Type="String" Name="CompanyName" />
        <asp:Parameter Type="String" Name="ContactName" />
        <asp:Parameter Type="String" Name="ContactTitle" />
        <asp:Parameter Type="String" Name="Address" />
        <asp:Parameter Type="String" Name="City" />
        <asp:Parameter Type="String" Name="Region" />
        <asp:Parameter Type="String" Name="PostalCode" />
        <asp:Parameter Type="String" Name="Country" />
        <asp:Parameter Type="String" Name="Phone" />
        <asp:Parameter Type="String" Name="Fax" />
        <asp:Parameter Type="String" Name="original_CustomerID" />
        <asp:Parameter Type="String" Name="original_CompanyName" />
        <asp:Parameter Type="String" Name="original_ContactName" />
        <asp:Parameter Type="String" Name="original_ContactTitle" />
        <asp:Parameter Type="String" Name="original_Address" />
        <asp:Parameter Type="String" Name="original_City" />
        <asp:Parameter Type="String" Name="original_Region" />
        <asp:Parameter Type="String" Name="original_PostalCode" />
        <asp:Parameter Type="String" Name="original_Country" />
        <asp:Parameter Type="String" Name="original_Phone" />
        <asp:Parameter Type="String" Name="original_Fax" />
    </UpdateParameters>
    <InsertParameters>
        <asp:Parameter Type="String" Name="CustomerID" />
        <asp:Parameter Type="String" Name="CompanyName" />
        <asp:Parameter Type="String" Name="ContactName" />
        <asp:Parameter Type="String" Name="ContactTitle" />
        <asp:Parameter Type="String" Name="Address" />
        <asp:Parameter Type="String" Name="City" />
        <asp:Parameter Type="String" Name="Region" />
```

Example 11-4. DataSource control with Optimistic Concurrency (continued)

```
            <asp:Parameter Type="String" Name="PostalCode" />
            <asp:Parameter Type="String" Name="Country" />
            <asp:Parameter Type="String" Name="Phone" />
            <asp:Parameter Type="String" Name="Fax" />
        </InsertParameters>
</asp:SqlDataSource>
```

Don't panic! The only difference between Examples 11-3 and 11-4 is that in the latter, the `Where` clause is extended to make sure the record has not been altered. The `DeleteCommand` illustrates this, and the `UpdateCommand` works the same way.

```
DeleteCommand="DELETE FROM [Customers]
WHERE [CustomerID] = @original_CustomerID
AND [CompanyName] = @original_CompanyName
AND [ContactName] = @original_ContactName
AND [ContactTitle] = @original_ContactTitle
AND [Address] = @original_Address
AND [City] = @original_City
AND [Region] = @original_Region
AND [PostalCode] = @original_PostalCode
AND [Country] = @original_Country
AND [Phone] = @original_Phone
AND [Fax] = @original_Fax"
```

You must, therefore, send in not only the parameter for the `customerID` but the original values of these fields:

```
<DeleteParameters>
    <asp:Parameter Type="String" Name="original_CustomerID" />
    <asp:Parameter Type="String" Name="original_CompanyName" />
    <asp:Parameter Type="String" Name="original_ContactName" />
    <asp:Parameter Type="String" Name="original_ContactTitle" />
    <asp:Parameter Type="String" Name="original_Address" />
    <asp:Parameter Type="String" Name="original_City" />
    <asp:Parameter Type="String" Name="original_Region" />
    <asp:Parameter Type="String" Name="original_PostalCode" />
    <asp:Parameter Type="String" Name="original_Country" />
    <asp:Parameter Type="String" Name="original_Phone" />
    <asp:Parameter Type="String" Name="original_Fax" />
</DeleteParameters>
```

All of that work is done for you by the wizard!

Displaying and Updating the Grid

Now that your `DataSource` object is ready to go, you have only to set up your `GridView`:

1. Click on the smart tag and choose Edit Columns, restoring the titles to the way you want (and while you are at it, enable sorting and paging).

2. Click the checkboxes to enable Editing and Deleting, as shown in Figure 11-13.

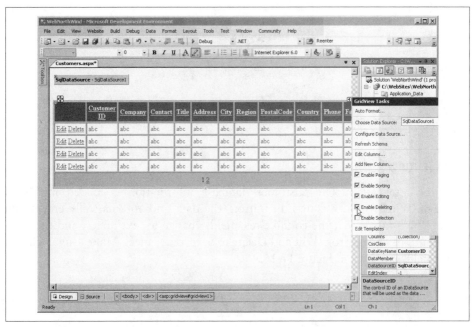

Figure 11-13. Enable Deleting and Editing

If you would prefer to have buttons for Edit and Delete, rather than links, click on the smart tag and click on Edit Columns…. When the fields dialog box opens, click in Selected Fields on the Command Field entry. This brings up the field properties in the righthand window, where you can change the ButtonType from Link to Button, as shown in Figure 11-14.

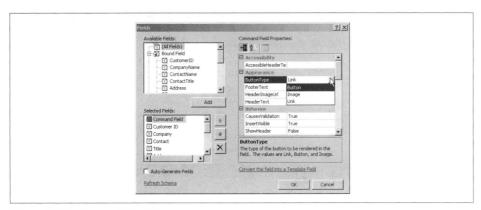

Figure 11-14. Change ButtonType

The result is that the commands (Edit and Delete) are now shown as buttons, as shown in Figure 11-15.

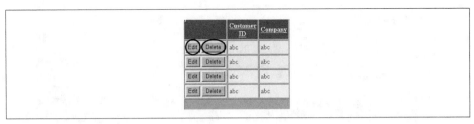

Figure 11-15. Button commands

Take It for a Spin

Start the application. The customer database information is loaded into your `GridView`. When you click the Edit button, the data grid automatically enters Edit mode. You'll notice that the editable text fields change to text boxes, and the command buttons change from Edit and Delete to Save and Cancel. Make a small change to one field, as shown in Figure 11-16.

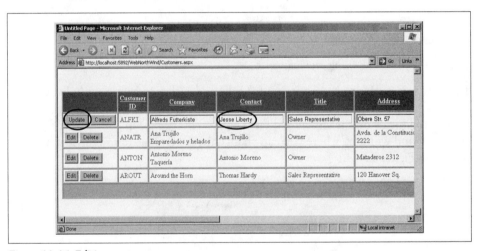

Figure 11-16. Editing

When you click Update, the grid and the database are both updated, as you can confirm by opening the table in the database, shown in Figure 11-17.

Figure 11-17. Updated database table

Tracking the Update with Events

Some programmers get very nervous when a control does so much work invisibly. After all, when all goes well, it is great not to have to sweat the details, but if something goes wrong, how can you tell whether your connection failed, no records were updated, an exception was thrown, or exactly what happened? Related to that, what if you want to modify the behavior of the control in some way?

The ASP.NET controls, in general, and the data controls, in particular, overcome these concerns by providing numerous events that you can handle. For example, the DataGrid has almost two dozen events. There is an event that fires when you press the Save button after editing a row (RowUpdating) and there is a second event that fires after the row has been updated (RowUpdated). There are events for when the data is about to be bound, and when it has been bound, when the row is created, when it is about to be deleted, and when it has been deleted, etc.

For example, after the Grid updates the row for you, the RowUpdated event is fired. To see this at work, create a handler:

1. Click on Design view.
2. Click on the DataGrid.
3. Click on the lightning bolt in the Properties window.
4. Double-click in the method name column (currently blank) to the right of the RowUpdated event.

Visual Studio 2005 will create an event handler named GridView1_RowUpdated and will place you in the code-behind page, within the skeleton of that method.

Notice that the second argument to this method is of type GridViewUpdatedEventArgs. This object has useful information about the update, including a Boolean property: ExceptionHandled, that will be True if an exception was thrown when updating the data. In that case, the GridViewUpdatedEventArgs object also contains the exception object itself.

Another property tells you how many rows were affected by your update (RowsAffected). Three ordered collections tell you what changes have taken place: Keys, OldValues, and NewValues. You can examine these in the debugger to see the values for each column in the row in turn, using the code shown in Example 11-5.

Example 11-5. Handling the RowUpdated event

```
Protected Sub GridView1_RowUpdated( _
    ByVal sender As Object, _
    ByVal e As System.Web.UI.WebControls.GridViewUpdatedEventArgs) _
    Handles GridView1.RowUpdated

    If e.ExceptionHandled = True Then
        Dim ex As String = e.Exception.Message
```

Example 11-5. Handling the RowUpdated event (continued)

```
    Else
        Dim numRowsChanged As Int32 = e.AffectedRows
        Dim returnValue As IOrderedDictionary
        returnValue = e.NewValues
        Dim myDE As DictionaryEntry
        For Each myDE In returnValue
            If myDE.Value IsNot Nothing Then
                Dim key As String = myDE.Key.ToString
                Dim val As String = myDE.Value.ToString
            End If

        Next myDE

    End If
End Sub
```

The `If` block tests to see if an exception was handled, and if so, sets a string (ex) to the value of the `Message` in that exception. You would, presumably, either display this message or log it, and then present the user with options on how to handle the exception.

If no exception has been thrown, you next get the number of rows that were affected, storing it in the local variable numRowsChanged. Again, you would presumably log this number and/or take action if it is zero (it might be zero because of a multiuser update conflict, as explained earlier).

Finally, in the example, you iterate through the `NewValues` collection to see that the values you updated on the grid are, in fact, the values that were in the collection passed back to the database. (Put these in the watch window to see their values as you step through the For Each loop.)

Modifying the Grid Based on Events

Suppose your client would like you to modify the grid so that the contents of the Title column are red when the person listed is the owner of the company. You can do so by handling the RowDataBound event (which fires after each row's data is bound), as shown in Example 11-6.

Example 11-6. Handling the RowDataBound event

```
Protected Sub GridView1_RowDataBound(ByVal sender As Object, _
ByVal e As System.Web.UI.WebControls.GridViewRowEventArgs) _
Handles GridView1.RowDataBound

    ' If the row passed in is a DataRow, and if its text is "OWNER"
    'then display the text in red
    If e.Row.RowType = DataControlRowType.DataRow Then
        Dim cell As TableCell = e.Row.Cells(4)
        If cell.Text.ToUpper( ) = "OWNER" Then
```

Example 11-6. Handling the RowDataBound event (continued)

```
        cell.ForeColor = Drawing.Color.Red
    End If      'end if text = owner
  End If        'end if is DataRow

End Sub
```

The first If statement tests whether the type of the Row passed in as a parameter is a DataRow (rather than a header, footer, separator, etc.):

```
If e.Row.RowType = DataControlRowType.DataRow Then
```

As you set up this test, IntelliSense will show you the various DataControlRowTypes that are available, as you see in Figure 11-18.

```
Protected Sub GridView1_RowDataBound(ByVal sender As Object, _
ByVal e As System.Web.UI.WebControls.GridViewRowEventArgs) _
Handles GridView1.RowDataBound

    ' If the row passed in is a DataRow, and if its text is "OWNER"
    'then display the text in red
    If e.Row.RowType =
                    DataControlRowType.DataRow
                    DataControlRowType.EmptyDataRow
                    DataControlRowType.Footer
                    DataControlRowType.Header
                    DataControlRowType.Pager
                    DataControlRowType.Separator
```

Figure 11-18. Picking the DataControlRowType

Once you know you are dealing with a DataRow, you can extract the cell you want to examine from that row (in this case, Title is the fifth cell, at offset 4).

You are ready to compare the cell's text field to the text string OWNER. If they match, set the forecolor for the cell itself to Red, rendering the word Owner in red.

```
If cell.Text.ToUpper( ) = "OWNER" Then
   cell.ForeColor = Drawing.Color.Red
```

It turns out that the row's Cells collection holds objects of type Table-Cell, but the actual type of the cell within the DataGrid is DataControlFieldCell (which derives from TableCell). If there are properties of DataControlFieldCell that are not available in TableCell (such as Containing Field, which gets the DataControlField that contains the current cell) you may safely cast to the "real" type:

```
Dim cell As DataControlFieldCell = _
    CType(e.Row.Cells(4), DataControlFieldCell)
```

Using IntelliSense to Help You Identify the Type to Declare

One question that might arise is, How do you know that the type of the cell is TableCell? This is another place where the development environment helps you. When you open the parentheses on the Cells collection to place the index, a tooltip opens that not only tells you that the index must be of type integer, and that explains what that index does, but also tells you the return type of the object obtained from the collection, as shown in Figure 11-19.

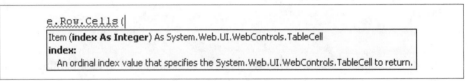

Figure 11-19. Indexing into the Cells Collection—Tooltip

Passing Parameters to the Select Query

Sometimes you do not want to display all the records in a table. For example, you might create a second grid on your current page that would display the Orders for the selected Company. To do so, you'll need a way to select a company, and a way to pass the ID of the selected company to a second grid to display that company's orders.

 To keep the downloadable source code clear, I've created a new web application named WebNorthwindTwoGrids, and used Web site → Copy Web Site to copy over the web site from the prior example, as previously described in Chapter 8.

Step one is to add a Select button on the existing Grid. You can do so by clicking on the smart tag on the grid and checking the Enable Selection checkbox. The grid immediately adds a Select button to the first cell, alongside Edit and Delete, as shown in Figure 11-20.

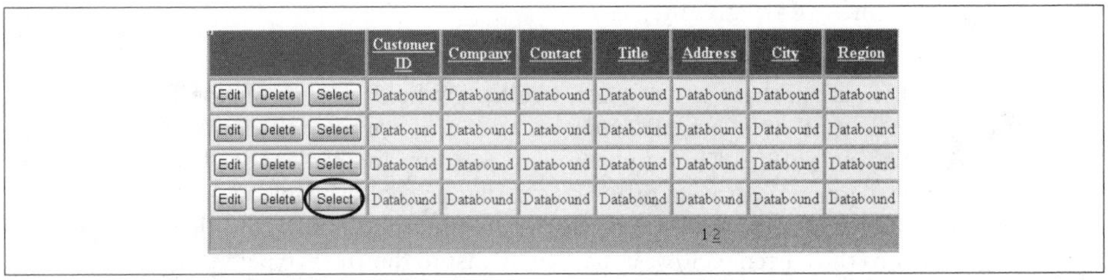

Figure 11-20. Adding the Select button

Step two is to create a second GridView object, that will be used to display the Orders. Drag the second grid onto the page, then open its smart tag. Create a new data source, but use the existing connection string. Choose all columns from the Orders table, then click the Where button, as shown in Figure 11-21.

The Add Where Clause dialog opens, as shown in Figure 11-22.

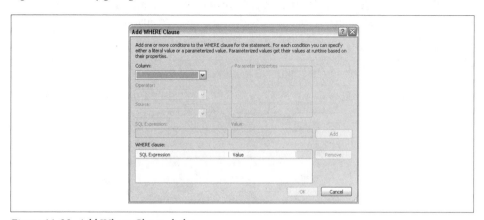

Figure 11-21. Configuring the Orders table

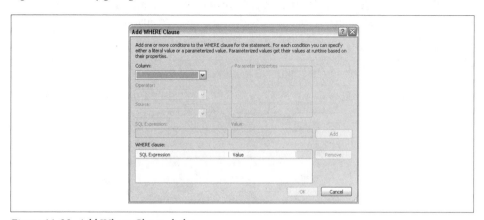

Figure 11-22. Add Where Clause dialog

Pick the column you want to match on; in this case, CustomerID, then pick the operator, which can be equals, less than/greater than, like, contains, etc. In this case, you'll use the default (=).

The third drop-down list lets you pick the source for the CustomerID. You can pick none if you will be providing a source, or you can obtain the source from the form, from a user's profile, from a QueryString or from Session state. In this case, however, you'll obtain the source of the CustomerID from the first GridView, so choose Control.

When you choose Control, the Parameter Properties window wakes up. You are asked to provide the ID of the Control providing the parameter; in this case, GridView1 and (optionally) a default value. Once you've made all your choices, the dialog will look like Figure 11-23.

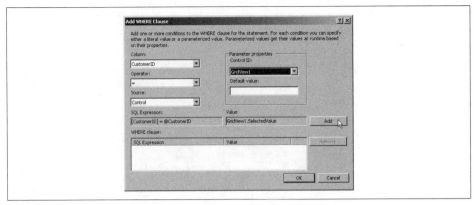

Figure 11-23. Adding a Where Clause

Now click add. When you do, the upper portion of the dialog returns to its initial (blank) state and the Where clause is added to the Where clause window, as shown in Figure 11-24.

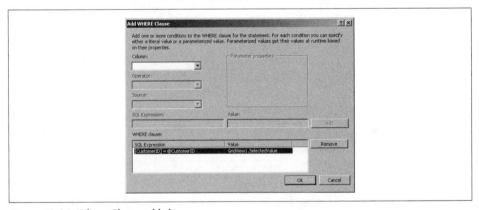

Figure 11-24. Where Clause added

Click OK until you are back at the Configure Select Statement dialog. While you are there, sort the results by the OrderDate column. You do this by clicking on the Order By button, which brings up the Add Order By Clause dialog, as shown in Figure 11-25.

After you finish creating this DataSource control, switch to Source view and look at the declaration created by Visual Studio 2005, as shown in Example 11-7.

Figure 11-25. Add Order By clause

Example 11-7. DataSource control source

```
<asp:SqlDataSource
ID="NorthWindOrders"
runat="server"
ConnectionString="<%$ ConnectionStrings:NorthwindConnectionString %>"
SelectCommand="SELECT * FROM [Orders]
WHERE ([CustomerID] = @CustomerID)
ORDER BY [OrderDate]">
    <SelectParameters>
        <asp:ControlParameter
        Name="CustomerID"
        ControlID="GridView1"
        PropertyName="SelectedValue"
        Type="String" />
    </SelectParameters>
</asp:SqlDataSource>
```

The Select statement now has a Where clause that includes a parameterized value (@CustomerID). In addition, within the definition of the DataSource is a definition of the SelectParameters, which includes one parameter of type asp:ControlParameter— that is, a parameter that knows how to get its value from a control. The asp: ControlParameter has a property, ControlID, that tells it which control to check for its value, and a second property, PropertyName, that tells it which property in the Grid to check. There is also a third property Type that tells it that the type of the value it is getting is of type String, so that it can properly pass that parameter to the Select statement.

You may now reformat your grid. Rebuild and run the application. Try out your new page; it should look something like Figure 11-26.

As you click on each Select button in the upper grid, the orders for that customer are displayed in the lower grid.

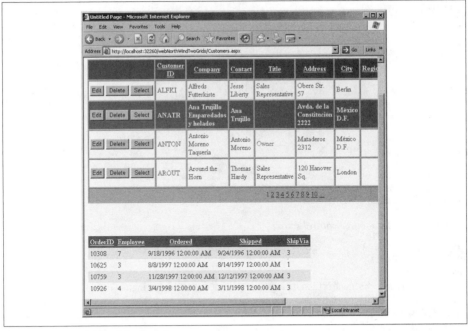

Figure 11-26. Order grid displayed

The DataList Control

The toolbox provides a `DataList` control for creating *templated* lists of data. A templated list is one in which you control the HTML used to render the list by defining templates: each template describes how to display one item in the list.

> `DataList` controls provide fairly simple templates; if you need very precise control of the layout, consider using the `Repeater` control.

To get started create a new web site called webNorthWindDataControls and copy the web site named WebNorthWind. Add a web form to your application named DataControls. Right-click on *DataControls.aspx* in the Solution explorer, and make it the start page for your application.

Switch to Design view and drag a `DataList` control onto *Datacontrols.aspx*. Notice that the smart tag opens, offering you an opportunity to choose a data source. Choose New Data Source and for this exercise, choose SQL Database, naming the new data source `DataListCustomerDataSources`. Use your existing connection to

Northwind, and specify that you want all the fields in the Customers table. When you finish, the DataList is populated with labels that represent the field names, and labels that are bound to the data control, as shown in Figure 11-27.

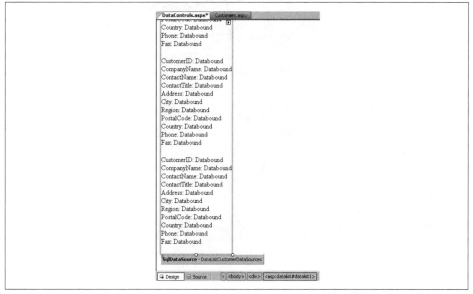

Figure 11-27. DataList bound to SQL data control

If you click on Source, you will see that the DataList has been defined with a number of attributes to identify its data source, as shown in Example 11-8.

Example 11-8. DataList control source

```
<asp:DataList
ID="DataList1"
runat="server"
DataKeyField="CustomerID"
DataSourceID="DataListCustomerDataSources">
```

Between the opening and closing tags of the DataList is an ItemTemplate tag that defines how each item will be displayed.

Click on the DataList's smart tag and choose Edit Templates. The ItemTemplate (the default) is opened, as shown in Figure 11-28.

Each column is represented as text, and the bound value is represented by a label. Click End Template Editing and examine the source produced. The label is populated using the Eval method on a column from the underlying data, as shown in Example 11-9.

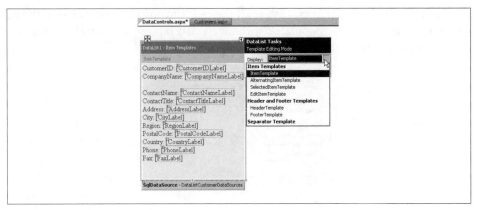

Figure 11-28. ItemTemplate editor

Example 11-9. Label control source

```
<asp:Label
    Text='<%# Eval("CustomerID") %>'
    runat="server"
    ID="CustomerIDLabel">
</asp:Label>
```

 Eval returns the value of the underlying data in the column whose name is passed in as a string.

There are a number of ways to improve the look and feel of this control. First, you can return to Design view, and click the Auto Format… link to choose a scheme (e.g., Classic). Doing so adds a number of styles to the DataList (after the opening tag but before the ItemTemplate tag).

```
<FooterStyle ForeColor="White" Font-Bold="True" BackColor="#507CD1" />
<SelectedItemStyle ForeColor="#333333" Font-Bold="True" BackColor="#D1DDF1" />
<AlternatingItemStyle BackColor="White" />
<ItemStyle BackColor="#EFF3FB" />
<HeaderStyle ForeColor="White" Font-Bold="True" BackColor="#507CD1" />
```

Once again you may return to the smart tag, and again choose Edit Templates. You are returned to Template Editing Mode (which continues until you click the link End Template Editing), and you may edit the layout of the template in any way you choose. Notice that there are different templates for Items, SelectedItems, and EditItems—so that you can display data as labels in Item mode, but as (for example) text boxes or drop-down lists in Edit mode, as shown in Figure 11-29. You can hand populate the EditItemTemplate (dragging in labels, text boxes, and drop-down lists) or, you can create the EditItemTemplate by ending Template editing and switching to Source view.

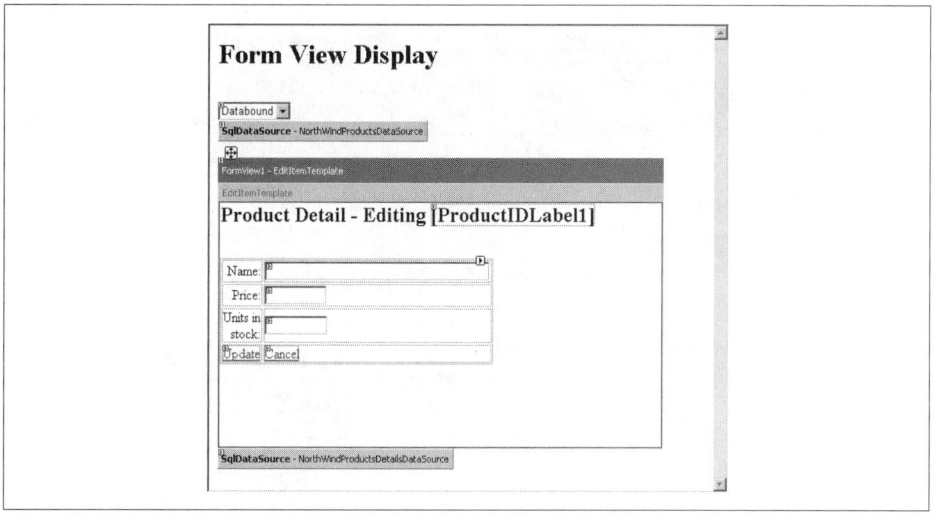

Figure 11-29. EditItem template

Copy the entire <ItemTemplate> section and in the copy, change the name from ItemTemplate to EditItemTemplate. Now modify the contents of the template by changing labels to text boxes. You can switch back and forth between editing in Source view and editing in the template Design view.

Organizing the Flow of the DataList

By default, each item is displayed below the next, in a vertical column. You may modify this by setting the RepeatDirection property of the DataList from Vertical to Horizontal and by setting the number of columns by setting the RepeatColumns property, as shown in Figure 11-30.

Editing Items in List Controls

To switch to the EditItemTemplate, you'll want a way to enter and to exit editing once the user has made changes. The easiest way is to drag buttons directly into the template form. For example, you might drag two buttons onto the ItemTemplate form. Set the ID for the first to ItemEditButton and for the second to ItemDeleteButton. Set the Text property appropriately (e.g., Edit and Delete), but be sure to set the CommandName property carefully. The Edit button's CommandName must be set to edit (case sensitive), and the Delete button's CommandName property must be set to delete. Setting the CommandName properly will cause the appropriate event to fire (e.g., the EditCommand event) for which you can create handlers (CancelCommand, EditCommand, UpdateCommand, DeleteCommand).

The easiest way to create the EditCommand, UpdateCommand, DeleteCommand, and CancelCommand event handlers is from Design view. Click on the DataList control; in

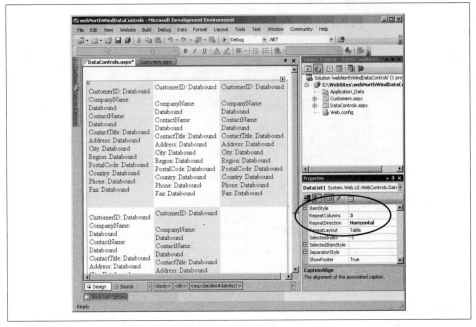

Figure 11-30. DataList column layout

the Properties window click on the lightning bolt to bring up the list of events, and you'll find the various commands. You can double-click as usual to have Visual Studio 2005 help you set up the event handlers.

The edit command and the delete command event handlers both receive a `DataListCommandEventArgs` object as their second parameter. The `DataListCommand-EventArgs` contains an `Item` property, representing the list item the user wants to edit (or delete). The `DataListItem` returned by the `Item` property, in turn, has an `ItemIndex` property, which, in the case of editing, you'll assign to the `EditItemIndex` property of the `DataList`. You'll then rebind the `DataList`. These changes are shown in Example 11-10.

Example 11-10. Edit command event handler
```
Protected Sub DataList1_EditCommand( _
ByVal source As Object, _
ByVal e As System.Web.UI.WebControls.DataListCommandEventArgs) _
Handles DataList1.EditCommand
    DataList1.EditItemIndex = e.Item.ItemIndex
    DataBind( )
End Sub
```

As you can see, it sounds harder than it is!

When you switch to Edit view, you'll want to have both a Save and a Cancel button. You'll need to add those buttons to the `EditItemTemplate`, either in Source view, as shown in Example 11-11 or by switching to Design view and dragging buttons into the EditItemTemplate.

Example 11-11. Save and Cancel button source

```
<asp:Button
    ID="ItemSaveButton"
    Text="Save"
    runat="server"
    CommandName="Update" />
<asp:Button
    ID="ItemCancelButton"
    Text="Cancel"
    runat="server"
    CommandName="Cancel" />
```

Notice the CommandName properties. These must be set to Update and Cancel (initial cap), respectively. Switch to Design view and click on the DataList itself. In the Properties window, click on the lightning bolt and you'll find both a CancelCommand and an UpdateCommand. Double-clicking on the space for the command name will create default command names and the skeletons for the event handlers. For example, you might implement the Cancel command, as shown in Example 11-12.

Example 11-12. Cancel command event handler

```
Protected Sub DataList1_CancelCommand( _
ByVal source As Object, _
ByVal e As System.Web.UI.WebControls.DataListCommandEventArgs) _
Handles DataList1.CancelCommand
    DataList1.EditItemIndex = -1
    DataBind( )
End Sub
```

The code to implement the Update command will be more complex, requiring that you read through the controls and update the appropriate fields in the database. For now, you can stub it out with the same code you use in the Cancel command.

Run the application and click the Edit button. You'll see the selected item switch to your EditItemTemplate view, as shown in Figure 11-31.

You can, of course, use other kinds of controls besides text boxes. For example, for some data items, a set of radio buttons or a checkbox might be a more appropriate choice. If you wish to control the data entry, you might use a drop-down list that is, itself, bound to data (perhaps from another table in the database).

Deleting Items from a List Control

To allow your user to delete a record, let's return to the Delete button you added to the ItemTemplate.

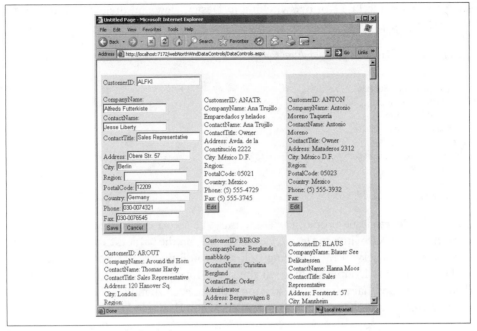

Figure 11-31. DataList in Edit mode

You'll need to drag another DataSource control onto the page to handle the Delete command (name it DataListCustomerDeleteDataSource). Configure the DataSource as you have previously, setting it up to select all the fields of the Customers table.

Next, set the Delete command by clicking on the DeleteQuery property, as shown in Figure 11-32.

Clicking the ellipsis shown in Figure 11-32 opens the Command and Parameter Editor in Figure 11-33.

Enter the Delete command:

```
Delete from Customers where CustomerID = @CustomerID
```

Click the Add Parameter button to add the parameter you'll need for the Delete command. Rename the parameter CustomerID and set its Parameter source to None and its Default Value to blank, as shown in Figure 11-33.

The complete source code for your new SQLDataSource object should look like Example 11-13.

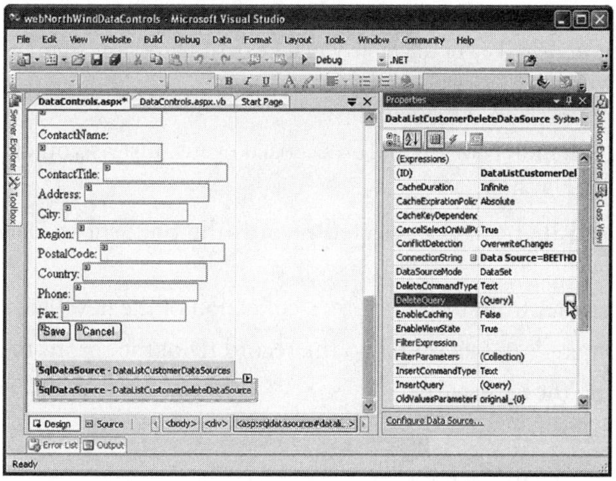

Figure 11-32. Creating the Delete query

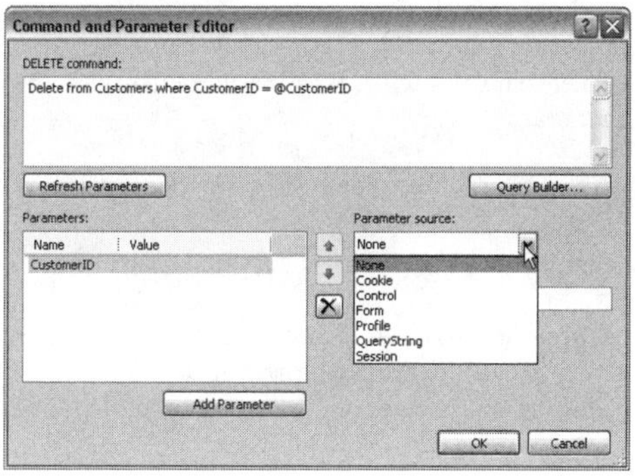

Figure 11-33. Command and Parameter Editor

Example 11-13. SQLDataSource source code

```
<asp:SqlDataSource
ID="DataListCustomerDeleteDataSource"
runat="server"
ConnectionString="<%$ ConnectionStrings:NorthwindConnectionString %>"
SelectCommand="Select * from Customers"
DeleteCommand="Delete from Customers where CustomerID = @CustomerID">
    <DeleteParameters>
        <asp:Parameter Name="CustomerID" />
    </DeleteParameters>
</asp:SqlDataSource>
```

Make sure you set the DataKeyField property of the DataList control to the primary key of the table you'll be deleting records from (it should already be set to CustomerID).

Create your event handler for the DeleteCommand event, just as you created a handler for the Edit event. The steps are:

1. Get the record ID from the selected record (the one whose Delete button was pushed).

2. Get the parameter from the Parameters collection of the new DataSource object.

3. Set the parameter's DefaultValue to the record ID of the record to be deleted.

4. Call Delete on the DataSource.

5. Rebind the DataList.

These steps are shown in Example 11-14.

Example 11-14. Deleting a record from a DataList

```
Protected Sub DataList1_DeleteCommand( _
ByVal source As Object, _
ByVal e As System.Web.UI.WebControls.DataListCommandEventArgs) _
Handles DataList1.DeleteCommand

    ' (1) Get the recordID from the selected item (a string)
    Dim recordID As String = _
        DataList1.DataKeys.Item(e.Item.ItemIndex).ToString( )

    ' (2) Get a reference to the CustomerID parameter
    Dim param As System.Web.UI.WebControls.Parameter = _
        DataListCustomerDeleteDataSource.DeleteParameters("CustomerID")

    ' (3) Set the parameter's default value to the value for
    ' the record to delete
    param.DefaultValue = recordID

    ' (4) Delete the record
    DataListCustomerDeleteDataSource.Delete( )

    ' (5) Rebind the list
    DataBind( )
End Sub
```

The first line is a bit tricky; let's break this out into a number of substeps to make it easier to understand:

```
Dim recordID As String = _
    DataList1.DataKeys.Item(e.Item.ItemIndex).ToString( )
```

You are given a `DataListCommandEventArgs` object (e) as a parameter. That `DataListCommandEventArgs` instance has an `Item` property of type `DataListItem`, which you can assign to a variable `theItem`.

```
' get the Item property from the parameter
Dim theItem As DataListItem = e.Item
```

You can ask that `DataListItem` for its `ItemIndex` (the index into the list for the selected item):

```
' get the itemIndex from the Item
Dim itemIndex As Integer = theItem.ItemIndex
```

Next, you can ask the `DataList` for its collection of `DataKeys`. Remember that you set the `DataKeyField` attribute of the list:

```
<asp:DataList
    DataKeyField="CustomerID"
```

so this collection contains all the `CustomerIDs`, one for each row:

```
' Get the DataKeys collection from the Data List
Dim keyCollection As DataKeyCollection = DataList1.DataKeys
```

With a reference to that collection and the index, you can extract the contents of the key collection at that index. Remember that what you get back is of type `Object`:

```
' Get the object stored at the ItemIndex inside the collection
Dim theRecordAsObject As Object = keyCollection(itemIndex)
```

You know that what you have is a string, so you can cast that returned object to string:

```
' Cast the result from object to string
Dim recordID As String = theRecordAsObject.ToString( )
```

All of this work is combined in the first line of the method:

```
Dim recordID As String = _
    DataList1.DataKeys.Item(e.Item.ItemIndex).ToString( )
```

The second line asks the `DataListCustomerDeleteDataSource` to index into its `DeleteParameters` for the parameter whose name is `CustomerID` and return a reference to that parameter:

```
Dim param As System.Web.UI.WebControls.Parameter = _
    DataListCustomerDeleteDataSource.DeleteParameters("CustomerID")
```

You can also search using an ordinal, so you could rewrite this line as:

```
Dim param As System.Web.UI.WebControls.Parameter = _
    DataListCustomerDeleteDataSource.DeleteParameters(0)
```

Using the name of the parameter is clearer, however.

The third line sets the `DefaultValue` property of this parameter to the `recordID` you extracted earlier, the fourth line calls the Delete method on the `DataSource` and the final line rebinds the control, now missing the record you've deleted.

Trying It Out

If you try this, however, it will almost certainly fail. The problem is that almost all the customer records have orders associated with them, and the Northwind database is set up to prevent deleting any customer who has associated orders (a good practice, to avoid data corruption).

You can work around this by creating a new customer, as shown in Figure 11-34.

Figure 11-34. Creating a dummy record

Once this record is added, place a break point on the first line of your new event handler (DataList1_DeleteCommand) and run the application. Scroll down to the new record you've added and click the Delete button, as shown in Figure 11-35.

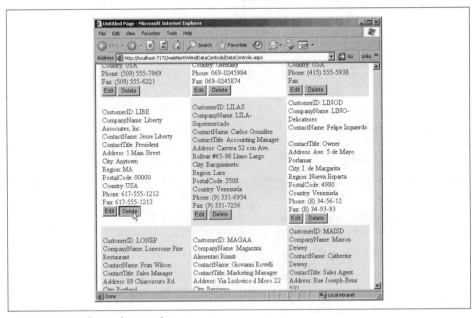

Figure 11-35. Deleting the record

Once the button is clicked, your application will stop at the break point you've set. As you step through, you can see that the record ID retrieved matches the record that you've asked to delete, and once the method completes, you can scroll down and see that the record has, in fact, been deleted (which you can also verify directly in the database).

Examining One Record at a Time: The DetailsView

Another way to look at your data is one record at a time. The Toolbox offers a control explicitly for this purpose: the DetailsView. Create a new page in your application (*DetailsView.aspx*) and drag a DetailsView object onto the page. Make *DetailsView.aspx* your new start page.

The smart tag will open and will offer you the opportunity to create a new DataSource. Call this one CustomersDetailsViewDataSource, and set it to get all the records in the Customers table. Use the Autoformat... smart tag menu choice on the DetailsView control to pick a nice color scheme, check the Enable Paging checkbox so that you can page through the records, and run the application.

It is easy to customize the UI for this control, using style properties (e.g., HeaderStyle, RowStyle, etc.) as well as by using templates.

In addition, you can set the AutoGenerateEditButton property to True, and the control will automatically render an Edit button.

Build and run the application. When you press the Edit button, the control enters Edit mode, and the currentMode property changes from ReadOnly to Edit. Each field of the control is rendered in its Edit User interface (which can be customized using styles and templates), as shown in Figure 11-36.

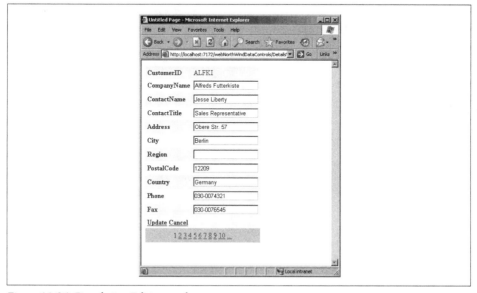

Figure 11-36. Detail view Editing mode

Notice that the edit text boxes were created for you automatically, as were the links for Update and Cancel. If you set the DataSource to create the Update and Delete commands (using the Advanced button in the configuration dialogs), the Update link works with no additional code. In addition, the wizard also generates the code to create the Insert and Delete buttons, as shown in the attributes of the DetailsView in Example 11-15.

Example 11-15. DetailsView control source

```
<asp:DetailsView
ID="DetailsView1"
runat="server"
Height="50px"
Width="125px"
DataSourceID="CustomersDetailsViewDataSource"
AutoGenerateRows="False"
DataKeyNames="CustomerID"
ForeColor="#333333" GridLines="None"
CellPadding="4" AllowPaging="True"
AutoGenerateEditButton="True"
AutoGenerateDeleteButton="True"
AutoGenerateInsertButton="True">
    <FooterStyle ForeColor="White" Font-Bold="True" BackColor="#990000" />
    <CommandRowStyle Font-Bold="True" BackColor="#FFFFC0" />
    <RowStyle ForeColor="#333333" BackColor="#FFFBD6" />
    <PagerStyle ForeColor="#333333" HorizontalAlign="Center"
    BackColor="#FFCC66" />
    <Fields>
        <asp:BoundField ReadOnly="True" HeaderText="CustomerID"
        DataField="CustomerID" SortExpression="CustomerID"/>
        <asp:BoundField HeaderText="CompanyName"
        DataField="CompanyName" SortExpression="CompanyName"/>
        <asp:BoundField HeaderText="ContactName"
        DataField="ContactName" SortExpression="ContactName"/>
        <asp:BoundField HeaderText="ContactTitle"
        DataField="ContactTitle" SortExpression="ContactTitle"/>
        <asp:BoundField HeaderText="Address"
        DataField="Address" SortExpression="Address" />
        <asp:BoundField HeaderText="City"
        DataField="City" SortExpression="City" />
        <asp:BoundField HeaderText="Region"
        DataField="Region" SortExpression="Region" />
        <asp:BoundField HeaderText="PostalCode"
        DataField="PostalCode" SortExpression="PostalCode" />
        <asp:BoundField HeaderText="Country"
        DataField="Country" SortExpression="Country" />
        <asp:BoundField HeaderText="Phone"
        DataField="Phone" SortExpression="Phone" />
        <asp:BoundField HeaderText="Fax"
        DataField="Fax" SortExpression="Fax" />
    </Fields>
    <FieldHeaderStyle Font-Bold="True" />
```

Example 11-15. DetailsView control source (continued)

```
    <HeaderStyle ForeColor="White" Font-Bold="True" BackColor="#990000" />
    <AlternatingRowStyle BackColor="White" />
</asp:DetailsView>
```

Examining Single Records with FormView (Master/Detail)

An alternative to the `DetailsView` is the `FormView`, which is built entirely with templates and, thus, gives you even greater control over the look and feel of the data. To demonstrate this, the next exercise will display details from the Products table, and will navigate to a specific record based on a value chosen by the user from a drop-down list of products.

Begin by creating a new page. Call it Products and make it your new start page.

Drag a drop-down list control from the Toolbox onto the form. Set its `ID` to `ddlProducts`. You'll note that the smart tag opens. Choose New Data Source, and for this exercise, name the new `DataSource` `NorthWindProductsDataSource`. You may use your existing connection, and choose the Product Name (to display) and the product ID (to identify which product was selected), as shown in Figure 11-37.

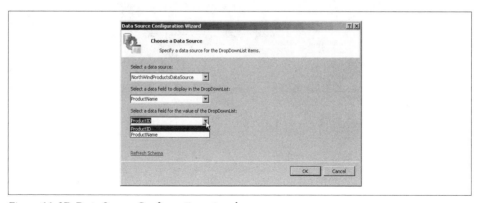

Figure 11-37. Data Source Configuration wizard

Don't forget to click AutoPostBack in the smart tag or in the Properties window to ensure that when the user makes a selection in the drop-down list, the page is posted back to the server for processing. You may want to run the application to test that the drop-down list is properly filled, as shown in Figure 11-38. Select a product, then watch to make sure the page is posted back and that the drop-down list is filled with the name of the selected product when the page is redrawn.

With the drop-down list working, you are now ready to drag a Form View control onto the form. Using the Form View's smart tag, create a new data source, this time named `NorthWindProductsDetailsDataSource`. Select the product details, as shown in Figure 11-39.

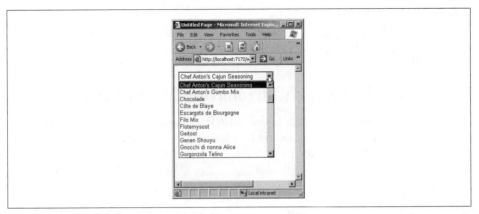

Figure 11-38. Testing the drop-down list

Figure 11-39. Configure Products data source

You want to display product details only for the product chosen by the user. Click the Where button to set the parameters for the Where clause. This brings up the Add Where Clause button. Set the column to ProductID and the Source to control. Set the ControlID to the name of the drop-down list (ddlProducts), and click Add to add the Where clause, as shown in Figure 11-40.

Click OK.

You'll want the control to support inserting and deleting records, as well as updating records. Click the Advanced button and Generate Insert, Update, and Delete statements, then click OK.

Finally, click Next and Finish to complete the configuration of the DataSource.

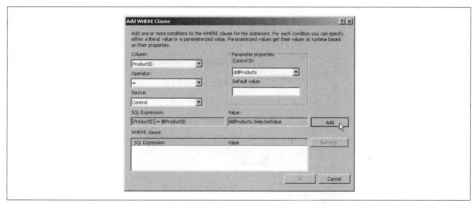

Figure 11-40. Adding drop-down list Where clause

Unlike the DetailsView, the FormView's display is entirely controlled by templates that you can modify using standard ASP.NET and HTML controls. Before editing the templates, switch to Source view and edit the page to type in a header just below the opening <div> tag: Product View Display, and set it to Heading 1.

```
<h1> Product View Display</h1>
```

Next, open the smart tag (or right-click on the control) and choose Edit Templates. The first template to edit is the ItemTemplate. You can click on the template box itself and grab the resizing handles to make it wider and taller.

Click in the top of the Item template, and hit enter a few times to make some room. Then type a heading such as Product Details. Select the title and set it to Heading 2 using the Toolbar, as shown in Figure 11-41.

Previously, you laid out the controls in a template by stacking them one over the other. Most web designers will use tables to control layout, and you can do so from within the template itself.

Click the menu choice Layout → Insert Table. In the Insert table dialog, set the Custom Layout to 5 rows (one for each of ProductID, ProductName, UnitPrice, Units in Stock, and the Edit/Delete/New buttons), and set two columns (one for display and one for the label). Set the cell width to 50 pixels and the cell height to 30 pixels, as shown in Figure 11-42.

Click OK.

To set the prompt for the productID just type *ID* into the upper-left cell. Then click and drag the ProductIDLabel control into the upper righthand cell. Your first row is now laid out with precision.

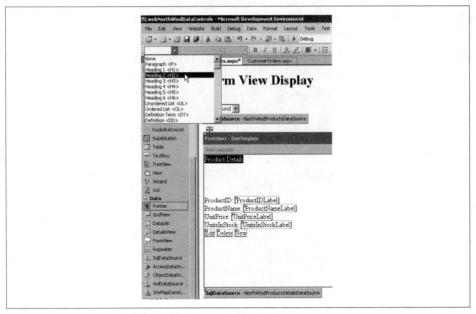

Figure 11-41. Setting the Product view ItemTemplate heading

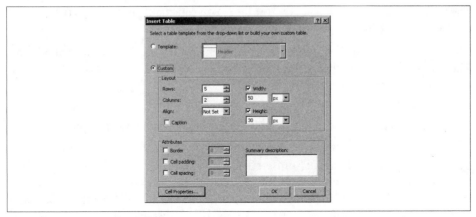

Figure 11-42. Insert Table dialog

Similarly, drag the `ProductNameLabel` control into the second row's righthand cell, and put a prompt (`Product:`) in the cell to its left. Do the same with the two remaining label controls.

To right align the prompts, click to highlight the left column, and then set the Align property in the Properties window. Be sure to expand the righthand column (highlight and then drag the column) to make room for large product names, as shown in Figure 11-43.

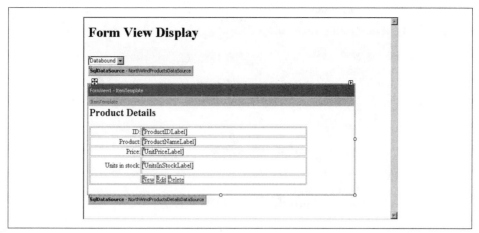

Figure 11-43. Editing the Product Item template

When the template is set the way you want, click on the smart tag and choose End Editing Templates.

Examine the source in Example 11-16. Everything you've done with wizards is reflected here, and you can, of course, edit the source directly.

Example 11-16. FormView control source

```
<asp:FormView
ID="FormView1"
runat="server"
DataSourceID="NorthWindProductsDetailsDataSource"
DataKeyNames="ProductID"
Width="410px">
```

Within the FormView (between the opening tag shown earlier, and the closing tag much later in the file) you'll find a series of ItemTemplates. The first dictates how the item should look when you first see it (not editing, etc.), as shown in Example 11-17.

Example 11-17. ItemTemplate source

```
<ItemTemplate>
    <h2>Product Details</h2>
    <table>
        <tr>
            <td style="width: 120px" align="right">
                ID:
            </td>
            <td style="width: 391px">
                <asp:Label ID="ProductIDLabel" runat="server"
                Text='<%# Eval("ProductID") %>' />
            </td>
        </tr>
        <tr>
```

Example 11-17. ItemTemplate source (continued)

```
            <td style="width: 120px" align="right">
                Product:
            </td>
            <td style="width: 391px">
                <asp:Label ID="ProductNameLabel" runat="server"
                Text='<%# Bind("ProductName") %>' />
            </td>
        </tr>
        <tr>
            <td style="width: 120px" align="right">
                Price:
            </td>
            <td style="width: 391px">
                <asp:Label ID="UnitPriceLabel" runat="server"
                Text='<%# Bind("UnitPrice") %>' />
            </td>
        </tr>
        <tr>
            <td style="width: 120px; height: 40px" align="right">
                Units in stock:
            </td>
            <td style="width: 391px; height: 40px">
                <asp:Label ID="UnitsInStockLabel" runat="server"
                Text='<%# Bind("UnitsInStock") %>' />
            </td>
        </tr>
        <tr>
            <td style="width: 120px; height: 21px" align="right">
            </td>
            <td style="width: 391px; height: 21px">
                <asp:LinkButton ID="NewButton"
                runat="server" Text="New"
                CommandName="New" />
                <asp:LinkButton ID="EditButton"
                runat="server" Text="Edit"
                CommandName="Edit" />
                <asp:LinkButton ID="DeleteButton"
                runat="server" Text="Delete"
                CommandName="Delete" />
            </td>
        </tr>
    </table>
</ItemTemplate>
```

Run the application to see how the items look. They should resemble what's shown in Figure 11-44.

Notice that the FormView includes links to create new records, edit records, or delete records. When you click Edit, the FormView will automatically enter Edit mode (you do not have to write code to make this happen), as shown in Figure 11-45. I've changed item 43 to my favorite coffee and set its price at something a bit more reasonable.

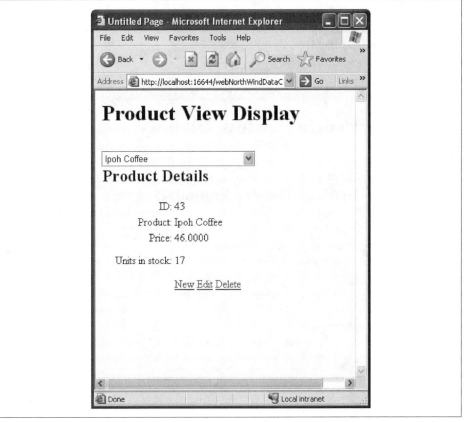

Figure 11-44. Testing the FormView display

You can check that the database was properly updated by returning to Visual Studio 2005, opening the database, and examining the products table, as shown in Figure 11-46.

Inserting New Records

Just as clicking Edit in the FormView put you in Edit mode and used the EditItems template, clicking New puts you in Insert mode, and uses the InsertItems template to insert items into the database.

Updating the Drop-Down List

When you change the name of a product, or add a new product, you want those changes reflected in the drop-down list. So you'll want to update the drop-down control after each edit. To do so, you'll handle the ItemInserted and the ItemUpdated events of the FormView to rebind the drop-down list with the new data, as shown in Example 11-18.

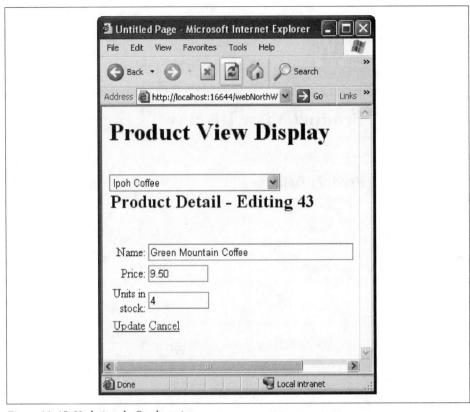

Figure 11-45. Updating the Product view

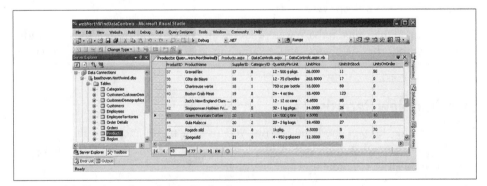

Figure 11-46. Checking the update in the database

Example 11-18. ItemInserted and ItemUpdated event handlers

```
Protected Sub FormView1_ItemInserted( _
ByVal sender As Object, _
ByVal e As System.Web.UI.WebControls.FormViewInsertedEventArgs) _
Handles FormView1.ItemInserted
```

Example 11-18. ItemInserted and ItemUpdated event handlers (continued)

```
    ddlProducts.DataBind( )
End Sub

Protected Sub FormView1_ItemUpdated( _
ByVal sender As Object, _
ByVal e As System.Web.UI.WebControls.FormViewUpdatedEventArgs) _
Handles FormView1.ItemUpdated
    ddlProducts.DataBind( )
End Sub
```

To test this, edit Green Mountain Coffee again (set its name to Green Mountain French Roast) and click Update. Notice that Green Mountain Coffee is no longer in the drop-down list, but Green Mountain French Roast is, as shown in Figure 11-47.

Figure 11-47. Drop-down menu updated

CHAPTER 12

Personalization

One of the hallmarks of a professional web site is the ability for users to *personalize* the site to their individual needs. Personalization means that the site remembers the user and the user's preferences, profile information, and so forth.

In addition to allowing users to personalize your site, you may want to limit their access based on their identity. To accomplish this, you may want your users to "log in." While you can use Windows security on an intranet, the harder task has always been to create a complete authentication and authorization system for Internet applications where you can't know in advance who will be logging in. This is called forms-based security, and Visual Basic 2005 makes it a snap, with a ready-to-go set of controls and a complete database for managing both your users login information and their preferences.

Implementing Forms-Based Security

To begin, create a new web application named FormsBasedSecurity. Click on Web-Site → ASP.NET Configuration to open the Web Site Administration Tool (WAT). Click on the Security tab, as shown in Figure 12-1.

Under Users, click on the link "Select authentication" and choose "From the Internet" as opposed to "From a local network." Then click the Done button. When you return to the Security tab, you'll find that the Users section has changed considerably, as shown in Figure 12-2.

Click on Create User and create one user for your site, as shown in Figure 12-3.

Figure 12-1. Web Site Administration Tool

Figure 12-2. User's section

 By default, passwords must be "strong," which is defined as having at least six characters and including at least one element of at least three of the four types of characters: English upper case, English lower case, Arabic numerals, and special characters (e.g., !, @, etc.). This is fully documented in the MSDN article "Strong Password Enforcement."

The CreateUserWizard has a PasswordRegularExpression property that allows you to substitute your own regular expression to determine the characteristics of acceptable passwords.

When you click the Create User button, you will receive confirmation that the user has been created. Click the Back button and you are returned to the WAT, which reports faithfully that one user has been created. Close the WAT for now.

The user has been added to the SqlExpress personalization database, as we'll explore in depth next. For an alternative approach, using IIS rather than the WAT, see the section "Creating the User Through IIS."

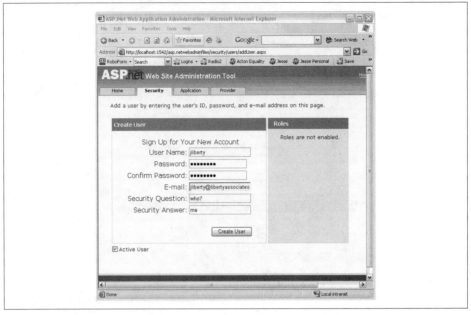

Figure 12-3. Creating the first user

Creating the User Through IIS

As an alternative to using the WAT, you can work through IIS to create the same effect.

To begin, create an new empty directory called FormsBasedSecurityIIS.

In IIS manager (accessed through the control panel), create a virtual directory named FormsBasedSecurityIIS, as shown in Figure 12-4.

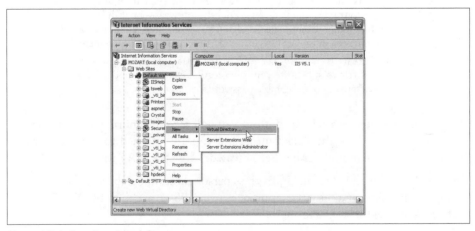

Figure 12-4. Creating virtual directory

Give the new virtual directory the alias "FormsBasedSecurityIIS" and on the second step of the wizard, browse to the physical FormsBasedSecurityIIS folder you just created. After the virtual directory is created, click Properties.

In the Properties window, click on the ASP.NET tab, and then click Edit Configuration. Within the Configuration settings dialog, click on the Authentication tab. Within that tab, set the Authentication mode to Forms, as shown in Figure 12-5. Confirm that the Membership provider class is set to AspNetSqlMembershipProvider.

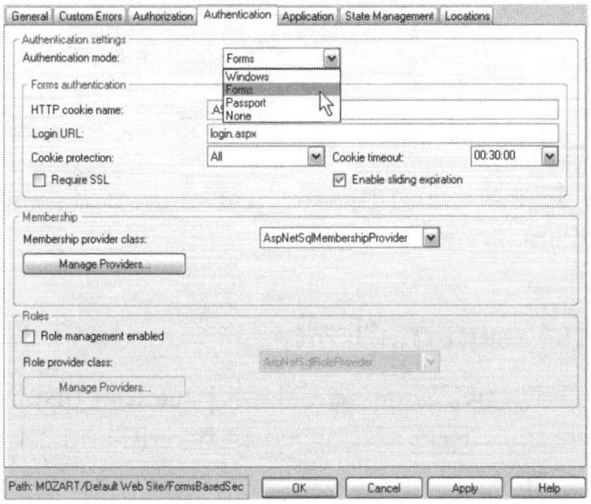

Figure 12-5. Set Authentication mode to Forms

Click OK to close all the dialogs. A *Web.config* file is created for you in the FormsBasedSecurityIIS directory, as shown in Example 12-1.

Example 12-1. Web.config file generated

```
<?xml version="1.0" encoding="utf-8"?>
<configuration xmlns="http://schemas.microsoft.com/.NetConfiguration/v2.0">
    <system.web>
        <authentication mode="Forms" />
    </system.web>
</configuration>
```

ASP.NET 2.0 Forms-built security is built on a set of tables that must be created in your database: typically SQL Server or SQL Server Express. Fortunately, ASP.NET provides a utility named *aspnet_regsql.exe*, located in the *<Drive:>\Windows\ Microsoft.NET\Framework\<versionNumber>* folder on your web server, which sets up the tables for you. This utility program will create the required database and all its tables.

The easiest way to use this utility is to run aspnet_regsql.exe from the .NET command box, with no arguments. A wizard will walk you through the process. For more details, see the MSDN article "Installing the SQL Server Provider Database."

You are now ready to create a new web site in the same location. A dialog box will warn you that you already have a web site in that location; choose Open Existing Site, as shown in Figure 12-6.

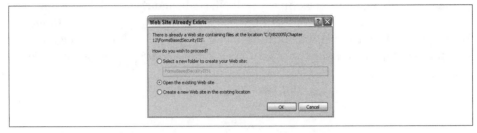

Figure 12-6. Open existing site

This instructs Visual Studio to use the site you've created, complete with the *Web. config* file already available for that site.

Creating Accounts Programatically

Your initial goal is to have two pages: a default page that displays different information depending on whether users are logged in or not, and a login page that allows the user to log in.

To have users log in, however, you must first create accounts. Create a new page called *CreateAccount.aspx*. (Right-click on the application and choose Add New Item. Choose web form and set the name to *CreateAccount.aspx*).

Click on the Design tab for your page, and then click on the Login tab in the Toolbox. Drag an instance of CreateUserWizard onto your page, as shown in Figure 12-7.

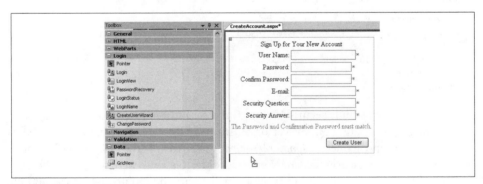

Figure 12-7. CreateUserWizard

The CreateUserWizard prompts the user for a username, a password (twice), an email address, and a security question and answer. All of this is configurable through the

HTML that is created by this control; through the Properties window; or, more commonly, through the smart tag, as shown in Figure 12-8.

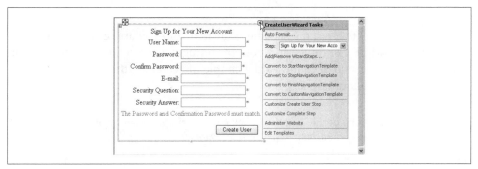

Figure 12-8. CreateUserWizard tasks

Click on the control and scroll through the properties to find the `ContinueDestinationPageURL`. Click the ellipses (…) button and choose the Create Account page itself (*CreateAccount.aspx*), so that you'll be brought back to the same page after the new user is confirmed. Click on the Document and scroll down the Properties window to the title of the page to Create User. Finally, set the *CreateAccount.aspx* page as your Start page, and fire up the application.

 Assuming you created this application, using the WAT as described earlier, you will be prompted to create a *Web.config* file. Click OK to add the new *Web.config* file with debugging enabled.

When the page opens, you will be prompted to add a new user, as shown in Figure 12-9.

Figure 12-9. Testing CreateAccountWizard

Remember to use a strong password, as explained earlier.

When you click Create User, the account is created, and you are brought to a confirmation screen. Click Continue, and you are brought back to the Create Account screen to create a second account. Add a couple of accounts, then stop the application and examine your database.

 To see the profile database, click on ServerExplorer and make a connection to *<machine>\sqlexpress.aspnetdb.dbo*.

You should find that a database named *aspnetdb* with many tables, including the aspnet_Users table. You can display it by right-clicking and choosing Show Table Data, as shown in Figure 12-10.

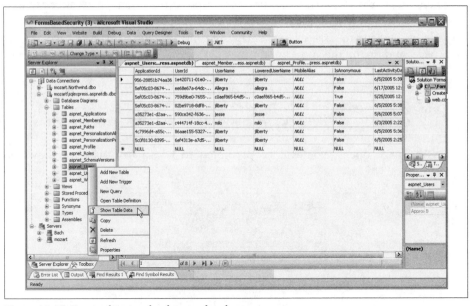

Figure 12-10. Personalization database updated

Creating the Welcome Page

With your user database in place, you are ready to create the page that will welcome the logged-in user.

Create a new page called *Welcome.aspx* and drag a LoginStatus control from the Login section of the Toolbox.

A link marked Login is placed on the page, whose smart tag indicates that you are looking at the template for when the user is not logged in, as shown in Figure 12-11.

Figure 12-11. Not logged in

You can set the properties of the `LoginStatus` control, for example, to change the text of the link. You can also drop down the view window to see the link and text for Logged In status.

Drag a `LoginView` control from the Toolbox, and drop it onto the page below the `LoginStatus` control. Here you may enter text and controls that will be displayed based on whether or not the user is logged in. Notice that this control has two views: Anonymous Template and Logged In Template. The template that will be displayed depends on whether the user has logged in.

Click on the smart tag and confirm that the view is set to Anonymous Template and type some text in the box, as shown in Figure 12-12.

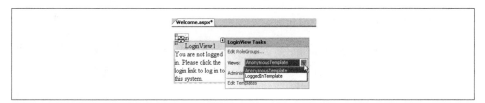

Figure 12-12. Not logged in view

Now set the `LoggedInTemplate`. Since the user will be logged in when this template is displayed, you can use the `LoginName` control to welcome the user by name. Drag the `LoginName` control onto the `LoginView` template, as shown in Figure 12-13.

Figure 12-13. The LoginName control

Create a Login Page

You are now ready to create the Login page for users to log in to the system (after having created an account). Add a new page named *Login.aspx*. Change to Design view, and drag a Login control onto the page. To make your page look more professional, click on the AutoFormat link from the smart tag, as shown in Figure 12-14.

Figure 12-14. Formatting the Login control

Pick one of the predefined formats for the control, as shown in Figure 12-15.

Figure 12-15. Pick a Format for the Login control

Make sure that the Welcome page is the Start page and run the application. The Welcome page will display its "Not Logged In" message. Click the link to go to the login page.

Enter a false name and/or incorrect password. The Login control will display an error message explaining your mistake; as shown in Figure 12-16.

Figure 12-16. Incorrect Logins are caught

Enter the correct name and password and you are brought back to the Welcome page. Your status is noted as logged in, you are greeted by name, and you are offered the opportunity to log out, as shown in Figure 12-17.

Figure 12-17. Logged In view

Adding a Password Reminder

To add a password reminder, you must first change your existing login control to a template by clicking on the smart tag and choosing "Convert to template," as shown in Figure 12-18.

Figure 12-18. Convert to template

The display will change to a template that you can modify. Add a link titled (for example) Recover Password, as shown in Figure 12-19.

Set the NavigateURL to the name of the page that will hold your PasswordRecovery control, then click the smart tag and choose End Editing.

Your next step, of course, is to create the new *.aspx* page, *RecoverPW.aspx*. Drag a PasswordRecovery control onto the page, and click the smart tag to choose the view you wish to edit, as shown in Figure 12-20.

Set the SuccessPageUrl property to *Login.aspx*. You may also want to confirm or change the Success Text as well as the other text fields (QuestionInstructionText, QuestionLabelText, etc.).

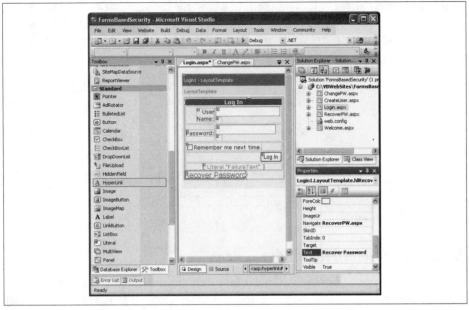

Figure 12-19. Adding password hyperlink to Login Template

Figure 12-20. Password Recovery control

Add Roles to ASP.NET Accounts

Authentication is the process of identifying a user; authorization is the process of deciding which parts of your application that user can see and interact with. The forms-based security controls and database that comes with Visual Basic 2005 allows you to set authorization for specific users based on their being assigned to a role (such as guest, member, manager, etc). You do so in three steps: create the roles, assign permissions to each *role*, and then assign users to the roles. Any given user may be in more than one role (e.g., administrator and manager). The permissions you assign to each role may determine access to a page, or may change the content of a given page displayed to members of that role.

Create a New Application with Roles

To demonstrate how to create roles and assign users to those roles, you'll need to create a new application, ASPSecurityRoles. Begin by copying over the web site you used in the previous exercise (FormBasedSecurity), as shown in Figure 12-21.

Figure 12-21. Copy web site

Set Welcome as the Start page and run the program to make sure you can still log in. Open the WAT and click on the Security tab. In the second column (Roles), you'll see that roles are not enabled. Click on Enable Roles, as shown in Figure 12-22.

Figure 12-22. Enabling roles in WAT

Open *Web.config* and you'll see that the WAT has updated it to add roles management:

```
<system.web>
    <roleManager enabled="true" />
    <authentication mode="Forms"/>
    <membership defaultProvider="AspNetSqlMembershipProvider"/>
    <compilation debug="true"/>
</system.web>
```

 Depending on how your machine is set up and which database you are using, you may or may not have the `defaultProvider` entry in your *Web.config*.

Once roles have been created, use the WAT to create your first Role: *Manager* (it is helpful to have an initial role and a user in that role so that you can have in your code a test to ensure that only Managers, for example, can create new roles or add users to roles).

 What you actually call that role—manager, adminstrator, tsar—is entirely up to you.

Under Add/Remove users, click the Manage link and navigate to one of your users (e.g., jliberty) and click the User Is In Role box to add that user to the role, as shown in Figure 12-23.

Using the LoginView's smart tag, click on Edit Templates and edit the Logged In Template. Add three hyperlinks to the Logged In Template on the Welcome page, as shown in Figure 12-24. Set the NavigateURL to *ChangePW.aspx, CreateAccount.aspx,* and *ManageRoles.aspx,* respectively. Be sure to click on End Template Editing when you are done.

Create the *ChangePW.aspx* page and drag a `ChangePassword` control onto the page. Use the smart tag to format the `ChangePassword` control, as shown in Figure 12-25.

Set the `ContinueDestinationPageURL` property to *Login.aspx*, and on *Login.aspx* make sure the `ContinueDestinationPageURL` of the Login control is set to *Welcome.aspx*. You may also want to confirm or change the Success Text as well as the other text fields (`ChangePasswordTitleText`, `ChangePasswordFailureText`, etc.)

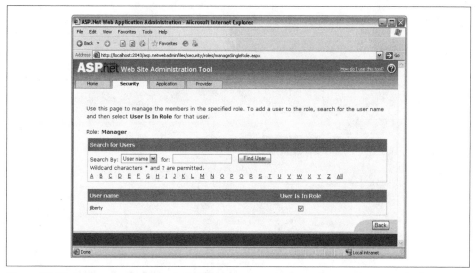

Figure 12-23. Adding users to roles in WAT

Figure 12-24. End Template Editing of Logged In Template

Figure 12-25. ChangePassword control

Create the *ManageRoles.aspx* page. This new page has a somewhat complex layout since it must display the list of roles and the list of users supported by your site, as well as which users have been assigned which roles. The page is shown in Figure 12-26, and the controls are listed in Table 12-1.

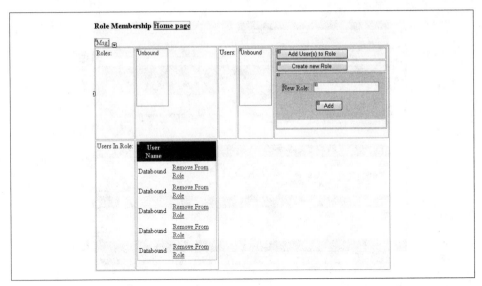

Figure 12-26. ManageRoles.aspx

Table 12-1. Controls in ManageRoles.aspx

Control name	Control type	Attributes
linkHome	Hyperlink	Inner HTML: Home Page NavigateURL= "Welcome.aspx"
Msg	Label	
RolesListBox	ListBox	Autopostback=true
UsersListBox	ListBox	Autopostback=true
btnAddUsersToRole	Button	Add User(s) to Role OnClick="AddUsers_OnClick"
btnCreateRole	Button	Create new Role OnClick="CreateRole_OnClick"
pnlCreateRole	Panel	Visible="False"
Label2	Label	New Role:
txtNewRole	TextBox	
btnAddRole	Button	Text="Add" OnClick="btnAddRole_Click"
UsersInRoleGrid	GridView	

The UsersInRoleGrid should look like Example 12-2.

Example 12-2. UserInRoleGrid source

```
<asp:GridView runat="server" CellPadding="4" id="UsersInRoleGrid"
              AutoGenerateColumns="false" Gridlines="None"
              CellSpacing="0"
```

Example 12-2. UserInRoleGrid source (continued)

```
OnRowCommand="UsersInRoleGrid_RemoveFromRole">
      <HeaderStyle BackColor="navy" ForeColor="white" />
      <Columns>
       <asp:TemplateField HeaderText="User Name">
         <ItemTemplate>
          <%# Container.DataItem.ToString( ) %>
         </ItemTemplate>
       </asp:TemplateField>
       <asp:ButtonField Text="Remove From Role" ButtonType="Link" />
      </Columns>
</asp:GridView>
```

All of these controls should be laid out in a table, with the text inserted into columns as well. The finished page is shown in Example 12-3.

Example 12-3. Manage Role Page source

```
<%@ Page Language="VB" AutoEventWireup="false" CodeFile="ManageRoles.aspx.vb"
Inherits="ManageRoles_aspx" %>

<!DOCTYPE html PUBLIC "-//W3C//DTD XHTML 1.1//EN" "http://www.w3.org/TR/xhtml11/DTD/
xhtml11.dtd">

<html xmlns="http://www.w3.org/1999/xhtml" >
<head runat="server">
   <title>Manage Roles</title>
</head>
<body>
   <form id="form1" runat="server">
   <h3>Role Membership
     <asp:HyperLink ID="linkHome" Runat="server" NavigateUrl="Welcome.aspx">
         Home page
     </asp:HyperLink>
   </h3>
   <asp:Label id="Msg" ForeColor="maroon" runat="server" /><BR>
   <table CellPadding="3" border="0">
    <tr>
     <td valign="top">Roles:</td>
     <td valign="top" style="width: 186px">
         <asp:ListBox id="RolesListBox"
             runat="server" Rows="8" AutoPostBack="True" />
     </td>
     <td valign="top">Users:</td>
     <td valign="top">
       <asp:ListBox id="UsersListBox" DataTextField="Username"
         Rows="8" SelectionMode="Multiple" runat="server" />
     </td>
     <td valign="top" visible="false">
         <table>
         <tr>
           <td>
              <asp:Button Text="Add User(s) to Role" id="btnAddUsersToRole"
```

Example 12-3. Manage Role Page source (continued)

```
                 runat="server" OnClick="AddUsers_OnClick" />
          </td>
      </tr>
      <tr>
         <td>
            <asp:Button Text="Create new Role" id="btnCreateRole"
            runat="server" OnClick="CreateRole_OnClick"
            Width="170px" Height="24px" />
         </td>
      </tr>
      <tr>
      <td>
    <asp:Panel ID="pnlCreateRole" Runat="server" Width="259px"
    Height="79px" Visible="False" BackColor="#E0E0E0">
       <br />
         
       <asp:Label ID="Label2" Runat="server" Text="New Role:"
        Width="72px" Height="19px"/>
       <asp:TextBox ID="txtNewRole" Runat="server"/> <br />
         <br />
                  
                 
       <asp:Button ID="btnAddRole" Runat="server"
         Text="Add" OnClick="btnAddRole_Click"
         Width="64px" Height="24px" /><br />
    </asp:Panel>

      </td>
      </tr>
      </table>
  </td>
</tr>
<tr>
 <td valign="top">Users In Role:</td>
 <td valign="top" style="width: 186px">
     <asp:GridView runat="server" CellPadding="4" id="UsersInRoleGrid"
                   AutoGenerateColumns="false" Gridlines="None"
                   CellSpacing="0"
     OnRowCommand="UsersInRoleGrid_RemoveFromRole">
           <HeaderStyle BackColor="navy" ForeColor="white" />
           <Columns>
            <asp:TemplateField HeaderText="User Name">
              <ItemTemplate>
              <%# Container.DataItem.ToString() %>
              </ItemTemplate>
            </asp:TemplateField>
            <asp:ButtonField Text="Remove From Role" ButtonType="Link" />
           </Columns>
     </asp:GridView>
  </td>
 </tr>
</table>
```

Example 12-3. Manage Role Page source (continued)

```
  </form>
</body>
</html>
```

 This page is not designed to be pretty, just useful. It is based on a demonstration *.aspx* page provided by Microsoft.

The code-behind page must implement five event handlers:

- Page_Load
- AddUsers_OnClick (adding users to roles)
- UsersInRoleGrid_RemoveFromRole (removing users from roles)
- CreateRole_OnClick (opening panel to create a new role)
- btnAddRole_Click (adding new role)

Your class will declare three *member variables*:

- A string array named rolesArray
- A string array named usersInRole
- An instance of MembershipUserCollection named users

The MembershipUserCollection is defined by the Framework to hold MembershipUser objects (surprise!). A MembershipUser object, in turn, is defined by the Framework to represent a single user in the membership data store (in this case, the tables created in SqlServerExpress). This class exposes information about the user such as the user's email address, and methods such as those needed to change or reset the user's password.

Here's how the code works. The first step is to override the Page_Load event handler, as shown in Example 12-4.

Example 12-4. Page_Load

```
Protected Sub Page_Load( _
ByVal sender As Object, _
ByVal e As System.EventArgs) Handles Me.Load
    If User.IsInRole("Manager") = False Then
        Response.Redirect("NoPrivs.aspx")
    End If
    Msg.Text = String.Empty
    If Not IsPostBack Then
        rolesArray = Roles.GetAllRoles( )
        RolesListBox.DataSource = rolesArray
        RolesListBox.DataBind( )
        users = Membership.GetAllUsers( )
        UsersListBox.DataSource = users
```

Example 12-4. Page_Load (continued)

```
    UsersListBox.DataBind( )
  End If
  If (RolesListBox.SelectedItem IsNot Nothing) Then
    usersInRole = Roles.GetUsersInRole(RolesListBox.SelectedItem.Value)
    UsersInRoleGrid.DataSource = usersInRole
    UsersInRoleGrid.DataBind( )
  End If
End Sub
```

First check that the current user is a manager. If he is, a redirect to an error page:

```
If User.IsInRole("Manager") = False Then
   Response.Redirect("NoPrivs.aspx")
End If
```

If this is the first time you are displaying the page, get the rolls and bind them to the list box, then get all the users and bind that collection to the Users List Box:

```
If Not IsPostBack Then
   rolesArray = Roles.GetAllRoles( )
   RolesListBox.DataSource = rolesArray
   RolesListBox.DataBind( )
   users = Membership.GetAllUsers( )
   UsersListBox.DataSource = users
   UsersListBox.DataBind( )
End If
```

If there is a selected item in the Roles List Box, get the list of users who are in that role and bind the list to the users in Roll Grid:

```
If (RolesListBox.SelectedItem IsNot Nothing) Then
   usersInRole = Roles.GetUsersInRole(RolesListBox.SelectedItem.Value)
   UsersInRoleGrid.DataSource = usersInRole
   UsersInRoleGrid.DataBind( )
End If
```

Step 2 is to implement the AddUsers_OnClick event handler, as shown in Example 12-5.

Example 12-5. AddUsers_OnClick handler

```
Protected Sub AddUsers_OnClick( _
ByVal sender As Object, _
ByVal e As System.EventArgs) Handles btnAddUsersToRole.Click

   ' A role must be selected
   If RolesListBox.SelectedItem Is Nothing Then
      Msg.Text = "Please select a role."
      Exit Sub
   End If

   ' At least one user must be selected
   If UsersListBox.SelectedItem Is Nothing Then
      Msg.Text = "Please select one or more users."
      Exit Sub
   End If
```

Example 12-5. AddUsers_OnClick handler (continued)

```
    ' Create list of users to be added to the selected role
    Dim sizeOfArray As Integer = UsersListBox.GetSelectedIndices.Length
    Dim newUsers(sizeOfArray - 1) As String

    'For i As Integer = 0 To newusers.Length - 1
    '    newusers(i) = _
    '    UsersListBox.Items( _
    '        UsersListBox.GetSelectedIndices( )(i)).Value
    'Next

    For i As Integer = 0 To newUsers.Length - 1
        ' get the array of selected indices from the (multiselect) list box
        Dim selectedIndices As Integer( ) = UsersListBox.GetSelectedIndices( )
        ' get the selectedIndex that corresponds to the counter (i)
        Dim selectedIndex As Integer = selectedIndices(i)
        ' get the ListItem in the UserListBox Items collection at that offset
        Dim myListItem As ListItem = UsersListBox.Items(selectedIndex)
        ' get the string that is that ListItem's value property
        Dim newUser As String = myListItem.Value
        ' add that string to the newUsers collection of string
        newUsers(i) = newUser
    Next


    ' Add users to the selected role
    Roles.AddUsersToRole(newUsers, RolesListBox.SelectedItem.Value)
    usersInRole = Roles.GetUsersInRole(RolesListBox.SelectedItem.Value)
    UsersInRoleGrid.DataSource = usersInRole
    UsersInRoleGrid.DataBind( )

End Sub
```

First, check to make sure that a role has been selected:

```
If RolesListBox.SelectedItem Is Nothing Then
    Msg.Text = "Please select a role."
    Exit Sub
End If
```

At least one user should be selected:

```
If UsersListBox.SelectedItem Is Nothing Then
    Msg.Text = "Please select one or more users."
    Exit Sub
End If
```

Create an array to hold the users to be added:

```
Dim sizeOfArray As Integer = UsersListBox.GetSelectedIndices.Length
Dim newusers(sizeOfArray - 1) As String
```

Iterate through the users, retrieving each selected user's name:

```
For i As Integer = 0 To newusers.Length - 1
    newusers(i) = _
```

```
    UsersListBox.Items( _
        UsersListBox.GetSelectedIndices( )(i)).Value
Next
```

This statement is pretty complicated. The best way to understand it is to rewrite it using interim variables, like this:

```
For i As Integer = 0 To newUsers.Length - 1
    ' get the array of selected indices from the (multiselect) list box
    Dim selectedIndices As Integer( ) = UsersListBox.GetSelectedIndices( )
    ' get the particular selectedIndex that corresponds to the counter (i)
    Dim selectedIndex As Integer = selectedIndices(i)
    ' get the ListItem in the UserListBox Items collection at that offset
    Dim myListItem As ListItem = UsersListBox.Items(selectedIndex)
    ' get the string that is that ListItem's value property
    Dim newUser As String = myListItem.Value
    ' add that string to the newUsers collection of string
    newUsers(i) = newUser
Next
```

The advantage of the interim variables is that you can set break points on them and see what their value is, and you can more easily document the code. The disadvantage is minimal, but many programmers (especially those from the "C" culture!) still prefer the terser version.

Next, call the static AddUsersToRole on the Roles class, passing in the array of usernames, and the role you want these users added to. Rebind the users who are in that role to the UsersInRoleGrid:

```
Roles.AddUsersToRole(newUsers, RolesListBox.SelectedItem.Value)
usersInRole = Roles.GetUsersInRole(RolesListBox.SelectedItem.Value)
UsersInRoleGrid.DataSource = usersInRole
UsersInRoleGrid.DataBind( )
```

As noted earlier, step 3 is to implement UsersInRoleGrid_RemoveFromRole as shown in Example 12-6.

Example 12-6. UsersInRoleGrid_RemoveFromRole

```
Protected Sub UsersInRoleGrid_RemoveFromRole( _
ByVal sender As Object, _
ByVal e As System.Web.UI.WebControls.GridViewCommandEventArgs) _
Handles UsersInRoleGrid.RowCommand

  ' get the user to remove
  Dim index As Integer = Convert.ToInt32(e.CommandArgument)
  Dim username As String = _
  CType(UsersInRoleGrid.Rows(index).Cells(0).Controls(0), _
      DataBoundLiteralControl).Text

  ' remove the user
  Roles.RemoveUserFromRole(username, RolesListBox.SelectedItem.Value)
```

Example 12-6. UsersInRoleGrid_RemoveFromRole (continued)

```
    ' Rebind the users in role to Gridview
    usersInRole = Roles.GetUsersInRole(RolesListBox.SelectedItem.Value)
    UsersInRoleGrid.DataSource = usersInRole
    UsersInRoleGrid.DataBind( )
End Sub
```

Step 4 is to add the Create Role_OnClick event handler, which makes the CreateRole panel visible, as shown in Example 12-7.

Example 12-7. CreateRole button Click event handler

```
Protected Sub CreateRole_OnClick( _
ByVal sender As Object, _
ByVal e As System.EventArgs) Handles btnCreateRole.Click
    pnlCreateRole.Visible = True
End Sub
```

The purpose of this is to present the panel, which contains a text box for the user to enter a new role and an Add button, as shown in Figure 12-27.

Figure 12-27. Create new role

Finally, implement the btnAddRole_Click event handler, shown in Example 12-8.

Example 12-8. AddRole button Click event handler

```
Protected Sub btnAddRole_Click( _
ByVal sender As Object, _
ByVal e As System.EventArgs) Handles btnAddRole.Click
    If txtNewRole.Text.Length > 0 Then
        Dim newRole As String = txtNewRole.Text

        ' if the role does not already exist, add it
        ' rebind the roles list box
        If Roles.RoleExists(newRole) = False Then
            Roles.CreateRole(newRole)
            rolesArray = Roles.GetAllRoles( )
            RolesListBox.DataSource = rolesArray
            RolesListBox.DataBind( )
        End If
    End If
    txtNewRole.Text = String.Empty
    pnlCreateRole.Visible = False
End Sub
```

Check to make sure there is text in the NewRole text box, and then check to make sure the role does not exist. If it does not, create the new role using the Shared CreateRole method of the Roles class, provided by the Framework.

 You do not need an instance of Roles to call CreateRole because CreateRole is Shared.

Get all the roles by calling the Shared method GetAllRoles and store the roles in the member array rolesArray, to which you bind the list box. When the role is added, the text box is cleared and the panel is made invisible.

Run the application and click on Manage Roles to add a couple of roles. Next, click on a role (to highlight it) and highlight one or more users; then click Add User(s) to Role. The results are shown in Figure 12-28.

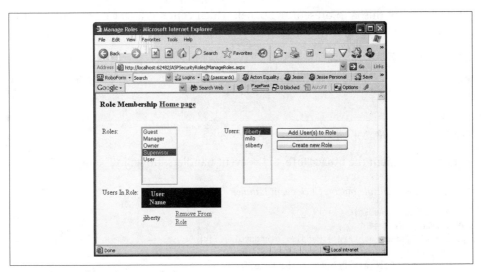

Figure 12-28. Adding users to roles

Add each user to one or more roles.

Restricting Access to Pages Based on Roles

There are two ways to restrict access to a page based on membership in a Role. The first is to test if the logged-in user is in a particular role, using the User.IsInRole() method:

```
Dim isManager as boolean  = User.IsInRole("Manager")
```

You might redirect the user to an error page if the user is not in the required role. As an example, let's add code that blocks nonmanagers from linking to the Manage Roles page. To do so, add a test in the Page_Load method of *ManageRoles.aspx.vb*:

```
Protected Sub Page_Load( _
ByVal sender As Object, _
ByVal e As System.EventArgs) Handles Me.Load
    If User.IsInRole("Manager") = False Then
        Response.Redirect("NoPrivs.aspx")
    End If
```

If the user is not in the role of "Manager," the user is redirected to the page *NoPrivs.aspx*. That page can display an error message and then allow the user to take other actions. A very simple example is shown in Figure 12-29.

Figure 12-29. NoPrivs.aspx

The code for the button (btnHome) on the *NoPrivs.aspx.vb* page, whose text is "Return to Welcome," is very simple and shown in Example 12-9.

Example 12-9. Return to Welcome button Click event handler

```
.Protected Sub btnHome_Click( _
ByVal sender As Object, _
ByVal e As System.EventArgs) Handles btnHome.Click
    Response.Redirect("Welcome.aspx")
End Sub
```

Restricting Access to a Set of Pages

You can also restrict access to a set of pages by adding an authorization section to a *Web.config* file. You place this file in a subdirectory to control access to all files in that subdirectory and all of its subdirectories, and you use the location element to control access to specific files:

```
<authorization>
  <deny users='?' />
  <allow roles='Manager' />
  <deny users='*' />
</authorization>
```

The first line (deny users = '?') prohibits access to anyone who is not logged in. The second line (allow roles='Manager') allows access to anyone in the Manager role, and the final line (deny users='*') disallows everyone, but is overridden by the allow roles.

Create Personalized Web Sites

Now that you have forms-based security working, you know who your user is and can store the user's preferences and, if appropriate, previous choices (e.g., "You have 3 items in your shopping cart").

To get started, you'll want a new project that duplicates the work you accomplished in the previous example. Create a new web site called SitePersonalization and use the CopyWebSite pattern described previously to make a copy of ASPSecurityRoles into the new site (copying over *all* the files and folders from the old site to the new.) Set *Welcome.aspx* as the Start page, and run the program to make sure you have a working duplicate.

Recording Personalization Information

The simplest form of personalization is to record information about the user, then make that information available whenever the user logs on. This requires a kind of persistence that goes beyond session state. To create true personalization, you'll want to store the user's choices and information in a database that associates the saved information with a particular user, and that persists indefinitely.

ASP.NET 2.0 provides all of the plumbing required. You do not have to design, edit, or manage the database tables; all of that is done for you.

Setting up profile handling

ASP.NET 2.0 has decoupled the Profile API (how you programmatically interact with profile data) from the underlying data provider (how you store the data). This allows you to use the default provider (SqlServerExpress), one of the other providers supplied (SQL server), or even write your own provider (e.g., for an existing Customer Relationship Management system) without changing the way you interact with the profile in the rest of your code.

If you wish to have the SQLExpress database handle the profile information, there are no additional steps; profile tables have already been created for you. To add data to the user's profile, alert the system about the data you wish to store by making an entry in *Web.config*. Add a profile section to the <system.web> element, as shown in Example 12-10.

Example 12-10. Adding a profile section to Web.config

```
<?xml version="1.0"?>
<configuration>
  <connectionStrings>
    <remove name="LocalSqlServer"/>
    <add name="LocalSqlServer" connectionString="data source=.\sqlExpress;Integrated
Security=SSPI;Initial Catalog=aspnetdb"/>
  </connectionStrings>
  <system.web>
    <authentication mode="Forms"/>
    <membership defaultProvider="AspNetSqlMembershipProvider"/>
    <roleManager enabled="True" defaultProvider="AspNetSqlRoleProvider"/>
    <compilation debug="true"/>
    <profile enabled="True" defaultProvider="AspNetSqlProfileProvider">
      <properties>
        <add name="lastName" />
        <add name="firstName" />
        <add name="phoneNumber" />
        <add name="birthDate" type="System.DateTime"/>
      </properties>
    </profile>
  </system.web>
</configuration>
```

 Your *Web.config* file may look somewhat different depending on your machine configuration and the databases you have installed (SQL Server, SQL Express, etc.)

The configuration shown in Example 12-10 causes the Profile API to create storage for four pieces of information: first and last name, phone number, and birth date. The default storage type is String. Notice, however, that you are storing the birth date as a DateTime object.

You can gather this personalization information any way you like. For this example, return to *Welcome.aspx* and click on the smart tag to choose EditTemplates and then choose the LoggedIn Template. Set the text to Add Profile Info and the NavigateURL property to ProfileInfo.aspx (which you will create shortly). Don't forget to click EndTemplateEditing when you are done.

Create the new page: *ProfileInfo.aspx*. Add a table, and within the table, labels and checkboxes, as well as a Save button, as shown in Figure 12-30.

The HTML code for the Profile Table is shown in Example 12-11.

Figure 12-30. Profile table

Example 12-11. HTML for profile table

```
<%@ Page Language="VB" AutoEventWireup="false" CodeFile="ProfileInfo.aspx.vb"
Inherits="ProfileInfo" %>


<!DOCTYPE html PUBLIC "-//W3C//DTD XHTML 1.1//EN" "http://www.w3.org/TR/xhtml11/DTD/
xhtml11.dtd">



<html xmlns="http://www.w3.org/1999/xhtml" >
<head id="Head1" runat="server">
    <title>ProfileInfo</title></head>
<body>
    <form id="form1" runat="server">
    <div>
        <table>
        <tr>
            <td>First Name: </td>
            <td style="width: 193px">
              <asp:TextBox ID="firstName" Runat="server" />
            </td>
        </tr>
        <tr>
            <td>Last Name: </td>
            <td style="width: 193px">
              <asp:TextBox ID="lastName" Runat="server" /></td>
        </tr>
        <tr>
            <td>Phone number: </td>
            <td style="width: 193px">
               <asp:TextBox ID="phone" Runat="server" />
            </td>
        </tr>
        <tr>
            <td>BirthDate</td>
            <td style="width: 193px">
               <asp:TextBox ID="birthDate" Runat="server" />
            </td>
        </tr>
         <tr>
            <td>
                <asp:Button ID="save" Text="Save" Runat="server"
```

Example 12-11. HTML for profile table (continued)

```
                        OnClick="save_Click" />
              </td>
           <td style="width: 193px"></td>
        </tr>
     </table>

   </div>
   </form>
</body>
</html>
```

All that remains to be done is to add an event handler for the Save button:

```
Protected Sub save_Click( _
ByVal sender As Object, _
ByVal e As System.EventArgs) Handles save.Click
    If Profile.IsAnonymous = False Then
        Profile.lastName = Me.lastName.Text
        Profile.firstName = Me.firstName.Text
        Profile.phoneNumber = Me.phone.Text
        Profile.birthDate = CType(Me.birthDate.Text, System.DateTime)
    End If
    Response.Redirect("Welcome.aspx")
End Sub
```

 The Profile.IsAnonymous property is explained in detail below

The Profile object has properties that correspond to the properties you added in *Web.config*. To test that the Profile object has, in fact, stored this date, you'll add a panel to the bottom of the Welcome page, as shown in Figure 12-31.

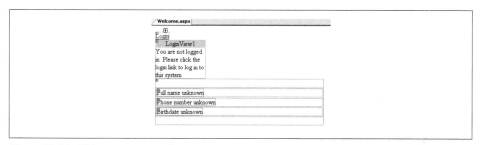

Figure 12-31. Welcome page panel

The panel has a table with three rows, and each row has a label that is initialized to say that the value is unknown (this is not normally needed, but is included here to ensure that the data you see is retrieved from the Profile object). When the page is loaded, you check to see if you have Profile data for this user and, if so, you assign that data to the appropriate controls.

Example 12-12 shows the source for the panel.

Example 12-12. Adding a panel to the Welcome page

```
<asp:Panel ID="pnlInfo" Runat="server" Visible="False" Width="422px" Height="63px">
  <br />
  <table width="100%">
    <tr>
      <td>
        <asp:Label ID="lblFullName" Runat="server"
        Text="Full name unknown">
        </asp:Label></td>
      </tr>
    <tr>
      <td>
        <asp:Label ID="lblPhone" Runat="server"
          Text="Phone number unknown">
        </asp:Label>
      </td>
    </tr>
    <tr>
      <td>
        <asp:Label ID="lblBirthDate" Runat="server"
            Text="Birthdate   unknown">
        </asp:Label>
      </td>
    </tr>
  </table>
</asp:Panel>
```

You'll need to add a bit of code to the *Welcome.aspx.vb* page, so that when the page loads it will check to see if you have a profile, and if so, it will make the panel visible, as shown in Example 12-13.

Example 12-13. Welcome page Page_Load method

```
Protected Sub Page_Load( _
ByVal sender As Object, _
ByVal e As System.EventArgs) Handles Me.Load
    If Not IsPostBack And Profile.UserName IsNot Nothing Then
        Me.pnlInfo.Visible = True
        If Profile.IsAnonymous = False Then
            Me.lblFullName.Text = Profile.firstName & " " & Profile.lastName
            Me.lblPhone.Text = Profile.phoneNumber
            Me.lblBirthDate.Text = Profile.birthDate.ToShortDateString( )
        End If
    Else
        Me.pnlInfo.Visible = False
    End If
End Sub
```

When you start the application, you are asked to log in. Once logged in, a new hyperlink appears: Add Profile Info. This was created by the hyperlink you added to the LoggedInTemplate earlier. Clicking on that link brings you to your new profile page, as shown in Figure 12-32.

Figure 12-32. Profile information page

When you click Save and return to the Welcome page, the Page_Load event fires. The Page_Load begins with an If statement:

```
If Profile.UserName IsNot Nothing And _
    Profile.IsAnonymous = False Then
```

Both parts of the If statement evaluate True: the UserName value in the profile is not Nothing, and the user is logged in, and thus not anonymous.

Your profile information is displayed, as shown in Figure 12-33.

Figure 12-33. Profile information displayed

Exploring the Profile Tables

Stop the application and open the Database Explorer window, and look at the Tables in the aspnetdb database. Open two tables, aspnet_Users (which lists all the users your database knows about) and aspnet_Profile (which lists the profile information for those users). To see these next to each other, click and drag the tab for one of the views, as shown in Figure 12-34.

Figure 12-34. Drag tab

When you let go, a menu will open offering to create a new tab group. Choose New Horizontal Tab Group, as shown in Figure 12-35.

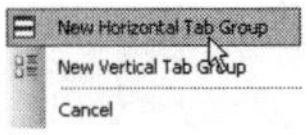

Figure 12-35. Create New Horizontal Tab Group

This done, you can see both the Profile tab and the Users tab in a single window. The Users tab shows you that each user has a unique `UserID`. The Profile tab has a foreign key added into that table (`UserID`) and lists the `PropertyNames` and `PropertyValues`, as shown in Figure 12-36.

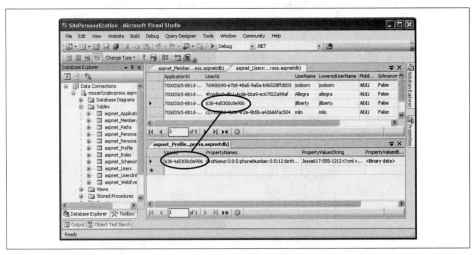

Figure 12-36. Profile tables

`PropertyNames` matches up with the entries you created in the `<profile>` section of *Web.config*:

```
<profile>
    <properties>
        <add name="lastName" />
        <add name="firstName" />
        <add name="phoneNumber" />
        <add name="birthDate" type="System.DateTime"/>
```

```
    </properties>
  </profile>
```

Each property is named (e.g., `phoneNumber`), given a type (`S` for string), a starting offset (`phoneNumber` begins at offset `5`), and a length (`phoneNumber`'s value has a length of `12`). This offset and value are used to find the value within the `PropertyValueString` field.

> Notice that `birthDate` is listed as a string, that begins at offset 17 and is 95 characters long; if you look at the `propertyValuesString` column, you'll find that the *birthDate* is encoded as XML.

Personalize with Complex Types

To make a useful commercial site, you often have to store complex user-defined types (classes) or collections.

In the next exercise, you'll edit the *Web.config* file to add a collection of strings called `CHOSENBOOKS`. Doing so will allow the user to choose one or more books, and have those choices stored in the user's profile.

Add a line to *Web.config* for your new property:

```
<profile>
  <properties>
    <add name="lastName" />
    <add name="firstName" />
    <add name="phoneNumber" />
    <add name="birthDate" type="System.DateTime"/>
    <add name="CHOSENBOOKS"
     type="System.Collections.Specialized.StringCollection" />
  </properties>
</profile>
```

To see this collection at work, edit the page *ProfileInfo.aspx*, inserting a row with a CheckBoxList just above the row with the Save button, as shown in Figure 12-37.

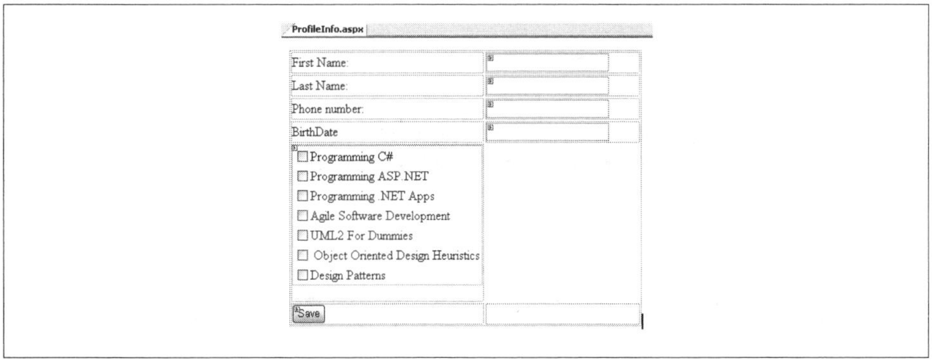
ProfileInfo.aspx
First Name:
Last Name:
Phone number:
BirthDate
Programming C#
Programming ASP.NET
Programming .NET Apps
Agile Software Development
UML2 For Dummies
Object Oriented Design Heuristics
Design Patterns
Save

Figure 12-37. Adding checkboxes to profile

Modify the Save button handler to add the selected books to the profile, as shown in Example 12-14.

Example 12-14. Code to modify Save button Click event handler

```
Profile.CHOSENBOOKS = New System.Collections.Specialized.StringCollection( )
For Each item As ListItem In Me.cblChosenBooks.Items
    If item.Selected Then
        Profile.CHOSENBOOKS.Add(item.Value.ToString( ))
    End If
Next
```

Each time you save the books, you create an instance of the String collection, and you then iterate through the checked list boxes, looking for the selected items. Each selected item is added to the string collection within the profile (the CHOSENBOOKS property).

You also need to override Page_Load so that this page will open with the user's profile information updated, as shown in Example 12-15.

Example 12-15. Modified ProfileInfo.aspx.vb

```
Partial Class ProfileInfo
    Inherits System.Web.UI.Page
    Protected Sub save_Click( _
    ByVal sender As Object, _
    ByVal e As System.EventArgs) Handles save.Click
        If Profile.IsAnonymous = False Then
            Profile.lastName = Me.lastName.Text
            Profile.firstName = Me.firstName.Text
            Profile.phoneNumber = Me.phone.Text
            Profile.birthDate = CType(Me.birthDate.Text, System.DateTime)
            Profile.CHOSENBOOKS =
                New System.Collections.Specialized.StringCollection( )
            For Each item As ListItem In Me.cblChosenBooks.Items
                If item.Selected Then
                    Profile.CHOSENBOOKS.Add(item.Value.ToString( ))
                End If
            Next
        End If
        Response.Redirect("Welcome.aspx")
    End Sub
    Protected Sub Page_Load(ByVal sender As Object, _
        ByVal e As System.EventArgs) Handles Me.Load
        If Not IsPostBack And Profile.UserName IsNot Nothing Then
            If Profile.IsAnonymous = False Then
                Me.lastName.Text = Profile.lastName
                Me.firstName.Text = Profile.firstName
                Me.phone.Text = Profile.phoneNumber
                Me.birthDate.Text = Profile.birthDate.ToShortDateString( )
            End If
```

Example 12-15. Modified ProfileInfo.aspx.vb (continued)

```
            If Profile.CHOSENBOOKS IsNot Nothing Then
                For Each theListItem As ListItem In Me.cblChosenBooks.Items
                    For Each theProfileString As String In Profile.CHOSENBOOKS
                        If theListItem.Text = theProfileString Then
                            theListItem.Selected = True
                        End If
                    Next
                Next
            End If
        End If
    End Sub
End Class
```

Each time you navigate to the Profile page, the values are updated from the existing profile (if any) in Page_Load and you are free to change them and save the new values, as shown in Figure 12-38.

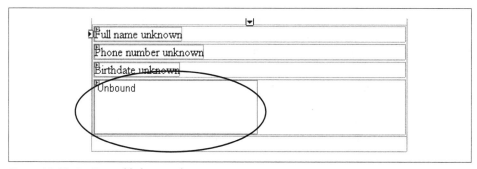

Figure 12-38. Profile Information page with CheckBoxList

To confirm that this data has been stored, add a ListBox (name it lbBooks) to the pnlInfo panel you added to *Welcome.aspx* page, as shown in Figure 12-39.

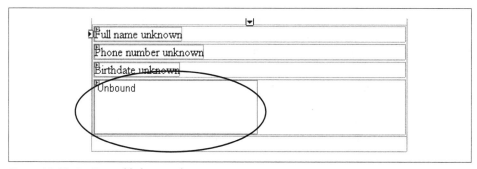

Figure 12-39. ListBox added to panel

Bind the ListBox to the collection in the profile, as shown in Example 12-16.

Example 12-16. Modified Page_Load in Welcome.aspx.vb

```
Protected Sub Page_Load( _
ByVal sender As Object, _
ByVal e As System.EventArgs) Handles Me.Load
   If Not IsPostBack And Profile.UserName IsNot Nothing Then
      Me.pnlInfo.Visible = True
      If Profile.IsAnonymous = False Then
         Me.lblFullName.Text = Profile.firstName & " " & Profile.lastName
         Me.lblPhone.Text = Profile.phoneNumber
         Me.lblBirthDate.Text = Profile.birthDate.ToShortDateString( )
      End If
      If Profile.CHOSENBOOKS IsNot Nothing Then
         For Each bookName As String In Profile.CHOSENBOOKS
            Me.lbBooks.Items.Add(bookName)
         Next
      End If
   Else
      Me.pnlInfo.Visible = False
   End If
End Sub
```

When you click Save in the Profile page and return to the Welcome page, your saved profile information is reflected, as shown in Figure 12-40.

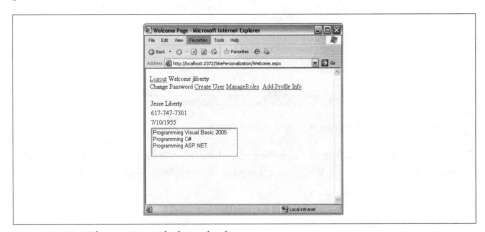

Figure 12-40. Welcome page with chosen books

Anonymous Personalization

It is common to allow your users to personalize your site before identifying themselves. A classic example of this is *Amazon.com*, which lets you add books to your shopping cart *before* you log in (you only need to log in when you are ready to purchase what is in your cart).

ASP.NET 2.0 supports personalization for anonymous users as well as the ability later to link anonymous personalized data with a specific user's. Once that user logs in, you don't want to lose what was in the user's cart.

To enable anonymous personalization, you must update your *Web.config* file adding:

```
<anonymousIdentification enabled="true" />
```

Add the attribute-value pair allowAnonymous="true" to the CHOSENBOOKS element of *Web.config*, as shown in Example 12-17.

Example 12-17. Modified Web.config for anonymous access

```
<?xml version="1.0"?>
<configuration xmlns="http://schemas.microsoft.com/.NetConfiguration/v2.0">
   <connectionStrings>
      <remove name="LocalSqlServer"/>
      <add name="LocalSqlServer" connectionString="data source=.\SqlExpress;Integrated
Security=SSPI;Initial Catalog=aspnetdb"/>
   </connectionStrings>
   <system.web>
      <anonymousIdentification enabled="true" />
      <roleManager enabled="true" />
      <authentication mode="Forms"/>
      <membership defaultProvider="AspNetSqlMembershipProvider"/>
      <compilation debug="true"/>
      <profile enabled="True" defaultProvider="AspNetSqlProfileProvider">
         <properties>
            <add name="lastName" />
            <add name="firstName" />
            <add name="phoneNumber" />
            <add name="birthDate" type="System.DateTime"/>
            <add name="CHOSENBOOKS" allowAnonymous="true"
              type="System.Collections.Specialized.StringCollection" />
         </properties>
      </profile>
   </system.web>
</configuration>
```

Redesign your *Welcome.aspx* page in two ways: first move the hyperlink to the profile Information page outside of the Logged In template. Second move the listbox (*lbBooks*) outside the panel. Thus, you can see both of these features whether or not you are logged in. Also, change the text on the Add Profile Info hyperlink to just Profile Info, since you will be using this link to add and edit the profile info.

When an anonymous user fills in the profile information, the user will automatically be assigned a Globally Unique Identifier (GUID), and an entry will be made in the database for that ID. However, note that only those properties marked with allowAnonymous may be stored, so you must modify your Save_Click event handler in *ProfileInfo.aspx.vb*. Bracket the entries for all the profile elements *except* CHOSENBOOKS in an If statement that tests whether the user is currently Anonymous. The new save_Click event handler for *ProfileInfo.aspx.vb* is shown in Example 12-18.

Example 12-18. Modified Save_Click event handler for ProfileInfo.aspx.vb

```
Protected Sub save_Click( _
ByVal sender As Object, _
ByVal e As System.EventArgs) Handles save.Click
   If Profile.IsAnonymous = False Then
       Profile.lastName = Me.lastName.Text
       Profile.firstName = Me.firstName.Text
       Profile.phoneNumber = Me.phone.Text
       Profile.birthDate = CType(Me.birthDate.Text, System.DateTime)
   End If
   Profile.CHOSENBOOKS = New System.Collections.Specialized.StringCollection( )
   For Each item As ListItem In Me.cblChosenBooks.Items
       If item.Selected Then
           Profile.CHOSENBOOKS.Add(item.Value.ToString( ))
       End If
   Next
   Response.Redirect("Welcome.aspx")
End Sub
```

The effect of the new code shown in Example 12-18 is that you check whether the IsAnonymous property is false. If it is, then you are dealing with a logged-in user, and you can get all of the properties; otherwise, you can get only those that are allowed for anonymous users.

Modify the *ProfileInfo* page so that the non-anonymous data is in a panel that will be invisible for users who are not logged in. The simplest way to do this may be to switch to Source view and bracket the nonanonymous code inside a panel (don't forget to end the table before ending the panel), as shown in Example 12-19.

Example 12-19. Adding a nonanonymous information panel to ProfileInfo.aspx.vb

```
<body>
    <form id="form1" runat="server">
    <div>
        <asp:Panel ID="pnlNonAnonymousInfo" runat="server">
            <table>
            <tr>
                <td>First Name: </td>
                <td style="width: 193px">
                  <asp:TextBox ID="FirstName" Runat="server" />
                </td>
            </tr>
            <tr>
                <td>Last Name: </td>
                <td style="width: 193px">
                  <asp:TextBox ID="LastName" Runat="server" /></td>
            </tr>
            <tr>
                <td>Phone number: </td>
                <td style="width: 193px">
                    <asp:TextBox ID="Phone" Runat="server" />
                </td>
```

```
            </tr>
            <tr>
                <td>BirthDate</td>
                <td style="width: 193px">
                    <asp:TextBox ID="BirthDate" Runat="server" />
                </td>
            </tr>
        </table>
    </asp:Panel>
```

Modify the Page_Load for *ProfileInfo.aspx* to hide the panel if the user is anonymous, as shown in Example 12-20.

Example 12-20. Modified page load—ProfileInfo.aspx.vb

```
Protected Sub Page_Load(ByVal sender As Object, _
  ByVal e As System.EventArgs) Handles Me.Load
    If Not IsPostBack And Profile.UserName IsNot Nothing Then
        If Profile.IsAnonymous = True Then
            Me.pnlNonAnonymousInfo.Visible = False
        Else
            Me.pnlNonAnonymousInfo.Visible = True
            If Profile.IsAnonymous = False Then
                Me.lastName.Text = Profile.lastName
                Me.firstName.Text = Profile.firstName
                Me.phone.Text = Profile.phoneNumber
                Me.birthDate.Text = Profile.birthDate.ToShortDateString()
            End If

            If Profile.CHOSENBOOKS IsNot Nothing Then
                For Each theListItem As ListItem In Me.cblChosenBooks.Items
                    For Each theProfileString As String In Profile.CHOSENBOOKS
                        If theListItem.Text = theProfileString Then
                            theListItem.Selected = True
                        End If
                    Next
                Next
            End If     'Profile.CHOSENBOOKS IsNot Nothing
        End If         'Profile.IsAnonymous = True
    End If             'Not IsPostBack And Profile.UserName IsNot Nothing
End Sub
```

Run the application. Do *not* log in, but do click the Profile Info link. Select a few books and click Save. When you return to the Welcome page, you are still not logged in, but your selected books are displayed, as shown in Figure 12-41.

Stop the application and reopen the database. You'll see that an ID has been created for this anonymous user (and the UserName has been set to the GUID generated). In addition, the profile information has been stored in the corresponding record, as shown in Figure 12-42.

Figure 12-41. Anonymous user information

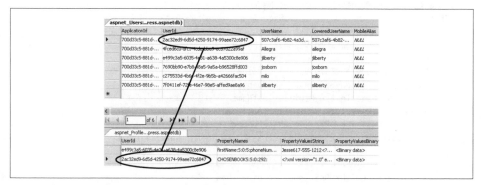

Figure 12-42. Anonymous user record in database

Migrating the Anonymous Data to the Actual User's Record

When the user *does* log in, you must migrate the Profile data you've accumulated for the anonymous user to the authenticated user's record (so that, for example, shopping cart items are not lost). You do this by writing a global handler in *global.asax*.

If your project does not yet have a *global.asax* file, right-click on the project and choose Add New Item. One of your choices will be Global Application Class, and it will default to the name *global.asax* (click Add). Within that class, add a method to handle the MigrateAnonymous event that is fired when a user logs in, as shown in Example 12-21.

Example 12-21. MigrateAnonymous event handler

```
Sub Profile_MigrateAnonymous( _
ByVal sender As Object, ByVal e As ProfileMigrateEventArgs)
    Dim anonymousProfile As ProfileCommon = _
        Profile.GetProfile(e.AnonymousId)
```

Example 12-21. MigrateAnonymous event handler (continued)

```
    If anonymousProfile IsNot Nothing And _
        anonymousProfile.CHOSENBOOKS IsNot Nothing Then
        For Each s As String In anonymousProfile.CHOSENBOOKS
            Profile.CHOSENBOOKS.Remove(s)   ' remove duplicates
            Profile.CHOSENBOOKS.Add(s)
        Next
    End If
End Sub
```

The first step in this method is to get a reference to the profile that matches the AnonymousID passed in as a property of ProfileMigrateEventArgs:

```
    Dim anonymousProfile As ProfileCommon = _
        Profile.GetProfile(e.AnonymousId)
```

If the reference is not Nothing, then you know that there is a matching anonymous profile, and that you may choose whatever data you need from that profile. In this case, you copy over the CHOSENBOOKS collection.

The user's profile is updated, and the books chosen as an anonymous user are now part of that user's profile, as shown in Figure 12-43.

Figure 12-43. Profiles merged

Themes and Skins

Many users like to personalize their favorite web sites by setting the look and feel to meet their own aesthetic preferences. ASP.NET 2.0 supports that requirement with "themes."

A *theme* is a collection of skins. A *skin* describes how a *control* should look. A skin can define style sheet attributes, images, colors, and so forth.

Having multiple themes allows your users to choose how they want your site to look by switching from one set of skins to another at the touch of a button. Combined with personalization, your site can remember the look and feel each user prefers.

There are two types of themes. The first, called *stylesheet themes*, define styles that may be overridden by the page or control. These are, essentially, equivalent to CSS style sheets. The second type, called *customization themes*, *cannot* be overridden. You set a stylesheet theme by adding the StyleSheetTheme attribute to the page directive, and, similarly, you set a customization theme by setting the Theme attribute in the page directive.

In any given page, the properties for the controls are set in this order:

- Properties are applied first from a stylesheet theme.
- Properties are then overridden based on properties set in the control.
- Properties are then overridden based on a customization theme.

Thus, the customization theme is guaranteed to have the final word in determining the look and feel of the control.

Skins themselves come in two flavors: default skins and explicitly named skins. Thus, you might create a Labels skin file with this declaration:

```
<asp:Label runat="server"
ForeColor="Blue" Font-Size="Large"
Font-Bold="True" Font-Italic="True" />
```

This is a default skin for all Label controls. It looks like the definition of an ASP:Label control, but it is housed in a skin file and, thus, is used to define the look and feel of all Label objects within that skin file's theme.

In addition, however, you might decide that some labels must be red. To accomplish this, create a second skin, but assign this skin a SkinID property:

```
<asp:Label runat="server" SkinID="RedLabel"
ForeColor="Red" Font-Size="Large"
Font-Bold="True" Font-Italic="True" />
```

Any label that does not have a SkinID attribute will get the default skin; any label that sets SkinID ="Red" will get your named skin.

The steps to providing a personalized web site are:

1. Create the test site.
2. Organize your themes and skins.
3. Enable themes and skins for your site.
4. Specify themes declaratively if you wish.

Create the Test Site

To demonstrate the use of themes and skins, you'll create a new web site (Themes) but you will use Copy Web Site to bring over all the personalization code from the previous example and set the start page to *Welcome.aspx*. Test the application to make sure it still works as expected.

To begin modifying your application, you'll need some controls whose look and feel you can set.

Open *Welcome.aspx*, and drag on some new controls, as shown in Figure 12-44.

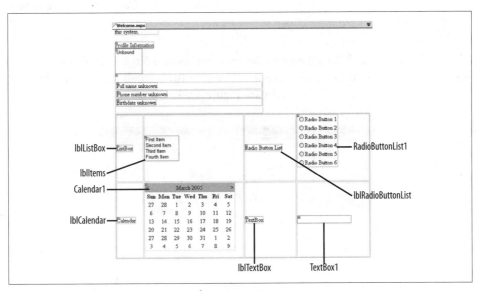

Figure 12-44. Welcome.aspx new controls

There are four labels (each with names beginning with lbl): ListBox, RadioButtonList, Calendar, and TextBox. Use the default properties (other than the names) for all, except remove all text from TextBox1's Text property.

You'll also need to click on the smart tag for both lbItems (the ListBox) and RadioButtonList1 (the RadioButtonList). For each of these, choose Edit the List items, as shown in Figure 12-45.

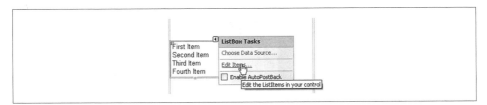

Figure 12-45. Choose Edit the List items

In the ListItem Collection Editor add four items to the list box, and six items to the RadioButtonList, as shown back in Figure 12-44.

You will use themes to change the look and feel of the new controls.

Organize Site Themes and Skins

Themes are stored in your project in a folder named App_Themes. To create this folder, go to Solution explorer, right-click on the project folder, and choose Add Folder → Theme Folder. Name the new folder *Dark Blue*—the folder *App_Themes* will be created automatically, with a Theme folder named *Dark Blue* immediately under it. Right-click on App_Themes and create a second theme folder, named *Psychedelic*.

Right-click on the *Dark Blue* theme folder and choose Add New Item. From the template lists, choose Skin File and name it *Button.skin* (to hold all the button skins for your Dark Blue theme), as shown in figure Figure 12-46.

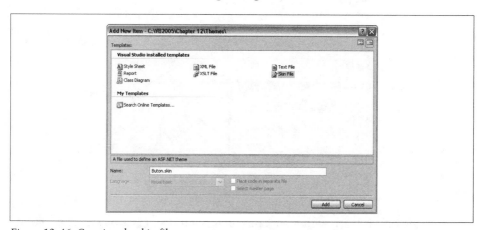

Figure 12-46. Creating the skin file

Each skin file is just a text file that contains a definition for the control type, but with no ID. Thus, your *Label.skin* file for the Dark Blue theme might look like this:

```
<asp:Label Runat="server"
ForeColor="Blue" Font-Size="Large"
Font-Bold="True" Font-Italic="True" />
```

Create skin files for each of the following types in both themes:

- *Button.skin*
- *Calendar.skin*
- *Label.skin*
- *ListBox.skin*
- *RadioButton.skin*
- *Text.skin*

At this point, your solution should look more or less like Figure 12-47.

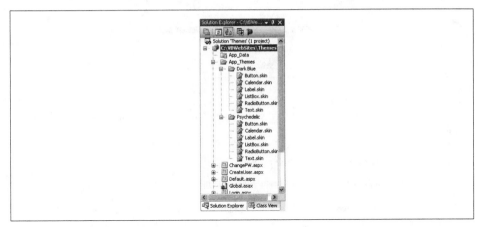

Figure 12-47. Themes and skins in your project

You can experiment with adding attributes to these new skin files and see the effects they produce on your user interface. Start by copying the text from *Label.skin*, then modifying it so it affects the appropriate control type (asp:Button in *Button.skin*, asp:Calendar in *Calendar.skin*, asp:ListBox in *ListBox.skin*, etc.).

Enable Themes and Skins

To let your users choose the theme they like and have their preference stored in their profile, you need to add a single line to the properties element in the profile element of *Web.config*:

```
<add name="Theme" />
```

Save and rebuild your application.

Specify Themes for Your Page

You can set the themes on your page either declaratively or programmatically. To set a theme declaratively, add the Theme attribute to the Page directive:

```
<%@ Page Language="VB" AutoEventWireup="true"
CodeFile="Default.aspx.vb" Inherits="Default_aspx" Theme="Dark Blue"%>
```

You can also set the theme programmatically, either by hard coding it or (even better) by setting it from the user's profile.

StyleSheet themes are set by overriding the StyleSheetTheme property for the page. IntelliSense will help you with this. Open *Welcome.aspx.vb* and scroll to the bottom of the class. Type the word **overrides** and all the overridable members are shown. Start typing *sty* and IntelliSense will scroll to the property you want: StyleSheetTheme, as shown in Figure 12-48.

Figure 12-48. Overriding a method

Once IntelliSense finds the property you want, press Tab to accept it. Fill in the accessors, as shown in Example 12-22.

Example 12-22. Setting a StylesheetTheme property

```
Public Overrides Property StyleSheetTheme() As String
    Get
        If Profile.IsAnonymous = False And Profile.Theme IsNot Nothing Then
            Return Profile.Theme
        Else
            Return "Dark Blue"
        End If
    End Get
    Set(ByVal value As String)
        Profile.Theme = value
    End Set
End Property
```

If you are going to set a *customization* theme programmatically, however, you must do so from the PreInit event handler for the page,* because the theme must be set before the controls are created. A PreInit event handler is shown in Example 12-23.

Example 12-23. Welcome page PreInit event handler

```
Protected Sub Page_PreInit( _
ByVal sender As Object, ByVal e As System.EventArgs) _
Handles Me.PreInit
    If Profile.IsAnonymous = False Then
        Page.Theme = Profile.Theme
    End If
End Sub
```

Setting the theme in PreInit creates a bit of a difficulty when you want to allow the user to change the theme at runtime. If you create a control that posts the page back with a new theme, the PreInit code runs *before* the event handler for the button that changes the theme, and so by the time the theme is changed, the controls have already been drawn.

---

* The pre-init event is new in Visual Basic 2005.

To overcome this you must, unfortunately, refresh the page again. An alternative is to set the themes in another page. For example, add two buttons to the *ProfileInfo.aspx* page (at the bottom of the table at the bottom of the page). Set the properties of the first button to:

```
ID="ThemeBlue" Text="Dark Blue" OnClick="Set_Theme"
```

Set the properties of the second button to:

```
ID="ThemePsychedelic" Text="Psychedelic" OnClick="Set_Theme"
```

Notice that the two buttons share a single Click event handler, Set_Theme, shown in Example 12-24. An easy way to have Visual Studio 2005 set up that event handler for you is to switch to Design view and click on one of the buttons. Click on the lightning bolt in the Properties window to go to the events, and double-click on the Set_Theme event. You are now ready to implement the event handler. You'll cast the sender to the button and check its text, setting the theme appropriately.

Example 12-24. Common Click event handler for ThemeBlue and ThemePsychedelic buttons

```
Protected Sub Set_Theme( _
ByVal sender As Object, _
ByVal e As System.EventArgs) Handles ThemePsych.Click
    Dim btn As Button = CType(sender, Button)
    If btn.Text = "Psychedelic" Then
        Profile.Theme = "Psychedelic"
    Else
        Profile.Theme = "Dark Blue"
    End If
End Sub
```

When the user is not logged on, the Welcome page's default theme will be used. Once the user sets a theme in the profile, that theme will be used when you return to the Welcome page. Create skins for your two themes and then run the application to see the effect of applying the themes.

Using Named Skins

You can override the theme for particular controls by using *named skins*.

Set the lblRadioButtonList label to be red even in the Deep Blue theme, by using a named skin. To accomplish this, create two Label skins in the *Label.skin* file within the *Deep Blue* folder.

```
<asp:Label Runat="server"
ForeColor="Blue" Font-Size="Large"
Font-Bold="True" Font-Italic="True" />

<asp:Label Runat="server" SkinID="Red"
ForeColor="Red" Font-Size="Large"
Font-Bold="True" Font-Italic="True" />
```

The first skin is the default; the second is a named skin, because it has a SkinID property set to Red. Click on the RadioButtonList control in Design view and set the SkinID property to Red. Or, open the source for *Welcome.aspx* and find the RadioButtonList and add the attribute SkinID="Red":

```
<asp:Label ID="lblRadioButtonList" Runat="server" Text="Radio Button List"
SkinID="Red"/>
```

When you log in and set your theme to Dark Blue, you'll find that the label for the RadioButtonList is Red, as shown in Figure 12-49. (You didn't get stuck with a black & white book, did you?)

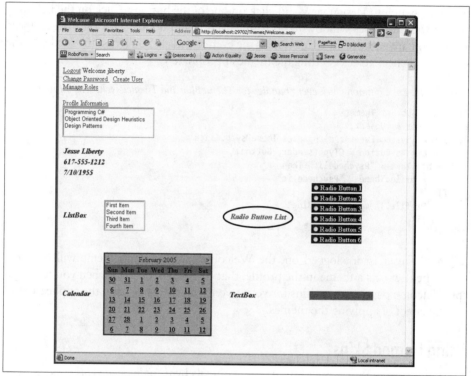

Figure 12-49. RadioButtonList label is Red

Web Parts

Web Parts allow your users to reconfigure sections of your site to meet their own needs and preferences. Many information providers allow the user to pick which content they want displayed and in which column to display it. Web Parts allow you to provide that functionality with drag-and-drop "parts" of your page.

Create a New Site

To learn about Web Parts, create a new web site (call it WebParts) and copy the SitePersonalization web site from the beginning of this chapter (not the Themes web site you just completed).

Set the Welcome page as the start page and make sure you can log in with an account you created previously (or, alternatively, set CreateAccount as the start page and create a new account to work with).

Web Parts Architecture

Web Parts are created and managed on top of personalization using the WebPartManager control to manage the interaction of Web Parts, and normal ASP UI Controls to create the user-managed interface.

Creating Zones

A page that uses Web Parts is divided into *zones*: areas of the page that can contain content and controls that derive from the Part class (Part controls). They can also contain consistent UI elements (header and footer styles, border styles, etc.) known as the *chrome* of the control.

It is typical (though certainly not required) to organize these zones using tables.

To see a simple example of Web Parts at work, follow these steps:

1. Create a new page called *WebPartsDemo.aspx*.
2. Open the WebParts section of your Toolbox, and drag a WebPartManager onto your page.

   The job of the WebPartManager is to track and coordinate all the Web Part controls on the page. It will not be visible when the page is running.
3. Add a new table, with two rows and three columns. Rearrange the columns so that they are not of even size.
4. Drag a WebPartZone into each of the six table cells. Each WebPartZone will have a default name (e.g., WebPartZone6) and a default heading. You can easily modify either or both of these properties in the Properties window, as shown in Figure 12-50.

Set the HeaderText property on the first Web Part control to News.

Adding Controls to Zones

Drag a Label control into the zone. The normal ASP.Label control is automatically wrapped in a Web Part control, and its title is set to Untitled, as shown in Figure 12-51.

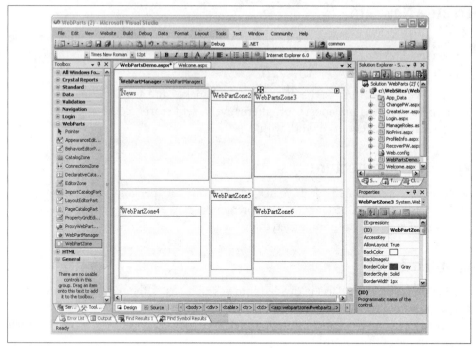

Figure 12-50. Web Parts Zones

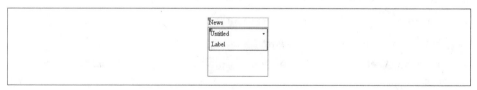

Figure 12-51. Label Web Part

Switch to Source view and set the `Title` property of the label to Today's News and the text to `<br/>New Translation of In Search Of <em>Lost Time</em> Sets English World On Fire`.

 Title is not normally a property of the Label control, and will not show up in the Properties window or IntelliSense. However, when you add it to a `WebPartZone` it is wrapped, at runtime, in a `GenericWebPart` control that does recognize this property. Ignore intelliSense and press on.

Switch back to Design view and drag a `ListBox` control into `WebPartZone3`. Set the header text for the `WebPartZone` to `Sponsors`. Click on the `ListBox`, and then on its smart tag and then click on Edit Items to open the ListItems Collection Editor. Add a few items to the `ListBox`. Back in Source view, set the `Title` property to Our

Sponsors. (This control, like the `Label` control, does not inherently have a `Title` property, so IntelliSense will complain, but as the note above explains, all will be well.)

Add a link in the `LoggedInTemplate` in *Welcome.aspx*, to take the user to your new page and run the program. Login using one of the accounts you set up previously and click on the link to the new Web Parts page.

You should see two Web Parts, as shown in Figure 12-52.

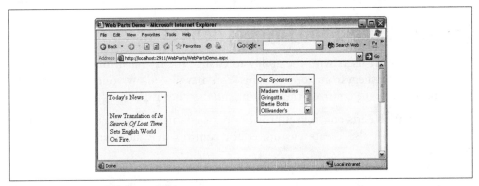

Figure 12-52. Two Web Parts visible

Minimizing and Restoring

Click on the tag next to the title and a menu appears allowing you to minimize or close the Web Part, as shown in Figure 12-53.

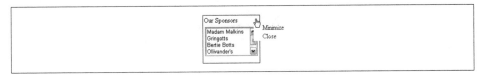

Figure 12-53. Minimize or Close

If you choose Minimize, the Web Part is minimized to its title, and the minimize tag offers the choices of Restore or Close, as shown in Figure 12-54.

Figure 12-54. Restore or close

Exit the application. Start it again, sign back in, and navigate back to these pages. Aha! The minimized zone remains minimized. Each individual's personalized Web Parts are automagically persisted through the personalization database.

Web Parts

Web Part controls derive from the Part class and are the essential UI of a Web Parts page. You can create custom Web Part controls or you can use existing ASP.NET server controls, user controls, and custom controls, all of which will be wrapped for you in a generic Web Parts control.

Enabling Editing and Layout Changes

Web Parts provide users with the ability to change the layout of the Web Part controls by dragging them from zone to zone. You may also allow your users to modify the appearance of the controls, their layout and their behavior.

The built-in Web Parts control set provides basic editing of any Web Part control on the page. You an also create custom editor controls that allow users to do more extensive editing.

Creating a User Control to Enable Changing Page Layout

To edit the contents of zones or move controls from one zone to another, you need to be able to enter Edit and Design mode. To do so, you will create a new user control called *DisplayModeMenu.ascx*, that will allow the user to change modes among Browse, Edit, and Design, as shown in Figure 12-55.

Figure 12-55. Display Mode user control

Right-click on the web project in the Solution explorer and choose Add New Item. Select Web User Control and name the new user control DisplayModeMenu.

 User controls are described in detail in Chapter 13.

Add the highlighted code listed in in Example 12-25 to the content file of your new user control.

Example 12-25. DisplayModeMenu .ascx file

```
<%@ Control Language="VB"
AutoEventWireup="false"
```

Example 12-25. DisplayModeMenu .ascx file (continued)

```
CodeFile="DisplayModeMenu.ascx.vb"
Inherits="DisplayModeMenu" %>
<div>
  <asp:Panel ID="Panel1" runat="server"
    Borderwidth="1"
    Width="230"
    BackColor="lightgray"
    Font-Names="Verdana, Arial, Sans Serif" >
    <asp:Label ID="Label1" runat="server"
      Text=" Display Mode"
      Font-Bold="true"
      Font-Size="8"
      Width="120" />
    <asp:DropDownList ID="ddlDisplayMode" runat="server"
      AutoPostBack="true"
      EnableViewState="false"
      Width="120"
      OnSelectedIndexChanged="ddlDisplayMode_SelectedIndexChanged" />
  </asp:Panel>
</div>
```

This code creates a panel, and within that panel it adds a single drop-down list (ddlDisplayMode). It also sets the event handler for when the Selected item changes in the drop-down list. To support this page, open the code-behind file (*DisplayModeMenu. ascx.vb*) and add the code shown in Example 12-26.

Example 12-26. DisplayModeMenu.ascx.vb

```
Imports System.Web.UI
Partial Class DisplayModeMenu
    Inherits System.Web.UI.UserControl

  Dim myWebPartManager As WebPartManager


  Protected Sub Page_Init( _
  ByVal sender As Object, _
  ByVal e As System.EventArgs) Handles Me.Init
    AddHandler Page.InitComplete, AddressOf Page_InitComplete
  End Sub

  Protected Sub Page_InitComplete( _
  ByVal sender As Object, _
  ByVal e As System.EventArgs)

  myWebPartManager = _
    WebPartManager.GetCurrentWebPartManager(Page)

  For Each mode As WebPartDisplayMode In _
    myWebPartManager.SupportedDisplayModes
    Dim modeName As String = mode.Name
```

Example 12-26. DisplayModeMenu.ascx.vb (continued)

```
    If mode.IsEnabled(myWebPartManager) Then
       Dim myListItem As ListItem = _
          New ListItem(modeName, modeName)
       ddlDisplayMode.Items.Add(myListItem)
    End If
  Next
End Sub


  Protected Sub ddlDisplayMode_SelectedIndexChanged( _
  ByVal sender As Object, _
  ByVal e As System.EventArgs) _
  Handles ddlDisplayMode.SelectedIndexChanged
     Dim selectedMode As String = ddlDisplayMode.SelectedValue
     Dim mode As WebPartDisplayMode = _
     myWebPartManager.SupportedDisplayModes(selectedMode)
     If (mode IsNot Nothing) Then
        myWebPartManager.DisplayMode = mode
     End If
  End Sub


  Protected Sub Page_PreRender( _
  ByVal sender As Object, _
  ByVal e As System.EventArgs) Handles Me.PreRender
     Dim items As ListItemCollection = ddlDisplayMode.Items
     Dim selectedIndex As Integer = _
     items.IndexOf(items.FindByText(myWebPartManager.DisplayMode.Name))
     ddlDisplayMode.SelectedIndex = selectedIndex
  End Sub
End Class
```

Open the WebPartsDemo page in Design mode and make a space between the WebPartManager and the table of zones. Drag the *DisplayModeMenu.ascx* file from the Solution explorer into that space. Change to Source view and notice that Visual Studio 2005 has done two things for you: it has registered the new control:

```
<%@ Register Src="DisplayModeMenu.ascx" TagName="DisplayModeMenul"
TagPrefix="uc1" %>
```

and it has placed the control into the form:

```
<div>
    <asp:WebPartManager ID="WebPartManager1" runat="server" />
    <uc1:DisplayModeMenul ID="DisplayModeMenul1" runat="server" />
```

Before testing this, delete the Web Part Zone in the lower righthand cell in the table and drag an Editor Zone into that cell. Drag an AppearanceEditorPart and a LayoutEditorPart onto the Editor Zone. To make the Editor Zone stand out, click on its smart tab and choose AutoFormat and then Professional. Your design page should look more or less like Figure 12-56.

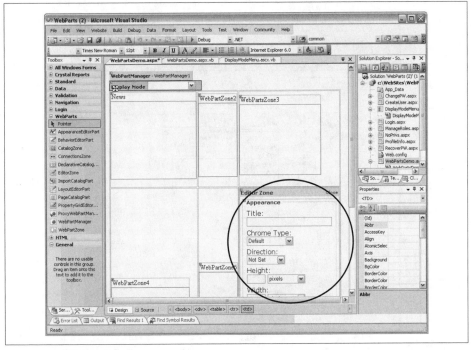

Figure 12-56. Editor Zone

Moving a Part

Run the application. When you log in and go to the Web Parts page, you are in Browse mode. Use the Display mode drop-down list to switch to Design mode and all the zones (except the Editing Zone) appear. You can now click on any Web Part (e.g., Today's News) and drag it to any other zone, as shown in Figure 12-57.

Editing a Part

Next, change the drop-down list to Edit mode. Nothing much happens, but click on the drop-down tag on one of the Web Part controls. A menu appears that now includes Edit, as shown in Figure 12-58.

Click Edit and the Edit Zone appears, allowing you to edit the current Web Part, as shown in Figure 12-59.

The Appearance editor lets you change the title and look of the Web Part, while the Layout lets you change, among other things, the zone where the Web Part will appear.

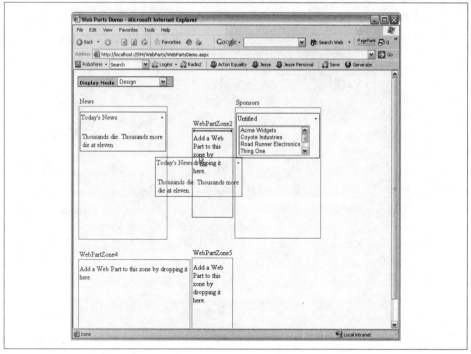

Figure 12-57. Dragging a Web Part

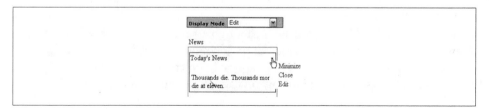

Figure 12-58. Edit mode

Adding Parts from a Catalog

You may want to provide a catalog of Web Parts that your users can add to the various zones. To do so, open *WebPartsDemo.aspx* and find Zone 4. Remove it from the cell so that the cell is empty. Next, drag a CatalogZone control into newly empty cell. Click on the zone and in the Properties window make sure the HeaderText property is set to Catalog Zone. Drag a DeclarativeCatalogPart control into the zone, as shown in Figure 12-60.

Click the smart tag on the DeclarativeCatalogPart and select Edit Templates. From the standard tab of the Toolbox drag on a Calendar and a File Upload control, as shown in Figure 12-61.

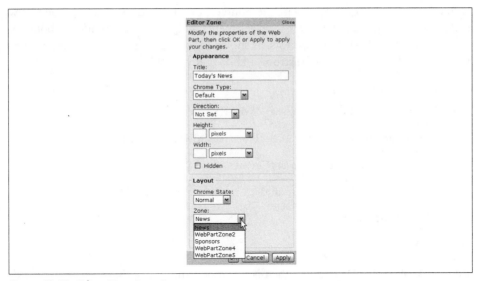

Figure 12-59. Editor Zone in action

Figure 12-60. Adding a DeclarativeCatalogPart control

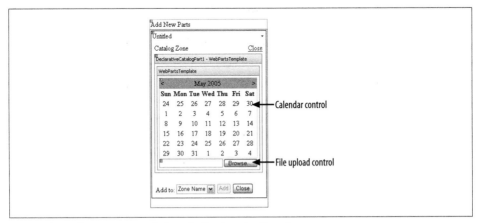

Figure 12-61. Dragging controls into the Declarative Template

Before you run your program, switch to Source view and find the catalog zone you've added. Within the `<WebPartsTemplate>` element, add a `Title` attribute to both the Calendar and the File Upload controls, as shown in Example 12-27. (Again, IntelliSense will not like this attribute, but be strong and do it anyway.)

Example 12-27. Catalog Zone

```
<asp:CatalogZone ID="CatalogZone1" runat="server">
   <ZoneTemplate>
      <asp:DeclarativeCatalogPart ID="DeclarativeCatalogPart1" runat="server">
         <WebPartsTemplate>
            <asp:Calendar ID="Calendar1" runat="server"
              title="Calendar" />
            <asp:FileUpload ID="FileUpload1" runat="server" title="Upload Files" />
         </WebPartsTemplate>
      </asp:DeclarativeCatalogPart>
   </ZoneTemplate>
</asp:CatalogZone>
```

Run the application. Drop down the display mode and notice that the Catalog mode has been added, as shown in Figure 12-62.

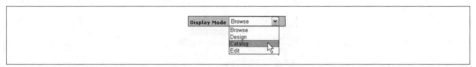

Figure 12-62. Catalog added to Display mode

When you select Catalog, the Catalog Zone is displayed. You may select one of the controls and decide which zone to place it in, as shown in Figure 12-63.

Figure 12-63. Adding a control from the catalog

Once you've picked your control and the zone to add it to, click Add and the control instantly appears in the designated zone.

CHAPTER 13

Custom Controls

In ASP.NET, Microsoft distinguishes between *user controls*, which are segments of ASP.NET pages that can be reused in other pages, and *custom controls*, which are compiled controls that act, from the client's perspective, much like web (ASP) controls. Custom controls can be created in one of three ways:

- By deriving a new custom control from an existing control (e.g., deriving your own specialized text box from asp:textbox). This is known as a *derived custom control*.

- By combining two or more existing controls into a new control. This is known as a *composite custom control*.

- By deriving from the base control class, thus creating a new custom control from scratch. This is known as a *full custom control*.

User Controls

User controls allow you to save a part of an existing ASP.NET page and reuse it in many other ASP.NET pages. A user control is almost identical to a normal *.aspx* page, with two differences: the user control has the *.ascx* extension rather than *.aspx*, and it cannot have <HTML>, <Body>, or <Form> tags.

The simplest user control is one that displays HTML only. A classic example of a simple user control is an HTML page that displays a copyright notice. To demonstrate this, create a new web application named UserControls. Once the application is open, right-click on the project and choose Add New Item. Highlight Web User Control and name your new control *Copyright.ascx*, as shown in Figure 13-1.

Example 13-1 shows the complete listing for *Copyright.ascx*, which you will notice is nothing but HTML.

Figure 13-1. Creating a user control

Example 13-1. Copyright user control

```
<%@ Control Language="VB" AutoEventWireup="false"
CodeFile="Copyright.ascx.vb" Inherits="Copyright_ascx" %>
<hr>
<table>
    <tr>
        <td align="center">Copyright 2005 Liberty Associates, Inc.</td>
    </tr>
    <tr>
        <td align="center">Support at http://www.LibertyAssociates.com</td>
    </tr>
</table>
```

To see your user control at work, you'll modify *Default.aspx*, adding a few controls as well as the user control (to provide a copyright at the bottom of the page). The first step is to register your copyright control at the top of the page with a `Register` statement:

```
<%@ Page Language="VB" AutoEventWireup="false"
CodeFile="Default.aspx.vb" Inherits="Default_aspx" %>
<%@Register tagprefix="OReilly" Tagname="copyright" src="copyright.ascx" %>
```

Notice that this consists of a `tagPrefix` (e.g., `"OReilly"`) and a `TagName`: `"copyright"` as well as a pointer to where this control is defined (`src="copyright.ascx"`).

The next step is to add the control to your page. Just as you have used a tagprefix (asp) and a tagname (Button) for web controls:

```
<asp:Button>
```

here you will use your own prefix and tagname:

```
<OReilly:copyright runat="server" ID="copyright1" />
```

Add this line to the bottom of your form, just above the closing `<div>` statement. Next, switch to Design view and you'll see the copyright in place.

Now, create a second page (*testUserControl.aspx*) and add controls to that page. Remember to register the user control at the top of the page using the same `Register` directive, and place the control in the page where you want it to appear. Create hyperlinks on both pages so that you can move from one to the other. You should see that the user control is displayed at the bottom of each page, serving as reusable code, as demonstrated in Figure 13-2.

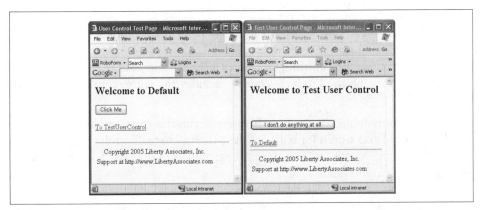

Figure 13-2. Basic user control on two pages

The copyright user control is shown at the bottom of both pages, as you would expect.

Adding Code to User Controls

So far, all you've put into the user control is straight HTML. This is simple, but also somewhat limited. In the next example, you'll create a user control that reuses your carefully developed and somewhat complex interface and code from a previous example.

Reopen the `WebNorthWindDataControls` application you developed in Chapter 10 (or use the downloaded source). Open the *Products.aspx* page and copy everything within the `<div>` tags to the clipboard.

Now return to your `UserControls` application and create a new User Control. Name it *NorthWindProductsControl.ascx*. Open the file in Source view, and paste the clipboard contents anywhere after the `<%@ Control>` directive.

Go back to `WebNorthWindDataControls`. Copy the code-behind for the methods used by this page, and paste them into the code-behind of your new user control.

Finally, open *TestUserControl.aspx* and add two lines. The first is the registration line for your new user control at the top of the page:

```
<%@Register tagprefix="OReilly" Tagname="Products" src="NorthWindProductsControl.ascx" %>
```

The second line inserts an instance of this control into the page:

```
<OReilly:Products runat="server" ID="Products1" />
```

To make the control stand out, I'll place it within an ASP:Panel:

```
<asp:Panel Height="50px" ID="Panel1" runat="server"
Width="125px" BackColor="#C0FFFF" BorderStyle="Groove">
    <OReilly:Products runat="server" ID="Products1" />
</asp:Panel>
```

The panel surrounds the control (and creates a border and background color) while the single line placing the Products control includes the entire control and its supporting code.

There is one more thing you must do before you run this program, however. Examine the *.ascx* file and search for either of the SqlDataSource controls. You'll find that both refer to the NorthwindConnectionString, which you created in the previous project, but not in this one:

```
<asp:SqlDataSource ID="NorthWindProductsDataSource" runat="server"
    SelectCommand="SELECT [ProductID], [ProductName] FROM [Products]"
    ConnectionString="<%$ ConnectionStrings:NorthwindConnectionString %>">
</asp:SqlDataSource>
```

This is easy to rectify, however. Return to WebNorthWindDataControls, and open the *Web.config* file. You'll find connectionString defined as follows:

```
<connectionStrings>
  <add name="NorthwindConnectionString"
    connectionString="Your connection string here"
    providerName="System.Data.SqlClient" />
</connectionStrings>
```

Open the *Web.config* on your new project and you'll find an empty connectionStrings element. (If you haven't yet run the application in Debug mode, you won't have a *Web.config* file. In this case, just press F5 to run the application, and tell Visual Studio to create a *Web.config* file when it asks what it should do.)

```
<connectionStrings />
```

Replace the empty element with the element you retrieved from WebNorthWindDataControls, and you are ready to run your application. It should look like Figure 13-3

Control properties

There can be only one @Control directive for each user control. This attribute is used by the ASP.NET page parser and compiler to set attributes for your user control. Possible values are shown in Table 13-1.

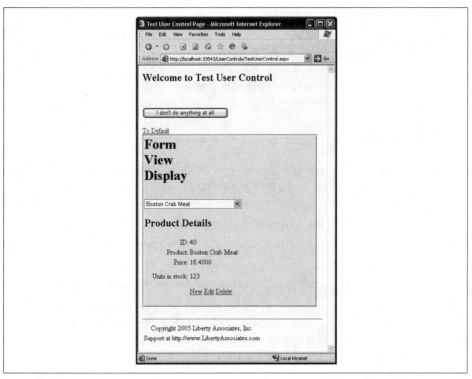

Figure 13-3. Product user control

Table 13-1. @Control directives

Attribute	Description	Possible values
AutoEventWireup	true indicates the page automatically posts back to the server. If false, the developer must fire the server event manually.	true or false; default is true.
ClassName	The class name for the page.	Any valid class name.
CompilerOptions	Passed to compiler.	Any string indicating valid compiler options.
Debug	Whether to compile with debug symbols.	true or false; default is false.
Description	Text description of the page.	Any valid text.
EnableViewState	Is view state maintained for the user control?	true or false; default is true.
Explicit	Should page be compiled with VB.NET option explicit?	true or false; default is false.
Inherits	Defines a code-behind class.	Any class derived from UserControl.
Language	The language used for inline rendering and server-side script blocks.	Any .NET-supported language.
Strict	Page should be compiled using VB.NET Strict option.	true or false; default is false. Set this true!

Table 13-1. @Control directives (continued)

Attribute	Description	Possible values
src	Name of the source file for the code-behind.	Any valid filename. Not used by Visual Studio 2005.
WarningLevel	Compiler warning level at which compilation will abort.	0–4.

Custom Controls

So far, you have created *user controls*, which are essentially reusable web page fragments.[*] You can also create your own compiled custom controls. As noted earlier, there are three ways to create custom controls:

- Create a derived custom control by deriving from an existing control.
- Create a composite control by grouping existing controls together into a new control.
- Create a full custom control by deriving from System.Web.UI.WebControls.WebControl.

The custom controls most similar to user controls are the composite controls. The key difference is that composite controls are compiled into a DLL and used as you would any server control you find in the Toolbox.

Creating a Web Control Library

To get started, you'll create a Web Control Library in which you'll place the various custom controls for this chapter. Open Visual Studio .NET and choose New Project. In the New Project Window, create a Web Control Library called CustomControls, as shown in Figure 13-4.

After clicking OK, you'll notice that Visual Studio has created a complete custom control named WebCustomControl1. Before examining this control, create a web application to test it. Right-click on the solution in the Solution explorer and choose Add → New Web Site. Set the name of your web site to CustomControlTester. Your solution now includes two projects: a web site (with *Default.aspx*) and a Custom Controls library (with *WebCustomControl1.vb*).

Web Custom Control 1

Web Custom Control 1 is a full custom control, derived from System.Web.UI.WebControls.WebControl. Even before you fully understand how this code works, you

---

[*] In fact, user controls were originally called "Pagelets"—a far better name in my opinion, but no one at Microsoft asked my opinion.

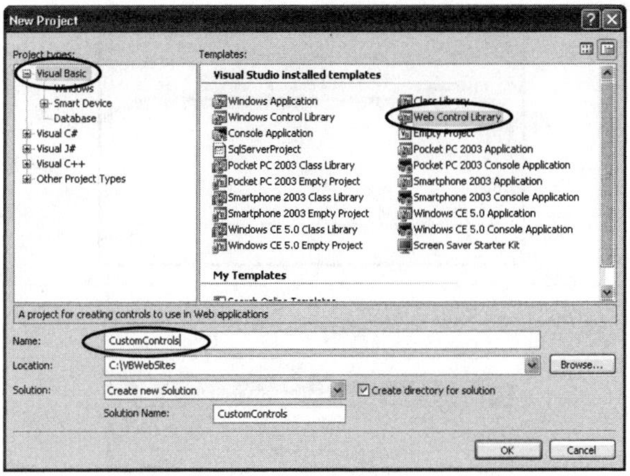

Figure 13-4. New Web Control Library

can test it in the test page you created. Open *Default.aspx* in the tester application and add a statement to register the new control:

```
<%@Register TagPrefix="OReilly"
Namespace="CustomControls"
Assembly="CustomControls" %>
```

This registers the custom control with the web page, similar to how you registered your user controls. Once again you use the @Register tag and provide a tag prefix (OReilly). Rather than providing a Tagname and src, however, you provide a Namespace and Assembly, which uniquely identify the control and the DLL that the page must use.

You now add the control to the page. The three attributes you must set are the Runat and ID attributes, which are needed for all server-side controls, and the Text attribute, which this custom control uses to determine how the control is displayed at runtime:

```
<OReilly:WebCustomControl1 Runat="Server" Text="Hello World!" Id="WC1" />
```

To build your new custom control, you must inform the CustomControlTester project about the CustomControls project. To do so, right-click on the CustomControlTester project and choose Add Reference. The Add Reference dialog opens. Select the Project tab, and choose the CustomControls project, as shown in Figure 13-5.

Click OK and then compile and run your test application. You will be asked to add a new *Web.config* file. As usual, click OK. When you view the page, the text you passed in as an attribute ("Hello World"):

```
<OReilly:WebCustomControl1 Runat="Server" Text="Hello World!" Id="WC1" />
```

is displayed, as shown in Figure 13-6.

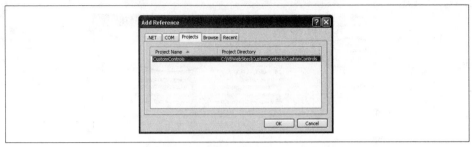

Figure 13-5. Add Reference to custom controls

Figure 13-6. Testing default custom control

Before proceeding, let's examine the code in *WebCustomControl1.vb*, created by Visual Studio 2005. This control contains a single property, Text, backed by a private string variable, _text:

```
Dim _text As String

<Bindable(True), Category("Appearance"), DefaultValue("")> _
Property [Text]() As String
    Get
        Return _text
    End Get

    Set(ByVal Value As String)
        _text = Value
    End Set
End Property
```

Notice that there are *attributes* (see the sidebar "Attributes") provided both for the property and for the class. These attributes are used by Visual Studio .NET and are not required when creating custom controls. The most common attributes for custom controls are shown in Table 13-2.

Table 13-2. Common attributes for custom controls

Attribute	Description
Bindable	Boolean. true indicates that VS.NET will display this control in the data bindings dialog box.
Browsable	Boolean. Is the property displayed in the designer?

Table 13-2. Common attributes for custom controls (continued)

Attribute	Description
Category	Determines in which category this control will be displayed when the Properties dialog is sorted by category.
DefaultValue	The default value.
Description	The text you provide is displayed in the description box in the Properties panel.

Attributes

Attributes are metadata—that is, information about the data itself. Often this data is used by tools (e.g., Visual Studio.NET).

There are two interesting facts about attributes:

- The metadata is compiled into the program (rather than into an associated file).
- You can examine that data either at runtime (using a technique called *reflection*) or independently using tools such as ILDASM.

Because all of this is fairly obscure, attributes and reflection are not covered in this book, except in so far as they are needed to accomplish specific tasks (such as COM interop, covered in Chapter 7).

Properties

Custom controls can expose properties just as any other class can. You access these properties in two ways:

1. Programmatically (e.g., in the code-behind)
2. Declaratively, by setting attributes of the custom control, as shown here:

```
<OReilly:WebCustomControl1 Runat="Server" Text="Hello World!" />
```

The Text property of the control is accessed through the Text attribute in the web page.

In the case of the Text property and the Text attribute, the mapping between the attribute and the underlying property is straightforward because both are strings.

ASP.NET will provide intelligent conversion of other types, however. For example, if the underlying type is an integer or a long, the attribute will be converted to the appropriate value type. If the value is an enumeration, ASP.NET matches the string value against the enumeration name and sets the correct enumeration value. If the value is a Boolean, ASP.NET matches the string value against the Boolean value; that is, it will match the string "True" to the Boolean value True.

The Render Method

The key method of the custom control is Render:

```
Protected Overrides Sub Render( _
ByVal output As System.Web.UI.HtmlTextWriter)
    output.Write([Text])
End Sub
```

This method is declared in the base class, and must be *overridden* in your derived class if you wish to take control of rendering to the page. In this example, the Render method uses the HtmlTextWriter object passed in as a parameter to write the string held in the Text property.

The HtmlTextWriter class derives from TextWriter and provides rich formatting capabilities. HtmlTextWriter will ensure that the elements produced are well-formed, and it will manage the attributes, including style attributes. Thus, if you want to set the text to red, you can add a color attribute, passing in an enumerated color object that you've translated to HTML, as shown in Example 13-2.

Example 13-2. Overriding the Render method

```
Protected Overrides Sub Render( _
ByVal output As System.Web.UI.HtmlTextWriter)
    output.AddStyleAttribute("color", ColorTranslator.ToHtml(Color.Red))
    output.Write([Text])
End Sub
```

 For the new line of code to compile, you will need to add an Imports statement at the top of the source code:

```
Imports System.Drawing
```

Rendering Text with Tags

You can set the text to be rendered within header (<h2>) tags with the HtmlTextWriter's RenderBeginTag and RenderEndTag methods:

```
output.RenderBeginTag("h2")
output.Write(Text)
output.RenderEndTag( )
```

The result is that when the text is output, the correct tags are created, as shown in Figure 13-7. (The source output that illustrates the HTML rendered by the Html-TextWriter is circled.)

Maintaining State

In the next example, you'll add a button to increase the size of the text in your custom control. To accomplish this, you'll eschew the rendering support of the

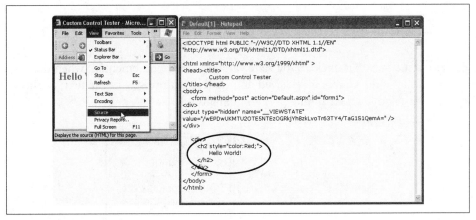

Figure 13-7. Output and source

`HtmlTextWriter`, instead writing the text yourself, using a new `Size` property (to set the size of the output text). Return to the `Render` method and replace the code you have with this new code.

```
Protected Overrides Sub Render(ByVal output As _
                            System.Web.UI.HtmlTextWriter)
    output.Write("<font size = " & Size & ">" & [Text] & "</font>")
End Sub
```

The `Size` property must maintain its state through the postback initiated by pressing the button.

```
Public Property Size( ) As Integer
    Get
        Return Convert.ToInt32(ViewState("Size"))
    End Get
    Set(ByVal Value As Integer)
        ViewState("Size") = Value.ToString( )
    End Set
End Property
```

The property `Get` method retrieves the value from `ViewState`, casts it to a string, and then converts that string to its integer equivalent. The property `Set` method stashes a string representing the size into `ViewState`.

To ensure that a valid value is in `ViewState` to start with, you'll also add a constructor to this control:

```
Public Sub New( )
    ViewState("Size") = "1"
End Sub
```

The constructor initializes the value held in `ViewState` to 1. Each press of the button will update the `Size` property. To make this work, drag a button onto *CustomControlTester.Default.aspx*, next to the custom control. Set its text to `Increase Size` and double-click on it to open the default (click) event handler.

```
Protected Sub Button1_Click( _
ByVal sender As Object, ByVal e As System.EventArgs) Handles Button1.Click
    WC1.Size += 1
End Sub
```

Each time the button is clicked, the state variable Size is incremented; when the page is drawn, the state variable is retrieved and used to set the size of the text, as shown by creating a copy of the running program in Figure 13-8.

Figure 13-8. Demonstrating event handling with custom controls

Creating Derived Controls

Most custom controls need not be created from scratch. If you are doing anything more than writing text, it is far easier to use the rendering capabilities of one or more existing controls.

Often, all you want to do is to extend the behavior of an existing control type. To do so, you will derive from that control just as you might derive from any class.

Imagine, for example, that you would like a button to maintain a count of the number of times it has been clicked. Such a button might be useful in any number of applications, but, unfortunately, the web Button control does not provide this functionality.

Create a new class in your custom controls library named CountedButton, as shown in Figure 13-9.

The Add New Item - CustomControls dialog will pop up. Select Web Custom Control and name it *CountedButton.vb*, as shown in Figure 13-10.

A new custom class is created for you. By default, it will inherit from System.Web. UI.WebControls.WebControl. Change the Inherits statement so it derives from System.Web.UI.WebControls.Button.

```
Public Class CountedButton
    Inherits System.Web.UI.WebControls.Button
```

This will allow your new custom control to inherit all the features of the standard button, which you can then extend. Your new class needs a Count property to keep track of the number of times the button is clicked. Since Count must survive the

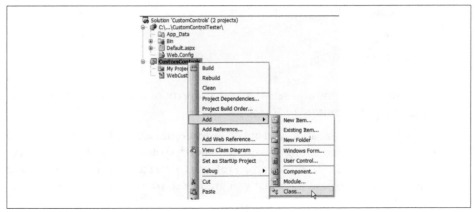

Figure 13-9. Adding new class to custom control library

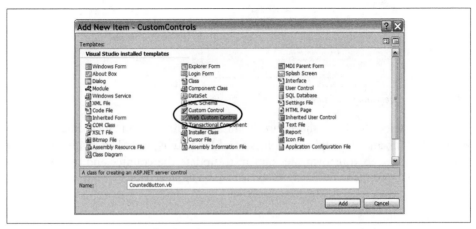

Figure 13-10. Creating CountedButton class

roundtrip to the server, you must store it in either Session or view state. Because the number of clicks is really a property of the CountedButton (rather than a value you might want to pass from page to page or persist for the life of the session), it is most appropriate to use view state, as shown in Example 13-3.

Example 13-3. Count property

```
Public Property Count( ) As Integer
    Get
        Return CInt(ViewState("Count"))
    End Get
    Set(ByVal Value As Integer)
        ViewState("Count") = Value
    End Set
End Property
```

Remember to initialize the Count to 0 in the constructor:

```
Public Sub New()
    Me.Text = "Click me"
    ViewState("Count") = 0
End Sub
```

Notice that the constructor also sets the Text property of the CountedButton (inherited from the base class button) to "Click Me".

The CountedButton also inherits, and must override, the OnClick event. Be careful here: you are not implementing an event handler, you are overriding an event declared in the base class. To do so, type Protected Overrides, and IntelliSense will offer all members of the base class that you are free to override. Choose OnClick, as shown in Figure 13-11.

Figure 13-11. Overriding OnClick event

When you select OnClick, the entire event is set up for you, including a call to MyBase.OnClick and the capitalization is fixed for you as well. This is just what you want. You'll put in your own mechanism to update the counter and to update the button's text, and then you'll call the base class (Button's) OnClick event to allow it to do whatever work it normally does.

```
Protected Overrides Sub OnClick(ByVal e As System.EventArgs)
    ViewState("Count") = CInt(ViewState("Count")) + 1
    Me.Text = ViewState("Count") & " clicks"
    MyBase.OnClick(e)
End Sub
```

When you extract the object whose key is "Count" from ViewState, what you get back is of type Object. You cast it to integer using CInt, then add 1 to that value. Finally, you store it back into ViewState using the same key: "Count".

```
ViewState("Count") = CInt(ViewState("Count")) + 1
```

Once you have the new count in ViewState, you can update the text of the button to reflect the number of clicks:

```
Me.Text = ViewState("Count") & " clicks"
```

Adding the Derived Custom Control to the ASPX Page

Return to the ASPX page to add an instance of your counted button. Since you've already registered your CustomControl library, you only have to add the actual CountedButton itself to the form:

```
<div>
    <OReilly:WebCustomControl1 Runat="Server" Text="Hello World!" Id="WC1" />
    <asp:Button ID="Button1" runat="server" Text="Increase Size" />
    <OReilly:CountedButton Runat="Server" id="CB1" />
</div>
```

When you run the application, you can click on the button, and it keeps track of the number of times it was clicked, as shown in Figure 13-12.

Figure 13-12. Testing the CountedButton

Creating Composite Controls

The third way to create a custom control is to combine two or more existing controls into a single bundled control. You can even combine custom controls with the controls provided by Microsoft.

In the next example, you'll create a somewhat advanced composite control to keep track of the number of inquiries you receive about books (perhaps books you sell on your web site). The architecture of your custom control is as follows:

- The BookInquiryList is a custom composite control that serves as a collection of BookCounter controls.
- The BookCounter is a custom control with two properties: BookName and Count.
- The (revised) CountedButton control is a derived control (derived from Button).

The BookCounter has an instance of CountedButton as a member in its Controls collection. The BookInquiryList has, in its Controls collection, zero or more instances of BookCounter.

The finished product is shown in Figure 13-13.

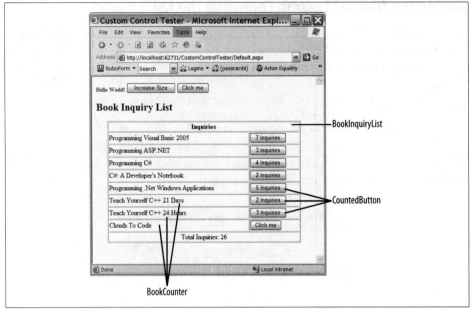

Figure 13-13. BookInquiryList

What is most interesting about this project is that you will declare the `BookCounter` members of the `BookInquiry` control *declaratively* in your aspx page. Just as you might write:

```
<asp:ListBox ID="ListBox1" runat="server">
    <asp:ListItem>Item 1</asp:ListItem>
    <asp:ListItem>Item 2</asp:ListItem>
    <asp:ListItem>Item 3</asp:ListItem>
</asp:ListBox>
```

so, with the `BookInquiry` control, you can write:

```
<OReilly:BookInquiryList Runat="Server" id="bookInquiry1">
    <OReilly:BookCounter Runat="server" BookName="Book 1" ID="B1" />
    <OReilly:BookCounter Runat="server" BookName="Book 2" ID="B2" />
    <OReilly:BookCounter Runat="server" BookName="Book 3" ID="B3" />
</OReilly:BookInquiryList>
```

This kind of declaration requires that you teach the ASP.NET parser how to create `BookCounter` objects based on their declaration; a topic covered later in this chapter. The best way to build this, however, is inside out: starting with the `CountedButton` control, then using that to build the `BookCounter`, and finally populating the `BookInquiry` control with `BookCounter` objects.

Modifying the CountedButton Derived Control

Modify the CountedButton class so that the *client* of your Countedbutton (any method that creates a CountedButton object) can pass in the string to be displayed on the button. That is, rather than displaying "5 clicks," the client can pass in (for example) the string "Inquiries" and the button will display "5 Inquiries."

Reopen the *CountedButton.vb* file and add a class member displayString of type String:

```
Private displayString As String
```

Modify the constructor to initialize displayString to the string "clicks" if no string is supplied, by creating both a default constructor (that takes no arguments) and a constructor that takes a string argument, as shown in Example 13-4.

Example 13-4. CountedButton constructors

```
Public Sub New( )
    Me.New("clicks")
End Sub

Public Sub New(ByVal displayString As String)
    Me.displayString = displayString
    If ViewState("Count") Is Nothing Then
        ViewState("Count") = 0
        Me.Text = "Click me"
    End If
End Sub
```

Rather than duplicating code in both constructors, the bulk of the work is done in the second constructor. The default constructor invokes the second constructor, passing in the string clicks. Modify the OnClick event to use the display string in its display, as shown in Example 13-5.

Example 13-5. CountedButton OnClick event handler

```
Protected Overrides Sub OnClick(ByVal e As System.EventArgs)
    ViewState("Count") = CInt(ViewState("Count")) + 1
    Me.Text = ViewState("Count") & " " & displayString
    MyBase.OnClick(e)
End Sub
```

With these changes, the CountedButton is ready to be used in the first composite control, BookCounter.

Creating the BookCounter Control

The BookCounter control is responsible for keeping track of and displaying the number of inquiries about an individual book. It does no rendering, it simply "holds" a book name (using ViewState) and a counted button (which is responsible for its own count).

Create a new class called BookCounter in your custom controls library, of type Web Custom Control, just as you did for CountedButton.

Replace the _text member variable with _countedButton of type CountedButton:

```
Dim _countedButton As CountedButton = New CountedButton("Inquiries")
```

Delete the methods provided by Visual Studio 2005 and add a property to hold the book name, as shown in Example 13-6.

Example 13-6. BookName property of Book counter

```
Public Property BookName() As String
    Get
        Return CStr(ViewState("BookName"))
    End Get
    Set(ByVal Value As String)
        ViewState("BookName") = Value
    End Set
End Property
```

The book name will be held in ViewState so that it persists across postback events. Book counter needs a second property, Count, but you'll implement Count by delegating responsibility to the member variable _countedButton, as shown in Example 13-7.

Example 13-7. Count property of Book counter

```
Public Property Count() As Integer
    Get
        Return _countedButton.Count
    End Get
    Set(ByVal Value As Integer)
        _countedButton.Count = Value
    End Set
End Property
```

You'll need a method to reset the CountedButton's count to 0, shown here in Example 13-8.

Example 13-8. Reset method of Book counter

```
Public Sub Reset()
    _countedButton.Count = 0
End Sub
```

In a moment, you'll create the BookInquiryList class which will consist of zero or more BookCounter objects. To make sure that the CountedButton is a control within each

BookCounter object created, you'll need to add _countedButton to the Controls collection of your BookCounter control. You do so by overriding the CreateChildControls method:

```
Protected Overrides Sub CreateChildControls( )
    Controls.Add(_countedButton)
End Sub
```

CreateChildControls is called in preparation for rendering and offers the BookCounter class the opportunity to add the CountedButton object as a contained control.

There is no need for BookCounter to override the Render method; the only thing it must render is the CountedButton, which can render itself. The default behavior of Render is to render all the child controls, so you don't need to do anything special to make this work.

INamingContainer

Because your BookCounter class contains a control, you must implement the INamingContainer interface. This is a "marker" interface that has no methods. The purpose of this interface is specifically to identify a control as a container control to ASP.NET. By implementing I Naming Container you instruct ASP.NET to create a new ID namespace for your BookCounter control, guaranteeing that all child controls have IDs that are unique to the page.

```
Public Class BookCounter
Inherits System.Web.UI.WebControls.WebControl
Implements INamingContainer
```

 For more on interfaces, please see Chapter 16.

To make this crystal clear, Example 13-9 has the complete definition of the BookCounter class.

Example 13-9. BookCounter class

```
Public Class BookCounter
Inherits System.Web.UI.WebControls.WebControl
Implements INamingContainer

    Dim _countedButton As CountedButton = New CountedButton("Inquiries")

    Public Property BookName( ) As String
        Get
            Return CStr(ViewState("BookName"))
        End Get
        Set(ByVal Value As String)
            ViewState("BookName") = Value
```

Example 13-9. BookCounter class (continued)

```
        End Set
    End Property

    Public Property Count() As Integer
        Get
            Return _countedButton.Count
        End Get
        Set(ByVal Value As Integer)
            _countedButton.Count = Value
        End Set
    End Property

    Public Sub Reset()
        _countedButton.Count = 0
    End Sub

    Protected Overrides Sub CreateChildControls()
        Controls.Add(_countedButton)
    End Sub
End Class
```

Creating the BookInquiryList Composite Control

You have now created a CountedButton and a custom control, BookCounter, that holds
the name of a book and an instance of CountedButton within it. All of this will be
wrapped within a BookInquiryList control that will be designed to hold zero or more
BookCounter instances.

To start, create a new custom control: BookInquiryList. Strip out the attributes created by Visual Studio 2005 and strip out all the code within the class. Once again,
have your class implement INamingContainer:

```
Public Class BookInquiryList
Inherits System.Web.UI.WebControls.WebControl _
Implements INamingContainer
```

Declaring the BookCounters in the .aspx File

As noted above, you want to be able to declare a BookInquiryList in your aspx page,
and then to declare BookCounter elements within the BookInquiry list, just as you do
with Lists and ListItems. You can type this right into the aspx file itself.

```
<OReilly:BookInquiryList Runat="Server" id="bookInquiry1">
    <OReilly:BookCounter Runat="server" BookName="Book 1" ID="B1" />
    <OReilly:BookCounter Runat="server" BookName="Book 2" ID="B2" />
    <OReilly:BookCounter Runat="server" BookName="Book 3" ID="B3" />
</OReilly:BookInquiryList>
```

Making this work with a Visual Studio collection editor is a much more advanced topic beyond the scope of this book.

For this to work, the ASP.NET parser must know how to create the BookCounter objects within the BookInquiryList. You accomplish this in two steps:

1. Declare a class BookCounterBuilder that inherits from ControlBuilder, and that knows how to "build" an instance of BookCounter (more on that below).

2. Add an attribute to the declaration of BookInquiryList indicating where to find the BookCounterBuilder.

To get started, create your BookCounterBuilder. It will inherit from ControlBuilder and override just two methods: GetChildControlType and AppendLiteralString. The latter will be left empty; its job is just to have the AppendLiteralString method do nothing.

```
Public Overrides Sub AppendLiteralString(ByVal s As String)
End Sub
```

The override of GetChildControlType is slightly more complicated. It is passed in a tagName by the ASP.NET parser (the tag you declare in the *.aspx* page) and a dictionary of attributes (attributes you add to the declaration in the *.aspx* page).

In this case, all you need to do is examine the tag name. If it is "BookCounter," you create a BookCounter object and return its type by calling its inherited GetType method:

```
Public Overrides Function GetChildControlType( _
    ByVal tagName As String, ByVal attributes As IDictionary) As Type
    If tagName = "BookCounter" Then
        Dim theBookCounter As BookCounter
        Return theBookCounter.GetType
    Else
        Return Nothing
    End If
End Function
```

With the BookCounterBuilder created, you are ready to add the required attributes to the BookInquiryList:

```
<ControlBuilder(GetType(BookCounterBuilder)), ParseChildren(False> _
Public Class BookInquiryList
Inherits System.Web.UI.WebControls.WebControl _
Implements INamingContainer
```

The ControlBuilder attribute specifies the ControlBuilder class for building a custom control within the ASP.NET parser that will parse your aspx page. The second attribute, ParseChildren, must be set to False. If the value were True, you'd be signaling that the nested values were properties of the object, rather than child controls.

Implementing BookInquiryList.Render

All that is left is to override the Render method. You'll start by declaring a local variable to keep track of the total number of clicks of all the buttons:

```
Dim totalClicks As Integer = 0
```

You'll then write out a table, complete with a header:

```
output.Write("<Table border='1' width='90%' cellpadding='1'" & _
    "cellspacing='1' align = 'center' >")
output.Write("<TR><TD colspan = '2' align='center'>")
output.Write("<B> Inquiries </B></TD></TR>")
```

You next create a table row for each BookCounter object you'll add. To determine how many books to add, you'll extract all the BookCounter objects in the BookInquiryList's Controls collection. Each time you extract one, you'll ask it for its count (which will, you remember, pass the query along to its counted button). You will then call RenderControl on the BookCounter, and the control will be rendered to the page within the table cell tags.

```
For Each current As BookCounter In Controls
    totalClicks += current.Count
    output.Write("<TR><TD align='left'>" & _
        current.BookName + "</TD>")
    output.RenderBeginTag("TD")
    current.RenderControl(output)
    output.RenderEndTag( )              ' end td
    output.Write("</tr>")
Next
```

Once you are done, you'll add one more row for the total:

```
Dim strTotalInquiries As String = totalClicks.ToString( )
output.Write("<TR><TD colspan='2' align='center'> " & _
    " Total Inquiries: " & _
    CStr(strTotalInquiries) & "</TD></TR>")
```

The complete Render method is shown in Example 13-10.

Example 13-10. Complete BookInquiryList.Render method

```
Protected Overrides Sub Render(ByVal output As HtmlTextWriter)

    Dim totalClicks As Integer = 0

    ' Write the header
    output.Write("<Table border='1' width='90%' cellpadding='1'" & _
        "cellspacing='1' align = 'center' >")
    output.Write("<TR><TD colspan = '2' align='center'>")
    output.Write("<B> Inquiries </B></TD></TR>")

    ' if you have no contained controls, write the default msg.
    If Controls.Count = 0 Then
        output.Write("<TR><TD colspan='2' align='center'>")
```

Example 13-10. Complete BookInquiryList.Render method (continued)

```
            output.Write("<B> No books listed </B></TD></TR>")
            ' otherwise render each of the contained controls
        Else
            ' iterate over the controls collection and
            ' display the book name for each
            ' then tell each contained control to render itself
            'Dim current As BookCounter

            For Each current As BookCounter In Controls
                totalClicks += current.Count
                output.Write("<TR><TD align='left'>" & _
                    current.BookName + "</TD>")
                output.RenderBeginTag("TD")
                current.RenderControl(output)
                output.RenderEndTag( )                ' end td
                output.Write("</tr>")
            Next
            Dim strTotalInquiries As String = totalClicks.ToString
            output.Write("<TR><TD colspan='2' align='center'> " & _
                " Total Inquiries: " & _
                CStr(strTotalInquiries) & "</TD></TR>")
        End If
        output.Write("</TABLE>")
End Sub
```

You are now ready to declare an instance of BookInquiryList within *Default.aspx*, adding any number of BookCounter entries, as shown in Example 13-11.

Example 13-11. Default.aspx with BookInquiryList declaration

```
<%@ Page Language="VB" AutoEventWireup="false" CodeFile="Default.aspx.vb"
Inherits="Default_aspx" %>
<%@Register TagPrefix="OReilly" Namespace="CustomControls" Assembly="CustomControls" %>

<!DOCTYPE html PUBLIC "-//W3C//DTD XHTML 1.1//EN" "http://www.w3.org/TR/xhtml11/DTD/
xhtml11.dtd">

<html xmlns="http://www.w3.org/1999/xhtml" >
<head runat="server">
    <title>Custom Control Tester</title>
</head>
<body>
    <form id="form1" runat="server">
    <div>
        <OReilly:WebCustomControl1 Runat="Server" Text="Hello World!" Id="WC1" />
        <asp:Button ID="Button1" runat="server" Text="Increase Size" />
        <OReilly:CountedButton Runat="Server" id="CB1" />

        <br /> <h2>Book Inquiry List </h2>

        <OReilly:BookInquiryList Runat="Server" id="bookInquiry1">
```

Example 13-11. Default.aspx with BookInquiryList declaration (continued)

```
        <OReilly:BookCounter Runat="server"
        BookName="Programming Visual Basic 2005"
        ID="Bookcounter9"/>

        <OReilly:BookCounter Runat="server"
        BookName="Programming ASP.NET"
        ID="Bookcounter1"/>

        <OReilly:BookCounter Runat="server"
        BookName="Programming C#"
        ID="Bookcounter2" />

        <OReilly:BookCounter Runat="server"
        BookName="C#: A Developer's Notebook"
        ID="Bookcounter10" />

        <OReilly:BookCounter Runat="server"
        BookName="Programming .NET Windows Applications"
        ID="Bookcounter11" />


        <OReilly:BookCounter Runat="server"
        BookName="Teach Yourself C++ in 21 Days"
        ID="BookCounter3" />

        <OReilly:BookCounter Runat="server"
        BookName="Teach Yourself C++ in 24 Hours"
        ID="Bookcounter4" />

        <OReilly:BookCounter Runat="server"
        BookName="Clouds to Code"
        ID="Bookcounter5" />

    </OReilly:BookInquiryList>

    </div>
    </form>
</body>
</html>
```

Assignment of Responsibilities

In this composite control the various responsibilities are spread among the participating objects illustrating good encapsulation. The BookInquiryList object assumes all responsibility for laying out the control, creating the table, and deciding what will be rendered where. However, it delegates responsibility for rendering the button object to the individual contained controls.

Similarly, the `BookInquiryList` is responsible for the total number of inquiries—because that information transcends what any individual `BookCounter` object might know. However, the responsibility for the count held by each `BookCounter` is delegated to the `BookCounter` itself. As far as the `BookInquiryList` is concerned, it gets that information directly from the `BookCounter`'s Count property. It turns out, however, that `BookCounter`, in turn, delegates that responsibility to the `CountedButton`.

CHAPTER 14

Web Services

Normal web pages allow interaction between the client browser and the web server hosting the web page. Many businesses, however, need to provide information not to users, but to other programs.

For example, Amazon.com has a service that allows applications to send in the ISBN of a book and get back information about the publisher, sale price, sales rank, and so forth. This service has no user interface: it is a way for your program to interact with their data. Such a service, providing information with no user interface, using standard web protocols, is called a *web service*.

Platform Independence

Unlike previous technologies for distributed computing (such as DCOM), web services make it unnecessary for both ends of the connection to be running the same operating system or to be programmed in the same language. For example, the server code might be written in VB.2005 on Windows 2000 while the client is a C++ program running on a Unix machine, or vice versa. In other words, while previous technologies required that the client and server be tightly coupled, web services permit them to be loosely coupled.

All that is necessary is that both server and client support the industry standard protocols HTTP, SOAP, and XML. HTTP is the protocol used by the Web. SOAP (Simple Object Access Protocol) is a lightweight, object-oriented protocol based on XML that, in turn, is a cross-platform standard for formatting and organizing information.

How Web Services Work

Microsoft has used web services to mimic RPC (remote procedure calls). You ask for an "object" from a web service, and what you get back provides the public interface to an object running on the web service's server. You can interact with that object, calling methods and examining or setting properties. In this model, web services allow an object on the server to expose program logic to clients over the Internet. Clients call exposed methods on the web service using standard Internet protocols.

Typically, both ends of the connection communicate using SOAP messages (see the sidebar "SOAP"), which consist of self-describing, text-based XML documents.*

SOAP

SOAP (Simple Object Access Protocol) is an XML grammar that's tailored for exchanging web service data. SOAP uses XML syntax to format its content. It is, by design, as simple as possible, and, it is very flexible. Since SOAP messages consist of XML, which is plain text, they can easily pass through firewalls, unlike many proprietary, binary formats.

SOAP is not limited to name/value pairs as HTTP-GET and HTTP-POST are. Instead, SOAP can also be used to send more complex objects, including datasets, classes, and other objects.

Creating a Web Service

There are two broad aspects to web service development: creating the web service and consuming the web service. You'll start by creating a simple web service that provides a simulated stock information service. Your web service will expose two methods:

```
Function GetName(stockSymbol As String) as String
Function GetPrice (stockSymbol As String) as Float
```

 If this web service were an actual production program, the data returned would be fetched from a live database. In order not to confuse web service issues with data access issues, the data in this chapter will be stored in a two-dimensional array of strings.

Begin by creating a new web site named StockPriceWebService. Be sure to click on ASP.NET Web Service in the templates window, as shown in Figure 14-1.

Visual Studio 2005 does a lot of the work of setting up your web service, including adding the necessary <WebService> attributes to your class, and creating a template method (HelloWorld) complete with <WebMethod> attributes. For more on attributes, see the note on attributes in Chapter 12.

---

* It is also possible to communicate via HTTP-GET or HTTP-POST requests.

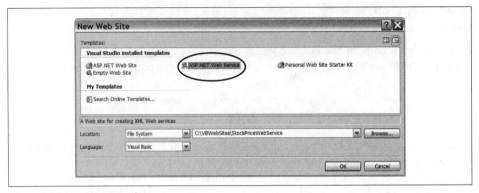

Figure 14-1. Creating a web service

You'll add a two dimensional array of stock symbols with their names and fictional prices, as shown in Example 14-1.

Example 14-1. Two-dimensional array of stock symbols and prices

```
Dim stocks As String(,) = _
{ _
    {"MSFT", "Microsoft", "25.22"}, _
    {"DELL", "Dell Computers", "42.12"}, _
    {"INTC", "Intel", "25.50"}, _
    {"YHOO", "Yahoo!", "30.81"}, _
    {"GE", "General Electric", "37.51"}, _
    {"IBM", "International Business Machine", "91.98"}, _
    {"GM", "General Motors", "64.72"}, _
    {"F", "Ford Motor Company", "25.05"} _
}
```

You are now ready to create your two web methods. Web methods are exposed to web clients by tagging them with the <WebMethod> attribute. The first method, GetPrice, takes a symbol as a string and returns the price, as shown in Example 14-2.

Example 14-2. GetPrice WebMethod

```
<WebMethod( )> _
Public Function GetPrice(ByVal StockSymbol As String) As Double
    Dim returnValue As Double = 0
    For counter As Integer = 0 To stocks.GetLength(0) - 1
        If (String.Compare(StockSymbol, stocks(counter, 0), True) = 0) Then
            returnValue = Convert.ToDouble(stocks(counter, 2))
        End If
    Next
    Return returnValue
End Function
```

You can imagine a two-dimensional array as an array of arrays. The first value passed into the offset operator for stocks (counter), ticks through each of the internal arrays in turn:

```
stocks(counter, 0)
```

The second value passed in, (offset 0), picks from within the internal array. The first field (offset 0) is the stock symbol, the second symbol (offset 1) is the stock name, and the third field (offset 2) is the price:

```
returnValue = Convert.ToDouble(stocks(counter, 2))
```

The GetName method is extremely similar, except that instead of returning a price, it returns the name of the stock, as shown in Example 14-3.

Example 14-3. GetName WebMethod

```
<WebMethod()> _
Public Function GetName(ByVal StockSymbol As String) As String
    Dim returnValue As String = "Symbol not found."
    For counter As Integer = 0 To stocks.GetLength(0) - 1
        If (String.Compare(StockSymbol, stocks(counter, 0), True) = 0) Then
            returnValue = stocks(counter, 1)
        End If
    Next
    Return returnValue
End Function
```

Notice that Visual Studio 2005 created an *.asmx* page, but it has only one line in it:

```
<%@ WebService Language="vb" CodeBehind="~/App_Code/Service.vb" Class="Service" %>
```

This determines that the code for the web service will be in the code behind (*Service.vb*) file. The Class attribute created by Visual Studio 2005 ties this *.asmx* page to the class defined in *Service.vb*.

Your new class derives from WebService. While this is the most common way to create a web service, it is optional. However, doing so does give you access to a variety of useful ASP.NET objects: Application and Session (for preserving state); User (for authenticating the caller); and Context (for access to HTTP-specific information about the caller's request, accessed through the HttpContext class).

WebMethod Properties

Each web method is preceded by the WebMethod attribute. You are free to add properties to this attribute. The following sections describe the valid WebMethod properties.

The BufferResponse Property

By default, ASP.NET buffers the entire response to a request before sending it from the server to the client. Under most circumstances, this is the optimal behavior. However, if the response is very lengthy, you might want to disable this buffering by setting the `WebMethod` attribute's `BufferResponse` property to `False`. If set to `False`, the response will be returned to the client in 16 KB chunks.

```
<WebMethod(BufferResponse:=False)>
```

The CacheDuration Property

Web services, like web pages, can cache the results returned to clients. If a client makes a request that is identical to a request made recently by another client, then the server will return the response stored in the cache. This can result in a huge performance gain, especially if servicing the request is an expensive operation (such as querying a database or performing a lengthy computation).

> For the cached results to be used, the new request must be *identical* to the previous request. If the web method has parameters, the parameter values must also be identical. For example, if the `GetPrice` web method of the `StockTicker` web service is called with a value of `msft` passed in as the stock symbol, that result will be cached separately from a request for `dell`.

The `CacheDuration` property defines how long the response is cached, in seconds. Once the `CacheDuration` period has expired, a new page is sent. To set the `CacheDuration` for 30 seconds, you'd write,

```
<WebMethod(CacheDuration:=30)>
```

The default value for `CacheDuration` is 0, which disables caching of results.

The Description Property

The `WebMethod` attribute's `Description` property allows you to attach a descriptive string to a web method. This description will appear on the web service help page when you test the web service in a browser.

When a representation of the web service is encoded into the SOAP message that is sent out to potential consumers, the `WebMethod Description` property is included:

```
<WebMethod(Description:="Returns the stock price for the input stock symbol.")>
```

The EnableSession Property

The WebMethod attribute's EnableSession property defaults to False.

If set to True and if your web service inherits from WebService, the session-state collection can be accessed with the WebService.Session property. If the web service does not inherit from the WebService class, then the session-state collection can be accessed directly from HttpContext.Current.Session.

To see this at work, you'll add a method that tells you how many times it has been called in the current session:

```
<WebMethod(Description:="Number of hits per session.", EnableSession:=True)> _
Public Function HitCounter() As Integer
    If Session("HitCounter") Is Nothing Then
        Session("HitCounter") = 1
    Else
        Session("HitCounter") = CInt(Session("HitCounter")) + 1
    End If
    Return CInt(Session("HitCounter"))
End Function
```

> Enabling session state adds additional performance overhead to the application.

Session state is implemented via HTTP cookies in ASP.NET web services, so if the transport mechanism is something other than HTTP (say, SMTP), then the session-state functionality will not be available.

The TransactionOption Property

ASP.NET web methods can use transactions, but only if the transaction originates in that web method. In other words, the web method can only participate as the *root object* in a transaction. This means that a consuming application cannot call a web method as part of a transaction and have that web method participate in the transaction.

The WebMethod attribute's TransactionOption property specifies whether or not a web method should start a transaction. There are five legal values of the property, all contained in the TransactionOption enumeration. However, because a web method transaction must be the root object, there are only two different behaviors: either a new transaction is started (Required or RequiresNew) or it is not (Disabled, NotSupported, or Supported).

To use transactions in a web service, you must take several additional steps.

Add a reference to *System.EnterpriseServices.dll*. In Visual Studio .NET, this is done through the Solution explorer or the Project → Add Reference menu item. Add the System.EnterpriseServices namespace:

```
Imports System.EnterpriseServices
```

You must also add a TransactionOption property with a value of RequiresNew or Required to the WebMethod attribute:

```
<WebMethod(TransactionOption:=TransactionOption.RequiresNew)>
```

If there are no exceptions thrown by the web method, then the transaction will automatically commit unless the SetAbort( ) method is explicitly called. If an unhandled exception is thrown, the transaction will automatically abort.

The MessageName Property

As with aux class, it is possible to have more than one method or function defined in your web service class with the same name (method overloading). They are differentiated by their *signature* (the number, data type, and order of their parameters).

Unfortunately, method overloading is not supported by the standard industry protocols, so if you do overload a web method, you must provide each overloaded version with its own unique MessageName property. When the overloaded method is referred to in SOAP messages, the MessageName will be used, and not the method name.

To see the MessageName property at work, you'll add an overloaded method named GetValue. The first overload accepts the stock name as a parameter (presumably it looks up the user's account in the database, and returns the value of that stock). The second overload passes in not only the stock name, but also the number of shares owned. The overloaded methods are shown in Example 14-4.

Example 14-4. Overloaded versions of the GetValue WebMethod

```
<WebMethod(Description:="Returns the value of the users holdings " & _
            "in a specified stock symbol.", _
        MessageName:="GetValueStockInPortfolio")> _
Public Function GetValue(ByVal StockSymbol As String) As Double
    ' Code stubbed out
    Return 0
End Function


<WebMethod(Description:="Returns the value of a specified number " & _
            "of shares in a specified stock symbol.", _
        MessageName:="GetValueThisManyShares")> _
Public Function GetValue( _
ByVal StockSymbol As String, _
ByVal NumShares As Integer) As Double
    ' Code stubbed out
    Return 0
End Function
```

Because you overloaded `GetValues` in the web service class, what you see displayed is the `MessageName` property, as shown in Figure 14-2).

Testing Your Web Service

Before you create a client for your web service, you can have Visual Studio 2005 create a test page for you. Just run the program in the debugger, as shown in Figure 14-2.

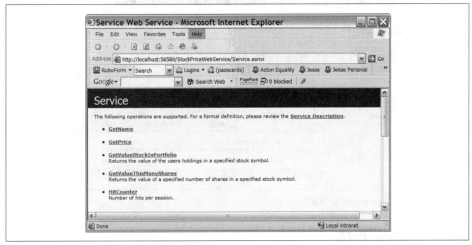

Figure 14-2. Testing the web services

Click on `GetName`, for example. You will be prompted to enter a stock symbol, as shown in Figure 14-3.

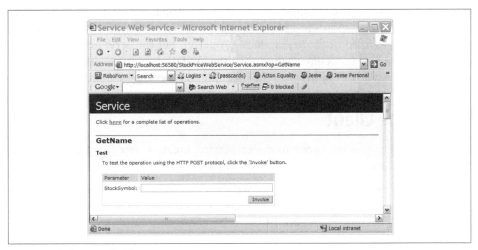

Figure 14-3. Testing GetName

Enter a valid stock symbol (one of the symbols in the array) and the stock's name is returned in an HTML document, as shown in Figure 14-4.

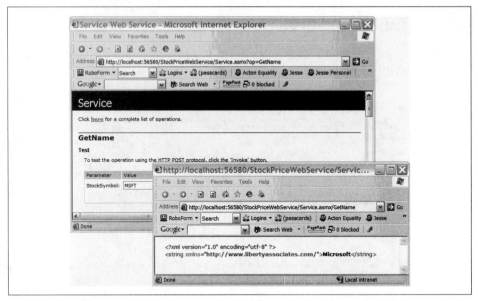

Figure 14-4. Value returned as XML

Examining the WSDL

You can examine the WSDL (Web Service Description Language) document for this web service by adding ?WSDL after the URL, as shown in Figure 14-5.

There are three things to notice in Figure 14-5. First, the URL is identical to the URL that brought up the test document, except that the string ?WSDL is appended. Second, both the GetValueStockInPorffolio and GetValueThisManyShares methods are shown (the names used in the MessageName property), but the GetValue method does not appear. The SOAP document (and thus the WSDL document) does not use the class's method name, but rather uses the unambiguous MessageName property.

Writing the Client

To create a client that uses your new web service, create a new (normal) ASP.NET web site called StockPriceClient, as shown in Figure 14-6.

Your client will need knowledge of your web service. The easiest way to provide that knowledge is to create a web reference. Right-click on your project and choose Add Web Reference, as shown in Figure 14-7.

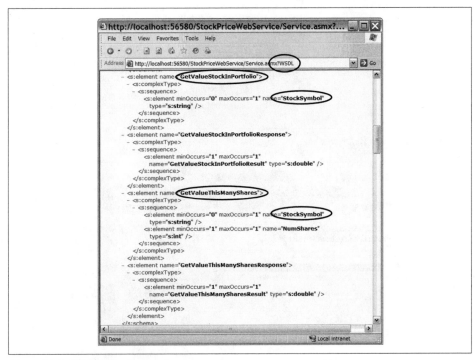

Figure 14-5. WSDL document

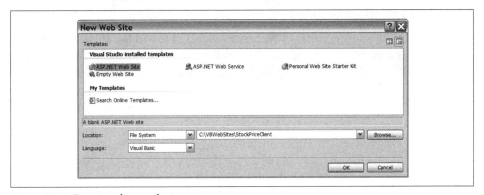

Figure 14-6. Creating client web site

The Add Web Reference dialog will open. If you have created the web service on the same machine as the client, click on "web services on the local machine," as shown in Figure 14-8.

> If you have been using file-based web applications, you'll need to create a virtual directory in IIS to point to the web service, for this web reference to work.

Figure 14-7. Add Web Reference

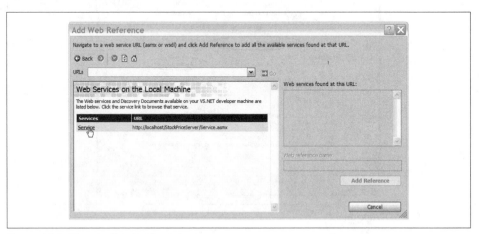

Figure 14-8. Choosing local web service

Once you click on Service, the Add Web Reference dialog will locate the service (and bring up the test page). Give your service a reference name (a name by which you can refer to it in your code) and click Add Reference, as shown in Figure 14-9.

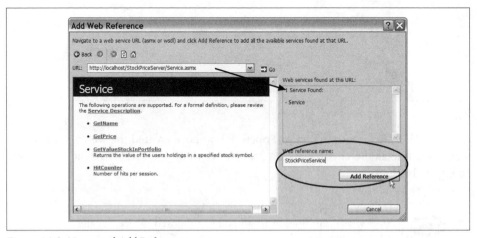

Figure 14-9. Name and Add Reference

When you click Add Reference, the web reference is added to your project, and reflected in the Solution explorer, as shown in Figure 14-10.

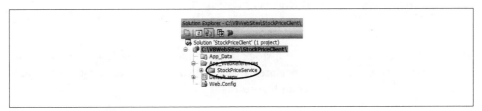

Figure 14-10. Client solution with web reference

Switch to Design view. Enter the words Stock Ticker and highlight them. Set them to Heading 1 and center them using the toolbar controls.

Move down on the page and enter the text **Please enter a stock symbol:**, then drag a text box into place. Name the text box txtStockSymbol. Add a button, name it btnSubmit, and set its text to Get Stock Info. Finally, add a label (lblMsg) and set its text to blank (see Figure 14-11).

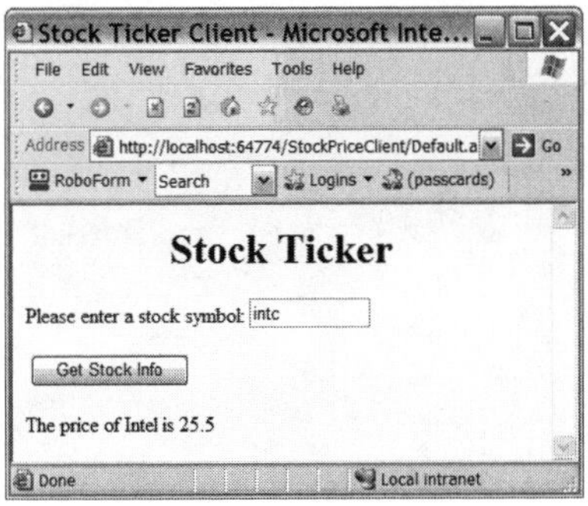

Figure 14-11. Running the Stock Ticker Client

Double-click on the button to create an event handler. In the event handler, you'll get the text from txtStockSymbol and send it to the GetName and GetPrice methods of your service. You'll then format the response and put it in the output label, as shown in Example 14-5.

Example 14-5. Submit button Click event handler

```
Protected Sub btnSubmit_Click( _
ByVal sender As Object, _
ByVal e As System.EventArgs) Handles btnSubmit.Click
    Dim proxy As StockPriceService.Service = New StockPriceService.Service()
    Dim symbol As String = Me.txtStockSymbol.Text
```

Example 14-5. Submit button Click event handler (continued)

```
    Dim stockName As String = proxy.GetName(symbol)
    Dim stockPrice As Double = proxy.GetPrice(symbol)
    Me.lblMsg.Text = "The price of " & stockName & " is " & stockPrice.ToString()
End Sub
```

The result is that when you put in a stock symbol and press the Get Stock Info button, the methods of the web service are called, and values are returned to your client application for display, as shown in Figure 14-11.

PART III

Programming with Visual Basic 2005

CHAPTER 15

Visual Studio 2005

As you've seen in Parts I and II, Visual Studio 2005 is an invaluable tool in creating robust, elegant Windows and Web applications in a minimum amount of time.

Visual Studio 2005 is a large and complex program, so it is impossible in this chapter to explore all of its nooks and crannies. Instead we will lay the foundation for understanding and using Visual Studio 2005, and will point out some of the nastier traps you might run into along the way.

Start Page

When you open Visual Studio 2005 for the first time you'll be asked to configure the tool for the type of development you do most often. Setting a specific Development environment (e.g., Visual Basic 2005) applies a predefined collections of internal settings that maximize your productivity. If you are unsure, you can choose General Development Settings, or if you will be focusing on building web apps you might choose Web Development Settings, as shown in Figure 15-1. However, as a Visual Basic 2005 developer, you'll most likely want to select Visual Basic Development settings.

Figure 15-1. Setting up Visual Studio

Once you've made your choice, you'll be presented with the Start page that lets you open and create windows projects and web sites and provides up-to-date news on MSDN and related products, as shown in Figure 15-2.

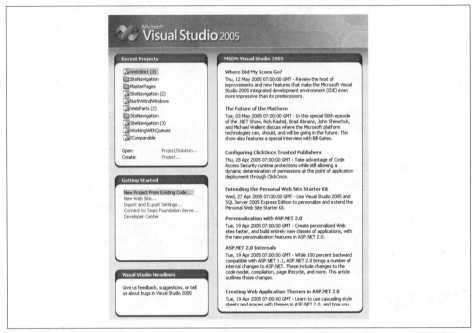

Figure 15-2. Visual Studio opening page

Along the top of the application window is a fairly typical collection of Windows menu items and buttons, plus several that are specific to the Visual Studio 2005 Integrated Development Environment. Specialized tabs that provide access to tools and controls, and to other servers and databases in the development environment, appear to the left of the application window, labeled Toolbox and Server Explorer, respectively. The Solution explorer, for exploring the files and classes associated with a particular project, appears on the righthand side. More windows are available through the Visual Studio 2005 menu bar (see the section "The Integrated Development Environment (IDE)").

At the center of the application window is the Start Page, which contains links for creating new projects or opening existing ones. It also contains several windows with links to helpful topics for getting started and up-to-date news items.

Projects and Solutions

Visual Studio .NET uses projects and solutions to organize your applications. A project contains user interface and source files, as well as other files such as data sources and graphics. Typically, the contents of a project are compiled into an assembly, e.g., an executable file (*.exe*) or a dynamic link library file (DLL).

You can create many types of projects in Visual Studio 2005, including:

- Windows application
- Windows service
- Windows Control Libray
- Web Control Library
- Class Library
- Pocket PC templates
- SmartPhone templates
- Windows CE templates
- Crystal Reports Windows application
- SQL Server project
- Word and Excel document and template
- Screen saver

Templates

When you create a new project by clicking the New Project… link on the Start Page or File → New Project…, you get the New Project dialog box, as shown in Figure 15-3.

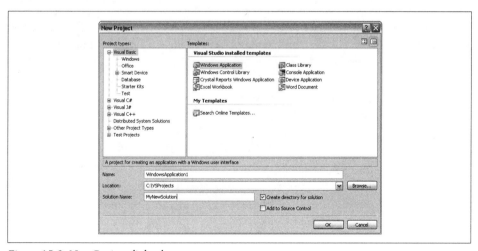

Figure 15-3. New Project dialog box

As described in the "Web Sites" section, web applications are not created by creating a new project, but by creating a new web site.

To create a new project, you select a project type and a template. There are a variety of templates for each project type. For example, the templates for Visual Basic 2005 Projects, shown in Figure 15-3, are different from the templates available to Other Project Types → Setup and Deployment. By selecting a Visual Studio Solutions project type, you can create an empty solution, ready to receive whatever items you want to add.

The template controls what items will be created automatically and included in the project, as well as default project settings. For example, if your project is a Visual Basic 2005 Web application, then web forms (*.aspx*) files and language-specific code-behind (*.vb*) files will be created as part of the project. If a different template is selected, then an entirely different set of files will be created.

Web Sites

A typical .NET web application is comprised of many items: content files (e.g., *.aspx* files), source files (e.g. *.vb* files), assemblies (e.g. *.exe* and *.dll* files) and assembly information files, data sources, references, and icons, as well as miscellaneous other files and folders. Visual Studio 2005 organizes these items into a folder that represents the web site. The web site folder is housed in a *solution*. When you create a new web site, Visual Studio 2005 automatically creates the solution.

To create a new web application, either click on New Web Site… from the Getting Started box on the Start Page, or go to File → New Web Site… In either case, you will get the New Web Site dialog box, as shown in Figure 15-4. It will present lists of available templates, described shortly.

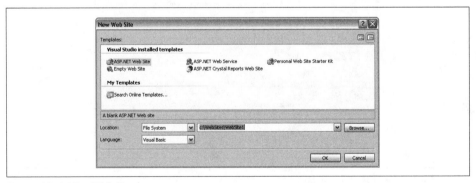

Figure 15-4. New Web Site

Below the list of templates are a set of controls for setting the location and language for your web site.

The first drop down, Location, allows you to work on web applications in three different manners, from three different types of locations. The choice here controls much more than just a physical location.

File System

The default, causes the new web site folder to be created somewhere on the physical file system accessible to this PC and this user, either on the local machine or the network.

The Browse... button and associated drop-down list allow you to browse the file system, and select any desired folder.

Choosing File System causes Visual Studio 2005 to run the web application using its own internal web server, rather than IIS. A persistent virtual directory for the web application is not created, and IIS is not part of the picture. In fact, IIS is not even required to be installed on the the development machine. (Of course, IIS is required on any deployment servers.)

The downside to using File System as the Location is that web pages created this way cannot be run from a browser, only through Visual Studio 2005 (since there is no virtual directory to reference after "localhost" in the browser address box). This is true even when redirecting users to another page programatically with the Response.Redirect or Server.Response methods. A URL such as *http://localhost/ myWebApp/default.aspx* referencing the target web site will not work unless you manually create a virtual directory called myWebApp in Computer Management on the local machine (right-click on My Computer and select Manage, then drill down to Services and Applications → Internet Information Services → Web Sites → Default Web Site, then right-click and select New → Virtual Directory...).

The advantage, however, is that it is very easy to share file-based solutions: you just copy the entire directory to the new machine and open it in Visual Studio. This will be the preferred approach for this book.

HTTP

This selection implies that IIS will be serving the pages. As such, it requires that the web application be located in an IIS virtual directory. Visual Studio 2005 will automatically create this virtual directory. This is evident when you open a browser on the local machine and enter a URL such as that shown in the previous description, which will now work fine.

The Browse... button and associated drop-down list allow you to browse and select from the contents, especially the virtual directories, on IIS running either locally or remotely (use the buttons on the left side of the dialog box to choose).

You can also see any virtual directories created by Visual Studio 2005 by opening Computer Management and looking under Default Web Site.

FTP

This selection allows you to develop your web site on a remote location accessible via the FTP protocol. You will be presented with an FTP Log On dialog box with a checkbox to allow Anonymous Log in, and textboxes for login user name and password, if necessary.

The Browse... button and associated drop-down list allows you to enter the information necessary to log in to an FTP site.

Solutions

Solutions typically contain one or more projects and/or web sites. They may contain other, independent items as well. These independent *solution items* are not specific to any particular project, but apply, or *scope*, to the entire solution. The solution items are not an integral part of the application, because they can be removed without changing the compiled output. They display in Solution explorer (described later in this chapter) in a Solution Items folder, and can be managed with source control.

Miscellaneous files are independent of the solution or project, but they may be useful to have handy. They are not included in any build or compile, but will display in the Solution explorer and may be edited from there. Typical miscellaneous files include project notes, database schemas, or sample code files. To display the Miscellaneous Files folder as part of the solution, go to Tools → Options → Environment → Documents, and check the checkbox for Show Miscellaneous Files in Solution explorer.

It is also possible to have a solution that does not contain any projects—just solution items or miscellaneous files, which can be edited using Visual Studio 2005.

Solutions are defined by a *solution file*, created by Visual Studio 2005 and named for the solution with a *.sln* extension. The *.sln* file contains a list of the projects that comprise the solution, the location of any solution-scoped items, and any solution-scoped build configurations. Visual Studio 2005 also creates a *.suo* file with the same name as the *.sln* file (e.g., *mySolution.sln* and *mySolution.suo*). The *.suo* file contains data used to customize the IDE on a per-user and per-solution basis.

In previous versions of Visual Studio, the *.suo* file was maintained only on a per-solution, not per-developer basis.

The solution file is placed in the Visual Studio projects location. By default it will look like the following (with your user name substituted):

```
c:\Documents and Settings\username\My Documents\Visual Studio\Projects
```

However, you can change it to something a little easier to navigate, such as:

```
c:\vsProjects
```

by going to Tools → Options → Projects and Solutions → General.

You can open a solution in Visual Studio 2005 by double-clicking the *.sln* file in Windows Explorer. Even if the *.sln* file is missing, you can still open a project in Visual Studio 2005. A new *.sln* file will be created when you save.

There is no project file, but there is a project folder. There are no solution folders, but there is a solution file that lives in a project folder. A solution file may reference multiple projects, including projects from other project folders.

Furthermore, the Solution explorer in Visual Studio 2005 (described in the following section) displays projects as though they are contained within solutions, even though the physical directory structure does not support this interpretation.

This can be a bit confusing, but it all comes together and works well enough once you get used to it.

The Integrated Development Environment (IDE)

The Visual Studio 2005 integrated development environment (IDE) consists of windows for visual design of forms, code-editing windows, menus and toolbars providing access to commands and features, Toolboxes containing controls for use on the forms, and windows providing properties and information about forms, controls, projects, and the solution.

Layout

Visual Studio 2005 is a multiple document interface (MDI) application. It consists of a single parent window, which contains multiple windows. All the menus, toolbars, design and editing windows, and miscellaneous other windows are associated with the single parent window.

Creating a Web Application

A typical layout of the IDE for a web application is shown in Figure 15-5. Basically, it consists of a menu and toolbar arrangement across the top and a work surface below, flanked by other toolbars and windows.

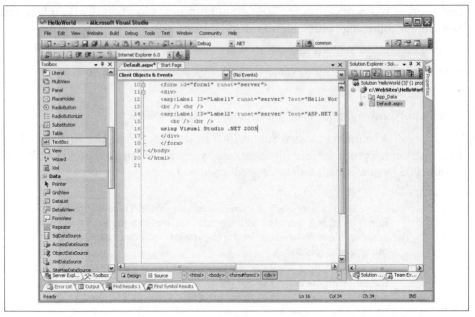

Figure 15-5. Typical IDE layout

 Users of previous versions of Visual Studio will notice that the IDE now opens by default in Source view rather than Design view. Also, new web pages start out in Flow Layout mode (like a word processor) rather than Grid Layout mode (absolute positioning).

Visual Studio 2005 has a title bar across the top with menus below. Under the menus are toolbars with buttons that duplicate many of the common menu commands. Nearly everything that can be done through menus can also be done with context-sensitive pop-up menus, as described in the discussion that follows. The menu and toolbars are easily customized by clicking on Tools → Customize.

The toolbars are docked along the top of the window by default. As with many Windows applications, they can be undocked and moved to other locations, either free-floating or docked along other window edges. You move the toolbars by grabbing them with the mouse and dragging them where you want.

Along the right side of the screen are two windows, both of which will be covered in more detail later in this chapter. The upper window is the Solution explorer. Below that is the Properties window. There are many other similar windows available to you, as will be described.

All of these windows, plus the Toolbox, are resizable and dockable. They can be resized by placing the mouse cursor over the edge you want to move. The cursor will change to a double-arrow resizing cursor, at which point you can drag the window edge one way or the other.

Right-clicking on the title bar of a dockable window pops up a menu with four mutually exclusive check items:

Floating
> The window will not dock when dragged against the edge of the Visual Studio 2005 window. The floating window can be placed anywhere on the desktop, even outside the Visual Studio 2005 window.

Dockable
> The window can be dragged and docked along any side of the Visual Studio 2005 window.
>
> While dragging a window to be docked, two sets of blue docking icons will appear in the window. One icon will be located at each edge of the application window and a set of five icons will be located in the center of the current window. Dragging and releasing the window to be docked over one of these docking icons will cause it to dock against the indicated edge. The center docking icon of the set of five will cause the window to be one of the tabbed windows on the central work surface.
>
> You can also double-click on either the title bar or the tab to dock and undock the window. Double-clicking on the title while docked undocks the entire group. Double-clicking on the tab just undocks the one window, leaving the rest of the group docked.

Tabbed Document
> The window occupies the work surface, with a tab for navigation, just the same as the code and design windows.

AutoHide
> The window will disappear, indicated only by a tab, when the cursor is not over the window. It will reappear when the cursor is over the tab. A pushpin in the upper-right corner of the window will be pointing down when AutoHide is turned off and pointing sideways when it is turned on.

Hide
> The window disappears. To see the window again (i.e., to unhide it), use the View main menu item.

Two icons are in the upper-right corner of the window:

Pushpin

> This icon toggles the AutoHide property of the window.
>
> When the pushpin is pointing down, the window is pinned in place; AutoHide is turned off. Moving the cursor off the window will not affect its visibility.
>
> When the pushpin is pointing sideways, AutoHide is turned on. Moving the cursor off the window hides the window. To see the window again, click on the tab, which is now visible along the edge where the window had been docked.

X

> Standard close window icon.

The work surface uses a tabbed metaphor (i.e., the tabs along the top edge of that window indicate there are other windows below it). You can change to an MDI style, if you prefer, in Tools → Options → Environment → General.

There are a number of navigational aids along the bottom of the work surface. Depending on the context, there may be one or more buttons. When looking at a web page, for example, as shown in Figures 15-5 and 15-6, two buttons labeled Design and Source allow switching between the Design view and underlying source code, i.e., HTML and script. There are also buttons representing the HTML hierarchy of the page. The cursor in the code window or the focus in Design view dictates which objects will be represented as buttons: one button for the current level and one more for each parent level. Clicking on any of the buttons highlights that level of code in the code window.

When you switch from a design window to a code window, the menu items, toolbars, and Toolbox change in a context-sensitive manner.

The code window has context-sensitive drop-down lists at the top of the screen for navigating around the application. In the HTML editor, the left drop down lists Client Objects & Events and Client Script, and the right drop down lists event handlers. In the Visual Basic 2005 code editor, the left drop down contains a list of all the classes in the code and the right drop down has a list of all the objects in the current class.

The left margin of a code window shows a yellow bar next to lines that have been changed and a green bar next to lines that have been saved. This color coding is per session; it resets when the project is first loaded.

Along the bottom edge of the IDE window is a status bar, which shows such information as the current cursor position (when a code window is visible), the status of the Insert key, and any pending shortcut key combinations.

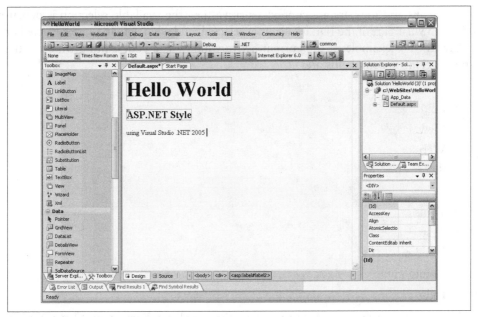

Figure 15-6. Design view window in IDE

Creating a Windows Application

The IDE for creating Windows Forms in Visual Basic 2005 is very similar to the IDE for creating web forms. Once again, Visual Studio 2005 has a title bar across the top with menus below and a toolbar that duplicates the most common menu commands.

Along the right side of the screen are the same two windows: Solution explorer and Properties.

With Windows applications, you do not have a Design and a Source window, you have only the Windows form, onto which you may drag controls from the Toolbox. The code behind page is reached by right-clicking on the form and choosing View Code.

Menus and Toolbars

The menus provide access to many of the commands and capabilities of Visual Studio 2005. The more commonly used menu commands are duplicated with toolbar buttons for ease of use.

The menus and toolbars are context-sensitive (i.e., the available selection is dependent on what part of the IDE is currently selected, and what activities are expected or allowed). For example, if the current active window is a code-editing window, the top-level menu commands are:

- File
- Edit
- View
- Website
- Build
- Debug
- Tools
- Test
- Window
- Community
- Help

If the current window is a design window, then the Data, Format, and Layout menu commands also become available.

Many of the menu items have keyboard shortcuts, listed adjacent to the menu item itself. These comprise one or more keys (referred to as a *chord*), pressed simultaneously. Shortcut keys can be a huge productivity boost, since you can perform common tasks quickly, without removing your hands from the keyboard.

The following sections describe some of the menu items and their submenus, focusing on those aspects that are interesting and different from common Windows commands.

File Menu

The File menu provides access to a number of file, project, and solution-related commands. Many of these commands are content-sensitive. Below are descriptions of the most commonly used file commands.

New

As in most Windows applications, the New menu item creates new items to be worked on by the application. In Visual Studio 2005, the New menu item has five submenu items, to handle the different possibilities. They are:

New Project... (Ctrl-Shift-N)
> The New Project command brings up the New Project dialog, shown in Figure 15-7.

New Web Site...
> The New Web Site command brings up the New Web Site dialog box shown in Figure 15-8.

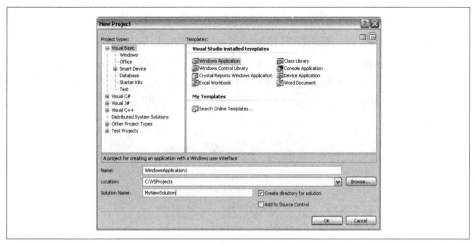

Figure 15-7. New Project window

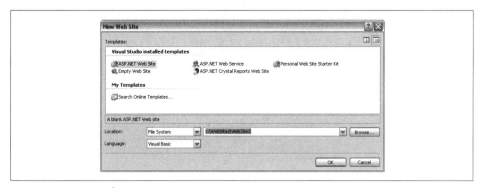

Figure 15-8. New Web Site

Edit Menu

The Edit menu contains the text editing and searching commands that one would expect, but also includes commands useful in editing code. The most useful are:

Cycle Clipboard Ring (Ctrl-Shift-V)

The Clipboard Ring is like copy and paste on steroids. Copy a number of different selections to the Windows clipboard, using the Edit → Cut (Ctrl-X) or Edit → Copy (Ctrl-C) commands. Then use Ctrl-Shift-V to cycle through all the selections, allowing you to paste the correct one when it comes around.

This submenu item is context-sensitive and is visible only when editing a code window.

Find and Replace → Quick Find (Ctrl-F) / Quick Replace (Ctrl-H)

These are just slightly jazzed names for slightly jazzed versions of the typical Find and Replace. Both commands call essentially the same dialog boxes, switchable by a tab at the top of the dialog box, as shown in Figures 15-9 and 15-10.

Figure 15-9. Find and Replace dialog box—Quick Find tab

Figure 15-10. Find and Replace dialog box—Quick Replace tab

The search string defaults to the text currently selected in the code window, or, if nothing is selected, to the text immediately after the current cursor location.

The Look in drop down offers the choice of the Current Document, All Open Documents, the Current Project, and the current method.

Search options can be expanded or collapsed by clicking on the plus/minus button next to Find Options. By default, Search hidden text is checked, which allows the search to include code sections currently collapsed in the code window. The Use checkbox allows the use of either regular expressions (see the sidebar "Regular Expressions") or wildcards. If the Use checkbox is checked, then the Expression Builder button to the right of the Find what textbox becomes enabled, providing a very handy way to insert valid regular expression or wildcard characters.

Once a search string has been entered in the Find what text box, the Find Next button becomes enabled. In Quick Find mode, there is also a Bookmark All button, which finds all occurrences of the search string and places a bookmark (described later) next to the code.

In Quick Replace mode, there is also a Replace with text box, and buttons for replacing either a single or all occurrences of the search string.

Find and Replace → Find in Files (Ctrl-Shift-F)

Find in Files is a very powerful search utility that finds text strings anywhere in a directory or subdirectory (subfolders). It presents the dialog box shown in Figure 15-11. Checkboxes present several self-explanatory options, including the ability to search using either wildcards or regular expressions.

Figure 15-11. Find and Replace dialog box—Find in Files tab

If you click on the Replace in Files tab at the top of the Find and Replace dialog box, you will get the Replace in Files dialog box shown in Figure 15-12 and described next.

Figure 15-12. Find and Replace dialog box—Replace in Files tab

Regular Expressions

Regular expressions are a language unto themselves, expressly designed for incredibly powerful and sophisticated searches. A full explanation of regular expressions is beyond the scope of this book. For a complete discussion of regular expressions, see the SDK documentation or *Mastering Regular Expressions*, Second Edition, by Jeffrey E. F. Friedl (O'Reilly).

Find and Replace → Replace in Files (Ctrl-Shift-H)

Replace in Files is identical to the Find in Files command, described in the previous section, except that it also allows you to replace the target text string with a new text string.

This command is extremely useful for renaming forms, classes, namespaces, projects, and so on. Renaming objects is a very common requirement, often because you don't want to be saddled with the default names assigned by Visual Studio 2005.

Renaming should not be difficult, but it can be. Object names are spread throughout a project, often hidden in obscure locations such as solution files, and throughout source code files. Although all of these files are text files and so can be searched and edited, it can be a tedious and error-prone task. The Replace in Files command makes it simple, thorough, and reasonably safe.

Find and Replace → Find Symbol (Alt-F12)

Clicking on this command will bring up the Find Symbol dialog box shown in Figure 15-13. This allows you to search for symbols (such as namespaces, classes, and interfaces) and their members (such as properties, methods, events, and variables). It also allows you to search in external components for which the source code is not available.

Figure 15-13. Find and Replace dialog box—Find Symbol tab

The search results will be displayed in a window labeled Find Symbol Results. From there, you can move to each location in the code by double-clicking on each result.

Go To...

This command brings up the Go To Line dialog box, which allows you to enter a line number and immediately go to that line. It is context-sensitive and is visible only when editing a text window.

Find All References

This is somewhat similar to Find Symbol under Find and Replace, except that rather than searching for any symbol, it only allows searches for methods which are referenced elsewhere in the project.

Insert File As Text...

This command allows you to insert the contents of any file into your source code, as though you had typed it in. It is context-sensitive and is visible only when editing a text window.

A standard file-browsing dialog box is presented for searching for the file to be inserted. The default file extension will correspond to the project language, but you can search for any file with any extension.

Advanced

The Advanced command is context-sensitive and is visible only when editing a code window. It has many submenu items. These include commands for:

- Creating or removing tabs in a selection (converting spaces to tabs and vice versa)
- Forcing selected text to uppercase or lowercase
- Deleting horizontal white space
- Viewing white space (making tabs and space characters visible on the screen)
- Toggling word wrap
- Commenting and uncommenting blocks of text
- Increasing and decreasing line indenting
- Incremental searching (see the next section)

Incremental search (Ctrl-I)

Incremental search allows you to search an editing window by entering the search string character by character. As each character is entered, the cursor moves to the first occurrence of matching text.

To use incremental search in a window, select the command on the Advanced submenu, or press Ctrl-I. The cursor icon will change to binoculars with an arrow indicating the direction of search. Begin typing the text string to search for.

The case sensitivity of an incremental search will come from the previous Find, Replace, Find in Files, or Replace in Files search (described earlier).

The search will proceed downward and left to right from the current location. To search backward, use Ctrl-Shift-I.

The key combinations listed in Table 15-1 apply to incremental searching.

Table 15-1. Incremental searching

Key combination	Description
Esc	Stop the search.
Backspace	Remove a character from the search text.
Ctrl-Shift-I	Change the direction of the search.
Ctrl-I	Move to the next occurrence in the file for the current search text.

Bookmarks

Bookmarks are useful for marking spots in your code and easily navigating from marked spot to marked spot. There are several context-sensitive commands on the Bookmarks submenu (listed in Table 15-2). Unless you add the item to the task list, bookmarks are lost when you close the file, although they are saved when you close the solution (so long as the file was still open).

Table 15-2. Bookmark commands

Command	Description
Toggle Bookmark	Place or remove a bookmark at the current line. When a bookmark is set, a blue rectangular icon will appear in the column along the left edge of the code window.
Previous Bookmark	Move to the previous bookmark.
Next Bookmark	Move to the next bookmark.
Previous Bookmark in Folder	Move to the previous bookmark in the folder.
Next Bookmark in Folder	Move to the next bookmark in the folder.
Clear Bookmarks	Clear all the bookmarks.
Previous Bookmark in Document	Move to the previous bookmark in the current document.
Next Bookmark in Document	Move to the next bookmark in the current document.
Add Task List Shortcut	Add an entry to the Task List (described later in the "View Menu" section) for the current line. When a task list entry is set, a curved arrow icon appears in the column along the left edge of the code window.

This menu item only appears when a code window is the current window.

Outlining

Visual Studio 2005 allows you to *outline*, or collapse and expand, sections of your code to make it easier to view the overall structure. When a section is collapsed, it appears with a plus sign in a box along the left edge of the code window. Clicking on the plus sign expands the region.

You can nest the outlined regions, so that one section can contain one or more other collapsed sections. There are several commands to facilitate outlining, shown in Table 15-3.

Table 15-3. Outlining commands

Command	Description
Hide Selection	Collapses currently selected text. In Visual Basic 2005 only, this command is visible only when automatic outlining is turned off or the Stop Outlining command is selected.
Toggle Outlining Expansion	Reverses the current outlining state of the innermost section in which the cursor lies.
Toggle All Outlining	Sets all sections to the same outlining state. If some sections are expanded and some collapsed, then all become collapsed.
Stop Outlining	Expands all sections. Removes the outlining symbols from view.
Stop Hiding Current	Removes outlining information for currently selected section. In Visual Basic 2005 only, this command is visible only when automatic outlining is turned off or the Stop Outlining command is selected.

Table 15-3. Outlining commands (continued)

Command	Description
Collapse to Definitions	Automatically creates sections for each procedure in the code window and collapses them all.
Start Automatic Outlining	Restarts automatic outlining after it has been stopped.
Collapse Block	In C++ only, similar to Collapse to Definitions, except applies only to the region of code containing the cursor.
Collapse All In	In C++ only, same as Collapse Block, except recursively collapses all logical structures in a function in a single step.

The default behavior of outlining can be set using the Tools → Options menu item. Go to Text Editor and select specific language for which you want to set the options. The outlining options can be set for Visual Basic 2005, under Visual Basic 2005 → Formatting.

IntelliSense

Microsoft IntelliSense technology simply makes programming. It provides real-time, context-sensitive help, which appears under your cursor. Code completion automatically completes your syntax, drastically reducing typing and errors. Drop-down lists provide all methods and properties possible in the current context.

IntelliSense works in all code windows, including not only the Visual Basic 2005 code-behind files, but also within both server- (i.e., script) and client-side (i.e., HTML) code in content files.

The default IntelliSense features can be configured by going to Tools → Options and then the language-specific pages under Text Editor.

Most of the IntelliSense features appear as you type inside a code window or allow the mouse to hover over a portion of the code. In addition, the Edit → IntelliSense menu item offers numerous commands, the most important of which are shown in Table 15-4.

Table 15-4. IntelliSense commands

Command	Description
List Members	Displays a list of all possible members available for the current context. Keystrokes incrementally search the list. Press any key to insert the highlighted selection into your code; that key becomes the next character after the inserted name. Use the Tab key to select without entering any additional characters.
	This can also be accessed by right-clicking and selecting List Member from the context-sensitive menu.
Parameter Info	Displays a list of number, names, and types of parameters required for a method, sub, function, or attribute.
Quick Info	Displays the complete declaration for any identifier (e.g., variable name or class name) in your code. This is also enabled by hovering the mouse cursor over any identifier.

Table 15-4. IntelliSense commands (continued)

Command	Description
Complete Word	Automatically completes the typing of any identifier once you type in enough characters to uniquely identify it. This only works if the identifier is being entered in a valid location in the code.
Insert Snippet	Displays a selection of code snippets to insert, such as the complete syntax for a switch-case block or an If block
Surround With	Displays a selection of code snippets to surround a block of code, such as a class declaration.

The member list presents itself when you type the dot following any class or member name.

Every member of the class is listed, and each member's type is indicated by an icon. There are icons for methods, fields, properties, events, and so forth. In addition, each icon may have a second icon overlaid to indicate the accessibility of the member: public, private, protected, and so on. If there is no accessibility icon, then the member is public.

 If the member list does not appear, you will want to ensure that you have added all the necessary using statements. Occasionally Visual Basic 2005 needs a rebuild before it will reflect the most recent changes.

Two of the subcommands under the IntelliSense menu item, Insert Snippet… and Surround With…., tap into a powerful feature to reduce typing and minimize errors: *code snippets*. A code snippet is a chunk of code that replaces an alias. A short alias is replaced with a much longer code snippet. For example, the alias SelectCase would be replaced with:

```
Select Case caseDiscriminant

    Case Else
End Case
```

with the case expression caseDiscriminant highlighted in yellow and the cursor in place, ready to type in your own expression. In fact, all the editable fields will be highlighted, and you can use the Tab key to navigate through them, or Shift-Tab to go backward. Any changes made to the editable field are immediately propagated to all the instances of that field in the code snippet. Press Enter or Esc to end the field editing and return to normal editing.

To do a straight alias replacement, either select Insert Snippet from the menu, or more easily, press Ctrl-K, Ctrl-X. Alternatively, just type an alias in the code window and an IntelliSense menu will pop up with a list of aliases, the current one highlighted. Press the Tab key to insert that code snippet.

Alternatively, a code snippet can surround highlighted lines of code, say with a for construct. To surround lines of code with a code snippet construct, highlight the code, then either select Surround With from the menu, or press Ctrl-K, Ctrl-S.

View Menu

The View menu is a context-sensitive menu that provides access to the myriad of windows available in the Visual Studio 2005 IDE. You will probably keep many of these windows open all the time; others you will use rarely, if at all.

The View menu is context-sensitive. For example, with a *.aspx* content file on the work surface, the first three menu items will be Code, Designer, and Markup, while the Code and Designer menu items will be omitted if looking at a code-behind file.

When the application is running, a number of other windows, primarily used for debugging, become visible or available. These windows are accessed via the Debug → Windows menu item, not from the View menu item.

Visual Studio 2005 can store several different window layouts. In particular, it remembers a completely different set of open windows during debug sessions than it does during normal editing. These layouts are stored per user, not per project or per solution.

Class View (Ctrl-Shift-C)

The Class View shows all the classes in the solution in a hierarchical manner. A typical Class View, somewhat expanded, is shown in Figure 15-14.

As with the Solution explorer, any item in the class view can be right-clicked, which exposes a pop-up menu with a number of context-sensitive menu items. This can provide a convenient way to sort the display of classes in a project or solution, or to add a method, property, or field to a class.

The button on the left above the class list allows for sorting the classes listed, either alphabetically, by type, by access, or grouped by type. Clicking on the button itself sorts by the current sort mode, while clicking on the down arrow next to it presents the other sort buttons and changes the sort mode.

The button on the right above the class list allows you to create virtual folders for organizing the classes listed. These folders are saved as part of the solution in the *.suo* file.

These folders are virtual (i.e., they are illusory). They are only used for viewing the list. As such, they have no effect on the actual items. Items copied to the folder are not physically moved, and if the folders are deleted, the items in them are not lost.

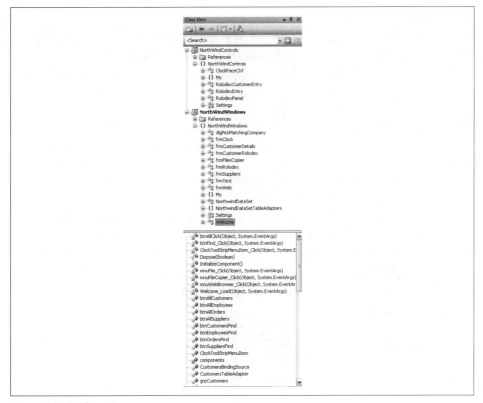

Figure 15-14. Class View

Note that if you rename or delete an object from the code that is in a folder, you may need to manually drag the item into the folder again to clear the error node.

Code Definition Window (Ctrl-W, D)

Available in either Design or Source view for a web page or user control file, this menu item displays the Code Definition window, which is a read-only display of the definition of a symbol in a code file. The display in this window is synchronized with the cursor location in the Code Editor window and the current selection in either the Class View or the Object Browser.

Error List (Ctrl-W, Ctrl-E)

Available in all editor views, The Error List window displays errors, warnings, and messages generated as you edit and compile your project. Syntax errors flagged by IntelliSense are displayed here, as well as deployment errors. Double-clicking on an error in this list will open the offending file and move the cursor to the error location.

Output (Ctrl-Alt-O)

The Output window displays status messages from the IDE, such as build progress. The Output window can be set to display by default when a build starts by going to Tools → Options → Projects and Solutions → General and checking "Show Output window when build starts."

Properties Windows (F4)

The Properties window displays all the properties for the currently selected item. Some of the properties (such as Font) may have subproperties, indicated by a plus sign next to their entries in the window. The property values on the right side of the window are editable.

One thing that can be confusing is that certain items have more than one set of properties. For example, a Form content file can show two different sets of properties, depending on whether you select the source file in the Solution explorer or the form as shown in the Design view.

A typical Properties window is shown in Figure 15-15.

Figure 15-15. Properties window

The name and type of the current object is displayed in the field at the top of the window. In Figure 15-15, it is an object named btnPage2 of type Button, contained in the System.Web.UI.WebControls namespace.

Most properties can be edited in place in the Properties window. The Font property has subproperties that may be set directly in the window by clicking on the plus sign to expand its subproperties, then editing the subproperties in place.

The Properties window has several buttons just below the name and type of the object. The first two buttons on the left toggle the list by category or alphabetically. The next two buttons from the left toggle between displaying properties for the selected item and displaying events for the selected item. The rightmost button displays property pages for the object, if there are any.

Some objects have both a Properties window and Property Pages. The Property Pages display additional properties from those shown in the Properties window.

The box below the list of properties displays a brief description of the selected property.

Solution Explorer (Ctrl-Alt-L)

Projects and solutions are managed using the Solution explorer, which presents the solution and projects, and all the files, folders, and items contained within them, in a hierarchical, visual manner. The Solution explorer is typically visible in a window along the upper-right side of the Visual Studio 2005 screen, although the Solution explorer window can be closed or undocked and moved to other locations, like all the windows accessible from the View menu. A typical Solution explorer is shown in Figure 15-16.

Figure 15-16. Solution explorer

It is also possible to display miscellaneous files in the Solution explorer. To do so, go to Tools → Options..., then go to Environment → Documents. Check the checkbox labeled Show Miscellaneous files in Solution explorer.

Most of the functionality of the Solution explorer is redundant with the Visual Studio 2005 menu items, although it is often easier and more intuitive to perform a given chore in Solution explorer rather than in the menus. Right-clicking on any item in the Solution explorer will pop up a context-sensitive menu.

Some of the context-sensitive menus are not redundant with any of the menu commands. These include:

Add Reference...
> The Add Reference command brings up the Add Reference dialog box. This allows you to reference assemblies or DLL's external to your application, making the public classes, methods, and members contained in the referenced resource available to your application.

Add Web Reference...
> The Add Web Reference command, also available in the Solution explorer by right-clicking a project, allows you to add a web reference to your project, thereby becoming a consuming application of a web service.

> Web services and distributed applications are covered in Chapter 14.

Task List (Ctrl-W, Ctrl-T)

In large applications, keeping a to-do list can be quite helpful. Visual Studio 2005 provides this functionality with the Task List window. You can provide shortcuts to comments in the Task List along with token strings, such as TODO, HACK, or UNDONE. Also, the compiler populates the Task List with any compile errors.

Toolbox (Ctrl-Alt-X)

Displays the Toolbox if it is not currently displayed. If it is currently displayed, nothing happens—it does not toggle the display. To undisplay the Toolbox, click on the X in the Toolbox title bar.

Other Windows

There are several other windows which have been relegated to a submenu called Other Windows. These include:

Bookmark window (Ctrl-K, Ctrl-W)
Command window (Ctrl-Alt-A)
> The Command window is used to enter commands directly, either bypassing the menu system or executing commands that are not contained in the menu system. (You can add any command to the menu or a toolbar button using Tools → Customize.)

> For a complete discussion of Command window usage, consult the SDK documentation.

Document Outline (Ctrl-Alt-T)
> The Document Outline displays the hierarchical structure of a web page or user control, including directives, script blocks, HTML elements, and server controls, as shown in Figure 15-17.

Macro Explorer (Alt-F8)

Visual Studio 2005 offers the ability to automate repetitive chores with macros. A macro is a set of instructions written in Visual Basic, either created manually or recorded by the IDE and saved in a file. The Macro Explorer is the one of the main tools for viewing, managing, and executing macros. It provides access into the Macro IDE.

Macros are described further in the section, "Tools Menu."

Object Browser (Ctrl-Alt-J)

The Object Browser is a tool for examining objects (such as namespaces, classes, and interfaces), and their members (such as methods, properties, variables, and events).

Performance Explorer
Resource View (Ctrl-Shift-E)

This window displays the resource files included in the project. Resources are nonexecutable data deployed with an application, such as icons and graphics, culture-specific text messages, and persisted data objects.

Server Explorer (Ctrl-Alt-S)

The Server Explorer allows you to access any server to which you have network access. If you have sufficient permissions, you can log on, access system services, open data connections, access and edit database information, access message queues and performance counters, and more. You can also drag nodes from the Server Explorer onto Visual Studio 2005 projects, creating components that reference the data source.

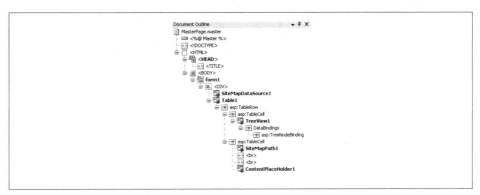

Figure 15-17. Document Outline

Refactor Menu

After you write your code you may find that two methods have a chunk of code that is identical. You can refactor that code into a method, and Visual Studio 2005 makes this exquisitely easy.

For expert details on refactoring, please see *Refactoring: Improving the Design of Existing Code* by Fowler et al. (Addison Wesley).

Refactoring modifies your code; for example, extracting common code to a new method and then calling that method in the place from which it was extracted. Refactoring can also be used to rename methods, and all references to the renamed method will automatically be updated, across all files in the project and across all projects of the same language. Before any changes are committed, an optional Preview Changes dialog box will appear, giving you the opportunity to either accept or cancel the changes. A project that is unable to build successfully can still be refactored, although ambiguous references might not update properly.

The following functions are available under the Refactor menu item:

Rename…(F2)

> To rename a code symbol such as a method, class, namespace, field, local variable, property, or type, click on the symbol in your code and select the Rename menu item, press F2, or right-click on the symbol and select Refactor → Rename… from the pop-up menu.

> The Rename dialog box will appear with a textbox for the new name to be entered. A read-only textbox will show the current cursor location. Several context-sensitive checkboxes will present options. "Preview reference changes" will be checked by default. Other options might include "Search in comments," "Search in strings," and "Rename overloads."

> After clicking on OK, the program will process for a bit before displaying the Preview Changes dialog box, if that option was left checked. The top pane will list all the files and lines of code where the symbol is to be renamed. Clicking on any of the lines will show the source code in context in the bottom pane of the dialog box.

> Click Apply to apply the changes or Cancel to cancel the operation.

> Alternatively, just type a new name, and then click the smart tag that appears at the end of the name and choose the Rename option.

Extract Method… (Ctrl-R,Ctrl-M)

> As described above, the extract method extracts duplicate code and turns it into a method, leaving a call to that new method in place of the old (duplicate) code.

> The new method is inserted into the source file in the same class immediately following the current method. If there is no instance data referenced by the new method, it will be declared as a static method.

> The Extract Method dialog box will preview the new method signature. You can click OK to create the new method or Cancel to cancel. If you wish to revert back after creating the new method, just use Edit → Undo (Ctrl Z).

Encapsulate Field… (Ctrl-R,Ctrl-F)

A public member variable can be accessed externally and its value altered without the knowledge or consent of its class, breaking encapsulation. A better practice is to declare private fields and then use properties with get and/or set accessors to control external access to the field.

The Encapsulate Field function creates a property from an existing public field and updates the code to refer to the new property rather than the field. The previously public field is converted to private, and the get and set accessors are created. If the original field had been declared as read-only, then the set accessor is not created.

Extract Interface

If multiple classes, structs, or interfaces use a common set of members, it can be beneficial to extract those common members into an interface that is then implemented by the original classes, structs, or interfaces.

This menu item is only available when the cursor is in the class, struct, or interface containing the members to extract into an interface. The new interface is created in a new file. The Extract Interface dialog lets you enter the name of the new interface, the new file name, and which public members to include in the new interface.

Promote Local Variable to Parameter (Ctrl-R,Ctrl-P)

This function converts a local variable to a parameter of a method, indexer, constructor, or delegate. It also updates all the calls to that local variable.

Remove Parameters… (Ctrl-R,Ctrl-V)

This function removes parameters from methods, indexers, constructors, or delegates. It also updates all the calls to the now defunct parameter. The easiest way to invoke this function is to right-click anywhere within the declaration of the object losing the parameter(s),then select Refactor → Remove Parameters… from the context menu.

Reorder Parameters… (Ctrl-R,Ctrl-O)

Similar to the Remove Parameters function, this menu item allows you to change the order of parameters in methods, indexers, constructors, or delegates. It also updates all the calls to the modified objects to reflect the new order of parameters.

Build Menu

The Build menu offers menu items for building the current project (highlighted in Solution explorer) or the solution. It also exposes the Configuration Manager for configuring the build process.

Debug Menu

The Debug menu allows you to start an application with or without debugging, set breakpoints in the code, and control the debugging session.

Data Menu

This context-sensitive menu is visible only when in Design mode. It is not available when editing code pages. The commands under it are only available when there are appropriate data controls on the form.

Format Menu

The Format menu is visible only when in Design mode, and furthermore, the commands under it are context-sensitive to the control(s) currently selected.

This menu offers the ability to control the size and layout of controls, although many of the menu options are grayed out for certain web form controls. You can:

- Align controls with a grid or with other controls six different ways
- Change the size of one or more controls to be larger, smaller, or all the same size
- Control the horizontal and vertical spacing
- Move controls forward or back in the vertical plane (Z order) of the form

To operate on more than one control, select the controls in one of several ways:

- Hold down the Shift or Ctrl key while clicking on controls to be selected.
- Use the mouse to click and drag a selection box around all the controls to be selected. If any part of a control falls within the selection box, then that control will be included.
- To unselect one control, hold down the Shift or Ctrl key while clicking that control.
- To unselect all the controls, select a different control or press the Esc key.

When operating on more than one control, the last control selected will be the baseline. In other words, if you are making all the controls the same size, they will become the same size as the last control selected. Likewise, if aligning a group of controls, they will align with the last control selected.

As controls are selected, they will display eight resizing handles. These resizing handles will be black for all the selected controls except the baseline, or last control, which will have white handles.

With that in mind, all of the commands under the Format menu are fairly self-explanatory.

Tools Menu

The Tools menu presents commands accessing a wide range of functionality, from connecting to databases to accessing external tools to setting IDE options. Some of the more useful commands are described in the following sections.

Connect to Device...

Brings up a dialog box that allows you to connect to either a physical mobile device or an emulator.

Connect to Database...

The Connect to Database command default brings up the dialog box that allows you to select a server, log in to that server, and connect to the database on the server. Microsoft SQL Server is the default database (surprise!), but the Change... button allows you to connect to any number of other databases, including any for which there are Oracle or ODBC providers.

Code Snippets Manager (Ctrl-K, Ctrl-B)

This command brings up the Code Snippets Manager dialog box, which allows you to maintain the code snippets, described earlier in the IntelliSense section. This dialog box allows you to add or remove code snippets for any of the supported languages. You can also import code snippets and search online for code snippets.

Choose Toolbox Items...

This command brings up the Choose Toolbox dialog box shown in Figure 15-18. The dialog box has two tabs: one for adding (legacy) COM components and one for adding .NET CLR-compliant components. All the components available on your machine (which include registered COM components and .NET components in specific directories—you can browse for .NET components if they are not listed) are listed in one or the other. In either case, check or uncheck the box in front of the component to include or not include the desired component.

 For adding .NET components to the toolbox, it is generally easier to drag them from Windows Explorer onto the toolbox.

You can sort the components listed in the dialog box by clicking on the column head by which you wish to sort.

Figure 15-18. Choose Toolbox Items dialog box

Macros

Macros are a wonderful feature that allow you to automate tasks in the IDE. Macros can either be hard-coded or recorded as you perform the desired task. If you allow the IDE to record the macro for you, then you can subsequently examine and edit the macro code it creates. This is very similar to the macro functionality provided as part of Microsoft Word or Microsoft Excel.

 Be aware that macro recording doesn't work for anything inside a dialog box. For example, if you record the changing of some property in a project's Property Pages, the recorded macro will open the Property Pages but won't do anything in there!

You can easily record a temporary macro by using the Macros → Record Temporary-Macro command, or by pressing Ctrl-Shift-R. This temporary macro can then be played back using the Macros → Run TemporaryMacro command, or by pressing Ctrl-Shift-P. It can be saved using the Macros → Save TemporaryMacro command, which will automatically bring up the Macro Explorer, described next.

Macros are managed using the Macro Explorer window, accessed via a submenu of the Macros command, or by pressing Alt-F8, shown in Figure 15-19 after recording a temporary macro.

Figure 15-19. Macro Explorer

Right-clicking on a macro in the Macro Explorer pops up a menu with four items:

Run
> Runs the highlighted macro. The macro can also be run by double-clicking on the macro name.

Edit
> Brings up the macro editing IDE, where all the macros for the user can be edited. The macro language is VB .NET, irrespective of the language used for the project. The macro editing IDE can also be invoked using the Macros → Macro IDE command, or by pressing Alt-F11.

Rename
> Allows the macro to be renamed.

Delete
> Deletes the macro from the macro file.

All the macros are contained in a *macro project* called, by default, MyMacros. This project is comprised of a binary file called *MyMacros.vsmacros* (unless you have elected to convert it to the multiple files format), which is physically located in a folder called VSMacros80 in the current projects directory for each user. You can create a new macro project by using the Macros → New Macro Project command or by right-clicking on the root object in the Macro Explorer and selecting New Macro Project. In either case, you will get the New Macro Project dialog box, which will allow you to specify the name and location of the new macro project file.

Macro projects contain modules, which are units of code. Each module contains subroutines, which correspond to the macros. So for example, the macro called TemporaryMacro shown in Figure 15-19 is the TemporaryMacro subroutine contained in the module named RecordingModule, which is part of the MyMacros project.

External Tools...

Depending on the options selected at the time Visual Studio 2005 was installed on your machine, you may have one or more external tools available on the Tools menu. These might include tools such as Create GUID or Dotfuscator Community Edition. (Use of these tools is beyond the scope of this book.)

The Tools → External Tools... command allows you to add additional external tools to the Tools menu. When selected, you are presented with the External Tools dialog box. This dialog box has fields for the tool title, the command to execute the tool, any arguments and the initial directory, as well as several checkboxes for different behaviors.

Performance Tools

This menu item exposes a wizard for benchmarking and tuning performance, as well as a command for starting a new performance session.

Import and Export Settings...

This command brings up the Import and Export Settings dialog box, which is a wizard for importing and exporting IDE environment settings. With this wizard, you can transfer your carefully wrought IDE settings from one machine to the next.

Customize...

The Customize... command allows you to customize many aspects of the IDE user interface. (The Options... command, described in the following section, allows you to set a variety of other program options.) It brings up the Customize dialog box, which has two different tabs plus one additional button, allowing customization in three different areas.

Toolbars

This tab, shown in Figure 15-20, presents a checkbox list of all the available toolbars, with checkmarks indicating those toolbars currently visible. You can control the visibility of specific toolbars by checking or unchecking them in this list, or alternatively, use the View → Toolbars command.

Figure 15-20. Customize dialog—Toolbars tab

You can also create new toolbars, rename or delete existing toolbars, or reset all the toolbars back to the original installation version on this tab. Checkboxes allow you to control tooltips and icons.

Commands

The Commands tab, shown in Figure 15-21, allows you to add or remove commands from a toolbar or modify buttons already on the toolbar.

To add a command to a toolbar, select the category and command from the lists in the dialog box, then use the mouse to drag the command to the desired toolbar.

To remove a command from a toolbar, drag it from the toolbar to anywhere in the IDE while the Customize Commands dialog is showing.

Figure 15-21. Customize dialog—Commands tab

The Modify Selection button is only active when a button on an existing toolbar is selected. It allows you to perform such chores as renaming or deleting the button, changing the image displayed on the button, changing the display style of the button (image only, text only, etc.), and organizing buttons into groups.

Keyboard...

The Keyboard... button brings up the Environment → Keyboard page, shown in Figure 15-22, also accessible under the Tools → Options command described below. This page allows you to define and change keyboard shortcuts for commands.

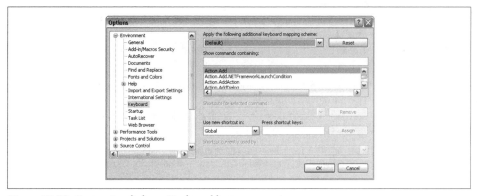

Figure 15-22. Customize dialog—Keyboard button

Options...

The Options... command also brings up the Options dialog box, shown in Figure 15-22. This dialog box allows setting a wide range of options, ranging from the number of items to display in lists of recently used items to HTML Designer options.

The dialog box displays a hierarchical list of categories on the left side. Selecting any category allows you to drill down through the tree structure. Clicking on a detail item brings up the available properties on the right side of the dialog box.

Most of the available options are fairly self-explanatory. If you have any questions about specific settings, clicking on the Help button at the bottom of the Options dialog box will bring up context-sensitive help about all the properties relevant to the current detail item.

Window Menu

The Window menu is a standard Windows application Window command. It displays a list of all the currently open windows, allowing you to bring any window to the foreground by clicking on it. Note that all the file windows currently displayed in the IDE also have tabs along the top edge of the work surface, below the toolbars (unless you have selected MDI mode in Tools → Options → Environment → General), and windows can be selected by clicking on a tab.

This is a context-sensitive menu. The menu items available for different circumstances are listed in Table 15-5.

Table 15-5. Window menu item commands

Current window	Description of available commands
Design	• AutoHide All hides all dockable windows. Clicking on window's pushpin icon turns AutoHide off for that window.
	• New Horizontal/Vertical Tab Group creates another set of windows with it own set of tabs.
	• Close All Documents is self-explanatory.
	• Window list.
Code	Same as for a Design window plus the following:
	• New Window creates a new window containing the same file as the current window (use this to open two windows to the same source file)
	• Split creates a second window in the current window for two different views of the same file
	• Remove Split removes a split window.
Dockable	This category of window includes the Solution explorer, the Properties window, the Class View window, the toolboxes, etc. These windows are dockable, as indicated by the pushpin icon in the upper-right corner of each.
	Available menu items are the same as for a Design window with the addition of commands to dock, hide, or float a window.

Help Menu

The Help menu provides access to a number of submenus. Those that are not self-explanatory are described here.

Dynamic Help (Ctrl-Alt-F4)

If you are developing on a machine with enough horsepower, Dynamic Help is a wonderful thing. Otherwise, it is quite a performance hog. (It can be disabled by unchecking all the checkboxes under Tools → Options → Environment → Dynamic Help) Alternatively, just closing the window is sufficient to prevent the performance hit, and that way it is still available when you need it.

That said, using Dynamic Help is very simple. Open a Dynamic Help window by clicking on this menu item or pressing Ctrl-F1. Then wherever the focus is, whether in a design, code, or dockable window, context-sensitive hyperlinks will appear in the Dynamic Help window. Click on any of these links to bring up the relevant help topic in a separate window.

Contents... (Ctrl-Alt-F1) / Index... (Ctrl-Alt-F2) / Search... (Ctrl-Alt-F3)

These three commands provide different views into the SDK help system, allowing you to search by a (pseudo) table of contents, an incremental index, or a search phrase, respectively. The first type of search is an indexed search, while the latter two are full text searches, so you may get different results using the different search types using the same phrase.

The Help system exposed by these commands is the exact same Help system exposed in two other places by the Start button:

```
Programs → Microsoft Visual Studio 2005 → Microsoft Visual Studio 2005
Documentation
Programs → Microsoft .NET Framework SDK v2.0 → Documentation
```

This Help tool uses a browser-type interface, with Forward and Back navigation and Favorites. The list of topics is displayed in the left-hand pane, and the help topic itself, including hyperlinks, is displayed on the right.

Index Results... (Shift-Alt-F2)

When searching for Help topics by Index, there are often many topics for a given index entry. In these cases, the multiple topics are listed in an Index Results window. This window will display automatically if this is the case. This command allows you to view the Index Results window if it has been closed.

Check for Updates

This command will check for service releases for your currently installed version of Visual Studio 2005. For this command to work, your machine must be connected to the Internet. If there is an update available, you will be prompted to close the IDE before the service release is installed.

Building and Running

You can run your application at any time by selecting either Start or Start Without Debugging from the Debug menu, or you can accomplish the same results by pressing either F5 or Ctrl-F5, respectively. In addition, you can start the program by clicking the Start icon on the Standard toolbar.

The program can be built (i.e., *.exe* and *.dll* files generated) by selecting a command under the Build menu. You have the option of building the entire solution or only the currently selected project.

CHAPTER 16

Visual Basic 2005 Fundamentals

One goal of this book is for you to pick up the language fundamentals of Visual Basic 2005 as you create applications. Thus, Chapter 1 starts right off with building applications and eschews the traditional introduction to programming elements such as If statements, While loops, and so forth.

That said, Visual Basic 2005 is a full programming language with its own complexities. This chapter is aimed at readers who would like to get the fundamentals under their belt *before* reading the rest of the book (feel free to read this chapter first), or readers who want to review the fundamentals *after* reading the book, as well as readers who want to dip in now and then, to check how certain things are done *as* they read the book.

While this book is aimed at VB6 programmers making the transition to .NET, this chapter does not assume prior experience with Visual Basic or any other programming language, though if you've never programmed at all you may find the pace a bit quick.

Types

Every object in Visual Basic 2005 has a type. Types come in two flavors:

- Those that are built into the language (called *fundamental* or *intrinsic* types)
- Types you create (classes, structs, and interfaces)

Visual Basic 2005 offers a number of intrinsic types, as shown in Table 16-1.

Table 16-1. The intrinsic types

Type	Size (in bytes)	.NET type	Description
Boolean	1	Boolean	true or false.
Byte	1	Byte	Unsigned (values 0–255).
Char	2	Char	Unicode characters.

Table 16-1. The intrinsic types (continued)

Type	Size (in bytes)	.NET type	Description
Date	8	DateTime	Midnight 1/1/0001 through 11:59:59 12/31/9999.
Decimal	12	Decimal	Fixed-precision up to 28 digits and the position of the decimal point. This is typically used in financial calculations. Requires the suffix "m" or "M."
Double	8	Double	Double-precision floating-point; holds the values from approximately $+/-5.0 * 10^{-324}$ to approximate $+/-1.8 * 10^{308}$ with 15–16 significant figures.
Integer	4	Int32	Integer values between –2,147,483,648 and 2,147,483,647.
Long	8	Int64	Integers ranging from –9,223,372,036,854,775,808 to 9,223,372,036,854,775,807.
Short	2	Int16	Integer values –32,768 to 32,767
Single	4	Single	Floating-point number. Holds the values from approximately $+/-1.5 * 10^{-45}$ to approximate $+/-3.4 * 10^{38}$ with 7 significant figures.
String		String	A sequence of Unicode characters.

Each type has a name (e.g., Integer) and a size (e.g., 4 bytes) The size tells you how many bytes each object of this type occupies in memory. Programmers generally don't like to waste memory if they can avoid it, but with the cost of memory these days, you can afford to be mildly profligate if doing so simplifies your program.

Each Visual Basic 2005 type corresponds to an underlying .NET type. Thus, what Visual Basic 2005 calls an Integer, .NET calls an Int32. This is interesting only if you care about sharing objects across languages, an important topic but one that is beyond the scope of this book. The description field of Table 16-1 tells you the minimum and maximum values you can hold in objects of each type.

Numeric Types

Most of the intrinsic types are used for working with numeric values (Byte, Short, Integer, Single, Double, Decimal, Long).

Another way to divide the types is into those used for integer (whole number) values, and those used for fractional values. The Short, Integer, and Long types all hold whole number values. Most of the time, you'll just use Integer for these values, unless there is a good reason to do otherwise.

The Single and Double types hold fractional values (rational numbers). For most uses, Single will suffice, unless you need to hold a really big fractional number, in which case you might use a Double. The Decimal value type was added to the language to support accounting applications, and is described in Table 16-1.

Nonnumeric types

In addition to the numeric types, the Visual Basic 2005 language offers four other primitive types: Char, String, Date, and Boolean.

The Char type is used from time to time when you need to hold a single character. For sequences of characters you'll use the String type. Date types are used to hold date and time values, and are most useful when working with databases from which you might extract a date-time value.

The one remaining type of importance is Boolean. A Boolean value is a value that is either True or False.

> The Boolean type was named after George Boole (1815–1864), an English mathematician who published "An investigation into the Laws of Thought, on Which Are Founded the Mathematical Theories of Logic and Probabilities," and thus created the science of Boolean algebra.

Understanding types

When you create a program under Visual Basic 2005, you may choose to set Option Explicit and Option Strict to On, by writing these lines at the top of your source code:

```
Option Strict On
Option Explicit On
```

> If you use Option Explicit or Option Strict, you must make them the first statements in your source code file.

Option Explicit requires that every variable be declared before it is used (variables are explained in the next section). Option Strict restricts the way you cast from one type to another. Both enable the compiler to help you find bugs in your program and together they make Visual Basic 2005 a strongly typed language; and that is a very good thing. This book assumes you will *always* set both Option Explicit and Option Strict on.

In a strongly typed language, every object you create or use must have a specific type (e.g., you must declare the object to be an Integer, a String, or a Dog). The type tells the compiler how big the object is and what it can do.

> Confusingly, a perfectly legitimate type is type Object, though this type is rarely used and tends to undermine type safety.

The size of an object is measured in bytes. An Integer, for example, is four bytes big. User-defined types have a size as well, measured as the sum of all their member variables.

When programmers talk about what an object can do, they typically mean the methods of the object. User-defined types have many methods. Intrinsic types have implicit methods. For example, the numeric types have the ability to be added together, multiplied, and so forth.

The compiler will help you by complaining if you try to use a type improperly. The compiler complains in one of two ways: it issues a warning or it issues an error.

 You are well advised to treat warnings as errors. That is, you ought to stop what you are doing and figure out why there is a warning and fix the problem. Never ignore a compiler warning.

Programmers talk about "design time," "compile time," and runtime." Design time is when you are designing the program. Compile time is when you compile the program, and runtime is (surprise!) when you run the program.

The earlier you find a bug, the better. It is best (and cheapest) to discover a bug in your logic at design time. It is better (and cheaper) to find bugs in your program at compile time rather than at runtime. Not only is it better, it is more reliable. A compile-time bug will fail every time you run the compiler, but a runtime bug can hide. Runtime bugs slip under a crack in your code, and lurk there (sometimes for months) biding their time, waiting to come out when it will be embarrassing to you.

It is a constant theme of this book that you *want* the compiler to find bugs. The compiler is your friend. The more bugs the compiler finds, the fewer bugs your users will find. Setting Option Strict On helps the compiler find bugs in your code. Here's how: suppose you tell the compiler that Milo is of type Dog. Some time later you try to use Milo to display text. Oops, Dog objects don't display text. Your compiler will stop with an error.

```
Dog does not contain a definition for 'showText'
```

Very nice. Now you can go figure out if you used the wrong object or you called the wrong method.

Visual Studio 2005 actually finds the error even before the compiler does. When you try to add a method that does exist, IntelliSense pops up to help you, as shown in Figure 16-1.

When you try to add a method that does not exist, it won't be in the list. That is a pretty good clue that you are not using the object properly.

Figure 16-1. IntelliSense

Variables

A variable is an object that holds a value:

```
Dim myVariable as Integer = 15
```

In this example, myVariable is an object of type Integer. It has been *initialized* with the value 15. The formal definition for how you create a variable is:

```
Access-Modifier Identifier As Type [= value]
```

Access modifiers are discussed later in this chapter; for now, you'll use Dim.

 The keyword Dim is short for dimension. This term dates back to the early days of BASIC programming, and is essentially vestigial.

An *identifier* is just a name for a variable, method, class, and so forth. In the case shown previously, the variable's identifier is myVariable. The keyword As signals that what follows is the type, in this case Integer. If you are initializing the variable, you follow the type with the assignment operators (=) followed by the value (e.g., 15)

Type characters

Variable identifiers may have a type character suffix that indicates the variable's type. For example, rather than writing as Integer you can use the suffix %.

```
Dim myVariable as Integer
Dim myVariable%
```

These two lines are identical in effect. Not every type is a character, but you are free to use them for those types that do. The complete set is shown in Table 16-2.

Table 16-2. Type characters

Type	Type character	Usage
Decimal	@	`Dim decimalValue@ = 123.45`
Double	#	`Dim doubleValue# = 3.14159265358979`
Integer	%	`Dim integerValue% = 1`
Long	&	`Dim longValue& = 123456789`
Single	!	`Dim singleValue! = 3.1415`
String	$	`Dim stringValue$ = "Hello world"`

 While type characters were preserved in the Visual Basic .NET language, many developers feel they should be avoided, and that spelling out the type makes for clearer and easier-to-maintain code.

Initializing variables

You are not required to initialize variables. You could write:

```
Dim myVariable as Integer
```

You can then assign a value to `myVariable` later in your program:

```
Dim myVariable as Integer
'some other code here
myVariable = 15   'assign 15 to myVariable
```

You can also change the value of a variable later in the program. That is why they're called variables, their values vary.

```
Dim myVariable as Integer
'some other code here
myVariable = 15   'assign 15 to myVariable
'some other code here
myVariable = 12   'now it is 12
```

Technically, a variable is a named storage location with a type. The value 12 is being stored in the named location. You can safely think of a variable as being an object of the type specified. You can assign values to that object and then you can extract those values later.

The use of variables is illustrated in Example 16-1. To test this program, open Visual Studio 2005 and create a Console application. Type in the code as shown.

WriteLine

The .NET Framework provides a useful method for displaying output on the screen in console applications. The details of this method, `System.Console.WriteLine()`, will become clearer as we progress through the book, but the fundamentals are straightforward. You call the method as shown in Example 16-1, passing in a string that you want printed to the console (the screen).

You can also pass in substitution parameters. Here's how it works. You place a number between braces:

```
System.Console.WriteLine("After assignment, myVariable: {0}", myVariable)
```

and you follow the quoted string with a comma and then a variable name. The value of the variable will be substituted into the parameter. Assuming `myVariable` has the value 15, the statement shown above causes the following to display:

```
After assignment, myVariable: 15
```

You can have more than one parameter, and the variable values will be substituted in order:

```
System.Console.WriteLine("After assignment, myVariable: {0} and
myOtherVariable: {1}", myVariable, myOtherVariable);
```

Assuming `myVariable` has the value 15, and `myOtherVariable` has the value 20, this will cause the following to display:

```
After
assignment, myVariable: 15 and myOtherVariable: 20.
```

Example 16-1. Initializing and assigning to variables

```
Sub Main( )
    Dim myInt As Integer = 7
    Console.WriteLine("Initialized myInt: {0}", myInt)
    myInt = 5
    Console.WriteLine("After assignment myInt: {0}", myInt)
End Sub
```

```
Output:
Initialized myInt: 7
After assignment myInt: 5
```

Here, we initialize the variable `myInt` to the value 7, display that value, reassign the variable with the value 5, and display it again. To display the value we call the shared `WriteLine` method on the console class (see the sidebar "WriteLine").

Default Values

Visual Basic 2005 does not require that you initialize your variables (though it is a very good idea to discipline yourself to do so). If you do not initialize your variable, it will be set to a default value, as shown in Table 16-3.

Table 16-3. Default values for uninitialized variables

Data type	Default value
All numeric types	0
Boolean	False
Date	01/01/0001 12:00:00 AM
Decimal	0
Object	Nothing
String	"" (zero length string)

 Object defaults to Nothing. This keyword indicates that the variable is not associated with any object. You can assign the keyword Nothing to a reference to an object of any type.

Constants

Variables are a powerful tool, but there are times when you want to manipulate a defined value, one whose value you want to ensure remains constant. For example, you might need to work with the Fahrenheit freezing and boiling points of water in a program simulating a chemistry experiment. Your program will be clearer if you name the variables that store these values FreezingPoint and BoilingPoint, but you do not want to permit their values to be reassigned. How do you prevent reassignment? The answer is to use a constant. A *constant* is like a variable except that its value cannot be changed once it is initialized.

A constant associates a name with a value, but you cannot change that value while the program runs. Hence, rather than varying, a constant is, well, constant.

Constants come in three flavors: *literals, symbolic constants*, and *enumerations*.

Literal constants

A literal constant is just a value, such as 32. It does not have a name, it is just a literal value. And you can't make the value 32 represent any other value. The value of 32 is always 32. You can't assign a new value to 32; and you can't make 32 represent the value 99 no matter how you might try.

When you write an integer as a literal constant, you are free just to write the number. The characters 32 are, together, a literal constant for the Integer value 32, and you can assign them accordingly:

```
Dim myValue as Integer = 32  'assign the literal value 32 to the variable myValue
```

If you want to assign a different type, however, you will want to use the correct format. For example, to designate the value 32 as a Double (rather than as an Integer) you will append the character R:

```
Dim myValue as Double = 32R 'assign literal value 32 as a Double
```

The complete list of literal formats is shown in Table 16-4.

Table 16-4. Literal formats

Type	Literal	Example
Boolean	True False	Dim booleanValue as Boolean = True
Char	C	Dim charValue as Char = "J"C
Decimal	D	Dim decimalValue as Decimal = 3.1415D
Double	Any floating-point number, or R	Dim doubleValue as Double = 3.1415 Dim doubleValue as Double = 3.1415R Dim doubleValue as Double = 5R
Integer	Any integer value in range, or I	Dim integerValue as Integer = 100 Dim integerValue as Integer = 100I
Long	Any integer value outside the range of type Integer, or L	Dim longValue as Long = 5000000000 Dim longValue as Long = 100L
Short	S	Dim shortValue as Short = 100S
Single	F	Dim singleValue as Single = 3.14F
String	" "	Dim stringValue as String = "Hello world"

Symbolic constants

Symbolic constants assign a name to a constant value. You declare a symbolic constant using the Const keyword and the following syntax:

```
access-modifier Const identifier as type = value;
```

Access modifiers are discussed later; for now, you will use Public.

The keyword Const is followed by an identifier (the name of the constant), the keyword As and the *type* of the constant (e.g., Integer). This is similar to declaring a variable, except that you add the keyword Const, and symbolic constants *must* be initialized. Once initialized, a symbolic constant cannot be altered. For example:

```
Public Const FreezingPoint As Integer = 32
```

In this declaration, 32 is a literal constant and FreezingPoint is a symbolic constant of type Integer. Example 16-2 illustrates the use of symbolic constants.

Example 16-2. Symbolic constants

```
    Sub Main( )
        Const FreezingPoint As Integer = 32 ' degrees Farenheit
        Const BoilingPoint As Integer = 212

        Console.WriteLine("Freezing point of water: {0}", FreezingPoint)
        Console.WriteLine("Boiling point of water: {0}", BoilingPoint)

        'FreezingPoint = 0
    End Sub
End Module
```

Example 16-2 creates two symbolic integer constants: `FreezingPoint` and `BoilingPoint`. See the sidebar "Naming Conventions" for symbolic constants.

Naming Conventions

Microsoft has promulgated white papers on how you should name the variables, constants, and other objects in your program. They define two types of naming conventions: camel notation and Pascal notation.

In camel notation, names begin with a lowercase letter. Multiword names (e.g., My Button) are written with no spaces and no underscore, but each word after the first begins with an uppercase letter (e.g., myButton).

Pascal notation is just like camel notation except that the first letter is also uppercase (e.g., `FreezingPoint`).

Microsoft suggests that variables be written with camel notation and constants with Pascal notation. Later on you'll learn that member variables and methods are named with camel notation, but classes are named with Pascal notation.

These constants serve the same purpose as always using the *literal* values 32 and 212 for the freezing and boiling points of water in expressions that require them, but because these constants have names, they convey far more meaning. Also, if you decide to switch this program to Celsius, you can reinitialize these constants at compile time, to 0 and 100, respectively; and all the rest of the code ought to continue to work.

To prove to yourself that the constant cannot be reassigned, try uncommenting the last line of the program (shown in bold). When you recompile, you should receive this error:

```
Constant cannot be the target of an assignment
```

Enumerations

Enumerations provide a powerful alternative to constants. An enumeration is a distinct value type, consisting of a set of named constants (called the *enumerator list*).

If you created two related constants:

```
Const FreezingPoint As Integer = 32
Const BoilingPoint As Integer = 212
```

you might wish to add a number of other useful constants as well, such as:

```
const LightJacketWeather As Integer = 60;
const SwimmingWeather As Integer = 72;
const WickedCold As Integer = 0;
```

This process is somewhat cumbersome, and there is no logical connection among these various constants. Visual Basic 2005 provides the *enumeration* to solve these problems:

```
Enum Temperatures
    CelsiusMeetsFahrenheit = -40
    WickedCold = 0
    FreezingPoint = 32
    LightJacketWeather = 60
    SwimmingWeather = 72
    BoilingPoint = 212
End Enum
```

Every enumeration has an underlying type, which can be any integral type (Byte, Short, Integer, and Long). The technical specification of an enumeration is:

```
[access modifiers] Enum identifier [As type]
    membername [ = constant expression]
end Enum
```

 In a specification statement like this, anything in square brackets is optional. That is, you can declare an Enum with no base type. The base type is optional, even if Strict is On, and if you don't define a base type, integer is assumed.

For now, let's focus on the rest of this declaration. An enumeration begins with the keyword Enum, which is followed by an identifier, such as:

```
Enum Temperatures
```

The AS keyword defines the underlying type for the enumeration. That is, are you declaring constant Integers, or constant Longs? If you leave out this optional keyword (and often you will) the underlying type will be integer.

Example 16-3 rewrites Example 16-2 to use an enumeration.

Example 16-3. Using an enumeration, not quite correctly

```
Enum Temperatures
    WickedCold = 0
    FreezingPoint = 32
    LightJacketWeather = 60
    SwimmingWeather = 72
    BoilingPoint = 212
End Enum 'Temperatures

Sub Main( )
    System.Console.WriteLine( _
        "Freezing point of water: {0}", _
        Temperatures.FreezingPoint)

    System.Console.WriteLine( _
        "Boiling point of water: {0}", _
        Temperatures.BoilingPoint)
End Sub
End Module
Output:
Freezing point of water: FreezingPoint
Boiling point of water: BoilingPoint
```

In Example 16-3, you declare enumerated constant `Temperatures`. `Temperatures` is an enumeration. The values of the enumeration must be qualified by the enumeration type. That means you cannot just refer to `FreezingPoint`, but you must use the prefix `Temperatures` followed by the dot operator. This is called qualifying the identifier `FreezingPoint`. Thus, to refer to the `FreezingPoint` you use the full identifier `Temperatures.FreezingPoint`.

Unfortunately, if you pass the name of an enumeration to `WriteLine` what is displayed is its name, not its value. To display the value of an enumerated constant, you must cast the constant to its underlying type (`Integer`), as shown in Example 16-4.

Example 16-4. Casting the enumerated value to fix Example 16-3

```
Sub Main( )
    System.Console.WriteLine( _
        "Freezing point of water: {0}", _
        CInt(Temperatures.FreezingPoint))

    System.Console.WriteLine( _
        "Boiling point of water: {0}", _
        CInt(Temperatures.BoilingPoint))
End Sub
End Module
```

When you cast a value (in this case, using the `CInt` function), you tell the compiler, "I know that this value is really of the indicated type." In this case, you are saying, "Treat this enumerated constant as an Integer." Since the underlying type is `Integer`, this is safe to do. See the section "Casting."

Casting

Objects of one type can be converted into objects of another type. This is called casting, and casting can be either narrowing or widening.

A widening conversion or cast is one in which the conversion is to a type that can accommodate every possible value in the existing variable type. For example, an Integer can accommodate every possible value held by a Short. Casting from Short to Integer is, thus, a widening conversion.

A narrowing cast is one in which the conversion is to a type that may not be able to accommodate every possible value in the existing variable type. For example, a Short can accommodate only some of the values that an Integer variable might hold. Casting from an Integer to a Short is thus a narrowing conversion.

Visual Basic 2005 conversions are either implicit or explicit. In an implicit conversion, the compiler makes the conversion, with no special action by the developer. With an explicit conversion, the developer must use a special function to signal the cast. For example, in Example 16-4 you use the Cint function to explicitly cast the enumerated value to an Integer.

The semantics of an explicit conversion are "Hey! Compiler! I know what I'm doing." This is sometimes called "hitting it with the big hammer" and can be very useful or very painful, depending on whether your thumb is in the way of the nail.

Whether a cast is implicit or explicit is affected by the Option Strict setting. If Option Strict is On (as it always should be) only widening casts can be implicit.

The explicit cast functions are:

CBool
> Converts any valid string (e.g., "True") or numeric expression to Boolean. Numeric nonzero values are converted to True; 0 is converted to False.

CByte
> Converts numeric expression in range 0 to 255 to Byte. Rounds any fractional part.

CChar
> Returns the first character of a string as a Char.

CDate
> Converts any valid representation of a date or time to Date (e.g., "January 1, 2002" is converted to the corresponding Date type).

CDbl
> Converts any expression that can be evaluated as a number to a Double if in the range of a Double.

CDec

Converts any expression that can be evaluated as a number to a Decimal if in the range of a Decimal.

CInt

Converts any expression that can be evaluated as a number to a `Integer` if in the range of a `Integer`, rounds fractional part.

CLng

Converts any expression that can be evaluated as a number to a `Long` if in the range of a `Long`, rounds fractional part.

CObj

Converts any expression that can be interpreted as an `Object` to an `Object`

CShort

Converts any expression that can be evaluated as a number to a `Short` if in the range of a `Short`

CStr

If Boolean, converts to the string "True" or "False." If the expression can be interpreted as a date, returns a string expression of the date. For numeric expressions, the returned string represents the number.

CType

This is a general purpose conversion function that uses the syntax

```
CType(expression, typename)
```

where expression is an expression or a variable, and typename is the data type to convert to. The first conversion in Example 16-4:

```
System.Console.WriteLine( _
    "Freezing point of water: {0}", _
    CInt(Temperatures.FreezingPoint))
```

can be rewritten as:

```
System.Console.WriteLine( _
    "Freezing point of water: {0}", _
    CType(Temperatures.FreezingPoint, Integer))
```

The value in the enumerated constant is cast to an integer, and that integer value is passed to WriteLine and displayed. If you don't specifically set it otherwise, the enumeration begins at 0 and each subsequent value counts up from the previous one.

If you create the following enumeration:

```
Enum SomeValues
    First
    Second
    Third = 20
    Fourth
End Enum
```

the value of First will be 0, Second will be 1, Third will be 20, and Fourth will be 21.

If `Option Strict` is set `On`, Enums are treated as formal types; that is, they are not just a synonym for another type, they are a type in their own right. Therefore, an explicit conversion is required to convert between Enum and an `Integer` types.

Strings

It is nearly impossible to write a Visual Basic 2005 program without creating strings. A string object holds a string of characters.

You declare a string variable using the `String` keyword much as you would create an instance of any object:

```
Dim myString as String
```

A string literal is created by placing double quotes around a string of letters:

```
"Hello World"
```

It is common to initialize a string variable with a string literal:

```
Dim myString as String = "Hello World"
```

Whitespace

In the Visual Basic 2005 language, spaces and tabs are considered to be *whitespace* (so named because you see only the white of the underlying "page"). Extra whitespace is generally ignored in Visual Basic 2005 statements. Thus, you can write:

```
Dim myVariable as Integer = 5
```

or:

```
Dim    myVariable    as    Integer    =    5
```

and the compiler will treat the two statements as identical.

The exception to this rule is that whitespace within strings is not ignored. If you write:

```
Console.WriteLine("Hello World")
```

each space between "Hello" and "World" is treated as another character in the string.

Most of the time, the use of whitespace is intuitive. The key is to use whitespace to make the program more readable to the programmer; the compiler is indifferent.

However, there are instances when the use of whitespace is quite significant. Although the expression:

```
Dim myVariable as Integer = 5 'no whitespace around = sign
```

is the same as:

```
Dim myVariable as Integer=5
```

it is not the same as:

```
DimmyVariable as Integer=5 'no white space around = sign
```

The compiler knows that the whitespace on either side of the assignment operator is extra, but the whitespace between the keyword `Dim` and the name of the variable is *not* extra, and is required.

This is not surprising; the whitespace allows the compiler to *parse* the keyword `Dim` rather than some unknown term `DimmyVariable`. You are free to add as much or as little whitespace between `Dim` and `myVariable` as you care to, but there must be at least one whitespace character (typically a space or tab).

Statements

In Visual Basic 2005, a complete program instruction is called a *statement*. Programs consist of sequences of Visual Basic 2005 statements. Each statement ends with a new line or a colon.

```
Dim myString As String = "Hello World"
Dim myVariable As Integer = 5 : Dim myVar2 As Integer = 7
```

The colon allows you to squeeze more than one statement on a single line, but is generally considered poor programming practice because it makes for code that is harder to read and thus harder to maintain.

If your code will not fit on a single line, you may use the *line continuation character*, the underscore: (_) to continue a single statement on more than one line, as shown here:

```
System.Console.WriteLine( _
    "Freezing point of water: {0}", _
    CInt(Temperatures.FreezingPoint))
```

All three lines are considered a single statement, because of the use of the line continuation character.

Be sure to add a space between any other code and the line continuation character.

Branching

Visual Basic 2005 statements are evaluated in order. The compiler starts at the beginning of a statement list and makes its way to the bottom. This would be entirely straightforward, and terribly limiting, were it not for branching.

Methods are executed from top to bottom. The compiler reads each line of code in turn, and executes one line after another. This continues in sequence until the method branches.

There are two ways a method can branch: unconditionally or conditionally. We'll look at each of these in turn.

Unconditional Branching Statements

The most common way to branch is by calling a method. This is an unconditional branch.

You call a method by writing its name. For example:

```
Method1()  'invokes Method1
```

 It is also legal to call a VB.NET method with the optional keyword call:

```
        call Method1()
```

If you do use call on a function, the return value is discarded. There is no advantage to this syntax, and it isn't used in this book.

Every time the compiler encounters a method call, it stops execution in the current method and branches to the newly called method. When that method returns, execution picks up in the original method on the line just below the method call, as illustrated schematically in Figure 16-2.

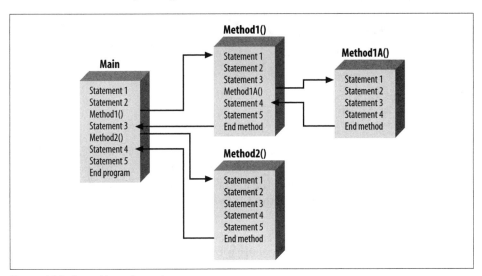

Figure 16-2. Branching schematic

In Figure 16-2, execution begins in Main. Statements 1 and 2 execute and then the compiler sees a call to Method1. Program execution branches to the start of Method1, where its first three statements are executed. At the call to Method1A execution again branches, this time to the start of Method1A.

The four statements in Method1A are executed and Method1A returns. Execution resumes on the first statement after the method call in Method1 (Statement 4). Execution continues until Method1 ends, at which time execution resumes back in Main at Statement 3. At the call to Method2, execution again branches; all the statements in Method2 execute and then Main resumes at Statement 4. When Main ends, the program itself ends.

You can see the effect of method calls in Example 16-5. Execution begins in Main, but branches to a method named SomeMethod. The WriteLine statements in each method assist you in seeing where you are in the code as the program executes.

Example 16-5. Calling a method

```
Option Strict On
Option Explicit On

Module Module1
    Sub Main( )
        Console.WriteLine("In Main! Calling SomeMethod...")
        SomeMethod( )
        Console.WriteLine("Back in Main.")
    End Sub 'Main

    Sub SomeMethod( )
        Console.WriteLine("Greetings from SomeMethod!")
    End Sub 'SomeMethod

End Module

Output:
In Main! Calling SomeMethod...
Greetings from SomeMethod!
Back in Main.
```

Program flow begins in Main and proceeds until SomeMethod is invoked (invoking a method is sometimes referred to as "calling" the method). At that point, program flow branches to the method. When the method completes, program flow resumes at the next line after the call to that method.

 Another way to create an unconditional branch is with one of the unconditional branch keywords: goto, exit, return, or throw.

Conditional Branching Statements

While method calls cause unconditional branching, often you will want to branch within a method depending on a condition that you evaluate while the program is running. This is known as conditional branching.

Conditional branching statements allow you to write logic, such as "If you are over 25, then you may rent a car."

If statements

The simplest branching statement is If. An If statement branches based on a condition. The condition is a *Boolean expression*. An expression is a statement that evaluates to a value. A Boolean expression evaluates to True or False.

An If statement says: if the condition evaluates to True, then execute the statement, otherwise, skip it. The formal description of an if statement is:

```
If expression Then
    statements
End If
```

An alternative one-line version is:

```
If expression Then statement
```

The use of the If statement is illustrated in Example 16-6.

Example 16-6. The If statement

```
Option Strict On
Module Module1

    Sub Main( )

        Dim valueOne As Integer = 10
        Dim valueTwo As Integer = 20
        Dim valueThree As Integer = 30

        Console.WriteLine("Testing valueOne against valueTwo...")
        If valueOne > valueTwo Then
            Console.WriteLine( _
                "ValueOne: {0} larger than ValueTwo: {1}", _
                valueOne, valueTwo)
        End If

        Console.WriteLine("Testing valueThree against valueTwo...")
        If valueThree > valueTwo Then
            Console.WriteLine( _
                "ValueThree: {0} larger than ValueTwo: {1}", _
                valueThree, valueTwo)
        End If
```

Example 16-6. The If statement (continued)

```
    Console.WriteLine("Testing is valueTwo > 15 (one line)...")
    If valueTwo > 15 Then Console.WriteLine("Yes it is")

  End Sub 'Main

End Module
Output:
Testing valueOne against valueTwo...
Testing valueThree against valueTwo...
ValueThree: 30 larger than ValueTwo: 20
Testing is valueTwo > 15 (one line)...
Yes it is
```

In this simple program, you declare three variables, valueOne, valueTwo, and valueThree. In the first If statement, you test whether valueOne is greater than valueTwo.

```
If valueOne > valueTwo Then
    Console.WriteLine( _
        "ValueOne: {0} larger than ValueTwo: {1}", valueOne, valueTwo)
End If
```

Because valueOne is less than valueTwo, this If statement fails (the condition returns False), and the body of the If statement (the statements between the If and the End If) never executes.

 The test for greater than uses the greater-than operator (>), which is discussed in detail later in this chapter.

You then test whether valueThree is greater than valueTwo:

```
If valueThree > valueTwo Then
    Console.WriteLine( _
        "ValueThree: {0} larger than ValueTwo: {1}", valueThree, valueTwo)
End If
```

Since valueThree (30) *is* greater than valueTwo (20), the test returns True and thus the statement executes. The statement in this case is the call to WriteLine( ), shown in bold.

Finally, Example 16-6 uses a one-line If statement to test whether valueTwo is greater than 15. Since this evaluates to True, the statement that follows executes, and the words "Yes it is" are displayed.

```
If valueTwo > 15 Then Console.WriteLine("Yes it is")
```

The output reflects that the first If statement fails, but the second and third succeed:

```
Testing valueOne against valueTwo...
Testing valueThree against valueTwo...
ValueThree: 30 larger than ValueTwo: 20
```

```
Testing is valueTwo > 15 (one line)...
Yes it is
```

 Many Visual Basic 2005 developers avoid the single line If statement because it can be confusing and difficult to maintain.

If...Else statements

Often you will find that you want to take one set of actions when the condition tests True, and a different set of actions when the condition tests False. This allows you to write logic such as "If you are over 25, then you may rent a car; *otherwise*, you must take the train."

The *otherwise* portion of the logic is executed in the *else* statement. For example, you can modify Example 16-6 to print an appropriate message whether or not valueOne is greater than valueTwo, as shown in Example 16-7.

Example 16-7. The Else clause

```
Option Strict On
Option Explicit On
Module Module1

    Sub Main( )

        Dim valueOne As Integer = 10
        Dim valueTwo As Integer = 20
        Dim valueThree As Integer = 30

        Console.WriteLine("Testing valueOne against valueTwo...")
        If valueOne > valueTwo Then
            Console.WriteLine( _
                "ValueOne: {0} larger than ValueTwo: {1}", valueOne, valueTwo)
        Else
            Console.WriteLine( _
                "Nope, ValueOne: {0} is NOT larger than valueTwo: {1}", _
                valueOne, valueTwo)
        End If
    End Sub 'Main
End Module
Output:
Testing valueOne against valueTwo...
Nope, ValueOne: 10 is NOT larger than valueTwo: 20
```

Because the test in the If statement fails (valueOne is *not* larger than valueTwo), the body of the If statement is skipped and the body of the Else statement is executed. Had the test succeeded, the If statement body would execute and the body of the Else statement would be skipped.

It is possible, and not uncommon, to nest If statements one within another, to handle complex conditions. It is also common to evaluate a sequence of expressions with the ElseIf construct. The first If/ElseIf statement to evaluate True will have its statements executed (and no others will even be evaluated). If none of the statements evaluates True, the final Else clause is executed.

Select Case Statements

Nested If statements and long sequences of ElseIf statements are hard to read, maintain, and debug. When you have a complex set of choices to make, the Select Case statement is a more powerful alternative. The logic of a Select Case statement is to "pick a matching value and act accordingly."

```
Select [ Case ] testExpression
[ Case expressionList
   [ statements ] ]
[ Case Else
   [ else statements] ]
End Select
```

It is easiest to understand this construct in the context of an example, as shown in Example 16-8.

Example 16-8. Select Case

```
Option Strict On
Module Module1

    Sub Main( )
        Dim targetInteger As Integer = 15

        Select Case targetInteger
           Case 5
              Console.WriteLine("5")
           Case 10
              Console.WriteLine("10")
           Case 15
              Console.WriteLine("15!")
           Case Else
              Console.WriteLine("Value not found")
        End Select
    End Sub 'Main
End Module
Output:
15!
```

In Example 16-8, a value (15) is assigned to targetInteger. The Select Case statement tests for the values 5, 10 and 15. If one matches, the associated statement is executed. The output shows that the value 15 matched, and the associated statement was executed, displaying the value. If none of the values matched, the `Else` select statement would be executed.

Checking for a range of values

You can check for a range of values (e.g., `Case 10 To 14`).

You are not restricted to just testing for a numeric value. You can also test for `String` values, and you can test ranges of string values, examining whether a target value fits alphabetically within the range (e.g., Case "Alpha To Lambda").

A single `Case` statement can test for more than one criterion: just separate them by commas:

```
Case "Fred", "Joe", Is < "Alpha"
    Console.WriteLine("Joe or Fred or < Alpha")
```

This case will match the strings "Fred" and "Joe" as well as any string that comes alphabetically before "Alpha."

Iteration Statements

In a VB.NET method, you will find many situations in which you want to do the same thing again and again, perhaps slightly changing a value each time you repeat the action. This is called iteration or looping. Typically, you'll iterate (or loop) over a set of items, taking the same action on each. This is the programming equivalent to an assembly line: take a hundred car bodies and put a windshield on each one as it comes by.

VB.NET provides an extensive suite of iteration statements, including `Do` and `For`.

The Do Loop

The semantics of a `Do` loop are "Do this work while a condition is true" or "Do this work until a condition becomes true." You can test the condition either at the top or at the bottom of the loop. If you test at the bottom of the loop, the loop will execute at least once.

The `Do` loop can even be written with no conditions; in which case, it will execute indefinitely, until it encounters an `Exit Do` statement.

Do loops come in the following flavors:

```
Do While BooleanExpression
    statements
Loop

Do Until BooleanExpression
    statements
Loop
```

```
Do
    statements
Loop while BooleanExpression

Do
    statements
Loop until BooleanExpression

Do
    statements
Loop
```

In each case, the BooleanExpression can be any expression that evaluates to a Boolean value of True or False.

Do While

The first kind of Do loop, Do While, executes only *while* the BooleanExpression returns True, as shown in Example 16-9.

Example 16-9. Using Do While

```
Option Strict On
Module Module1

    Sub Main( )
        Dim counterVariable As Integer = 0

        Do While counterVariable < 10
            Console.WriteLine("counterVariable: {0}", counterVariable)
            counterVariable = counterVariable + 1
        Loop ' While counterVariable < 10

    End Sub 'Main
End Module

Output:
counterVariable: 0
counterVariable: 1
counterVariable: 2
counterVariable: 3
counterVariable: 4
counterVariable: 5
counterVariable: 6
counterVariable: 7
counterVariable: 8
counterVariable: 9
```

Do Until

The second version of Do:

```
Do Until BooleanExpression
    statements
Loop
```

executes *until* the BooleanExpression returns True.

 Be very careful when looping to a specific value. If the value is never reached or is skipped over, your loop can continue without end, causing your program to "hang."

The two constructs are closely related; which one you use will depend on the semantics of the problem you are trying to solve. That is, use the construct that represents how you think about the problem. If you are solving this problem: "keep winding the box until the Jack pops up," then use a Do Until loop. If you are solving this problem: "As long as the music plays, keep dancing," then use a Do While loop, though either construct will work ("keep dancing until the music stops.")

The two variants:

```
Do
    statements
Loop while BooleanExpression

Do
    statements
Loop until BooleanExpression
```

are used when you want to ensure that the loop runs at least once, whatever the starting conditions. Thus, although your counterVariable might be initialized to 100, you want to make sure the loop runs once anyway. You'll use the Do... *Loop* While construct.

Breaking out of a Do loop

You can break out of any Do loop with the Exit Do statement. You *must* break out of the final Do construct:

```
Do
    statements
Loop
```

because otherwise it will never terminate. You typically use this construct when you do not know in advance what condition will cause the loop to terminate (e.g., the termination may be in response to user action).

While Loops

As further proof that there are many ways to accomplish the same thing, VB.NET also offers a While loop construct that is closely related to the Do...While loops. The syntax is:

```
while BooleanExpression
    statements
End While
```

The For loop

When you need to iterate over a loop a specified number of times, you can use a For loop with a counter variable. The syntax of the For loop is:

```
For variable = expression to expression [ step expression ]
    statements
Next [ variable-list ]
```

The simplest and most common form of this statement creates a loop variable to count through the iterations of the loop. For example, you might create an integer variable loopCounter that you will use to step through a loop ten times, as shown in Example 16-10.

Example 16-10. For loop

```
Option Strict On
Module Module1

    Sub Main( )

        Dim loopCounter As Integer
        For loopCounter = 0 To 9
            Console.WriteLine("loopCounter: {0}", loopCounter)
        Next

    End Sub 'Main

End Module
Output:
loopCounter: 0
loopCounter: 1
loopCounter: 2
loopCounter: 3
loopCounter: 4
loopCounter: 5
loopCounter: 6
loopCounter: 7
loopCounter: 8
loopCounter: 9
```

The variable (loopCounter) can be of any numeric type. For example, you might initialize a Single rather than an Integer, and step up through the loop from 0.5 to 9.

You can also modify multiple variables on each Next statement. This allows you to nest one For loop within another. You might use an outer and an inner loop to iterate through the contents of collections. A simple example of this technique is shown in Example 16-11.

Example 16-11. Multiple updates with one Next statement

```
Option Strict On
Module Module1
```

Example 16-11. Multiple updates with one Next statement (continued)

```
Sub Main()

    Dim outer As Integer
    Dim inner As Integer

    For outer = 3 To 6
        For inner = 10 To 12
            Console.WriteLine("{0} * {1} = {2}", _
                outer, inner, outer * inner)
    Next inner, outer

    End Sub 'Main

End Module

3 * 10 = 30
3 * 11 = 33
3 * 12 = 36
4 * 10 = 40
4 * 11 = 44
4 * 12 = 48
5 * 10 = 50
5 * 11 = 55
5 * 12 = 60
6 * 10 = 60
6 * 11 = 66
6 * 12 = 72
```

As an alternative to updating both counters in the same Next statement, you can provide each nested For loop with its own Next statement:

```
For outer = 3 To 6
    For inner = 10 To 12
        Console.WriteLine("{0} * {1} = {2}", _
            outer, inner, outer * inner)
    Next inner
Next outer
```

When you update a single value in a Next statement, you are free to leave off the variable you are updating. Thus, the previous code is identical to this code:

```
For outer = 3 To 6
    For inner = 10 To 12
        Console.WriteLine("{0} * {1} = {2}", _
            outer, inner, outer * inner)
    Next
Next
```

Using the variable name in Next statements is generally preferred by VB.NET programmers because it makes for code that is easier to understand and maintain.

Operators

An *operator* is a symbol (e.g., =, >, +) that causes VB.NET to take an action. That action might be assignment (=), addition of two values (+), or comparison of two values (>).

The simplest is the assignment operator:

```
myVariable = 15;
```

The single equal sign (=) is used to assign a value (15) to a variable (myVariable). If statements often use comparison operators:

```
if ( valueOne > valueTwo )
```

This If statement compares valueOne with valueTwo, and if the former is larger than the latter, the test evaluates True, and the If statement executes.

Arithmetic Operators

VB.NET uses seven arithmetic operators, six for standard calculations (+, -, *, ^, /, and \) and a seventh to return the remainder when dividing integers.

VB.NET offers *two* division operators: / and \. The right-facing division operator (/) returns a floating-point answer. If you divide 12/5, the answer is 2.4, as you would expect. This answer is returned as a Double. If you assign the returned value to an Integer, the decimal part is lopped off, and the result will be 2. If Option Strict is On (as it should be), you cannot assign the result to an Integer without explicitly casting, because you would lose the decimal portion of the answer.

The left-facing division operator (\) returns an Integer value. If you divide 12\5, the result is returned with a truncated integer: 2. No cast is needed (even with Option Strict On) because you've explicitly asked for the integer value.

The modulus operator (Mod) to return remainders

To find the remainder in integer division, use the modulus operator (Mod). For example, the statement 17 Mod 4 returns 1 (the remainder after integer division).

The modulus operator is more useful than you might imagine. When you perform modulus n on a number that is a multiple of n, the result is zero. Thus, 80 Mod 10 = 0 because 80 is an even multiple of 10. This allows you to set up loops in which you take an action every nth time through the loop, by testing a counter to see if Mod n is equal to zero.

The exponentiation (^) operator

The final arithmetic operator is the exponentiation operator, which raises a number to the power of the exponent:

```
2^8 = 1024 ' 2 to the 8th power is 1,024.
```

Relational Operators

Relational operators are used to compare two values, and then return a Boolean (True or False). The greater-than operator (>), for example, returns True if the value on the left of the operator is greater than the value on the right. Thus, 5 > 2 returns the value True, while 2 > 5 returns the value False.

The relational operators for VB.NET are shown in Table 16-5. This table assumes two variables: bigValue and smallValue, in which bigValue has been assigned the value 100 and smallValue the value 50.

Table 16-5. Relational operators assumes bigValue = 100 and smallValue = 50

Name	Operator	Given this statement	The expression evaluates to
Equals	=	bigValue = 100 bigValue = 80	True False
Not Equals	<>	bigValue <> 100 bigValue <> 80	False True
Greater than	>	bigValue > smallValue	True
Greater than or equals	>= or =>	bigValue >= smallValue smallValue => bigValue	True False
Less than	<	bigValue < smallValue	False
Less than or equals	<= or =<	smallValue <= bigValue bigValue =< smallValue	True False

Notice that some operators are composed of two characters. For example, greater than or equal to is created with the greater-than symbol (>) and the equal sign (=). You may place these symbols in either order (>= or =>)

The VB.NET equality operator (=) and assignment operator (=) use the same symbol.

When you write:

```
If myX = 5 Then myX = 7
```

the first use of the = symbol is the equality operator (if myX is equal to 5), the second use is the assignment operator (set myX to the value 7). The compiler figures out which is meant by context. (Eat your heart out, C# programmers!)

Use of Logical Operators with Conditionals

If statements test whether a condition is True. Often you will want to test if two conditions are both True, only one is True, or none is True. VB.NET provides a set of logical operators for this, as shown in Table 16-6. This table assumes two variables, x and y, in which x has the value 5 and y the value 7.

Table 16-6. Logical operators given x = 5 and y = 7

Operator	Given this statement	The expression evaluates to	Logic
And	x = 3 And y = 7	False	Both must be True, to evaluate True.
AndAlso	X = 3 AndAlso y = 7	False	Short circuits the test, y is never tested. If the left side fails, the right is not tested.
Or	x = 3 Or y = 7	True	Either or both must be True to evaluate True.
OrElse	X = 5 or y = 9	True	Short circuited, since x is equal to 5, no need to evaluate y.
Xor	X = 5 Xor y = 7	False	True only if one (and only one) statement is True.
Not	Not x = 3	True	Expression must be False for test to evaluate True.

The And operator tests whether two statements are both True. The first line in Table 16-6 includes an example that illustrates the use of the And operator:

    x = 3 And y = 7

The entire expression evaluates False because one side (x = 3) is False.

With the Or operator, either or both sides must be True; the expression is False only if both sides are False. So, in the example in Table 16-6:

    x = 3 Or y = 7

the entire expression evaluates to True because one side (y = 7) is True.

The Xor logical operator is used to test if one (and only one) of the two statements is correct. Thus:

    x = 5 Xor y = 7

evaluates to False, because both statements are True. The Xor statement is False if both statements are True, or if both statements are False; it is True only if one and only one statement is True.

With a Not operator, the statement is True if the expression is False, and vice versa. So, in the accompanying example:

    Not x = 3

the entire expression is True because the tested expression (x = 3) is False. (The logic is: "it is True that it is not True that x is equal to 3.")

Operator Precedence

The compiler must know the order in which to evaluate a series of operators. For example, if I write:

```
myVariable = 5 + 7 * 3
```

there are three operators for the compiler to evaluate (=, +, and *). It could, for example, operate left to right, which would assign the value 5 to myVariable, then add 7 to the 5 (12) and multiply by 3 (36). Since we're evaluating left to right, the assignment has been done, so the value 36 is thrown away. This is clearly not what is intended.

The rules of precedence tell the compiler which operators to evaluate first. As is the case in algebra, multiplication has higher precedence than addition, so 5 + 7 * 3 is equal to 26 rather than 36. Both addition and multiplication have higher precedence than assignment, so the compiler will do the math, and then assign the result (26) to myVariable only after the math is completed.

In VB.NET, parentheses are used to change the order of precedence much as they are in algebra. Thus, you can change the result by writing:

```
myVariable = (5+7) * 3
```

Grouping the elements of the assignment in this way causes the compiler to add 5 + 7, multiply the result by 3, and then assign that value (36) to myVariable.

Within a single line of code, operators are evaluated in the following order:

- Parentheses
- Arithmetic
- Concatenation
- Comparison
- Logical
- Assignment

Comparison operators are evaluated left to right. Arithmetic operators are evaluated in this order:

- Exponentiation (^)
- Division and multiplication (/, *)
- Integer division (\)
- Modulo operator (Mod)
- Addition and subtraction (+,-)

The logical operators are evaluated in this order:

- Not
- And
- Or
- Xor

CHAPTER 17

Using Collections and Generics

The .NET Framework provides a rich suite of collection classes. With the advent of Generics in 2.0, most of these collection classes are now type safe, making for a greatly enhanced programming experience. The collection classes include the List, Dictionary, Sorted Dictionary, Queue, and Stack.

The simplest collection is the Array, the only collection type for which Visual Basic 2005 provides built-in support. In this chapter, you will learn to work with single, multidimensional, and jagged arrays. Arrays have built-in indexers, allowing you to request the *n*th member of the array.

The .NET Framework provides a number of interfaces, such as IEnumerable and ICollection, whose implementation provides you with standard ways to interact with collections. In this chapter, you will see how to work with the most essential of these. The chapter concludes with a tour of commonly used .NET collections, including List, Dictionary, Queue, and Stack.

> In previous versions of Visual Basic.NET, the collection objects were not type safe (you could, for example, mix strings and integers in a Dictionary). The non-type-safe version of List (ArrayList), Dictionary, Queue, and Stack are still available for backward compatibility, but will not be covered in this book because their use is very similar to the Generics-based versions, and because they are obsolete and deprecated.

Arrays

An *array* is an indexed collection of objects, all of the same type. Arrays are both built into the language and implemented as *types*, with properties, fields, and methods.

> Arrays do not use the new Generic syntax. Generics are covered later in this chapter.

Visual Basic 2005 provides native syntax for the declaration of Arrays. What is actually created, however, is an object of type System.Array. Arrays in Visual Basic 2005 provide you with the best of both worlds: easy-to-use array syntax underpinned with an actual class definition, so that instances of an array have access to the methods and properties of System.Array. These appear in Table 17-1.

Table 17-1. System.Array methods and properties

Method or property	Purpose
BinarySearch	Overloaded public static method that searches a one-dimensional sorted array.
Clear	Public static method that sets a range of elements in the array either to zero or to a null reference.
Copy	Overloaded public static method that copies a section of one array to another array.
CreateInstance	Overloaded public static method that instantiates a new instance of an array.
IndexOf	Overloaded public static method that returns the index (offset) of the first instance of a value in a one-dimensional array.
LastIndexOf	Overloaded public static method that returns the index of the last instance of a value in a one-dimensional array.
Reverse	Overloaded public static method that reverses the order of the elements in a one-dimensional array.
Sort	Overloaded public static method that sorts the values in a one-dimensional array.
IsFixedSize	Required because Array implements ICollection. With Arrays, this will always return True (all arrays are of a fixed size).
IsReadOnly	Public property (required because Array implements IList) that returns a Boolean value indicating whether the array is read-only.
IsSynchronized	Public property (required because Array implements ICollection) that returns a Boolean value indicating whether the array is thread safe.
Length	Public property that returns the length of the array.
Rank	Public property that returns the number of dimensions of the array.
SyncRoot	Public property that returns an object that can be used to synchronize access to the array.
GetEnumerator	Public method that returns an IEnumerator.
GetLength	Public method that returns the length of the specified dimension in the array.
GetLowerBound	Public method that returns the lower boundary of the specified dimension of the array.
GetUpperBound	Public method that returns the upper boundary of the specified dimension of the array.
Initialize	Initializes all values in a value type array by calling the default constructor for each value. With reference arrays, all elements in the array are set to null.
SetValue	Overloaded public method that sets the specified array elements to a value.

Declaring Arrays

Declare a Visual Basic 2005 array with the following syntax:

```
Dim array-name( ) as type
```

For example:

```
Dim intArray( ) as Integer
```

 You are not actually declaring an array. Technically, you are declaring a variable (intArray) that will hold a reference to an Array of integers. As always, we'll use the shorthand and refer to intArray as the array, knowing that what we really mean is that it is a varaible that holds a reference to an (unnamed) array on the heap.

The parentheses tell the Visual Basic 2005 compiler that you are declaring an array, and the type specifies the type of the elements it will contain. In the previous example, intArray is an array of integers.

You instantiate an array using the new keyword. For example:

```
intArray = new Integer(5) { }
```

 The braces are required and indicate that you are not explicitly initializing the array with any values at this time.

The effect of this declaration is to create and intialize an array of six integers, all of which are initialized to the value zero.

 VB6 Warning: Although the value in VB6 designated the upper bound of the array, as it does in VB.NET, the array indexes were one based (by default). Therefore, the upper bound was also the size of the array. in Visual Basic 2005, arrays are zero-based, and so the size of the array is one more than the upper bound.

C# Warning: In Visual Basic 2005, the value passed into the parentheses is not the size of the array, but the upper bound.

It is important to distinguish between the array itself (which is a collection) and the elements of the array. intArray is the array (or, more accurately, the variable that holds the reference to the array); its elements are the six integers it holds.

Visual Basic 2005 arrays are reference types, created on the heap. Thus, the array to which intArray refers is allocated on the heap. The *elements* of an array are allocated based on their own type. Since Integers are value types, the elements in intArray will be value types, *not* boxed integers, and, thus, all the elements will be created inside the block of memory allocated for the array.

The block of memory allocated to an array of reference types will contain references to the actual elements, which are themselves created on the heap in memory separate from that allocated for the array.

Understanding Default Values

When you create an array of value types, each element initially contains the default value for the type stored in the array. The statement:

```
intArray = new Integer(5) { }
```

creates an array of six integers, each of whose value is set to 0, which is the default value for integer types.

On the other hand reference types in an array are *not* initialized to their default value. Instead, the references held in the array are initialized to *null*. If you attempt to access an element in an array of reference types before you have specifically initialized the elements, you will generate an exception.

Assume you have created a Button class. Declare an array of Button objects with the following statement:

```
Dim myButtonArray( ) as Button
```

and instantiate the actual array like this:

```
myButtonArray = new Button(3)
```

You can shorten this to:

```
Dim myButtonArray( ) as Button = new Button(3)
```

This statement does *not* create an array with references to four Button objects. Instead, this creates the array myButtonArray with four null references. To use this array, you must first construct and assign the four Button objects, one for each reference in the array.

Accessing Array Elements

Access the elements of an array using the index operator (( )). Arrays are zero-based, which means that the index of the first element is always zero—in this case, myArray(0).

As explained previously, arrays are objects and, thus, have properties. One of the more useful of these is Length, which tells you how many objects are in an array. Array objects can be indexed from 0 to Length-1. That is, if there are five elements in an array; their indices are 0, 1, 2, 3, and 4.

Example 17-1 is a console application named *Arrays*, that illustrates the array concepts covered so far.

Example 17-1. Working with Arrays

```
Module Module1

    Public Class Employee
        Private _empID As String
```

Example 17-1. Working with Arrays (continued)

```
        Public Sub New(ByVal empID As Integer)
            Me._empID = empID
        End Sub
        Public Overrides Function ToString() As String
            Return _empID
        End Function
    End Class

    Sub Main()
        Dim empArray() As Employee
        empArray = New Employee(3) {}
        Dim intArray() As Integer = New Integer(5) {}

        For index As Integer = 0 To empArray.Length - 1
            empArray(index) = New Employee(index + 5)
        Next

        For index As Integer = 0 To intArray.Length - 1
            Console.WriteLine(intArray(index).ToString())
        Next

        For index As Integer = 0 To empArray.Length - 1
            Console.WriteLine(empArray(index).ToString())
        Next
    End Sub

End Module

Output:
0
0
0
0
0
0
5
6
7
8
```

The example starts with the definition of an Employee class, which implements a constructor taking a single integer parameter. The ToString() method inherited from Object is overridden to print the value of the Employee object's employee ID.

The test method declares and then instantiates a pair of arrays. The integer array is automatically filled with integers whose value is set to 0. The Employee array contents must be constructed by hand.

Finally, the contents of the arrays are printed to ensure that they are filled as intended. The six integers print their value (zero) first, followed by the four Employee objects.

Initializing Array Elements

It is possible to initialize the contents of an array at the time it is instantiated by providing a list of values delimited by curly braces ({ }). Visual Basic 2005 provides a longer and a shorter syntax:

```
Dim firstArray()  As Integer = New Integer(5) {1, 2, 3, 4, 5, 6}
Dim secondArray() As Integer = {1, 2, 3, 4, 5, 6}
```

There is no practical difference between these two statements, and most programmers will use the shorter syntax.

Multidimensional Arrays

Arrays can be thought of as long rows of slots into which values can be placed. Once you have a picture of a row of slots, imagine 10 rows, one on top of another. This is the classic two-dimensional array of rows and columns (often referred to as a Matrix).*

A third dimension is possible, but somewhat harder to imagine. Okay, now imagine four dimensions. Now imagine 10.

Those of you who are not string-theory physicists have probably given up, as have I. Multidimensional arrays are useful, however, even if you can't quite picture what they would look like.

Visual Basic 2005 supports two types of multidimensional arrays: rectangular and jagged. In a rectangular array, every row is the same length. A jagged array, however, is an array of arrays, each of which can be a different length.

Rectangular arrays

A *rectangular array* is an array of two (or more) dimensions. In the classic two-dimensional array, the first dimension is the rows and the second dimension is the columns.

To declare a two-dimensional array, use the following syntax:

```
Dim identifier(,) As type
```

For example, to declare and instantiate a two-dimensional rectangular array named theMatrix that contains four rows and three columns of integers, you would write:

```
Dim theMatrix(,) As Integer = New Integer(3,2) { }
```

---

* "The Matrix is everywhere. It is all around us. Even now in this very room. You can see it when you look out your window. Or when you turn on your television. You can feel it when you go to work. When you go to Church. When you pay your taxes. It is the world that has been pulled over your eyes to blind you from the truth." (Morpheus, *The Matrix*, Warner Brothers, 1999)

Example 17-2 declares, instantiates, initializes, and prints the contents of a two-dimensional array. In this example, a nested For loop is used to initialize the elements of the array.

Example 17-2. theMatrix

```
Module Module1

    Sub Main()
        Const rows As Integer = 3
        Const columns As Integer = 2

        Dim theMatrix(,) As Integer = New Integer(rows, columns) { }
        For index As Integer = 0 To rows
            For internalIndex As Integer = 0 To columns
                theMatrix(index, internalIndex) = _
                        (index + 1) * (internalIndex + 1)
            Next
        Next

        For index As Integer = 0 To rows
            For internalIndex As Integer = 0 To columns
                Console.WriteLine("theMatrix({0})({1}) = {2}", _
                index, internalIndex, theMatrix(index, internalIndex))
            Next
        Next


    End Sub

End Module

Output:
theMatrix(0)(0) = 1
theMatrix(0)(1) = 2
theMatrix(0)(2) = 3
theMatrix(1)(0) = 2
theMatrix(1)(1) = 4
theMatrix(1)(2) = 6
theMatrix(2)(0) = 3
theMatrix(2)(1) = 6
theMatrix(2)(2) = 9
theMatrix(3)(0) = 4
theMatrix(3)(1) = 8
theMatrix(3)(2) = 12
```

In this example, you declare a pair of constant values:

```
Const rows As Integer = 3
Const columns As Integer = 2
```

that are then used to set the size of the dimensions the array:

```
Dim theMatrix(,) As Integer = New Integer(rows, columns) { }
```

Notice the syntax. The parentheses in the theMatrix(,) declaration indicate that the array has two dimensions. (Two commas would indicate three dimensions, and so on.) The actual instantiation of theMatrix with New Integer(rows, columns) { } allocates the memory and sets the size of each dimension.

The program fills the rectangle with a pair of nested For loops, iterating through each column in each row. Thus, the first element filled is theMatrix(0,0), followed by theMatrix(0,1), and theMatrix(0,2). Once this is done, the program moves on to the next rows: theMatrix(1,0), theMatrix(1,1), theMatrix(1,2), and so forth, until all the columns in all the rows are filled.

Just as you can initialize a one-dimensional array using lists of values, you can initialize a two-dimensional array using similar syntax. Thus, you can modify the previous example to initialize the values at the same time you declare them:

```
Dim theMatrixReloaded(,) As Integer = New Integer(rows, columns) _
{ _
    {0, 1, 2}, {3, 4, 5}, {6, 7, 8}, {9, 10, 11} _
}
```

Jagged Arrays

A *jagged array* is an array of arrays. It is called "jagged" because the rows need not be the same size, and thus a graphical representation of the array would not be square.

When you create a jagged array, you declare the number of rows in your array. Each row will hold an array, which can be of any length. These arrays must each be declared. You can then fill in the values for the elements in these "inner" arrays.

In a jagged array, each dimension is a one-dimensional array. To declare a jagged array, use the following syntax, where the number of parentheses indicates the number of dimensions of the array:

```
Dim identifier( )( ) as type
```

For example, you would declare a two-dimensional jagged array of integers named myJaggedArray as follows:

```
Dim myJaggedArray( )( ) as Integer = new Integer(5)
```

Access the fifth element of the third array by writing myJaggedArray(2)(4).

Example 17-3 creates a jagged array named myJaggedArray, initializes its elements, and then prints their content. To save space, the program takes advantage of the integer array elements automatically initializing to zero, and it initializes the values of only some of the elements.

Example 17-3. Working with a jagged array

```
Module Module1

    Sub Main( )
        Const rows As Integer = 3

        ''declare the jagged array as 4 rows high
        Dim jaggedArray As Integer()() = New Integer(rows)() { }

        '' the first row has 3 elements
        jaggedArray(0) = New Integer(2) { }

        '' the second row has 2 elements
        jaggedArray(1) = New Integer(1) { }

        '' the third row has 4 elements
        jaggedArray(2) = New Integer(3) { }

        '' the fourth row has 5 elements
        jaggedArray(3) = New Integer(4) { }

        '' fill some (not all) elements of the rows
        jaggedArray(0)(2) = 15
        jaggedArray(1)(1) = 12
        jaggedArray(2)(1) = 9
        jaggedArray(2)(2) = 99
        jaggedArray(3)(0) = 10
        jaggedArray(3)(1) = 11
        jaggedArray(3)(2) = 12
        jaggedArray(3)(3) = 13
        jaggedArray(3)(4) = 14

        For index As Integer = 0 To jaggedArray(0).Length - 1
            Console.WriteLine("jaggedArray(0)(" & index & "): {0}", _
                jaggedArray(0)(index))
        Next

        For index As Integer = 0 To jaggedArray(1).Length - 1
            Console.WriteLine("jaggedArray(1)(" & index & "): {0}", _
                jaggedArray(1)(index))
        Next

        For index As Integer = 0 To jaggedArray(2).Length - 1
            Console.WriteLine("jaggedArray(2)(" & index & "): {0}", _
                jaggedArray(2)(index))
        Next

        For index As Integer = 0 To jaggedArray(3).Length - 1
            Console.WriteLine("jaggedArray(3)(" & index & "): {0}", _
                jaggedArray(3)(index))
        Next

    End Sub
```

Example 17-3. Working with a jagged array (continued)

```
End Module
```

```
Output:
jaggedArray(0)(0): 0
jaggedArray(0)(1): 0
jaggedArray(0)(2): 15
jaggedArray(1)(0): 0
jaggedArray(1)(1): 12
jaggedArray(2)(0): 0
jaggedArray(2)(1): 9
jaggedArray(2)(2): 99
jaggedArray(2)(3): 0
jaggedArray(3)(0): 10
jaggedArray(3)(1): 11
jaggedArray(3)(2): 12
jaggedArray(3)(3): 13
jaggedArray(3)(4): 14
```

In this example, a jagged array is created with four rows:

```
Dim jaggedArray As Integer()() = New Integer(rows)() { }
```

Notice that the second dimension is not specified. Each row holds an array and each of these arrays can have a different size. Indeed, you see that the first has three rows, the second has two, and so forth.

Once an array is specified for each row, you need only populate the various members of each array and then print their contents to ensure that all went as expected.

When you access the members of the rectangular array, you put the indexes all within one set of parentheses:

```
theMatrixtheMatrix(index, innerIndex)
```

while with a jagged array you need a pair of parentheses:

```
jaggedArray(3)(index)
```

You can keep this straight by thinking of the first as a single array of more than one dimension and the jagged array as an array *of arrays*.

Generics

The goal of generics is to create collections that are "type safe" but that can be reused at design time with any type. Thus, the designer of a generic List would like to be able to designate that the List class can hold any type of data, but a specific type will be declared when the List class is used, and the compiler will enforce the type safety.

Generic List Class

The classic problem with the `Array` type is its fixed size. If you do not know in advance how many objects an array will hold, you run the risk of declaring either too small an array (and running out of room) or too large an array (and wasting memory).

Suppose you create a program that gathers input from a web site. As you find objects (strings, books, values, etc.), you will add them to the array, but you have no idea how many objects you'll collect in any given session. The classic fixed-size array is not a good choice, as you can't predict how large an array you'll need.

The `List` class is like an array whose size is dynamically increased as required. `List`s provide a number of useful methods and properties. Some of the most important are shown in Table 17-2.

Table 17-2. List methods and properties

Method or property	Purpose
Capacity	Property to get or set the number of elements the `List` can contain. This value is increased automatically if count exceeds capacity. You might set this value to reduce the number of reallocations, and you may call `Trim` to reduce this value to the actual `Count`.
Count	Property to get the number of elements currently in the array.
Item	Gets or sets the element at the specified index. This is the indexer for the `List` class.[a]
Add	Public method to add an object to the `List`.
AddRange	Public method that adds the elements of an `ICollection` to the end of the `List`.
BinarySearch	Overloaded public method that uses a binary search to locate a specific element in a sorted `List`.
Clear	Removes all elements from the `List`.
Contains	Determines if an element is in the `List`.
CopyTo	Overloaded public method that copies a `List` to a one-dimensional array.
Exists	Determines if an element is in the `List`.
Find	Returns the first occurrence of the element in the `List`.
FindAll	Returns all the specified elements in the `List`.
GetEnumerator	Overloaded public method that returns an enumerator to iterate through a `List`.
GetRange	Copies a range of elements to a new `List`.
IndexOf	Overloaded public method that returns the index of the first occurrence of a value.
Insert	Inserts an element into `List`.
InsertRange	Inserts the elements of a collection into the `List`.
LastIndexOf	Overloaded public method that returns the index of the last occurrence of a value in the `List`.
Remove	Removes the first occurrence of a specific object.
RemoveAt	Removes the element at the specified index.
RemoveRange	Removes a range of elements.

Table 17-2. List methods and properties (continued)

Method or property	Purpose
Reverse	Reverses the order of elements in the List.
Sort	Sorts the List.
ToArray	Copies the elements of the List to a new array.
TrimToSize	Sets the capacity to the actual number of elements in the List.

a The idiom in the Framework Class Library is to provide an Item property for collection classes that is implemented as an indexer in Visual Basic 2005.

When you create a List, you do not define how many objects it will contain. Add to the List using the Add method, and the List takes care of its own internal bookkeeping, as illustrated in Example 17-4.

Example 17-4. Working with a List

```
Imports System.Collections.Generic
Module Module1

    Sub Main( )
        Dim empList As New List(Of Employee)
        Dim intList As New List(Of Integer)

        For counter As Integer = 0 To 4
            empList.Add(New Employee(counter + 100))
            intList.Add(counter + 5)
        Next


        For Each val As Integer In intList
            Console.Write(val.ToString( ) + " ")
        Next
        Console.WriteLine(Environment.NewLine)

        For Each emp As Employee In empList
            Console.Write(emp.ToString( ) + " ")
        Next
        Console.WriteLine(Environment.NewLine)
        Console.WriteLine("empList.Capacity: {0}", empList.Capacity)

    End Sub

End Module

Public Class Employee

    Private employeeID As Integer

    Public Sub New(ByVal theID As Integer)
        Me.employeeID = theID
    End Sub
```

Example 17-4. Working with a List (continued)

```
Public Overrides Function ToString( ) As String
   Return employeeID.ToString( )
End Function
Public Property EmpID( ) As Integer
   Get
       Return employeeID
   End Get
   Set(ByVal value As Integer)
      employeeID = value
   End Set
End Property

End Class

Output:
0 5 10 15 20
100 101 102 103 104
empArray.Capacity: 8
```

With an Array class, you define how many objects the array will hold. If you try to add more than that, the Array class will throw an exception. With a List, you do not declare how many objects the List will hold. The List has a property, Capacity, which is the number of elements the List is capable of storing:

```
public int Capacity { get; set; }
```

The default capacity is eight. When you add the ninth element, the capacity is automatically doubled to 16. If you change the For loop to:

```
For counter As Integer = 0 To 8
```

the output looks like this:

```
5 6 7 8 9 10 11 12 13
100 101 102 103 104 105 106 107 108
empList.Capacity: 16
```

You can manually set the capacity to any number equal to or greater than the count. If you set it to a number less than the count, the program will throw an exception of type ArgumentOutOfRangeException.

Implementing IComparable

Like all collections, the List implements the Sort method, which allows you to sort any objects that implement IComparable. In the next example, you'll modify the Employee object to implement IComparable:

```
Public Class Employee
    Implements IComparable(Of Employee)
```

To implement the IComparable interface, the Employee object must provide a CompareTo method:

```
Function CompareTo(ByVal rhs As Employee) As Integer _
Implements IComparable(Of IComparable.Employee).CompareTo
   Return Me.employeeID.CompareTo(rhs.employeeID)
End Function
```

The CompareTo method has been implemented to take an Employee as a parameter. The current Employee object must compare itself to the parameter and return -1 if it is smaller than the parameter, 1 if it is greater than the parameter, and 0 if it is equal to the parameter.

It is up to Employee to determine what smaller than, greater than, and equal to actually mean. In the next example, you'll compare the EmployeeID (so that Employees can be sorted by EmployeeIDs.).

You are ready to sort the list of employees, empList. To see if the sort is working, you'll need to add integers and Employee instances to their respective lists with (pseudo)random values. To create the random values, you'll instantiate an object of class Random and call the Next method on the Random to return a pseudo-random number.

The Next method is overloaded; one version allows you to pass in an integer that represents the largest random number you want. In this case, you'll pass in the value 10 to generate a random number between 0 and 10:

```
Random r = new Random( );
r.Next(10);
```

Example 17-5 creates and then sorts the two lists.

Example 17-5. Sorting generic Lists usng IComparable

```
Imports System.Collections.Generic
Module Module1

   Sub Main( )
      Dim empList As New List(Of Employee)
      Dim intList As New List(Of Integer)

      Dim r As New Random( )

      For counter As Integer = 0 To 8
         empList.Add(New Employee(r.Next(10) + 100))
         intList.Add(r.Next(10))
      Next


      For Each val As Integer In intList
         Console.Write(val.ToString( ) + " ")
      Next
      Console.WriteLine(Environment.NewLine)
```

Example 17-5. Sorting generic Lists usng IComparable (continued)

```
        For Each emp As Employee In empList
            Console.Write(emp.ToString( ) + " ")
        Next
        Console.WriteLine(Environment.NewLine)

        intList.Sort( )
        empList.Sort( )
        Console.WriteLine("Sorted: ")
        For Each val As Integer In intList
            Console.Write(val.ToString( ) + " ")
        Next
        Console.WriteLine(Environment.NewLine)

        For Each emp As Employee In empList
            Console.Write(emp.ToString( ) + " ")
        Next

    End Sub

End Module
Public Class Employee
    Implements IComparable(Of Employee)

    Private employeeID As Integer

    Public Sub New(ByVal theID As Integer)
        Me.employeeID = theID
    End Sub
    Public Overrides Function ToString( ) As String
        Return employeeID.ToString( )
    End Function
    Public Property EmpID( ) As Integer
        Get
            Return employeeID
        End Get
        Set(ByVal value As Integer)
            employeeID = value
        End Set
    End Property

    Function CompareTo(ByVal rhs As Employee) As Integer _
        Implements IComparable(Of IComparable.Employee).CompareTo
        Return Me.employeeID.CompareTo(rhs.employeeID)
    End Function

End Class
Output:
5 3 7 8 3 8 4 9 7
102 106 100 106 101 107 109 109 106
```

Example 17-5. Sorting generic Lists usng IComparable (continued)

```
Sorted:
3 3 4 5 7 7 8 8 9
100 101 102 106 106 106 107 109 109
```

The output shows that the integer array and Employee array were generated with random numbers. When sorted, the display shows the values have been ordered properly.

Queues

A *queue* represents a first-in, first-out (FIFO) collection. The classic analogy is to a line (or queue if you are British) at a ticket window. The first person in line ought to be the first person to come off the line to buy a ticket.

A queue is a good collection to use when you are managing a limited resource. For example, you might want to send messages to a resource that can only handle one message at a time. You would then create a message queue so that you can say to your clients: "Your message is important to us. Messages are handled in the order in which they are received."

The Queue class has a number of member methods and properties, as shown in Table 17-3.

Table 17-3. Queue methods and properties

Method or property	Purpose
Count	Public property that gets the number of elements in the Queue
Clear	Removes all objects from the Queue
Contains	Determines if an element is in the Queue
CopyTo	Copies the Queue elements to an existing one-dimensional array
Dequeue	Removes and returns the object at the beginning of the Queue
Enqueue	Adds an object to the end of the Queue
GetEnumerator	Returns an enumerator for the Queue
Peek	Returns the object at the beginning of the Queue without removing it
ToArray	Copies the elements to a new array

Add elements to your queue with the Enqueue command and take them off the queue with Dequeue. You can also see what is next in the queue (without removing it) using Peek. Example 17-6 illustrates.

Example 17-6. Working with a queue

```
Imports System.Collections.Generic
Module Module1
```

Example 17-6. Working with a queue (continued)

```
Sub Main( )
    Dim empQueue As New Queue(Of Employee)
    Dim intQueue As New Queue(Of Integer)

    Dim r As New Random( )

    For counter As Integer = 0 To 8
        empQueue.Enqueue(New Employee(r.Next(10) + 100))
        intQueue.Enqueue(r.Next(10))
    Next

    '' Display the queues
    Console.Write("intQueue: ")
    PrintValues(intQueue)
    Console.WriteLine( )
    Console.Write("empQueue: ")
    PrintValues(empQueue)
    Console.WriteLine( )

    '' remove one element from the queues
    Console.WriteLine(vbCrLf + "intQueue.Dequeue {0}" + vbTab, _
        intQueue.Dequeue( ))
    Console.WriteLine("empQueue.Dequeue {0}" + vbTab, empQueue.Dequeue( ))


    '' Display the queues
    Console.Write("intQueue: ")
    PrintValues(intQueue)
    Console.WriteLine( )
    Console.Write("empQueue: ")
    PrintValues(empQueue)
    Console.WriteLine( )

    '' remove another element from the queues
    Console.WriteLine(vbCrLf + "intQueue.Dequeue {0}" + vbTab, _
        intQueue.Dequeue( ))
    Console.WriteLine("empQueue.Dequeue {0}" + vbTab, empQueue.Dequeue( ))

    '' Display the queues
    Console.Write("intQueue: ")
    PrintValues(intQueue)
    Console.WriteLine( )
    Console.Write("empQueue: ")
    PrintValues(empQueue)
    Console.WriteLine( )

    '' peek at the first element remaining
    Console.WriteLine(vbCrLf + "intQueue.Peek {0}" + vbTab, _
        intQueue.Peek( ))
    Console.WriteLine("empQueue.Peek {0}" + vbTab, empQueue.Peek( ))
```

Example 17-6. Working with a queue (continued)

```
    '' Display the queues
    Console.Write("intQueue: ")
    PrintValues(intQueue)
    Console.WriteLine( )
    Console.Write("empQueue: ")
    PrintValues(empQueue)
    Console.WriteLine( )



  End Sub
  Public Sub PrintValues(ByVal myCollection As IEnumerable(Of Integer))
      Dim myEnumerator As IEnumerator(Of Integer) = _
        myCollection.GetEnumerator( )
      While myEnumerator.MoveNext( )
        Console.Write("{0} ", myEnumerator.Current)
      End While
  End Sub

  Public Sub PrintValues(ByVal myCollection As IEnumerable(Of Employee))
      Dim myEnumerator As IEnumerator(Of Employee) = _
        myCollection.GetEnumerator( )
      While myEnumerator.MoveNext( )
        Console.Write("{0} ", myEnumerator.Current)
      End While
  End Sub



End Module
Public Class Employee
    Implements IComparable(Of Employee)
    Private employeeID As Integer

    Public Sub New(ByVal theID As Integer)
      Me.employeeID = theID
    End Sub

    Public Overrides Function ToString( ) As String
      Return employeeID.ToString( )
    End Function

    Public Property EmpID( ) As Integer
      Get
          Return employeeID
      End Get
      Set(ByVal value As Integer)
        employeeID = value
      End Set
    End Property
```

Example 17-6. Working with a queue (continued)

```
Function CompareTo(ByVal rhs As Employee) As Integer _
    Implements IComparable(Of WorkingWithQueues.Employee).CompareTo
    Return Me.employeeID.CompareTo(rhs.employeeID)
End Function

End Class
```

Output:
```
intQueue: 7 2 6 3 6 6 8 6 2
empQueue: 108 101 106 101 100 107 108 103 108

intQueue.Dequeue 7
empQueue.Dequeue 108
intQueue: 2 6 3 6 6 8 6 2
empQueue: 101 106 101 100 107 108 103 108

intQueue.Dequeue 2
empQueue.Dequeue 101
intQueue: 6 3 6 6 8 6 2
empQueue: 106 101 100 107 108 103 108

intQueue.Peek 6
empQueue.Peek 106
intQueue: 6 3 6 6 8 6 2
empQueue: 106 101 100 107 108 103 108
```

 VB6 Tip: In this example, I've used the traditional VbCrLf constants rather than Environment.NewLine as in previous examples. Visual Basic 2005 supports both. There is no Environment class equivalent to vbTab.

Because the Queue class is enumerable, you can pass it to the PrintValues method, which expects a reference to an IEnumerable interface. The conversion is implicit. In the PrintValues method you call GetEnumerator, which you will remember is the single method of all IEnumerable classes. This returns an IEnumerator, which you then use to enumerate all the objects in the collection.

Stacks

A *stack* is a last-in, first-out (LIFO) collection, like a stack of dishes at a buffet table, or a stack of coins on your desk. The last dish added to the top of the stack is the first dish you take off the stack.

The principal methods for adding to and removing from a stack are Push and Pop; Stack also offers a Peek method, very much like Queue. The significant methods and properties for Stack are shown in Table 17-4.

Table 17-4. Stack methods and properties

Method or property	Purpose
Count	Public property that gets the number of elements in the Stack
Clear	Removes all objects from the Stack
Clone	Creates a shallow copy
Contains	Determines if an element is in the Stack
CopyTo	Copies the Stack elements to an existing one-dimensional array
GetEnumerator	Returns an enumerator for the Stack
Peek	Returns the object at the top of the Stack without removing it
Pop	Removes and returns the object at the top of the Stack
Push	Inserts an object at the top of the Stack
ToArray	Copies the elements to a new array

Dictionaries

A *dictionary* is a collection that associates a *key* with a *value*. A language dictionary, such as *Webster's*, associates a word (the key) with its definition (the value).

To see the benefit of dictionaries, start by imagining that you want to keep a list of the state capitals. One approach might be to put them in an array:

```
Dim stateCapitals(50) As String
```

The stateCapitals array will hold 50 state capitals. Each capital is accessed as an off-set into the array. For example, to access the capital for Arkansas, you need to know that Arkansas is the fourth state in alphabetical order:

```
Dim capitalOfArkansas As String = stateCapitals(4)
```

It is inconvenient, however, to access state capitals using array notation. After all, if I need the capital for Massachusetts, there is no easy way for me to determine that Massachusetts is the 21st state alphabetically.

It would be far more convenient to store the capital with the state name. A dictionary allows you to store a value (in this case, the capital) with a key (in this case, the name of the state).

A .NET Framework generic dictionary can associate any kind of key (string, integer, object, etc.) with any kind of value (string, integer, object, etc.). Typically, of course, the key is fairly short, the value fairly complex.

The most important attributes of a good dictionary are that it is easy to add values and that it is quick to retrieve values and some of the most important properties methods of the Dictionary class are shown in Table 17-5.

Table 17-5. Dictionary methods and properties

Method or property	Purpose
Count	Public property that gets the number of elements in the Dictionary.
Item	The indexer for the Dictionary.
Keys	Public property that gets a collection containing the keys in the Dictionary. (See also Values.)
Values	Public property that gets a collection containing the values in the Dictionary. (See also Keys.)
Add	Adds an entry with a specified Key and Value.
Clear	Removes all objects from the Dictionary.
ContainsKey	Determines whether the Dictionary has a specified key.
ContainsValue	Determines whether the Dictionary has a specified value.
GetEnumerator	Returns an enumerator for the Dictionary.
GetObjectData	Implements ISerializable and returns the data needed to serialize the Dictionary.
Remove	Removes the entry with the specified Key.

The key in a Dictionary can be a primitive type, or it can be an instance of a user-defined type (an object). Objects used as keys for a Dictionary must implement GetHashCode as well as Equals. In most cases, you can simply use the inherited implementation from Object.

IDictionary<K,V>

Dictionaries implement the IDictionary<K,V> interface (where K is the key type and V is the value type).

Example 17-7 demonstrates adding items to a Dictionary and then retrieving them.

Example 17-7. The Item property as offset operators

```
Module Module1

    Sub Main()
        Dim dict As Dictionary(Of String, String) = New Dictionary(Of String, String)
        dict.Add("Alabama", "Montgomery")
        dict.Add("Alaska", "Juneau")
        dict.Add("Arizona", "Phoenix")
        dict.Add("Arkansas", "Little Rock")
        dict.Add("California", "Sacramento")
        dict.Add("Colorado", "Denver")
        dict.Add("Connecticut", "Hartford")
        dict.Add("Delaware", "Dover")
        dict.Add("Florida", "Tallahassee")
        dict.Add("Georgia", "Atlanta")
        dict.Add("Hawaii", "Honolulu")
        dict.Add("Idaho", "Boise")
        dict.Add("Illinois", "Springfield")
```

Example 17-7. The Item property as offset operators (continued)

```
        dict.Add("Iowa", "Des Moines")
        dict.Add("Kansas", "Topeka")
        dict.Add("Kentucky", "Frankfort")
        dict.Add("Louisiana", "Baton Rouge")
        dict.Add("Maine", "Augusta")
        dict.Add("Maryland", "Anapolis")
        dict.Add("Massachusetts", "Boston")
        dict.Add("Michigan", "Lansing")
        dict.Add("Minnesota", "St. Paul")
        dict.Add("Mississippi", "Jackson")
        dict.Add("Missouri", "Jefferson City")
        dict.Add("Montana", "Helena")
        dict.Add("Nebraska", "Lincoln")
        dict.Add("Nevada", "Carson City")
        dict.Add("New Hampshire", "Concord")
        dict.Add("New Jersey", "Trenton")
        dict.Add("New Mexico", "Santa Fe")
        dict.Add("New York", "Albany")
        dict.Add("North Carolina", "Raleigh")
        dict.Add("North Dakota", "Bismark")
        dict.Add("Ohio", "Columbus")
        dict.Add("Oklahoma", "Oklahoma City")
        dict.Add("Oregon", "Salem")
        dict.Add("Pennsylvania", "Harrisburg")
        dict.Add("Rhode Island", "Providence")
        dict.Add("South Carolina", "Columbia")
        dict.Add("South Dakota", "Pierre")
        dict.Add("Tennessee", "Nashville")
        dict.Add("Texas", "Austin")
        dict.Add("Utah", "Salt Lake City")
        dict.Add("Vermont", "Montpelier")
        dict.Add("Washington", "Olympia")
        dict.Add("West Virginia", "Charleston")
        dict.Add("Wisconsin", "Madison")
        dict.Add("Wyoming", "Cheyenne")

        ' access a state
        Console.WriteLine("The capital of Massachusetts is {0}", _
            dict("Massachusetts"))
    End Sub
End Module
```

Output:
```
The capital of Massachussetts is Boston
```

Example 17-7 begins by instantiating a new Dictionary. The key and the value are both declared to be strings.

I got a bit carried away and added the key/value pairs for all 50 states. The key is the state name, the value is the capital (often the values associated with a key will be more complex than simple strings) then accessed the capital of Massachusetts, using the string Massachusetts as the key, and retrieving the string Boston as the value.

 If you use a reference type as a key you must be careful not to change the value of the key object once you are using it in a Dictionary. (This can happen by changing another reference to the same object and inadvertently changing the value of the key)

If, for example, you were using an Employee object as a key, changing the employeeID in another reference to the same object would create problems in the Dictionary if that property were used by the Equals or GetHashCode methods; the Dictionary consults these methods.

CHAPTER 18

Object-Oriented Visual Basic 2005

A true object-oriented language supports the following features, all found in Visual Basic 2005: programmer-defined types, encapsulation, specialization, and polymorphism. This chapter will briefly review how these hallmarks of object-oriented programming are implemented in Visual Basic 2005.

Chapter 15 discussed the myriad primitive types built into the Visual Basic 2005 language, such as Integer, Long, and Single. The heart and soul of Visual Basic 2005, however, is the ability to create programmer-defined types.

You specify new types in Visual Basic 2005 by declaring and defining classes. *Instances* of a class are called *objects*. The difference between a class and an object is the same as the difference between the concept of a Dog and the particular dog who is sitting at your feet as you read this. You can't play fetch with the definition of a Dog, only with an instance (unless your instance is lazy and would prefer to sleep on the sofa that you just vacuumed thank you very much, and whose only interest is in eating and going out in the snow and then you have to clean his feet and, well, just don't get me started, okay?)

A Dog class describes what dogs are like: they have weight, height, eye color, hair color, disposition, and so forth. They also have actions they can take, such as eat, walk, bark, and sleep. A particular dog (such as my dog, Milo) will have a specific weight (62 pounds), height (22 inches), eye color (black), hair color (yellow), disposition (angelic), and so forth. All dogs implement the same behaviors (though the yap method is optional).

The huge advantage of classes in object-oriented programming is that classes *encapsulate* the characteristics and capabilities of a type in a single, self-contained, and self-sustaining *unit of code*. When you want to sort the contents of an instance of a Windows list box control, for example, you tell the list box to sort itself. How it does so is of no concern; *that* it does so is all you need to know.

An old programming joke asks, how many object-oriented programmers does it take to change a light bulb? Answer: none; you just tell the light bulb to change itself.[*]

This chapter explains the Visual Basic 2005 language features that are used to specify new classes. The elements of a class—its behaviors and properties—are known collectively as its *class members*. Methods are used to define the behaviors of the class, and the state of the class is maintained in member variables (often called *fields*).

Defining Classes

To define a new type or class you first declare it, and then define its methods and fields. You declare a class using the Class keyword. The complete syntax is:

```
[attributes] [access-modifiers] Class identifier
[inherits classname]
    {class-body}
End Class
```

Attributes are used to provide special metadata about a class (that is, information about the structure or use of the class). You will not need attributes for routine Visual Basic 2005 programming.

Access modifiers are discussed later in this chapter. (Typically, your classes will use the keyword Public as an access modifier.)

The identifier is the name of the class that you provide. The optional Inherits statement implements specialization, and is explained below. The class body is defined until the End Class statement.

```
Public Class Dog
    Dim age as Integer       'the dog's age
    Dim weight as Integer    'the dog's weight
    Public Sub Bark( )
       '….
    End Sub
End Class
```

All the things a dog can do (as far as your program is concerned) are described within the class definition of Dog, as are all the Dog's attributes (age and weight).

---

[*] How many Microsoft engineers does it take to change a light bulb? None. They changed the standard to dark.

Instantiating Objects

To make an actual instance of Dog, you must declare the object and you must allocate memory for the object. You declare an object much as you declare a variable of a primitive type.

```
Dim milo as Dog  'declare a Dog object
```

The declaration shown doesn't actually create an instance, however. To create an instance of a class you must allocate memory for the object by using the keyword New:

```
milo = New Dog( ) 'allocate memory for milo
```

You typically combine the declaration and the creation of the new instance into a single line:

```
Dim milo As New Dog( )
```

This declares milo to be an object of type Dog, and creates a new instance of Dog. You'll see what the parentheses are for later in this chapter when we discuss the constructor.

In Visual Basic 2005, *everything* happens within a class. "But wait!" I hear you cry, "Don't we create modules?" Yes, Visual Studio .NET does create modules, but when you compile your application, a class is created for you from that module. This allows Visual Studio .NET to continue to use modules (as Visual Basic did) but still comply with the .NET approach that everything is a class.

No methods can run outside of a class, not even Main, the entry point for your program. Typically, you'll create a small module to house Main:

```
Module modMain
    Public Sub Main( )
        ...
    End Sub
End Module
```

The compiler will turn this into a class for you. A somewhat more efficient alternative is for you to declare the class yourself:

```
Public Class Tester
    Public Sub Main( )
        Dim testObject As New Tester( )
    End Sub
    ' other members
End Class
```

In this example, you create the class Tester explicitly. Even though Tester was created to house the Main method, you've not yet *instantiated* any objects of type Tester. To do so, you would write:

```
Dim testObject As New Tester( ) 'make an instance of Tester
```

Creating an instance allows you to call other methods on testObject, as you'll see later in this chapter.

Scope

You will remember that in Visual Basic 2005 objects declared within methods are called local variables. They are local to the method, as opposed to belonging to the object, as member variables do.

Local variables of intrinsic types such as Integer are created on the "stack." The stack is a portion of memory that is allocated as methods are invoked and freed as methods end. When you start a method, all the local variables are created on the stack. When the method ends, all the local variables are destroyed.

These variables are referred to as local because they exist (and are visible) only during the lifetime of the method. They are said to have *local scope*. When the method ends, the variable *goes out of scope* and is destroyed.

.NET divides the world of types into value types and reference types. Value types are created on the stack. All the intrinsic types (Integer, Long, etc.) are value types and thus are created on the stack.

Classes, on the other hand, are reference types. Reference types are created on the heap.

The Heap

The heap is an undifferentiated block of memory; an area of RAM in which your objects are created. When you declare an object (e.g., milo) you are actually declaring a reference to an object that will be located on the heap.

A reference is a variable that refers to another object. The reference acts like an alias for the object. When you allocate memory on the heap with the New operator, what you get back is a reference to the new object:

```
Dim milo As New Dog()
```

Your new Dog object is on the heap. The reference milo refers to that object. The reference milo acts as an alias for that unnamed object, and you can treat milo as if it *were* the Dog object.

You can have more than one reference to the same object. This difference between creating value types and reference types is illustrated in Example 18-1. The complete analysis follows the output.

Example 18-1. Heap versus stack

```
Module Module1

    Public Class Dog
        Public weight As Integer
    End Class


    Public Sub Main( )
        ' create an integer
        Dim firstInt As Integer = 5

        ' create a second integer
        Dim secondInt As Integer = firstInt

        ' display the two integers
        Console.WriteLine( _
            "firstInt: {0} second Integer: {1}", firstInt, secondInt)

        ' modify the second integer
        secondInt = 7

        ' display the two integers
        Console.WriteLine( _
            "firstInt: {0} second Integer: {1}", firstInt, secondInt)

        ' create a dog
        Dim milo As New Dog( )

        ' assign a value to weight
        milo.weight = 5

        ' create a second reference to the dog
        Dim fido As Dog = milo

        ' display their values
        Console.WriteLine( _
          "Milo: {0}, fido: {1}", milo.weight, fido.weight)

        ' assign a new weight to the second reference
        fido.weight = 7

        ' display the two values
        Console.WriteLine( _
            "Milo: {0}, fido: {1}", milo.weight, fido.weight)
    End Sub

End Module

Output:
firstInt: 5 second Integer: 5
firstInt: 5 second Integer: 7
```

Example 18-1. Heap versus stack (continued)

```
Milo: 5, fido: 5
Milo: 7, fido: 7
```

Main begins by creating an integer, firstInt, and initializing it with the value 5. The second integer, secondInt, is then created and initialized with the value in firstInt. Their values are displayed.

```
firstInt: 5 second Integer: 5
```

Because Integer is a value type, a copy of the value is made, and secondInt is an independent second variable, as illustrated in Figure 18-1.

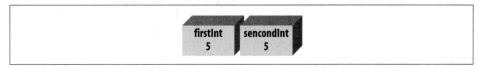

Figure 18-1. A copy of firstInt

When you assign a new value to secondInt:

```
secondInt = 7
```

the first variable is unaffected. Only the copy is changed, as illustrated in Figure 18-2.

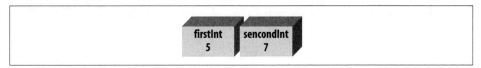

Figure 18-2. Only the copy is changed

The values are displayed and they are now different:

```
firstInt: 5 second Integer: 7
```

Your next step is to create a simple Dog class with only one member: a Public variable weight.

 Generally, you will not make member variables Public, as explained below. The field weight was made Public to simplify this example.

You instantiate a Dog, and save a reference to that Dog in the reference milo:

```
Dim milo As New Dog( )
```

You assign the value 5 to milo's weight field:

```
milo.weight = 5
```

You commonly say that you've set milo's weight to 5, but actually you've set the weight of the unnamed object on the heap to which milo refers, as shown in Figure 18-3.

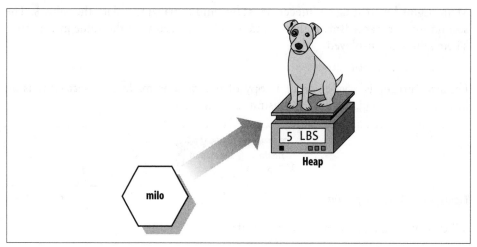

Figure 18-3. milo is a reference

You next create a new reference to Dog (fido) and initialize it by setting it equal to milo. This creates a new reference *to the same object* on the heap.

```
Dim fido As Dog = milo
```

Notice that this is syntactically similar to creating a second Integer variable and initializing it with an existing Integer, as you did before:

```
Dim secondInt As Integer = firstInt
Dim fido As Dog = milo
```

The difference is that Dog is a reference type, so fido is not a copy of milo, it is a copy of the reference. Thus, fido is a second reference to the same object to which milo refers. That is, you now have an object on the heap with two references to it, as illustrated in Figure 18-4.

When you change the weight of that object through the fido reference, you are changing the weight of the same object to which milo refers. This is reflected in the output:

```
milo: 7, fido: 7
```

It isn't that fido is changing milo, it is that fido is changing the same (unnamed) object on the heap to which milo refers.

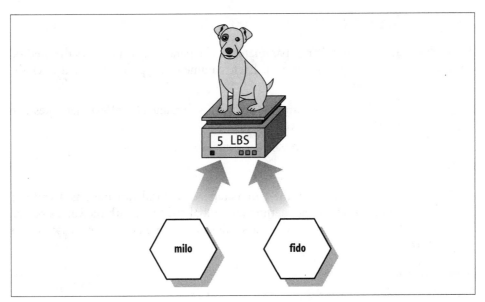

Figure 18-4. *fido is also a reference*

Access Modifiers

An access modifier determines which class methods—including methods of other classes—can see and use a member variable or method within a class. Table 18-1 summarizes the Visual Basic 2005 access modifiers.

Table 18-1. *Access modifiers*

Access modifier	Restrictions
Public	No restrictions. Members marked `Public` are visible to any method of any class.
Private	The members in class A which are marked `Private` are accessible only to methods of class A.
Protected	The members in class A which are marked `Protected` are accessible to methods of class A and also to methods of classes derived from class A.
Friend	The members in class A which are marked `Friend` are accessible to methods of any class in A's assembly.
Protected Friend	The members in class A which are marked `Protected Friend` are accessible to methods of class A, to methods of classes derived from class A, and also to any class in A's assembly. This is effectively `Protected` OR `Friend` (There is no concept of `Protected` AND `Friend`.)

The `Protected` access modifier is used with derived classes, as explained below in the discussion on inheritance. The `Friend` accessor says that the members are visible to any method within the Assembly. An assembly is a collection of files that appear to the programmer as a single executable (*.exe*) or DLL.

It is good programming practice to explicitly set the accessibility of all methods and members of your class.

Method Arguments

Methods can take any number of parameters.* The parameter list follows the method name and is enclosed in parentheses. Each parameter's type is identified after the name of the parameter.

For example, the following declaration defines a sub named MyMethod that takes two parameters: an Integer and a Button:

```
Sub MyMethod (firstParam as Integer, secondParam as Button)
    ' ...
End Sub
```

Within the body of the method, the parameters act as local variables, as if you had declared them in the body of the method and initialized them with the values passed in. Example 18-2 illustrates how you pass values into a method, in this case, values of type Integer and Single.

Example 18-2. Passing parameters

```
Public Class TestClass
    Sub SomeMethod( _
        ByVal firstParam As Integer, _
        ByVal secondParam As Single)

        Console.WriteLine( _
            "Here are the parameters received: {0}, {1}", _
            firstParam, secondParam)

    End Sub
End Class

Module Module1

    Sub Main( )
        Dim howManyPeople As Integer = 5
        Dim pi As Single = 3.14F

        Dim tc As New TestClass( )
        tc.SomeMethod(howManyPeople, pi)

    End Sub

End Module

Output:
Here are the parameters received: 5, 3.14
```

* The terms "argument" and "parameter" are used interchangeably in this book, though some programmers prefer to differentiatie between the parameter declaration and the arguments passed in when the method is invoked.

Visual Studio will mark your parameters as ByVal:

```
ByVal firstParam As Integer
```

This indicates that the parameter is passed "by value"—that is, a copy is made.

 Note that, if Strict is On, (which is should be) when you pass in a Single with a decimal part (3.14) you must append the letter f (3. 14f) to signal to the compiler that the value is a Single, and not a Double.

The method SomeMethod( ) takes an Integer and a Single and displays them using Console.WriteLine( ). The parameters, firstParam and secondParam, are treated as local variables within SomeMethod( ).

In the calling method (Main( )), two local variables (howManyPeople and pi) are created and initialized. These variables are passed as the arguments to SomeMethod( ). The compiler maps howManyPeople to firstParam and pi to secondParam, based on their relative positions in the parameter list.

Constructors

In that example, you will create a new instance of the Time class.

```
Dim timeObject As New Time( );
```

The parentheses look a lot like a method call. In fact, a method *is* invoked whenever you instantiate an object. This method is called a *constructor*. If you don't define one as part of your class definition, the compiler will provide one on your behalf.

The job of a constructor is to create the object specified by a class and to put it into a *valid* state. Before the constructor runs, the object is just a blob of memory; after the constructor completes, the memory holds a valid instance of the class.

 Any constructor that takes no arguments is called a *default constructor*. It turns out that the constructor provided by the compiler takes no arguments, and, hence, is a default constructor. This terminology has caused a great deal of confusion. You can create your own default constructor, and if you do not create a constructor at all, the compiler will create a default constructor for you, by default.

If you do not explicilty initialize your member variables, they are initialized to their default values based on their type (integers to 0, strings to the empty string, etc.). Table 18-2 lists the default values assigned to various types.

Table 18-2. Types and their default values

Type	Default value
Numeric (Integer, Long, etc.)	0
Boolean	False
Char	The Unicode character whose code point is 0
Enum	0
Reference	Nothing

Typically, you'll want to define your own constructor and provide it with arguments, so that the constructor can set the initial state for your object. In Example 18-3, you will pass in the current year, month, date, and so forth, so that the Time object is created with meaningful data.

Example 18-3. Defining a constructor

```
Public Class Time
    ' Private variables
    Private year As Integer
    Private month As Integer
    Private dayOfMonth As Integer
    Private hour As Integer
    Private minute As Integer
    Private second As Integer

    ' Public methods
    Public Sub DisplayCurrentTime( )
        System.Console.WriteLine("{0}/{1}/{2} {3}:{4}:{5}", _
            month, dayOfMonth, year, hour, minute, second)
    End Sub 'DisplayCurrentTime

    ' Constructor
    Public Sub New( _
     ByVal theYear As Integer, _
     ByVal theMonth As Integer, _
     ByVal theDate As Integer, _
     ByVal theHour As Integer, _
     ByVal theMinute As Integer, _
     ByVal theSecond As Integer)

        year = theYear
        month = theMonth
        dayOfMonth = theDate
        hour = theHour
        minute = theMinute
        second = theSecond
    End Sub

End Class 'Time

Module Module1
```

Example 18-3. Defining a constructor (continued)

```
Sub Main( )
    Dim timeObject As New Time(2008, 7, 10, 9, 35, 20)
    timeObject.DisplayCurrentTime( )
End Sub

End Module
```

```
output:
7/10/2008 9:35:20
```

You declare a constructor like any other sub except: the constructor is always named New.

If there are arguments to be passed, you define an argument list just as you would for any other method.

Example 18-3 declares a constructor for the Time class that accepts six integers.

In this example, the constructor (Sub New) takes a series of Integer values, and initializes all the member variables based on these parameters. When the constructor finishes, the Time object exists and the values have been initialized. When DisplayCurrentTime is called in Main, the values will be displayed.

Try commenting out one of the assignments and running the program again. You'll find that each member variable is initialized by the compiler. Integer member variables are set to 0 if you don't otherwise assign them. Remember, value types (e.g., integers) must be initialized one way or another; if you don't tell the constructor what to do, it will set innocuous values.

Initializers

It is possible to initialize the values of member variables in an *initializer*, instead of having to do so in the constructor. You create an initializer by assigning an initial value to a class member:

```
Private second As Integer = 30
```

Copy Constructors

A *copy constructor* creates a new object by copying variables from an existing object of the same type. For example, you might want to pass a Time object to a Time constructor so that the new Time object has the same values as the old one.

Visual Basic 2005 does not provide a copy constructor, so if you want one you must provide it yourself. Such a constructor copies the elements from the original object into the new one, as shown in Example 18-4.

Example 18-4. Copy constructor

```
Public Sub New(ByVal existingObject As Time)
    year = existingObject.year
    month = existingObject.month
    dayOfMonth = existingObject.dayOfMonth
    hour = existingObject.hour
    minute = existingObject.minute
    second = existingObject.second
End Sub
```

A copy constructor is invoked by instantiating an object of type Time and passing it the name of the Time object to be copied:

```
Dim t2 As New Time(timeObject)
```

The Me Keyword

The keyword Me refers to the current instance of an object. The Me reference is a hidden reference to every non-Shared method of a class (Shared methods are discussed later). Each method can refer to the other methods and variables of that object by way of the Me reference.

The Me reference may be used to distinguish instance members that have the same name as parameters, as in the following:

```
Public Sub SomeMethod(ByVal hour As Integer)
    Me.hour = hour
End Sub
```

In this example, SomeMethod takes a parameter (hour) with the same name as a member variable of the class. The Me reference is used to resolve the ambiguity. While Me.hour refers to the member variable, hour refers to the parameter.

 The argument in favor of this style, which is often used in constructors, is that you pick the right variable name and then use it both for the parameter and for the member variable. The counter-argument is that using the same name for both the parameter and the member variable can be confusing.

Another use of the Me reference is to pass the current object as a parameter to another method. For example:

```
Public Sub myMethod( )
    Dim someObject As New SomeType( )
    someObject.SomeMethod(Me)
End Sub
```

In this code snippet, you call a method on an object, passing in the Me reference. This allows the method you're calling access to the methods and properties of the current object.

You can also use the Me reference to make the copy constructor more explicit:

```
Public Sub New(ByVal that As Time)
    Me.year = that.year
    Me.month = that.month
    Me.dayOfMonth = that.dayOfMonth
    Me.hour = that.hour
    Me.minute = that.minute
    Me.second = that.second
End Sub
```

In this snippet, Me refers to the current object (the object whose constructor is running) and that refers to the object passed in.

Using Shared Members

The properties and methods of a class can be either *instance members* or *Shared members*. Instance members are associated with instances of a type, while Shared members are associated with the class, and not with any particular instance.

You may access a Shared member through the name of the class in which it is declared. For example, suppose you have a class named Button and have instantiated objects of that class named btnUpdate and btnDelete.

Suppose that the Button class has an instance method Draw and a Shared method GetButtonCount. The job of Draw is to draw the current button; the job of GetButtonCount is to return the number of buttons currently visible on the form.

You access an instance method through an instance of the class; that is, through an object:

```
btnUpdate.SomeMethod( )
```

You access Shared methods through the class name (rather than through an instance):

```
Button.GetButtonCount( )
```

The Shared method is considered a method of the class rather than of an instance of the class, and you do not need an instance of the class to access the method.

 Methods are instance methods unless you explicitly mark them with the keyword Shared.

A common use of Shared member variables is to create utility classes with useful methods and not force clients to create an instance if the class just to access the method.

Destroying Objects

The .NET Framework provides garbage collection. Your objects are destroyed when you are done with them. You do not need to worry about cleaning up after your objects unless you use unmanaged resources. An unmanaged resource is an operating system feature outside of the .NET Framework, such as a file handle or a database connection. See Sidebar on Finalize.

Overloading Methods and Constructors

Often you'll want to have more than one function with the same name. The most common example of this is to have more than one constructor.

It is possible to create a Time object by passing in the year, month, date, hour, minute, and second values, but it would be convenient also to allow the user to create a new Time object by passing in a Framewok DateTime object. Some clients might prefer one or the other constructor; you can provide both and the client can decide which best fits the situation.

Overloaded Methods—Different Signatures

The *signature* of a method is defined by its name and its parameter list. Two methods differ in their signatures if they have different names or different parameter lists. Parameter lists can differ by having different numbers of parameters or different types of parameters. For example, in the following code, the first method differs from the other methods by having a different name. The second differs from the third in the number of parameters, and the third differs from the fourth in the types of parameters:

```
Public Sub SomeMethod(p1 as Integer)
Public Sub MyMethod(p1 as Integer)                'different name
Public Sub MyMethod(p1 as Integer, p2 as Integer) 'different number
Public Sub MyMethod(p1 as Integer, s1 as String)  'different types
```

A class can have any number of methods, as long as each one's signature differs from that of all the others.

Encapsulating Data with Properties

It is generally desirable to designate the member variables of a class as Private. This means that only member methods of that class can access their value. You make member variables Private to support *data hiding*. Data hiding is part of the encapsulation of a class, and allows you to change how you store your data without breaking other classes that interact with your class.

Finalize

If you do control an unmanaged resource, it is best to explicitly free that resource as soon as you are done with it. Implicit control over this resource is provided with a finalize method, which will be called by the garbage collector when your object is destroyed.

```
Protected Overrides Sub Finalize()
  ' release non-managed resources
  MyBase.Finalize()
End Sub
```

It is not legal to call finalize explicitly. Finalize will be called by the garbage collector. If you do handle precious unmanaged resources (such as file handles) that you want to close and dispose of as quickly as possible, you ought to implement the IDisposable interface. (You will learn more about interfaces later in this chapter.)

The IDisposable interface requires you to create a method named Dispose which will be called by your clients.

If you provide a Dispose method, you should stop the garbage collector from calling your object's destructor. To stop the garbage collector, you call the Shared method GC. SuppressFinalize, passing in the Me reference for your object. Your Finalize method can then call your Dispose method. Thus, you might write:

```
Public Class Testing
    Implements IDisposable
    Dim is_disposed As Boolean = False

    Protected Sub Dispose(ByVal disposing As Boolean)
        If Not is_disposed Then
            If disposing Then
                Console.WriteLine("Not in destructor, OK to reference other
objects")
            End If
            ' perform cleanup for this object
            Console.WriteLine("Disposing...")
        End If
        Me.is_disposed = True
    End Sub

    Public Sub Dispose() Implements IDisposable.Dispose
        Dispose(True)
        'tell the GC not to finalize
        GC.SuppressFinalize(Me)
    End Sub

    Protected Overrides Sub Finalize()
        Dispose(False)
        Console.WriteLine("In destructor.")
    End Sub

End Class
```

The public members of your class constitute a contract between your class and *clients* of your class, (any object that interacts with your class is a client.) Your public methods promise that if the client calls them with the right parameters, they will perform the promised action. *How* your methods perform that object is not part of the public contract. That is up to your class.

Properties allow clients to access class state as if they were accessing member fields directly, while actually implementing that access through a class method.

This is ideal. The client wants direct access to the state of the object. The class designer, however, wants to hide the internal state of his class in private class fields, and provide indirect access through a method. The property provides both: the illusion of direct access for the client and the reality of indirect access for the class developer.

By decoupling the class state from the method that accesses that state, the designer is free to change the internal state of the object as needed, without breaking the client.

You create a property with this syntax:

```
Property Identifier( ) As Type
  Get
     Statements
  End Get

  Set(ByVal Value As Type)
     Statements
  End Set
End Property
```

For example:

```
Private mHour As Integer

Property Hour( ) As Integer
    Get
        Return mHour
    End Get
    Set(ByVal Value As Integer)
        mHour = Value
    End Set
End Property
```

If you create the property in Visual Studio .NET, however, the editor will provide extensive help with the syntax. Once you type, for example:

```
Property Minute as Integer
```

the IDE will reformat your property properly:

```
Property Minute( ) As Integer
    Get

    End Get
    Set(ByVal Value As Integer)
```

```
      End Set
   End Property
```

The Get Accessor

The body of the Get accessor is similar to a class method that returns an object of the type of the property. In the example, the accessor for Hour is similar to a method that returns an Integer. It returns the value of the private member variable in which the value of the property has been stored:

```
Get
    Return mHour
End Get
```

In this example, the value of a private Integer member variable is returned, but you could just as easily retrieve an Integer value from a database, or compute it on the fly.

Whenever you reference the property (other than to assign to it), the Get accessor is invoked to read the value of the property:

```
Dim time1 As New Time(currentTime)
Dim theHour As Integer = time1.Hour
```

The Set Accessor

The Set accessor has one parameter, Value, that represents the assigned value. That is, when you write:

```
Minute = 5
```

the compiler passes the value you are assigning (5) to the Set accessor as the Value parameter. You can then set the member variable to that value:

```
mMinute = Value
```

The advantage of this approach is that the client can interact with the properties directly, without sacrificing the data hiding and encapsulation sacrosanct in good object-oriented design.

Specialization and Generalization

Classes and their instances (objects) do not exist in a vacuum, they exist in a network of interdependencies and relationships, just as we, as social animals, live in a world of relationships and categories.

One of the most important relationships among objects in the real world is *specialization,* (the *is-a* relationship). When we say that a dog *is-a* mammal, we mean that the dog is a specialized kind of mammal. It has all the characteristics of any mammal (it bears live young, nurses with milk, has hair), but it specializes these characteristics to the familiar characteristics of *canis domesticus*. A cat is also a mammal. As such we expect it to share certain characteristics with the dog that are generalized in Mammal, but to differ in those characteristics that are specialized in Cat.

The specialization and generalization relationships are both reciprocal and hierarchical. They are reciprocal because specialization is the reverse side of the coin from generalization. Thus, Dog and Cat specialize Mammal, and Mammal generalizes from Dog and Cat.

These relationships are hierarchical because they create a relationship tree, with specialized types branching off from more generalized types. As you move up the hierarchy, you achieve greater *generalization*. You move up toward Mammal to generalize that Dogs and Cats and Horses all bear live young. As you move down the hierarchy you specialize. Thus, the Cat specializes Mammal in having claws (a characteristic) and purring (a behavior).

Similarly, when you say that ListBox and Button *are* Windows, you indicate that there are characteristics and behaviors of Windows that you expect to find in both of these types. In other words, Window generalizes the shared characteristics of both ListBox and Button, while each specializes its own particular characteristics and behaviors.

Inheritance

In Visual Basic 2005, the specialization relationship is implemented using inheritance. Saying that ListBox inherits from (or derives from) Window indicates that it specializes Window. Window is referred to as the *base* class, and ListBox is referred to as the *derived* class. That is, ListBox derives its characteristics and behaviors from Window and then specializes to its own particular needs.

Implementing Inheritance

In Visual Basic 2005, you create a derived class by using the key word Inherits followed by the name of the base class:

```
Public Class ListBox
    Inherits Window
```

This code declares a new class, ListBox, that derives from Window. The derived class inherits all the members of the base class, both member variables and methods.

Calling Base Class Constructors

ListBox derives from Window and has its own constructor. The ListBox constructor invokes the constructor of its parent by calling MyBase.New and passing in the appropriate parameters:

```
Public Sub New( _
    ByVal top As Integer, _
```

```
      ByVal left As Integer, _
      ByVal theContents As String)
   MyBase.New(top, left) ' call base constructor
   mListBoxContents = theContents
End Sub 'New
```

Because classes cannot inherit constructors, a derived class must implement its own constructor and can only make use of the constructor of its base class by calling it explicitly.

Polymorphism

There are two powerful aspects to inheritance. One is code reuse. When you create a ListBox class, you're able to reuse some of the logic in the base (Window) class.

What is arguably more powerful, however, is the second aspect of inheritance: *polymorphism*.

When the phone company sends your phone a ring signal, it does not know what type of phone is on the other end of the line. You might have an old-fashioned Western Electric phone which energizes a motor to ring a bell, or you might have an electronic phone which plays digital music.

As far as the phone company is concerned, it knows only about the "base type" phone and expects that any "instance" of this type knows how to ring. When the phone company tells your phone to *ring*, it simply expects the phone to "do the right thing." Thus, the phone company treats all the phones it connects to polymorphically.

Creating Polymorphic Types

Because a ListBox *is-a* Window and a Button *is-a* Window, we expect to be able to use either of these types in situations that call for a Window. For example, a form might want to keep a collection of all the instances of Window it manages so that when the form is opened, it can tell each Window to draw itself. For this operation, the form does not want to know which windows are actually ListBoxes and which are Buttons; it just wants to tick through its collection and tell each to "Draw." In short, the form wants to treat all its Window objects polymorphically.

Creating Polymorphic Methods

To create a method that supports polymorphism, you need only mark it as Overridable in its base class. For example, to indicate that the method DrawWindow of the window class is polymorphic, simply add the keyword Overridable to its declaration, as follows:

```
Public Overridable Sub DrawWindow( )
```

Now, each derived class is free to implement its own version of DrawWindow and the method will be invoked polymorphically. To do so, you simply override the base class overridable method by using the keyword Overrides in the derived class method definition, and then add the new code for that overridden method:

```
Public Overrides Sub DrawWindow( )
    MyBase.DrawWindow( ) ' invoke the base method
    Console.WriteLine( _
      "Writing string to the listbox: {0}", listBoxContents)
End Sub 'DrawWindow
```

The keyword Overrides tells the compiler that this class has intentionally overridden how DrawWindow works. Similarly, you'll override this method in another class, Button, also derived from Window.

 See the sidebar "Versioning with New and Override" for more information on the Overrides keyword.

Abstract Classes

Every subclass of Window *should* implement its own DrawWindow method—but nothing requires that it do so. To require subclasses to implement a method of their base, you need to designate that method as *abstract*.

An abstract method has no implementation. An abstract method creates a method name and signature that must be implemented in all derived classes. Furthermore, making one or more methods of any class abstract has the side effect of making the entire class abstract.

Abstract classes establish a base for derived classes, but it is not legal to instantiate an object of an abstract class. Once you declare a method to be abstract, you prohibit the creation of any instances of that class.

NotInheritable Class

The opposite side of the design coin from abstract is NotInheritable. Although an abstract class is intended to be derived-from and to provide a template for its subclasses to follow, a NotInheritable class does not allow classes to derive from it at all. The NotInheritable keyword placed before the class declaration precludes derivation. Classes are most often marked NotInheritable to prevent accidental inheritance.

The Root of All Classes: Object

All Visual Basic 2005 classes, of any type, ultimately derive from System.Object. Interestingly, this includes value types!

Versioning with New and Override

In Visual Basic 2005, the programmer's decision to override an overridable method is made explicit with the overrides keyword. This helps with versioning.

Here's how: assume for a moment that the Window base class of the previous example was written by Company A. Suppose also that the ListBox and RadioButton classes were written by programmers from Company B, using a purchased copy of the Company A Window class as a base. The programmers in Company B have little or no control over the design of the Window class, including future changes that Company A might choose to make.

Now suppose that one of the programmers for Company B decides to add a Sort method to ListBox:

```
Public Class ListBox
  Inherits Window
   Public Overridable Sub Sort()
     '…
   End Sub
```

This presents no problems until Company A, the author of Window, releases Version 2 of its Window class, and it turns out that the programmers in Company A have also added a Sort method to their Public Class Window:

```
Public Class Window
   Public Overridable Sub Sort()
     '…
   End Sub
```

In other object-oriented languages (such as C++), the new overridable Sort method in Window would now act as a base method for the Sort method in ListBox. The compiler would call the Sort method in ListBox when you intend to call the Sort in Window. In Java, if the Sort in Window had a different return type, the class loader would consider the Sort in ListBox to be an invalid override and would fail to load.

Visual Basic 2005 prevents this confusion. In Visual Basic 2005, an overridable function is always considered to be the root of dispatch; that is, once Visual Basic 2005 finds an overridable method, it looks no further up the inheritance hierarchy. If a new overridable Sort function is introduced into Window, the runtime behavior of ListBox is unchanged.

When ListBox is compiled again, however, the compiler generates a warning:

```
Module1.vb(31) : warning BC40005: sub 'Sort' shadows an overridable method in a
base class. To override the base method, this method must be declared
'Overrides'.
```

—continued—

To remove the warning, the programmer must indicate what she intends. She can mark the ListBox Sort method Shadows, to indicate that it is *not* an override of the Sort method in Window:

```
Public Class ListBox
    Inherits Window

    Public Shadows Sub Sort()
        '...
    End Sub 'Sort
```

This action removes the warning. If, on the other hand, the programmer does want to override the method in Window, she need only use the Override keyword to make that intention explicit:

```
Public Class ListBox
    Inherits Window

    Public Overrides Sub Sort()
        '...
    End Sub 'Sort
```

To avoid this warning, it might be tempting to add the keyword Shadows to all your overridable methods. This is a bad idea. When Shadows appears in the code, it ought to document the versioning of code. It points a potential client to the base class to see what it is that you are not overriding. Using Shadows scattershot undermines this documentation. Further, the warning exists to help identify a real issue.

A base class is the immediate "parent" of a derived class. A derived class can be the base to further derived classes, creating an inheritance "tree" or hierarchy. A root class is the top-most class in an inheritance hierarchy. In Visual Basic 2005, the root class is Object. The nomenclature is a bit confusing until you imagine an upside-down tree, with the root on top and the derived classes below. Thus, the base class is considered to be "above" the derived class.

Object provides a number of methods that subclasses can and do override. These include Equals to determine if two objects are the same; GetType, which returns the type of the object; and ToString, which returns a string to represent the current object. Table 18-3 summarizes the methods of Object.

Table 18-3. The Object class

Method	What it does
Equals	Evaluates whether two objects are equivalent
GetHashCode	Allows objects to provide their own hash function for use in collections
GetType	Provides access to the type object

Table 18-3. The Object class (continued)

Method	What it does
ToString	Provides a string representation of the object
Finalize	Cleans up nonmemory resources; implemented by a destructor
MemberwiseClone	Creates copies of the object; should never be implemented by your type
ReferenceEquals	Evaluates whether two objects refer to the same instance

Boxing and Unboxing Types

Boxing and *unboxing* are the processes that enable value types (e.g., integers) to be treated as reference types (objects). The value is "boxed" inside an Object, and subsequently, "unboxed" back to a value type.

Boxing Is Implicit

Boxing is an implicit conversion of a value type to the type Object. Boxing a value allocates an instance of Object and copies the value into the new object instance, as shown in Figure 18-5.

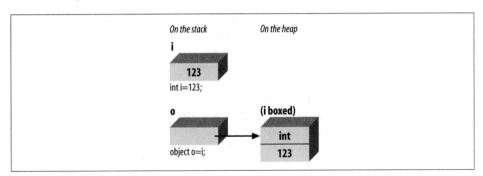

Figure 18-5. Boxing reference types

Boxing is implicit when you provide a value type where a reference is expected and the value is implicitly boxed. You can, of course, explicitly cast the value type to a reference type:

```
Dim myIntegerValue as Integer = 5
Dim myObject as Object = myIntegerValue ' explicitly cast to object
myObject.ToString()
```

This is not necessary, however, since the compiler will box the value for you:

```
Dim myIntegerValue as Integer = 5
myIntegerValue.ToString() ' boxed for you
```

Unboxing Must Be Explicit

To return the boxed object back to a value type, you must explicitly unbox it if Option Strict is On (as it should be). You will typically unbox by using the DirectCast( ) function or the CType( ) function.

Figure 18-6 illustrates unboxing.

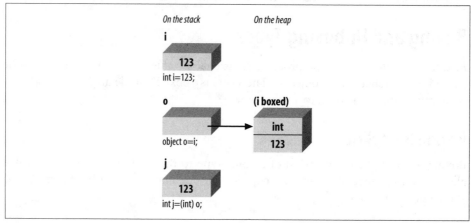

Figure 18-6. Unboxing

Interfaces

There are times when a designer does not want to create a new type. Rather, the designer wants to describe a set of behaviors that any number of types might implement. For example, a designer might want to describe what it means to be storable (i.e., capable of being written to disk) or printable.

Such a description is called an interface. An *interface* is a contract; the designer of the interface says "if you want to provide this capability, you must implement these methods." The *implementer* of the interface agrees to the contract and implements the required methods.

When a class implements an interface, it tells any potential *client*, "I guarantee I'll support the methods, properties, and events of the named interface." The interface details the return type from each method and the parameters to the methods.

It is easy to get confused about who is responsible for what with interfaces. There are three concepts to keep clear:

The interface
> This is the contract. By convention, interface names begin with a capital I, and so your interface might have a name like IPrintable. The IPrintable Interface might describe a method Print. (Creating and using interfaces is described below.)

The implementing class
> This is the class that agrees to the contract described by the interface. For example, Document might be a class that implements IPrintable and thus implements the Print method.

The client class
> This is a class that calls methods on the implementing class. For example, you might have an Editor class that calls the Document's Print method.

Interfaces Versus Abstract Base Classes

Programmers learning Visual Basic 2005 often ask about the difference between Interfaces and Abstract Base Classes. The key difference is in the semantics, the meaning of the two constructs. An abstract base class serves as the base class for a family of derived classes, while interfaces are meant to be mixed in with other inheritance trees.

Inheriting from an abstract class implements the *is-a* relationship. Implementing an interface defines a different relationship: the *implements* relationship. These two relationships are subtly different. A car *is-a* vehicle, but it might *implement* the CanBeBoughtWithABigLoan capability (as can a house, for example).

Defining an Interface

The syntax for defining an interface is as follows:

```
[attributes] [access-modifier] Interface identifier
[InterfaceBases]
   interface-body
End Interface
```

The keyword Interface is followed by an identifier (the interface name). It is common (but not required) to begin the name of your interface with a capital I. Thus, IStorable, ICloneable, IAndThou, etc.

The body of the interface is terminated with the keywords `End Interface`.

Suppose you wish to create an interface to define the contract for being stored. Your interface will define the methods and properties a class will need to be stored to a database or file. You decide to call this interface `IStorable`. The purpose of this interface is to define the capabilities that you want to have available in any class that can be stored.

In the `IStorable` interface you might specify two methods: `Read` and `Write`, and a property `Status`:

```
Interface IStorable
    Sub Read( )
    Sub Write(ByVal obj As Object)
    Property Status( ) As Integer
End Interface
```

Note that when declaring the methods of the interface you provide a prototype:

```
Sub Read( )
```

but no implementation and no `End Function`, `End Sub`, or `End Property` statement. Notice also that the `IStorable` method declarations do not include access modifiers (e.g., public, protected, internal, private). In fact, providing an access modifier generates a compile error. Interface methods are implicitly public because an interface is a contract meant to be used by other classes.

Implementing an Interface

Imagine that you are the author of a `Document` class. It turns out that `Document` objects can be stored in a database, so you decide to have `Document` implement the `IStorable` interface.

To do so, you must do two things:

- Declare the class to implement the interface.
- Implement each of the interface methods, events, properties, and so forth, and explicitly mark each as implementing the corresponding interface member.

To declare that the class implements the interface, you use the keyword `Implements` on the line below the class definition:

```
Public Class Document
    Implements IStorable
```

Visual Studio 2005 will help you with the available interfaces, as shown in Figure 18-7.

As soon as you write that your class implements the `IStorable` interface, Visual Studio 2005 will fill in all the required methods and properties of the interface, as shown in Figure 18-8!

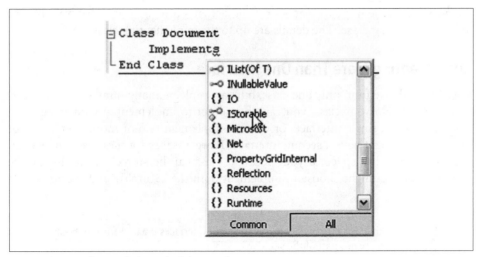

Figure 18-7. IntelliSense helping find the interface

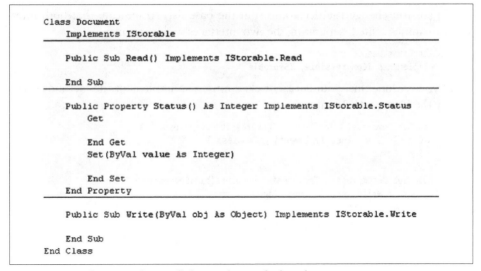

Figure 18-8. IntelliSense stubs out all the interface methods and properties

All you have to do is fill in the stubbed out methods and properties and the Interface contract is fulfilled.

You cannot create an instance of an interface; instead you instantiate a class that implements the interface. The class implementing the interface must fulfill the contract exactly and completely. Document must provide both a Read and a Write method and the Status property.

How it fulfills these requirements, however, is entirely up to the Document class. Although IStorable dictates that Document must have a Status property, it does not know or care whether Document stores the actual status as a member variable, or looks it up in a database. The details are up to the implementing class.

Implementing More Than One Interface

Classes can derive from only one class, but can implement any number of interfaces. When you design your class, you can choose not to implement any interfaces, you can implement a single interface, or you can implement two or more interfaces. For example, you might have a second interface: ICompressible for files that can be compressed to save disk space. If your Document class can be stored and it also can be compressed, you might choose to implement both the IStorable and ICompressible interfaces.

Both IStorable and ICompressible are interfaces created for this book and are not part of the standard .NET Framework.

To do so, you change the declaration (in the base list) to indicate that both interfaces are implemented, separating the two interfaces with commas:

```
Public Class Document
    Implements ICompressible, IStorable
```

Once you've done this, your Document class must also implement the methods specified by the ICompressible interface:

```
Public Sub Compress() Implements ICompressible.Compress
    Console.WriteLine("Implementing Compress")
End Sub 'Compress

Public Sub Decompress() Implements ICompressible.Decompress
    Console.WriteLine("Implementing Decompress")
End Sub 'Decompress
```

All of this is illustrated in Example 18-5.

Example 18-5. Demonstrating interfaces

```
Module Module1

    Sub Main()
        Dim doc As New Document("Test Document")
        doc.Status = -1
        doc.Read()
        doc.Compress()
        Console.WriteLine("Document Status: {0}", doc.Status)

    End Sub

End Module
Interface IStorable
```

Example 18-5. Demonstrating interfaces (continued)

```
    Sub Read( )
    Sub Write(ByVal obj As Object)
    Property Status( ) As Integer
End Interface 'IStorable

' here's the new interface
Interface ICompressible
    Sub Compress( )
    Sub Decompress( )
End Interface 'ICompressible


' Document implements both interfaces
Public Class Document
    Implements ICompressible, IStorable

    ' the document constructor
    Public Sub New(ByVal s As String)
        Console.WriteLine("Creating document with: {0}", s)
    End Sub 'New

    ' implement IStorable
    Public Sub Read( ) Implements IStorable.Read
        Console.WriteLine("Implementing the Read Method for IStorable")
    End Sub 'Read


    Public Sub Write(ByVal o As Object) Implements IStorable.Write
        Console.WriteLine( _
          "Implementing the Write Method for IStorable")
    End Sub 'Write

    Public Property Status( ) As Integer Implements IStorable.Status
        Get
            Return myStatus
        End Get
        Set(ByVal Value As Integer)
            myStatus = Value
        End Set
    End Property

    ' implement ICompressible
    Public Sub Compress( ) Implements ICompressible.Compress
        Console.WriteLine("Implementing Compress")
    End Sub 'Compress

    Public Sub Decompress( ) Implements ICompressible.Decompress
        Console.WriteLine("Implementing Decompress")
    End Sub 'Decompress
```

Example 18-5. Demonstrating interfaces (continued)

```
    ' hold the data for IStorable's Status property
    Private myStatus As Integer = 0
End Class 'Document
```

```
Output:
Creating document with: Test Document
Implementing the Read Method for IStorable
Implementing Compress
Document Status: -1
```

Casting to an Interface

You can access the members of the IStorable interface through the Document object, as if they were members of the Document class:

```
Dim doc As New Document("Test Document")
doc.Status = -1
doc.Read()
```

Alternatively, you can create a reference to an object that implements an interface, and then use that interface to access the methods:

```
Dim isDoc As IStorable = doc
isDoc.status = 0
isDoc.Read()
```

You will, from time to time, create collections of objects that implement a given interface (e.g., a collection of IStorable objects). You may manipulate them without knowing their real type; so long as they all implement IStorable. Similarly, you can declare a method to take an IStorable as a parameter, and you can pass in any object that implements IStorable.

As stated earlier, you cannot instantiate an interface directly. That is, you cannot write:

```
IStorable isDoc as New IStorable()
```

You can, however, create an instance of the implementing class, and then create an instance of the interface:

```
Dim isDoc as IStorable = doc;
```

This is considered a widening conversion (from Document to the IStorable interface), so the compiler makes it work with no need for an explicit cast.

Index

We'd like to hear your suggestions for improving our indexes. Send email to *index@oreilly.com*.

---

fully qualifying names, 24
functions
    casting, 453
    CBool, 453
    CByte, 453
    CChar, 453
    CDate, 453
    CDbl, 453
    CDec, 454
    CInt, 454
    CLng, 454
    CObj, 454
    CShort, 454
    CStr, 454
    CType, 454
    Encapsulate Field, 431
    Extract Interface, 431
    Extract Method, 430
    Promote Local Variable to Parameter, 431
    Remove Parameters, 431
    Rename, 430
    Reorder Parameters, 431

G

garbage collection, 510
GDI+
    Graphics class, 116–119
    implementing controls, 119–146
generalization, 513
generating methods, 41
generics, 482–488
    IComparable, implementing, 485
    List classes, 483
    sorting, 486
Get accessor, 513
GetCheckedFiles method, 91
GetHeight method, 124
GetHourRotation method, 142
GetName WebMethod, 391
GetParentString method, 90
GetPrice WebMethod, 390
GetSin method, 127
GetWidth method, 124
global.asax file
    Application directive and, 213
    Assembly directive and, 214
    session-scoped application objects, 210
Go To Line dialog box, 419
GoToURL helper class, 69
Graphics class, 116–119
    implementing controls, 119–146
GraphicsUnit enumeration, 118

GridLayout mode, adding controls to Web
        Forms, 188
grids
    comparing, 265
    executing, 267
    features, adding, 266
    modifying, 278
    updating, 274
    viewing, 274
group boxes, adding, 9

H

handing profiles, 330
handlers, event (see event handlers)
handles, 13
Handles keyword, 48
hands, drawing, 137
headers, rendering text with, 372
HeaderText attribute, ValidationSummary
        control, 226
heaps, 499–502
Hello World, ASP.NET, 186
Help menu, Visual Studio, 438
helper classes, GoToURL, 69
helper methods
    CreateFont, 155
    FillDirectoryTree, 82
    FillRows, 108
    LoadFromDB, 55
    moving, 150
    StopEditing, 55
hiding
    AutoHide, 411
    windows, 411
hierarchies, control trees, 210
history, URLs, 70
Home button Click event handler, 71
hooking Masked Text Boxes, 73
HTML (Hypertext Markup Language)
    controls, adding, 187
    formatting, 193
    profile tables, 332
    text, rendering with tags, 372
HTTP (Hypertext Transfer Protocol), Visual
        Studio, 407
Hungarian Notation, 10
Hypertext Markup Language (see HTML)
Hypertext Transfer Protocol (HTTP), Visual
        Studio, 407

About the Author

Jesse Liberty is the bestselling author of *Programming C#*, *Programming ASP.NET*, *Learning C#*, and a dozen other books on web and object-oriented programming. He is the president of Liberty Associates, Inc., where he provides contract programming, consulting, and on-site training in ASP.NET, Visual Basic, C#, and related topics. He is a former vice president of Citibank and a former Distinguished Software Engineer and Software Architect for AT&T, Ziff Davis, Xerox, and PBS.

Colophon

Our look is the result of reader comments, our own experimentation, and feedback from distribution channels. Distinctive covers complement our distinctive approach to technical topics, breathing personality and life into potentially dry subjects.

The animal on the cover of *Programming Visual Basic 2005* is a crested grebe. Grebes are sleek freshwater birds that inhabit lakes, rivers, and estuaries on every continent on Earth, except Antarctica. The crested variety (*Podiceps cristatus*) is 46 to 51 centimeters long and has a wingspan of 59 to 73 centimeters. In the summer months, adults can be recognized by their colorful head and neck plumage. As winter approaches, these decorations turn white. Grebes are powerful swimmers and can pursue fish underwater. They also dine on aquatic insects, tiny vertebrates, crustaceans, and snails.

Grebes are monogamous during the mating season. Both males and females can initiate courtship. A grebe attracts a prospective mate with extravagant water dances (they will often mirror each other's behavior, sometimes in displays of synchronized swimming or by running next to each other along the surface of the water) and over a dozen distinct vocalizations that include wails, chirps, peeps, and whistles. Both sexes aid in the construction of the nest, and both incubate the eggs. Once the chicks are born, the mother and father share in the feeding duties and carry the chicks from place to place on their backs.

The grebe's primary predators are ferrets, gulls, falcons, hawks, bass, pike, and humans. These days, grebes are hunted for food. However, in 19th-century Great Britain, the species was hunted almost to extinction for their colorful "fur," which was used to adorn hats.

Matt Hutchinson was the production editor for *Programming Visual Basic 2005*. Octal Publishing, Inc. provided production services. Darren Kelly, Genevieve d'Entremont, and Claire Cloutier provided quality control.

Karen Montgomery designed the cover of this book, based on a series design by Edie Freedman. The cover image is a 19th-century engraving from the Dover Pictorial Archive. Karen Montgomery produced the cover layout with Adobe InDesign CS using Adobe's ITC Garamond font.

David Futato designed the interior layout. This book was converted by Keith Fahlgren to FrameMaker 5.5.6 with a format conversion tool created by Erik Ray, Jason McIntosh, Neil Walls, and Mike Sierra that uses Perl and XML technologies. The text font is Linotype Birka; the heading font is Adobe Myriad Condensed; and the code font is LucasFont's TheSans Mono Condensed. The illustrations that appear in the book were produced by Robert Romano, Jessamyn Read, and Lesley Borash using Macromedia FreeHand MX and Adobe Photoshop CS. The tip and warning icons were drawn by Christopher Bing. This colophon was written by Matt Hutchinson.

Better than e-books

Buy *Programming Visual Basic 2005* and access
the digital edition FREE on Safari for 45 days.

Go to www.oreilly.com/go/safarienabled
and type in coupon code AIGL-VWXI-SYCA-Q7IU-CBH3

Search
thousands of
top tech books

Download
whole chapters

Cut and Paste
code examples

Find
answers fast

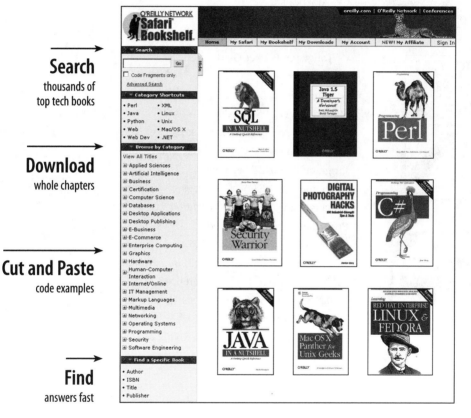

Search Safari! The premier electronic reference
library for programmers and IT professionals.

Related Titles from O'Reilly

.NET

.NET and XML

.NET Framework Essentials, *3rd Edition*

ADO.NET in a Nutshell

ADO.NET Cookbook

ASP.NET 2.0: A Developer's Notebook

C# Cookbook

C# Essentials, *2nd Edition*

C# in a Nutshell, *2nd Edition*

C# Language Pocket Guide

Learning C#

Learning Visual Basic.NET

Mastering Visual Studio.NET

Mono: A Developer's Notebook

Programming .NET Components, *2nd Edition*

Programming .NET Security

Programming .NET Web Services

Programming ASP.NET, *3rd Edition*

Programming C#, *4th Edition*

Programming Visual Basic 2005

VB.NET Language in a Nutshell, *2nd Edition*

VB.NET Language Pocket Reference

Visual Basic 2005: A Developer's Notebook

Visual Basic 2005 Jumpstart

Visual C# 2005: A Developer's Notebook

Visual Studio Hacks

Keep in touch with O'Reilly

Download examples from our books

To find example files from a book, go to: *www.oreilly.com/catalog* select the book, and follow the "Examples" link.

Register your O'Reilly books

Register your book at *register.oreilly.com* Why register your books? Once you've registered your O'Reilly books you can:

- Win O'Reilly books, T-shirts or discount coupons in our monthly drawing.
- Get special offers available only to registered O'Reilly customers.
- Get catalogs announcing new books (US and UK only).
- Get email notification of new editions of the O'Reilly books you own.

Join our email lists

Sign up to get topic-specific email announcements of new books and conferences, special offers, and O'Reilly Network technology newsletters at:

elists.oreilly.com

It's easy to customize your free elists subscription so you'll get exactly the O'Reilly news you want.

Get the latest news, tips, and tools

www.oreilly.com

- "Top 100 Sites on the Web"—PC Magazine
- CIO Magazine's Web Business 50 Awards

Our web site contains a library of comprehensive product information (including book excerpts and tables of contents), downloadable software, background articles, interviews with technology leaders, links to relevant sites, book cover art, and more.

Work for O'Reilly

Check out our web site for current employment opportunities:

jobs.oreilly.com

Contact us

O'Reilly Media, Inc.
1005 Gravenstein Hwy North
Sebastopol, CA 95472 USA
Tel: 707-827-7000 or 800-998-9938
    (6am to 5pm PST)
Fax: 707-829-0104

Contact us by email

For answers to problems regarding your order or our products:
order@oreilly.com

To request a copy of our latest catalog:
catalog@oreilly.com

For book content technical questions or corrections: **booktech@oreilly.com**

For educational, library, government, and corporate sales: **corporate@oreilly.com**

To submit new book proposals to our editors and product managers:
proposals@oreilly.com

For information about our international distributors or translation queries:
international@oreilly.com

For information about academic use of O'Reilly books:
adoption@oreilly.com
or visit:
academic.oreilly.com

For a list of our distributors outside of North America check out:
international.oreilly.com/distributors.html

Order a book online

www.oreilly.com/order_new

 **O'REILLY®**